DONALD   y Holgate
Gramma   g the war
he serve   at Trinity
College,   e, before
becomin   University
of Essex.   hairs, first
at Stanfo   rn home
in 1988;   ed in the
1950s bo   s *Purity of*
Diction in   ell as this
Collected   9), *Slavic*
Excursion   2), *With*
the Grain

NEIL PO   evenoaks
School a   owned a
booksho   tor. His
Carcanet   (1977), *A*
Season of   *Thorpeness*
Beach (19   *ht* (1979),
Roy Fulle   97). He
lives in S   e.

Also by Donald Davie from Carcanet

POETRY

To Scorch or Freeze
Poems and Melodramas
Selected Poems

CRITICISM

Under Briggflatts
Slavic Excursions
Studies in Ezra Pound
Older Masters
Purity of Diction and *Articulate Energy*
With the Grain
Two Ways Out of Whitman

DONALD DAVIE

Collected Poems

Edited by Neil Powell

CARCANET

This edition first published in 2002 by
Carcanet Press Limited
4th Floor, Conavon Court
12–16 Blackfriars Street
Manchester M3 5BQ

A CIP catalogue record for this book
is available from the British Library
ISBN 1 85754 579 6 (library edition)
ISBN 1 85754 406 4 (trade paperback)

The publisher acknowledges financial assistance
from the Arts Council of England

Set in Monotype Bembo by XL Publishing Services, Tiverton
Printed and bound in England by SRP Ltd, Exeter

Contents

Introduction   xvii

Early Poems

Pelican   1
A Song for These Crusaders   1
Glaphira III   2
Kites   2
Duplicity in Prayer   3
Tiger at the Movie-Show   3
Landfall among Friends   4
Condolence   5
Christmas Week, 1948   6
Protesilaus and Laodamia   7
Homage to William Cowper   8
At Knaresborough   8
The Bride of Reason   9
The Poet-Scholar   10
Elders and Betters   10

Brides of Reason (1955)

Among Artisans' Houses   12
Three Moral Discoveries   13
Twilight on the Waste Lands   14
Demi-Exile, Howth   15
Hypochondriac Logic   16
Creon's Mouse   17
Poem as Abstract   17
Mamertinus on Rhetoric, AD 291   19
Evening on the Boyne   19
Thyestes   20
Belfast on a Sunday Afternoon   21
Zip!   21
On Bertrand Russell's 'Portraits from Memory'   22
The Garden Party   22
The Owl Minerva   23
Heart Beats   24

Machineries of Shame   24
Pushkin. A Didactic Poem   25
At the Synod in St Patrick's   27
Remembering the 'Thirties   28
The Evangelist   29
An English Revenant   30
Hawkshead and Dachau in a Christmas Glass   32
Eight Years After   36
Selina, Countess of Huntingdon   36
Method. For Ronald Gaskell   37
Woodpigeons at Raheny   37

Love-Poems: for Mairi MacInnes   39
Jacob's Ladder   39

A Winter Talent and Other Poems (1957)

Time Passing, Beloved   40
Dream Forest   40
Obiter Dicta   41
Mens Sana in Corpore Sano   43
At the Cradle of Genius   44
The Mushroom Gatherers   45
    ENGLAND
The Wind at Penistone   46
Under St Paul's   47
Derbyshire Turf   49
Dissentient Voice   50
    IRELAND
The Priory of St Saviour, Glendalough   54
Samuel Beckett's Dublin   55
North Dublin   55
Corrib. An Emblem   56
The Wearing of the Green   56
    ITALY
Going to Italy   57
Tuscan Morning   58
Mr Sharp in Florence   58
Via Portello   59
The Tuscan Brutus   59
The Pacer in the Fresco. John the Baptist   60

The Fountain   61
Chrysanthemums   62

Cherry Ripe   63
Hearing Russian Spoken   63
Limited Achievement   64
A Winter Talent   65
Under a Skylight   65

Gardens no Emblems   66
The Nonconformist   67
Rejoinder to a Critic   67
Heigh-ho on a Winter Afternoon   68

Poems of 1955–6
On Sutton Strand   69
Aubade   70
Dudwood   70
Dublin Georgian   71
Dublin Georgian (2)   72
Eden   72
The Waterfall at Powerscourt   73

The Forests of Lithuania (1959)
Foreword. Mickiewicz in England   74
I.   The Homestead   75
II.   The Castle   79
III. The Gathering of Mushrooms   85
IV.   The Forest   92
V.   The Quarrel   104
VI.   The Year 1812   107
Epilogue   115

from *New and Selected Poems* (1961)
Against Confidences   116
Nineteen-Seventeen   117
To a Brother in the Mystery   118
Killala   119
With the Grain   120
Red Rock of Utah   122
Reflections on Deafness   123
For an Age of Plastics   124
The Life of Service   125
The 'Sculpture' of Rhyme   126

A Sequence for Francis Parkman (1961)

The Jesuits in North America 127
Lasalle 128
Frontenac 129
Montcalm 131
Pontiac 132
Bougainville 133
A Letter to Curtis Bradford 134

For Doreen. A Voice from the Garden 136

Events and Wisdoms (1964)

Two Dedications
  1 Wide France 137
  2 Barnsley Cricket Club 137
Resolutions 138
Life Encompassed 139
Hornet 139
Housekeeping 140
Low Lands 141
Green River 141
House-martin 142
Treviso, the Pescheria 143
The Prolific Spell 143
A Battlefield 144
The Cypress Avenue 145
Humanly Speaking 146
The Hill Field 147
The Feeders 147
A Lily at Noon 148
Love and the Times 148
Across the Bay 150
A Christening 150
Agave in the West 151
In California 152
New York in August 153
Viper-Man 154
In Chopin's Garden 154
Poreč 155
Barnsley and District 156
Right Wing Sympathies 157
Hyphens 159
A Meeting of Cultures 160
Metals 161

Homage to John L. Stephens   162
The Vindication of Jovan Babič   162
Bolyai, the Geometer   163
After an Accident   164
The Hardness of Light   167

Poems of 1962–3
On Not Deserving   169
Autumn Imagined   169
Hot Hands   170
Where Depths are Surfaces   170
Vying   171

from *The Poems of Doctor Zhivago* (1965)
March   172
Fairy Story   172
The Miracle   175
Magdalene   176

Essex Poems (1969)
Rodez   178
The North Sea   179
July, 1964   180
The Blank of the Wall   181
Out of East Anglia   181
January   182
Pietà   182
Sunburst   184
The God of Details   184
Ezra Pound in Pisa   185
Tunstall Forest   186
Orford   187
Thanks to Industrial Essex   188
Expecting Silence   188
A Winter Landscape near Ely   189
A Death in the West   189
From the New World   190
Stratford on Avon   192
Barnsley, 1966   193
A Conditioned Air   194
Sylvae   194
Amazonian   196
Intervals in a Busy Life   196

FROM THE NEW WORLD
Iowa 197
Back of Affluence 198
Or, Solitude 199

More Essex Poems (1964–8)
My Father's Honour 200
Rain on South-East England 201
Pentecost 201
Winter Landscapes 202
Behind the North Wind 203
Revulsion 204
Oak Openings 204
New Year Wishes for the English 205
Preoccupation's Gift 206
The North Sea, in a Snowstorm 206
To Certain English Poets 207
Democrats 207
Epistle. To Enrique Caracciolo Trejo 208
Cold Spring in Essex 209

Los Angeles Poems (1968–9)
To Helen Keller 210
Christmas Syllabics for a Wife 211
Idyll 212
Brantôme 212
Looking out from Ferrara 213
An Oriental Visitor 214
'Abbeyforde' 215
England 216
Emigrant, to the Receding Shore 230
The Break 231
Pilate 234
Trevenen 235
Vancouver 244
Commodore Barry 247
Lady Cochrane 249

Other Poems of the 1960s
England, for Ezra Pound 253
T.S. Eliot (1928) 254
Cowper's 'Yardley Oak': A Continuation 255
Midsummer's Eve 256

August, 1968   257
Energies   258
Boyhood Misremembered   259
Fatherhood   259
Reticence   260

Six Epistles to Eva Hesse (1970)   261

The Shires (1974)
Bedfordshire   299
Berkshire   299
Buckinghamshire   300
Cambridgeshire   300
Cheshire   301
Cornwall   302
Cumberland   303
Derbyshire   303
Devonshire   304
Dorset   305
County Durham   305
Essex   306
Gloucestershire   307
Hampshire   307
Herefordshire   308
Hertfordshire   309
Huntingdonshire   309
Kent   310
Lancashire   310
Leicestershire   311
Lincolnshire   312
Middlesex   313
Monmouthshire   313
Norfolk   314
Northamptonshire   314
Northumberland   315
Nottinghamshire   315
Oxfordshire   316
Rutland   317
Shropshire   317
Somerset   318
Staffordshire   318
Suffolk   319
Surrey   319
Sussex   320

Warwickshire 321
Westmorland 321
Wiltshire 322
Worcestershire 322
Yorkshire 323

In the Stopping Train and other poems (1977)

Father, the Cavalier 325
The Harrow 326
The Departed 327
Rousseau in his Day 327
After the Calamitous Convoy (July 1942) 327
Depravity: Two Sermons 329
Seeing Her Leave 331
Mandelstam, on Dante 332
Death of a Painter 334
Portland 335
Orpheus 335
Ars Poetica 336
In the Stopping Train 337
His Themes 344
To Thom Gunn in Los Altos, California 346
Seur, near Blois 348
Gemona–del–Friuli, 1961–1976 348
An Apparition 349
Horae Canonicae 350
Morning 352
To a Teacher of French 353
Widowers 354
Some Shires Revisited 354
Grudging Respect 356
A Spring Song 357
Townend, 1976 358

Other Poems of the 1970s

Mandelstam in the Crimea 361
Robinson Jeffers at Point Sur 361
Berryman 362
Replying to Reviewers 363

Three for Water-Music (1981)

The Fountain of Cyanë 364
Wild Boar Clough 368
The Fountain of Arethusa 371

The Battered Wife and other poems (1982)

The Battered Wife	376
G.M.B.	377
Short Run to Camborne	377
Livingshayes	378
The Admiral to his Lady	379
Screech-owl	380
Fare Thee Well	381
Grace in the Fore Street	382
Some Future Moon	383
Ox-bow	385
A Late Anniversary	385
No Epitaph	386
Utterings	387
Skelpick	388
Strathnaver	389
Winter's Talents	390
To Londoners	391
A Liverpool Epistle	392
Well-found Poem	395
Artifex in Extremis	398
The Bent	400
Catullus on Friendship	401
Two from Ireland	402
Penelope	404
Devil on Ice	405
Advent	406
Having No Ear	407
Siloam	408
A Christian Hero	410
An Anglican Lady	411
Mandelstam's Hope for the Best	411
Three Beyond	415
A Garland for Ronsard	416
'Pastor Errante'	423
Summer Lightning	428
Death of a Voice	432
Mandelstam's 'Octets'	434

To Scorch or Freeze (1988)

The Thirty-ninth Psalm, Adapted	438
Benedictus	439
Poet Redeemed & Dead	440
Attar of Roses	440

Sing Unto The Lord a New Song	441
'So make them melt as the dishousèd snail'	441
God Saves the King	442
Meteorologist, September	443
Vengeance Is Mine, Saith The Lord	444
Standings	444
Church Militant	445
Curtains!	446
'And Our Eternal Home'	446
Zion	447
Felicity's Fourth Order	449
Put Not Your Trust in Princes	449
Their Rectitude Their Beauty	450
Except The Lord Build The House	451
Inditing A Good Matter	452
The Creature David	453
Saw I Never The Righteous Forsaken	453
The Elect	454
The Zodiac	455
'Just You Wait!'	456
Bowing the Head	457
Widower	458
Master & Man	459
Levity	459
Witness	460
Our Lady	461
The Ironist	462
'Thou Art Near At Hand, O Lord'	463
The Nosegay	464
Gripping Serial	465
I Have Said, Ye Are Gods	465
David Dancing	466
Dancing Measures	466
Being Angry With God	467
The Comforter	468
Cannibals	469
Woe Unto Thee!	470
Kingship	471
Ordinary God	472
Nashville Mornings	473
If I Take The Wings Of The Morning	475

Other Poems of the 1980s

Kavyria	476

Sorting Old Papers 478
Sonnet 479
After Pasternak, in Byron's Manner 479

from *Collected Poems* (1990)
North & South 480
They, to Me 481
By the Road to Upper Midhope 483
Dule of a Dewsbury Matron 484
Black Hoyden 484
The Right Lads 485
Grazia Deledda, young 486
Hermes and Mr Shaw 488
Articulacy. Hints from the Koran 489
Reminded of Bougainville 491
A Measured Tread 493
Northern Metres 494
Church of Ireland 495
The Scythian Charioteers 496
Mother 497
At the Café Parnasse 498
Though dry, not dry 499
To a Bad Poet 501
On a Proposed Celebration of Ezra Pound 501
Revenge for Love 502
A Garland for Ivor Gurney 503
Wombwell on Strike 505
After the Match 506
Mustered into the Avant-Garde 507
Sculptures in Hungary 508
Sounds of a Devon Village 509
On Generous Lines 511
Equestrian Sestina 511
Homage to George Whitefield 512
Two Widows in Tashkent 513
Helena Morley 514
Sorting the Personae 515
'1945' 517

Goodbye to the USA (1990)
Sunday Morning 519
The University of the South 521
Savannah 522

To an American Classicist   523
H. D.   524
The Gardens of the Savoy   524
Alzheimer's Disease   533
Recollections of George Oppen in a letter to an English friend   534
West Virginia's Auburn   536
Through Bifocals   538

from *Poems and Melodramas* (1996)
    SEVEN MELODRAMAS
After a Change of Régime   540
A Heroine of the Academy   551
Bella & Rosa   556
Three Pastors in Berlin   561
Chernobyl. A Disaster   567
Balancing Acts   572
Another Old Bolshevik   579
    POEMS
Bits and Pieces   585
The Knave of Hearts   585
The Lost Bride   586
Orvieto. The King of Clubs   587
On the Final Day   588
To C. T.   589
To a Staffordshireman, from a Devon Villa   589
Jottings, not so Random   590
Sea of Tiberias   591
Seeing through Me   592
Toby to Aguecheek   593
War Criminal   594
Ecclesiastical Polity   594
Women and War   595
'Our Father'   596
On Edmund Spenser's House in Ireland   601
Two Intercepted Letters   601
Immortal Longings. Before Surgery   602
Thomas and Emma   603

Notes   605

Index of First Lines   615
Index of Titles   625

Introduction

1

During his lifetime, Donald Davie published two – or, more precisely, two and a half – volumes of *Collected Poems*. The first, which appeared in 1972 to mark the author's fiftieth birthday, contained over 300 pages and covered the years 1950 to 1970: although it thus excluded some uncollected early work as well as 'poems published in periodicals which I have lost sight of', it represented a remarkable poetic output for someone who was also a full-time university teacher, a prolific academic author and an energetic literary journalist. The 'half' volume, a supplementary *Collected Poems 1971–1983*, added an astonishing further 172 pages. Lastly, the second *Collected Poems*, published in 1990, managed to include much new material in just under 500 pages; but it did so at the cost of excluding Davie's versions of Mickiewicz and of Pasternak, the authorial notes from the 1972 edition, and the indexes of first lines and titles.

While all three of these books remain valuable, none of them is entirely satisfactory or complete: this edition is therefore an attempt to provide as full a *Collected Poems* as can be contained in a fairly hefty single volume. It differs most obviously from the 1990 *Collected* in its restorations and rediscoveries. For example, the *Doctor Zhivago* poems reappear, and so does the whole of *The Forests of Lithuania*, which in 1972 was included only in puzzlingly abbreviated form. Some poems are now for the first time collected in their fullest or most authoritative versions – 'The Gardens of the Savoy', which includes both 'Brilliance' and 'The Trip to Huntsville', is the most striking instance – and various minor corrections or modifications which Donald Davie made to the 1990 text have been incorporated, as have the slightly rearranged contents of the posthumous *Poems and Melodramas*. Perhaps most interestingly of all, this edition includes over two dozen poems which, mostly no doubt having been 'lost sight of' in a busy life, have not been previously published in any of Davie's slim volumes nor in the earlier editions of his *Collected Poems*.

One of the mysteries which impertinent, or just ordinarily curious, readers sense about Davie's poetic career concerns its beginning. His start is so unnervingly clear and purposeful: both the 1972 and the 1990 *Collected Poems* open with 'Homage to William Cowper', the poem in which he famously describes himself as 'A pasticheur of late-Augustan styles', setting the agenda for one of his own poetic selves as well as for his contemporaries in The Movement. That poem was designated (in 1990) as 'of the 1950s', and it seems safe to assume that most if not all the poems in his earliest full-length collection, *Brides of Reason* (1955), were similarly written during the first half of the decade: that this is 'probably' the case is confirmed by the author's own note to 'Hypochondriac Logic'. But Davie had gone up to Cambridge as long ago as 1940; he then spent four years on active service in the Royal Navy before he returned to marry Doreen John and to complete his degree, graduating in 1947 and staying on to read for his PhD. Could a poet who was subsequently to prove so prolific have written nothing at all during these years of study, travel and marriage? Or could it be – and here curiosity begins to shade towards impertinence – that the mature Donald Davie carefully suppressed the work of some wildly apocalyptic younger self?

The answer is (as it usually is) yes and no. One notably free, unMovementish poem, 'Tiger at the Movie-Show', published in the magazine *Prospect* in 1949, was included in *Poems and Melodramas* and is here restored to its proper chronological place. But the early poems which are now collected for the first time – from *Poetry from Cambridge in Wartime*, *Poetry London*, *Prospect* and *Essays in Criticism* – tell a rather different story. The five earliest, written during the war years and anthologised in 1946, are both disciplined and dense: while they prove beyond doubt that the young Davie was largely immune to sprawling rhetoric, they lack the terse lucidity and careful diction which would be among his hallmarks a decade later. They are fascinating and valuable in the same sort of way as Philip Larkin's early work in *The North Ship*: the manner, the voice we would come to know is fleetingly in evidence, but it is still trapped within the wrong sort of poem.

The other hitherto uncollected early poems represent huge advances. For instance, the overlapping rhyme-scheme of 'Landfall among Friends' (which first appeared in September 1949) is a typical Movement device, and the phrase 'dissentient coast' startlingly prefigures a major strand in Davie's imagery and thought – the poem 'Dissentient Voice', the dissenting emphasis of his Augustan anthologies, the answering 'protestant sea' of *Essex Poems* and of course the theme of his 1976 Clark Lectures, *A Gathered Church*. Its strikingly Hardyesque companion-piece in that issue of *Poetry London*, 'Condolence', points forward to Davie's famous assertion, some thirty years later, 'that in British poetry of the last fifty years (as not in American) the most far-reaching influence, for good and ill, has been not Yeats, still less Eliot or Pound, not Lawrence, but *Hardy*'. Equally prescient is 'The Poet-Scholar', first published in 1955 but curiously excluded from both *Brides of Reason* and *A Winter Talent*. 'The scholar's pleasure is the poet's vice,' Davie writes; and, a little later, 'The poet-scholar cannot keep apart / The gift and the investment.' He may even then have suspected that this was too true for comfort: certainly, his reputation with the reading public was to be coloured by the inaccurate perception of him as only, or primarily, an 'academic' poet.

A number of later poems have been added: they are clearly grouped in the text and their sources are given in the notes at the end of the book. They date from the 1960s to the 1980s – the years in which Davie, moving back and forth between England and America and publishing work in magazines on both sides of the Atlantic, might very easily have 'lost sight of' some quite important poems. Many of them touch on his recurrent literary interests – Cowper, Pound, Eliot, Mandelstam, Robinson Jeffers, Berryman, Pasternak. Others provide typically oblique shafts of auto-biographical light. And some clearly belong as part of the late twentieth-century record: 'August, 1968', for instance, is a response to that year's events in Czechoslovakia, while 'Replying to Reviewers' came at the end of a memorable controversy – which had begun with Davie's review of *The Oxford Book of Twentieth-Century Verse* – in the pages of *The Listener*. However, there are certainly other poems which remain ungathered, as well as one deliberate editorial exclusion. In his memoir *These the Companions* (1982), Davie published for the first time a longish poem written in 1972/3, called 'Petit-Thouars (Guide-Michelin)', which, he said, 'I must probably learn to think of as a folly of my middle age'; he did not include it in his subsequent *Collected Poems* (1990), so it seems reasonable to assume that this was indeed his considered opinion (as it is, dare I add, mine).

This edition restores the notes which Donald Davie provided for his 1972 *Collected Poems* – among them, the crucially 'vulnerable' one on 'With the Grain' – and adds to these a few brief quotations from *These the Companions*, which provide background information about some specific poems, as well as editorial notes on the sources of all previously uncollected material.

2

The sheer extent of Donald Davie's *Collected Poems* puts him among the twentieth-century heavyweights – though weight is not a particularly useful yardstick for judging poetry – in marked contrast to his friend and contemporary Philip Larkin, whose mature poetic output comprised three slim volumes. Some readers find the scope and, at times, the complexity of Davie's poetry daunting; for them, a mildly diverting, if ultimately pointless, exercise might involve winnowing it down to the equivalent of those three volumes by Larkin. That could, up to a point, be done; and the daunted reader would then discover a poet as approachable as Larkin: a poet of wry Northern retrospects ('The Garden Party', 'Barnsley Cricket Club'), perfectly-judged intimacies ('Time Passing, Beloved', 'Heigh-ho on a Winter Afternoon'), sculpted anger ('Right-Wing Sympathies', 'July, 1964') and, in the wonderful *Essex Poems*, pared-down passionate eloquence. Around here, however, our reader would have to concede that Davie's post-Movement trajectory was beginning to look more Gunnish than Larkinesque. And indeed it would soon become plain that the poems I've just cited, admirable starting-points though they would be for any as yet unconvinced reader, are just that: starting-points. The poet they map out is clearly a significant one, but he is not the complete Donald Davie.

The challenge Davie sets his readers is the challenge he sets himself: to move on, as a rigorous and restless intelligence must, continually seeking different forms of articulate energy. And in fact his quest, despite its apparently wayward lurches of style, is remarkably consistent in its purpose. From the start, Davie is a writer whose poetry is dense with ideas and information rather than with description; the models he chooses – the causes he champions – are invariably those whose poems are alive with intellectual urgency rather than placid with expansive evocation. That is the common factor which unites the Augustans with the allusive modernists and with the geographical-historical Black Mountaineers: they are all impatient to cram their poems with whatever awkward and intractable stuff is rattling about in their heads. Davie is that sort of poet all the way through. As early as 1956, he was infuriated by the reluctance of other Movement poets (and English literary life in general) to share the inescapably intellectual scope of his project: 'Isn't the reading of a poem, or the seeing of a picture, an experience like an other? Isn't such an experience, for many people, unusually intense and meaningful? And what is the "life" which you oppose to "art"?' A quarter of a century later, in *These the Companions*, he would write of 'an enterprise which I suppose I have never given up – the incorporating into verse of more and more of the prose virtues, so as to see how near to prose poetry can come while still remaing poetry'. These two principles – the centrality of cultural-intellectual life and the need to make poetry as effective a discursive medium as prose – are consistent in Davie's work. That a poet who subscribes them is also likely to be a moralist almost goes without saying.

Davie gives his readers a fairly bumpy ride: it is hard to think of a major poet who offers a smooth one. There are times when a kind of information overload threatens to derail a poem; but then he brilliantly transforms this very pressure into his subject, as he does in 'In the Stopping Train' – a poem which, he tells us, refers to a journey from Tours to Paris and back, but which surely embodies an ironic nod towards that other literary stopping train, the one Larkin caught in 'The Whitsun Weddings' – or in 'Summer Lightning'. There are moments, especially in the difficult years of the late 1960s and early 1970s, when articulacy seems to crack and the poems become fragmentary and exclamatory with impatient fury. And, of course, there are the poems which are difficult because the poet is alluding to things which the reader hasn't read – as all poets do, without ever being at all sure when they are doing it: most of us, if for example we hope to understand that fine long poem 'Trevenen', will need to visit the *DNB* or a decent eighteenth-century history, but the effort will be repaid. As is ever the case, poems which at first seem puzzling usually become less opaque when read in the context of the author's other work. That, among other things, is what a *Collected Poems* is for.

I am especially grateful to Doreen Davie, for allowing me to edit this book and for providing advice, information and copies of several newly-collected poems; to Bernard Bergonzi, who very kindly unearthed many of the earliest poems here, including those from *Poetry from Cambridge in Wartime* and *Poetry London*; to Clive Wilmer, who drew my (baffled) attention to 'T.S. Eliot (1928)'; and to Martin Wright, who thirty years ago supervised my postgraduate work and generously handed on his own Donald Davie cuttings file to me.

NEIL POWELL
January 2002

EARLY POEMS

Pelican

Obtrusive and absurd, the guilty mind
Haggles about and cracks forbearance,
Pride to self-torture still before, behind,
Its closed and comic sequence, in the dance,
Twitching and turning, burning, unconfined
Fierce uncontrollable pelican.

A barren forest without bridle ways,
Continual cross-roads, or the dwarf forest,
Ridge behind ridge mounting, and no rest;
This is the road beginning, this is best,
The noble doing, or the no-pride at the doing.

Oh, heckling spirit whistle not
The will that has its way in me.
Your wayward eyes are the will's undoing,
For will is blind, and has forgot
All worlds but what you let him see.

A Song for These Crusaders

Joe, little serpentine white boy,
The baby of our company;
Thin-lipped with grinning wide, provocative,
Sitting on knees, solemn and childishly preoccupied,
Loud-mouthed, savage, and unkind;
Doing violence to servant-girls in alley-ways,
Befriending none, on friends depending,
Exploiting all forbearance, faithlessly,
How shall I see, whose gracelessness
Cries to high heaven above the blood
For pardon, and the verse
Is halt and tumbling, whose purport

So far outstrips felicity? But O
Gentlest of men, thou certain Christ,
Here is no still resolve – where now
The passion without the fury?

Glaphira III

The circle of her arms could be
A circle of tall trees for me.
Not arms of Walden's conifers,
Nor Binsey's aspens, singing tree,
Were ever havens safe as hers
For speculation, free
As sensuous bright birds.
Caresses, not words,
Applaud, in her perfection, perfect worlds,
By perfect hands made up.
These involute companions, these lips,
Lying, strange bow to shadowed tips,
Together, in their curves conceal
All proofs, all marvels; and who sips
Their jealous sweets, to him reveal
How adoration slips
Free, as freed bright birds.
As falcons, fierce birds,
Slip from the fowler, hair uncurled
Patterns the modes of worlds.

Kites

A village of kite-flyers, we
Let loose the gorgeous, powerful box,
To fly fast, and obscure the stars.
By rocks and snow then, and over hills
Stumble, weighing on the grapnel.
Some totem kites drag men from cliffs,
Some grapnels gouge the heart. Beware
Of kites too lovely, or will fly too fast.

Duplicity in Prayer

It will not help, my heart
To ransack through.
This lonely hunted heart
The mind finds two,
Poor culprits, doubling from the dart,
Apparently, and in vain, untrue.

Turn, two-faced heart,
By mind caught out.
So heart and heart, and heart
That mind doth flout,
A keener compound smart
Will breed, and deeper doubt.

Tiger at the Movie-Show

I was never impressed, when they presented
'Culture' as a mesh of learned letters,
Weaving a basket for Europe, to keep together fragments
Against a future dawn. Of course, from time to time,
After 'Mädchen in Uniform', after
'Marie-Louise' (to take a couple of films),
I felt what the beaky poet had implied
With his broken columns, and the pigeons pecking
And the rough basket, piled on a cart
With the parrot and the family bible, when the bombers come.

At bottom it will all become a question
Of procédé, of talent and tradition, of the sense
Of 'saying', meaning an event, in the first place
And secondly what is said. And very often
We don't consider the created thing
But the ceremonies of creation.

For instance this 'Mädchen', this admirable film
Should pad about the precincts of my soul
A dangerous animal, answering no law
But those of its constitution, and appearing
With a shocking pertinence, on quite another trail
From where I marked it last. Instead
Two hours of the tiger's playing have become
Stuffed to a cypher, packed to a point to
Stand for something other than itself.
The difference is between the carnivore and the carved,
                              snarling from thickets
Or else on a pedestal, yawning.

The singing robe of Europe is shrugged on
By every would-be poet. Some are weighed and stifled.
More seem ridiculous, and a few
Are dignified. Which has, as a spectacle,
Its own impressiveness, but which is never,
Properly speaking, Art.

To say you will stand by Art, with no farrago
Of decadence, and no wish to be clever
Or a superior person, means an intention
To outface the tiger, never to make him decorous
In stone or silk.

As for the pieces of Europe, caught up in a basket,
The thousands of Europe are starving, and ask for
Just what is left of the fishes
And a few small loaves. They will not pause to examine
The wickerwork of the roundsman and Redeemer.

Landfall among Friends

At that time, two friends stood
On that dissentient coast, like lights that would,
Compared, pin-point me in the darkling sea.

One stood for (or, in life and blood,
Engrossed) whole tracts, saying, 'This church, that wood
Stand so, behind, or else oblique to me.'

The sentimental counties he implied
Were those called 'Style', lying along one side
Of that small estuary where I was bound.

The other tower, on a spit of land
Continually clouded, rose on my other hand,
And grave and sober forests hedged it round.

Through sober and magnificent, between
The gay and insolent flash, the charitable gleam,
I nose her now. The lights are high above.

Between the assertive 'I', the tender 'They',
What little town winks in the close of day?
A needful pride, an equal, fluent love.

Condolence

When he came back from saying good-bye
For the last time in that foreign town
To his foreign woman, was it I
    Who was suddenly drawn
To touch him and say 'My dear'?

Of passionate comradely men, and their ways
Of mutual comfort, I had learned
Nothing at all. Yet the warmest phrase
    I suddenly turned,
And the only acceptable movement made.

No tongue's sufficient. There is none
So noble and so intimate;
Unless that ancient stilted one,
    With its Delphic beat,
Could act condolence through the hand.

There was the tact in it! Brush of a wing,
The touching was the happy ruse,
A quiet and time-honoured thing
    Quite out of use,
Articulation by the bone.

I never did so. Never I
Pulled down the wild head to the nest
In one quick warmth of arm and eye,
        And the moment's rest
Of a flickering hand, and a word.

But it was I, resuming then
The usual day, who rejoicing went
At the ease and grace of comradely men,
        And full of content
At my hand that lay light like a wing.

Christmas Week, 1948

'The uncontrollable mystery on the bestial floor.' W.B. Yeats

That Christmas quite the animal
I made occasions serve my heat.
Mistletoe-kisses and sherry wine
Warm rooms and roasted meat.

These fumes, becoming rational
Defined the nature of the feast:
About the God's mysterious birth
The stink of stabled beast.

That image, dwelt upon with passion
Pumped blood into the ox-eye lens.
The pupil of the brute and flower
Reviewed experience.

That scrutiny, grown introspective,
Blurred as soon as brought to bear.
The brutal mystery was gone
From that self-conscious air.

That agony, my wilful habit,
Made me the stranger at the board.
I was keeping Easter when
The simple carol was heard.

That difference, by concentration,
Created what it could not be.
And rank as ox or fox or badger,
I made the mystery.

Protesilaus and Laodamia

The streaming simile, the plume,
The legend and the flying hair
All indifferently assume
Life in Homer's heavy air.

His heroes wish it. They applaud
When from the shades they hear him sing
The only conquest they implored,
The heavy status of a thing.

Upon the bosom of his love
The dedicated bosom heaves,
Aspiring to the denseness of
His sword, his corslet, casque, and greaves.

He sees, before the assembled power
(His flange between her dreaming thighs)
His time come round, his timeless hour
Solid in all their armour, rise.

The beaks of Greece that mob the town
Lie idling in a bay of time;
Who'll turn the hour-glass upside-down
Now that the sands no longer climb?

They only seem to cut the sea,
All stems but one, where stands the one,
Once slave of fate, of destiny
Now the self-appointed son.

The tragic hero jumps to death,
Kissing the day that gives at once,
Free of the accident of breath,
A life in legendary bronze.

But Laodamia, his love,
Is only less substantial, wed
To no true man, and dreaming of
A metal beak, no human head.

Homage to William Cowper

Mrs Throckmorton's bull-finch sang a song.
(Domesticate that comfortable bird!)
But still the deer has wandered from the herd,
The bard was not articulate for long.

A pasticheur of late-Augustan styles,
I too have sung the sofa and the hare,
Made nightmare ride upon a private air
And hearths, extinguished, send a chill for miles.

This costive plan, this dense upholstery,
These mice and kittens, this constrictive rhyme,
These small Infernos of another time –
What's all this modish Hecuba to me?

Most poets let the morbid fancy roam.
The squalid rat broke through the finch's fence,
Which was a cage, and still was no defence:
For Horror starts, like Charity, at home.

At Knaresborough

'Broad acres, sir.' You hear them in my talk.
As tell-tale as a pigment in the skin,
Vowels as broad as all the plain of York
Proclaim me of this country and your kin.

And, gratified to have your guess endorsed,
You warm to me. I thaw, and am approved.
But, to be frank, the sentiment is forced,
When I pretend, for your sake, to be moved.

To feel so little, when his sympathies
Would be so much engaged (he would have said),
Surprised the poet too. But there it is,
The heart is not to be solicited.

Believe me, sir, I only ply my trade,
Which is to know when I am played upon.
You might have moved, you never shall persuade.
You grow too warm. I must be moving on.

The Bride of Reason

Pragmatical old Capulet, the head,
So long has ruled, or seemed to rule, the heart,
That Juliet muse, to County Paris wed,
Lets his good sense determine all her art.

Charmed with his manners towards alternatives,
The unacceptable Romeos she has kissed,
The heart with this judicious husband lives,
And, wed to Reason, seems a moralist.

Some who have loved the lady are dismayed;
Some who have loved her first love, Romeo,
Think that impulsive gallant is betrayed,
Now Juliet's voice is so demure and low.

Only her father thinks the wench is sly,
And sees in her docility her treason;
She loves the truth he thought she must deny,
Her lyric to the music of his reason.

The Poet-Scholar

That proper ghoul, the scholar, may exhume
A bony reputation that the nice
And rigorous poet must again entomb.
The scholar's pleasure is the poet's vice;
For looking backwards Orpheus met his doom.

It's little that the poet can afford
In the indulgent, antiquarian way.
Like other people, he prefers to hoard;
But has to learn, if dogs must have their day,
The next day they deserve to be ignored.

The poet-scholar cannot keep apart
The gift and the investment. In the least
Anticipated movement of his heart,
He finds a pleasure that reverts, increased,
To season what was selfish from the start.

But in a way he cannot understand,
By sheer good luck, his studies burst their frame.
Scholarship was its own reward, and planned
Its own dishonest pleasures. Yet there came,
Just here, to touch him, Truth's imperious hand!

Elders and Betters

To Mr Graves on his Clark Lecture

A cuckoo in the singing nest betrays
The confidences of the singing masters,
Himself no songster of a single phrase
But variously, brilliantly endowed
Among the best. And we who have been proud
To emulate his throat that so surpassed us,
Ashamed for him, avoid his beady gaze.

There are more kinds of cuckoldry than one,
As many as the meanings of espousal;
Our muse was chaste, though wed to more than one,
While those were true. One lover, who espoused
His jealousies, has cuckolded the rest;
Ours are the sheets his indiscretions tousle,
Our occupation, like Othello's, gone.

BRIDES OF REASON

Among Artisans' Houses

High above Plymouth, not so high
But that the roof-tops seem to sweat
In the damp sea-mist, the damp sea-sky
Lowers on terraced houses, set
Like citadels, so blank and high;
Clothes-lines run to a handy cleat,
And plots are furiously neat.

There are not many notice this
Resourcefulness of citizens,
And few esteem it. But it is
An outcome of the civil sense,
Its small and mean utilities;
A civilization, in its way,
Its rudiments or its decay.

And if civility is gone,
As we assume it is, the moulds
Of commonwealth all broken down,
Then how explain that this still holds,
The strong though cramped and cramping tone
Of mutual respect, that cries
Out of these small civilities?

It could occur, perhaps, only here,
On these hills over Plymouth Sound,
Where continuity is clear
From Drake to now, where life is bound
Still, though obscurely, to the gear
Traditionally maritime,
And sanctioned by the use of time.

There is no moral to the scene,
Curious relic from the past.
What has and not what might have been
It serves to show now. And at last,
Shortly, nothing will be seen
By which historians may fix
The moral shape of politics.

Three Moral Discoveries

1

Oh I can praise a cloistered virtue, such
As knows it cannot fear itself too much;
That though innate corruption breaks the laws,
Woman, for instance, is the efficient cause.
The genuine prayer, when all is said and done,
Is 'Lead us not into temptation'.

2

As Will and I went down the hill
Who should we meet, dressed up to kill,
        But a sexual misdemeanour.

When Will and I got into the train,
There was a loose-limbed wench again,
        An inconsiderate action.

As I left the station, I missed my pipe,
And I turned on Will. He began to weep.

It wasn't until I was nearly thirty,
I noticed the will resents being dirty.

3

I dared occasion, and came off intact,
Unharmed, not therefore ashamed. The act
Is unimportant; and the times I fell
In fact, in thought, in wish, in all but will,
Reflect how little credit falls to me,
At fault just there, in will's obduracy.

Twilight on the Waste Lands

Some quickly-weathering rock, perhaps,
Eroded by a sandy wind,
Conceals a carving, in the lapse
Of centuries so often skinned
That more than patinas escape,
And from the crag the chiselled shape
Disperses on the desert wind.

The traveller, at dusk or dawn,
Adverted by a trick of light,
Starts at a meaning, hints a form
So fugitive, the doubtful sight
Suspects no hand of man at all,
An artefact so natural
It seems the work of air and light.

Conceive of such a poem, planned
With such a nicety of touch
It quite conceals the maker's hand
And seems a votive fragment, such
As patient scholars make unclear
And, hazarding their guesses, fear
They have read into it too much.

Strung to the dominant, the voice
Guys all the intervals of speech.
Time-honoured forms present a choice
Of parody or else pastiche.
In all but what seems inchoate
We quiz the past. To see it straight
Requires a form just out of reach:

Such form as, see, the setting sun
Behind the shoulder of the bluff
Brings out there! But the beam is gone;
Old Rocky-face there in the rough,
Asleep again, has wiped the slate,
A God, a shape, that must await
A light that's sensitive enough.

Sand–blast the friable. Concede
Skin after skin, but frayed not flayed,
Not chipped to chastened bone, but freed
From every play but light and shade,
Invertebrate. The marble chills;
Be no more shapely than the hills.
See, there again, the sense betrayed!

Demi-Exile. Howth

Daisy and dandelion, speedwell, daffodil,
Lean from the parks on this sea-ward hill,
In Queen Victoria's Anglo-Ireland,
Lean from the lawns to my English hand
In Anglo-India, Anglo-Ireland,
Cities drowning in drifted sand.

Division of loyalties, dolour of exile,
Do you command a quizzical smile
Here, at the roof that once defended
Jonathan Swift's demented head?
Here, in the suburb that Hopkins visited,
Strangled in sand of its famous dead?

Flowers of England, flowers of Ireland,
Lean from earth to my empty hand.
Hands acknowledging no allegiance,
Gloved for good against brutal chance,
Pluck the shadow and not the substance,
Grasp no nettle of circumstance.

Hypochondriac Logic

Appendicitis is his worst
Obsession, mordant from the first
And unannounced. For who but he,
By curious failing schooled to see
The tiniest pain, can hope to be
Fore-warned of appendectomy?
So thinking, he thinks pain to be
More real as more illusory.

So argue all men who have thought
A truth more true as more remote,
Or in poetic worlds confide
The more their air is rarefied.
This the Shelleyan failing is,
Who feared elephantiasis,
Whose poems infect his readers too,
Who, since they're vague, suppose them true.

But lagging down a crippled street
Like fugitives from their own feet,
Some who are whole can yet observe
Disease is what we all deserve,
Or else disdain a painless life
While any squeal beneath the knife.
So, if you trace the impulse back,
The best are hypochondriac.

So poets may astonish you
With what is not, but should be, true,
And shackle on a moral shape
You only thought you could escape;
And if their scenery is queer,
Its prototype may not be here,
Unless inside a frightened mind,
Which may be dazzled, but not blind.

Creon's Mouse

Creon, I think, could never kill a mouse
When once that dangerous girl was put away,
Shut up unbridled in her rocky house,
Colossal nerve denied the light of day.

Now Europe's hero, the humaner King
Who hates himself, is humanized by shame,
Is he a curbed or a corroded spring?
A will that's bent, or buckled? Tense, or tame?

If too much daring brought (he thought) the war,
When that was over nothing else would serve
But no one must be daring any more,
A self-induced and stubborn loss of nerve.

In itching wainscot having met his match,
He waits unnerved, and hears his caverned doom,
The nausea that struggles to dispatch
Pink-handed horror in a craggy room.

The absolute endeavour was the catch;
To clean the means and never mind the end
Meant he had not to chasten but to scotch
The will he might have managed to amend.

You that may think yourselves not proud at all,
Learn this at least from humble Creon's fall:
The will that is subject, not overthrown,
Is humbled by some power not its own.

Poem as Abstract

'To write about a tree… you must first *be* a tree.' (W.R. Rodgers)

1

A poem is less an orange than a grid;
It hoists a charge; it does not ooze a juice.
It has no rind, being entirely hard.

All drumming yards and open, it asserts
That clouds have way upon them, and that hills
Breast into time behind a singing strut.

A sheer abstraction, apt upon the grass
Of London parks, has emulated oak
And aped the ramage that it could surpass.

That construct, ribbed with wire across a quern,
Is caging such serenity of stress
As boughs, or fruit that breaks them, cannot learn.

For gods are gathered from the styles they wear,
And do they curl, a fœtus in a fruit,
Or, like Orion, pinned upon the air?

2

No trowelled matron but a rigger's mate,
The pile-high poet has no time to brood.
He steps the mast; it does not germinate.

Not for ingestion but to frame the air
He flies the spar that even winter's tree
In green ambition cannot grow so spare.

The orange dangles, drops, and comes again.
To make a fruit he has to be a fruit,
A globe of pulp about a pip of pain.

But tip-toe cages lofted in a day
(To make a grid he has to *make* a grid)
Have come unprecedented, and to stay.

If poems make a style, a way of walking
With enterprise, should not a poet's gait
Be counties-wide, this stride, the pylons stalking?

Mamertinus on Rhetoric, AD 291

Personae seek provisional assent.
Perversities of unforeseen address
Obliquely murmur, and a sentiment
Finds not expression but expressiveness.

This is the entry of the chamberlains
To Diocletian and his fictive son.
They speak through masks. The double image feigns
To share the dye too dangerous for one.

Urbanities of Danube and Milan
(Himself at Nicomedia, at York
Constantius Chlorus) baffle, if they can,
And drown the edict in a buzz of talk.

But virtue has to rule the world alone
And scorns assistance from a trick of light,
Her ceremonies rectitude, her tone
Not florid nor austere, but coming right.

A poor decorum? So it seems, my lord,
There in your palace planted like a camp.
The Roman style, however, can afford
To think seven hills an all-sufficient ramp.

Evening on the Boyne

The Boyne at Navan swam in light,
Where children headlong through the trees
Plunged down the sward, and nicked the bright
Precarious evening with unease.

Swans at the bottom of a vale,
Sailing rapidly from sight,
Made the sweet arrangements fail
And emptied all the precious light.

A moment later all was well,
The light was full, the ranks were closed;
The fields of flags, the wading mill
Withdrew again, once more composed.

But what had happened? Who had made
This mirror tremble and subside?
The evening by what eye betrayed
Winced, like a curtain drawn aside?

The shutter of some active mind,
Panicked by a glide of swans,
Closing, made all nature blind,
Then photographed itself at once.

O bleak and lunar emptiness,
How many eyes were then belied?
A god's, a man's, a swan's, and – yes,
The very flags were iris-eyed!

Thyestes

Brush of a raven's, not an eagle's wing!
No wonder older classicists could wish
For something more cathartic than this King
Who spooned his baked-meat children from a dish.

With Jung and Frazer, Tylor, Graves and Lang,
The scholiast can wash the blood away.
But what's the use? The savage poets sang
Enormities that happen every day.

No talons raven in a titan's gut
When dreadful fathers of a fortnight's date
Are drowning kittens in a water-butt.
But see, a baby's finger in the plate!

Belfast on a Sunday Afternoon

Visiting Belfast at the end of June,
We found the Orange Lodge behind a band:
Sashes and bearskins in the afternoon,
White cotton gloves upon a crippled hand.

Pastmasters pale, elaborately grim,
Marched each alone, beneath a bowler hat:
And, catapulted on a crumpled limb,
A lame man leapt the tram-lines like a bat.

And first of all we tried to laugh it off,
Acting bemusement in the grimy sun;
But stayed to worry where we came to scoff,
As loud contingents followed, one by one.

Pipe bands, flute bands, brass bands and silver bands,
Presbyter's pibroch and the deacon's serge,
Came stamping where the iron Mænad stands,
Victoria, glum upon a grassy verge.

Some brawny striplings sprawled upon the lawn;
No man is really crippled by his hates.
Yet I remembered with a sudden scorn
Those 'passionate intensities' of Yeats.

Zip!

I'd have the silence like a heavy chock
That's kicked away as you begin to read;
And sense, responding to the tiny shock,
Roll forward, fire, and smoothly gather speed.

Lines should be hoops that, vibrantly at rest,
Devolve like cables as the switches trip,
Each syllable entailing all the rest,
And rhymes that strike, exploding like a whip.

I'd have the spark that leaps upon the gun
By one short fuse, electrically clear;
And all be done before you've well begun.
(It is reverberations that you hear.)

On Bertrand Russell's 'Portraits from Memory'

Those Cambridge generations, Russell's, Keynes'…
And mine? Oh mine was Wittgenstein's, no doubt:
Sweet pastoral, too, when some-one else explains,
Although my memories leave the eclogues out.

The clod's not bowed by sedentary years,
Yet, set by Thyrsis, he's a crippled man:
How singularly naked each appears,
Beside the other on this bosky plan.

Arrangements of the copse and cloister seem,
Although effective, still Utopian,
For groves find room, behind a leafy screen,
For sage and harvester, but not for man.

I wonder still which of the hemispheres
Infects the other, in this grassy globe;
The chumbling moth of Madingley, that blears
The labourer's lamp, destroys the scarlet robe.

It was the Muse that could not make her home
In that too thin and yet too sluggish air,
Too volatile to live among the loam,
Her sheaves too heavy for the talkers there.

The Garden Party

Above a stretch of still unravaged weald
In our Black Country, in a cedar-shade,
I found, shared out in tennis courts, a field
Where children of the local magnates played.

And I grew envious of their moneyed ease
In Scott Fitzgerald's unembarrassed vein.
Let prigs, I thought, fool others as they please,
I only wish I had my time again.

To crown a situation as contrived
As any in 'The Beautiful and Damned',
The phantom of my earliest love arrived;
I shook absurdly as I shook her hand.

As dusk drew in on cultivated cries,
Faces hung pearls upon a cedar-bough;
And gin could blur the glitter of her eyes,
But it's too late to learn to tango now.

My father, of a more submissive school,
Remarks the rich themselves are always sad.
There is that sort of equalizing rule;
But theirs is all the youth we might have had.

The Owl Minerva

The muse that makes pretensions to discourse,
Not sage nor sybil but a piece of both,
Astute in form, oracular in force,
Can make a proposition sound an oath.

Rapid, abrupt and violent like a blow,
An exclamation or ecstatic howl,
Still it asserts, and shows it is not so,
Articulates the hooting of an owl.

Can spells or riddles be articulate?
We take our stand, to make the music heard,
And only speech aspires to music's state.
The Owl Minerva was no singing bird.

Heart Beats

If music be the muses' paragon,
Where mostly pure relation is expressed,
The poet looks accusingly upon
This cramped performer drumming in his breast.

'Why brag,' he cries, 'of buffetings survived
To make the high-pitched harmonies of strain?
You suffered, but some colder thing contrived,
Articulated, and endorsed the pain.'

As from a cellar, unrepentant comes
The virtuoso's lunatic tattoo,
Beating to parley in a school of drums:
'I plot the passions, and endure them too.'

Machineries of Shame

Decaying teeth, before they start to ache,
Start up obscure machineries of shame,
As if the mind were fool enough to take
This, and the soul's corruption, for the same.

This is to make debility a crime;
So, too, a mere discomfiture can start
A blush as hot as, at another time,
A black place in the mouth or in the heart, –

And justly, too. Guilt, sleeping in the cell,
Sparks out upon the throwing of a switch.
If sins can do it, blunders serve as well,
And jumping nerves can make a conscience twitch.

Pushkin. A Didactic Poem

'he did not yet know well those hidden mechanisms of the person by which it achieves its isolation from others and withdraws into itself; he was entirely surrendered to his genius, disarmed by his own power; and if his pride led him to challenge God, he cancelled by that very act his own right to deny Him.'   (Wladimir Weidlé)

What with hounds and friends and, in the winter,
Skating, he was seldom bored.
He had learned to be wary, was at pains, I think,
To remain amused?

In the matter of Pushkin, Emily Brontë
Is the best analogy in some ways
Among our poets. As in her verse,
In Pushkin's we assume the truth
That for life to be tolerable, man must
Be wary, ingenious, quick to change
Among diversions, grave or frivolous,
To keep off spleen; although for her,
As she was a woman, a narrower range
Presented itself, and so she is less
Various, flexible, fiery, though as noble
As Pushkin was, more stoical.

Pushkin's draughts-playing and his drinking,
His friends, his travelling, even some
Of his mistresses, he considered as
So many improvisations against
Boredom. But the boredom was
No vacancy nor want of occupation
Nor lack of resources. It was the spleen,

And Pushkin certainly fled before it
Or circumvented it. His poems
Record the circumventions as
Hours when the mind, turned outwards, knew
Friendships or the approach of death
As gifts. The poet exhibits here
How to be conscious in every direction
But that of the self, where deception starts.
This is nobility; not lost
Wholly perhaps, if lost to art.

Grateful tears, delicious sorrow,
Said the Russian gentleman,
Mozart will be dead tomorrow
Of this confusion.

As Byron said of Keats, 'I don't
mean he is indecent, but
viciously soliciting
his own ideas.'

(Schiller and Dostoievsky, oysters
Pearling their own disease, the saints
Full of self-help)

Long before Shakespeare wrote, or Donne,
In the modern manner, there were minds
Aware of themselves, and figuring this
In psychomachia. But the Greeks
Knew states of innocence, the will
Turned always outwards, courage the gift
Counting for virtue, and control,
As of the craven self, a notion
Lost in the social usage. Thus
Self-consciousness is not at fault
In itself. It can be kept
Other than morbid, under laws
Of disciplined sensibility, such
As the seventeenth-century Wit.
But all such disciplines depend
On disciplines of social use,
Now widely lost. Yet there are those
Few men remaining, gifted, or
Especially heroic, or,
Like Pushkin, brilliantly both.

Ask when we are diseased, and these
Will answer: When the moral will
Intervenes to sap the heart,
When the difficult feelings are
Titillated and confused
For novel combinations, or
Ransacked for virtue.

Remains the voice that moves on silence
In moral commonplace, where yet
Some thwart and stern communal sense
Whispers, before we all forget.

What need dissection of the thrust
Which motivates the skating feet,
When that can always be deduced
From the figure of eight?

What need dissection of the thrust
Which motivates the skating feet,
Skating with friends in the winter,
He foretold our defeat.

At the Synod in St Patrick's

This head meant to be massive and therefore,
Being a woman's, less than beautiful,
Is, being young and animated, more
Engaging than a less emphatic skull.

Late flowering, like a cleft-encompassed bush,
To this tradition time has left behind,
Can it be long before her fibres push
At barren rock, the backward-looking mind?

Yet, mollified not merely by their youth,
The jowl too full, the brows like heavy eaves
Bespeak, within, the climate of the truth,
Like Eden's crags with honey in their caves.

The bland and sparkling weather of the good
Extends its dry elation, and disarms
Across two pews my Lucifer that would
Learn why such light should sadden as it charms.

Remembering the 'Thirties

1

Hearing one saga, we enact the next.
We please our elders when we sit enthralled;
But then they're puzzled; and at last they're vexed
To have their youth so avidly recalled.

It dawns upon the veterans after all
That what for them were agonies, for us
Are high-brow thrillers, though historical;
And all their feats quite strictly fabulous.

This novel written fifteen years ago,
Set in my boyhood and my boyhood home,
These poems about 'abandoned workings', show
Worlds more remote than Ithaca or Rome.

The Anschluss, Guernica – all the names
At which those poets thrilled or were afraid
For me mean schools and schoolmasters and games;
And in the process some-one is betrayed.

Ourselves perhaps. The Devil for a joke
Might carve his own initials on our desk,
And yet we'd miss the point because he spoke
An idiom too dated, Audenesque.

Ralegh's Guiana also killed his son.
A pretty pickle if we came to see
The tallest story really packed a gun,
The Telemachiad an Odyssey.

2

Even to them the tales were not so true
As not to be ridiculous as well;
The ironmaster met his Waterloo,
But Rider Haggard rode along the fell.

'Leave for Cape Wrath tonight!' They lounged away
On Fleming's trek or Isherwood's ascent.
England expected every man that day
To show his motives were ambivalent.

They played the fool, not to appear as fools
In time's long glass. A deprecating air
Disarmed, they thought, the jeers of later schools;
Yet irony itself is doctrinaire,

And curiously, nothing now betrays
Their type to time's derision like this coy
Insistence on the quizzical, their craze
For showing Hector was a mother's boy.

A neutral tone is nowadays preferred.
And yet it may be better, if we must,
To praise a stance impressive and absurd
Than not to see the hero for the dust.

For courage is the vegetable king,
The sprig of all ontologies, the weed
That beards the slag-heap with his hectoring,
Whose green adventure is to run to seed.

The Evangelist

'My brethren...' And a bland, elastic smile
Basks on the mobile features of Dissent.
No hypocrite, you understand. The style
Befits a church that's based on sentiment.

Solicitations of a swirling gown,
The sudden vox humana, and the pause,
The expert orchestration of a frown
Deserve, no doubt, a murmur of applause.

The tides of feeling round me rise and sink;
Bunyan, however, found a place for wit.
Yes, I am more persuaded than I think;
Which is, perhaps, why I disparage it.

You round upon me, generously keen:
The man, you say, is patently sincere.
Because he is so eloquent, you mean?
That test was never patented, my dear.

If, when he plays upon our sympathies,
I'm pleased to be fastidious, and you
To be inspired, the vice in it is this:
Each does us credit, and we know it too.

An English Revenant

1

From easterly crepuscular arrivals
Come with me by the self-consuming north
(The North is spirit), to the loam-foot west
And opulent departures of the south.

You that went north for geysers or for grouse,
While Pullman sleepers lulled your sleeping head,
You never saw my mutilated house
Flame in the north by Sheffield as you fled.

You that went west, young man, behind the range
('Westward the course of Empire takes its way')
You never knew my west that cannot change
Its stolid dream and violent feet of clay.

And what became of Waring in the east?
He learnt what traitors generous feelings are,
And lost his nerve, and knew no Samarcand,
In Vishnu-land no hopeful Avatar.

But in the nub of war, a sullen soldier,
He saw the south, its orchards and its wine;
A rich wrap slipping from a Mayfair shoulder,
Successful chromium on his future shine.

In passing, be it understood
Most revenants are flesh and blood.

My home is in the west,
But not in the far west;
And though I was born in the north,
It was not in the far north;
I am lately returned from the east,
But from the middle east;
My songs aspire to the south,
But not to the deep south.

I have cured my breast
Of its need for action;
I have taught it to rest
This side of the Western passes;
Its deeds are commendable,
Not noble.

I have laughed my mind
Out of its need for abstraction;
I have taught it not to find
Shrines in the Orient;
Its thoughts are in tune with the time;
They are not exalted.

I have cheated my will
Out of its need for command;
I have taught it not to kill
Free water into ice;
Its ways are adaptable,
Not unswerving.

Now only my singing mouth
Thirsts for the springs of the south.

3

A craning lamb that craves an empty dug;
A murdered trunk still twitching on the ground;
A water-wheel inertly turning round
Beneath a stream that would not fill a jug.

Such mere momentum moves me still to you,
Supposed a court, a region of reward;
Cannot this wreck of compasses afford
Some south at last, deserved, and coming true?

'My country 'tis of thee…' What can I say?
'Gone in the teeth,' sang Owen and Sassoon,
Or Ezra Pound who parodied their tune.
'London, Thou art of townes A per se.'

It is, my dear, an intimate inquires
(Indigenous, with hard provincial mouth),
What news of all the olives of the south,
Since Owen's bugles blew from saddened shires?

England, we wheel and fly about you still,
The dead of that and of another war.
It is a laurel we are looking for,
Or bounty of the horn we thought to fill.

Hawkshead and Dachau in a Christmas Glass

1

At home with my infirmities I fare
Forth to the nightfall on bald avenues,
Whose charities I shall no more refuse,
However cheaply on the blue-black air
Proffered from lighted windows, such as once,
Though more sporadic, from the mountain-road
　　　　　Welcomed, where Hawkshead glowed.
　　　　Panels of domestic light!
　　　　Like labels pasted on the night,
　　　　(Pasted, opaque, rectangular,
Cut out of paper like a tinsel star –)
I see the sleigh that rocks, the bells that chime
Upon the plate-glass of suburban groceries,
Flatly announcing coming Christmas-time,
The holy time honoured in parodies.

When Hawkshead's poet chose to be humane
And praise the homestead beaming from afar
His Michael's cottage was 'The Evening Star',
            An elevated strain –
Oh Wordsworth! when we walked the mountain-road
So long ago, in quite another mood
     We crested every contour of the fell,
Dark-blue and frost-white on the darker blue,
Our spirits swelling with the upland swell
To bulky heights and knolls we never knew.
Now these lean trees, over the parkland wall,
     Delicate brush-work on a darkling ground;
That deep blue ground that, feathered by the tall
And springing brushes, seems a felted pall;
Its matt and nap as dense as if it lay
A shielding wing over the sharpest day;
     I see the aspirations they invite,
     I lean towards, but dare not launch in flight.

            As I shall not aspire
            To wear the coat of fire
Which (we have proved) incinerates the heart;
            Because the human mind
            Cannot be far refined,
But must admit its grossness from the start;
I hope for no dark elbow-room, to win
Accommodation with the night within.

Making these faces in a Christmas glass
May terrify some others as they pass;
For window-gazers, when a God is dead,
Abide no dreamed-up artefact of mind,
But by reflection from a human head
When most it lacks divinity, they find,
That is, invent, perfection in its stead.
For not by what we want is God defined,
            Only by what we lack;

By what is wanting to us; what we need,
Not what we know we need. And at our back
His eye augments our window-shopping greed.

5

Insatiable proud buyers who could rest
      With nothing but the best,
Who pressed through to the other side
Of every flaring window, and defied
Tragedy even to reflect them right,
Still asked too little, and at best supplied
Only their aspirations. Far too bright
A light shone through the glass; their dazzled sight
Losing the lens, they put us in a fright,
Claiming it was God's face they brought to light.
      Outside the bleakest pane,
Bulging like water in a rippled glass,
My face makes such pretensions as surpass
      Insane self-deified
Projectors of a private pantheon,
Purveyors' voices from the other side
Of window-panes that heaven was pasted on.

6

There was a time I would have scorned to think
My self-aversions so entirely eased
By neighbour windows. Such a night of ink
Required, I thought, supernal light at least.
To be believers, let us not forget
How cheaply all our petty needs are met,
All that we know of. If we blow them up
And push away the off-hand proffered cup,
      Each time we raise our price
Some unimagined need is given up,
And we are gulled, intending to be nice.
In such a time, antediluvian,
We came to Hawkshead. It was long ago,
In our own youth and in the youth of Man,
Not long ago in years, but since we know
At Dachau Man's maturity began
And that was earlier, it was long ago,

A time we could not easily outgrow.
At Dachau Yeats and Rilke died. We found,
    In those who lived before,
Our growing pains. A groaning, cracking sound,
Exploding now through each exclusive store,
Starred what we thought light of uncommon day
And damned it glass. Yet some endured the ray,
Wordsworth for one, who may have hoped for light
That never was on sea or land, but knew
The brittle thing that he was looking through,
A waving pane projected on the night.

7

No wind, please God, will rise tonight. The trees
Still sprig the velvet on the pelt of night.
Still, stuck about the raw estate, one sees
The coloured labels of a Christmas light.
Still, in the stillness, only smoke aspires.
(The movement in the stillness is not ours.)

    We shut up shop, and there's
No glimmer now by which to see the wares
Banked behind glass; but in the early hours
Some mooning hobo, by inhuman fires
Of stars or moon, may, glancing in the glass,
Observe his insufficiencies, and find
A supplement there hinted, to surpass
The dearest purchase that he had in mind.

    Natural pieties,
    Unthought-of charities
Grow up about the newest housing-scheme;
    Curtained or not, the light
    Is tempered to our sight,
And poorest taste can dress the dearest theme,
Where cotton-wool can simulate the snow
And coloured bulbs make Bethlehem a show.

Eight Years After

If distance lends enchantment to the view,
Enormities should not be scrutinized.
What's true of white, holds of black magic too;
And, indistinct, evil is emphasized.

Gilfillan, telling how the poet Churchill
'Indulged in nameless orgies', makes us smile;
We think such large unutterables fill
Vapid lacunæ in a frowzy style.

A case however can be made for this:
The queasy Levite need not be ashamed
To have no stomach for atrocities.
We brook them better, once they have been named.

For fearsome issues, being squarely faced,
Grow fearsomely familiar. To name
Is to acknowledge. To acquire the taste
Comes on the heels of honouring the claim.

'Let nothing human be outside my range.'
Yet horrors named make exorcisms fail:
A thought once entertained is never strange,
But who forgets the face 'beyond the pale'?

Selina, Countess of Huntingdon

Your special witness, as I recollect,
Was, in your fervour, elegance; you yearned
For Grace, but only gracefully, and earned,
By sheer good taste, the title of 'elect'.

So perfectly well-bred that in your hands
All pieties were lavender, that scent
Lingered about your college, where you spent
Your fragrance on the burly ordinands.

In your communion, virtue was uncouth;
But now that rigour lost its cutting edge,
As charm in you drove its schismatic wedge
Between your church's beauty and its truth.

Method. For Ronald Gaskell

For such a theme (atrocities) you find
My style, you say, too neat and self-possessed.
I ought to show a more disordered mind.

But Wesley's sermons could be methodized
According to a Ramist paradigm;
Enthusiasts can never be surprised.

The method in the madness of their zeal
Discounts their laceration of the wounds
That, though so bloodied, have had time to heal.

Cassandra plays her frenzied part too well
To be convincing in hysteria.
Has discourse still its several heads, in Hell?

It has, of course; and why conceal the fact?
An even tenor's sensitive to shock,
And stains spread furthest where the floor's not cracked.

Woodpigeons at Raheny

One simple and effective rhyme
Over and over in the April light;
    And a touch of the old time
In the serving-man, stooping, aproned tight,
At the end of the dappled avenue
To the easy phrase, 'tereu-tereu',
Mulled over by the sleepy dove –
This was the poem I had to write.

White wall where the creepers climb
Year after year on the sunny side;
    And a touch of the old time
In the sandalled Capuchin's silent stride
Over the shadows and through the clear
Cushion-soft wooing of the ear
From two meadows away, by the dove –
This was the poem that was denied.

For whether it was the friar's crime,
His lean-ness suddenly out of tune;
    Or a touch of the old time
In the given phrase, with its unsought boon
Of a lax autumnal atmosphere,
Seemed quaint and out of keeping here,
I do not know. I know the dove
Outsang me down the afternoon.

Love-Poems: for Mairi MacInnes

from *Poets of the 1950s* (1955)

All these love-poems…!
Love in its place
Is simple, therefore interesting;
Inscrutable face,
Looming through leaves or water,
Unlooked-for aisle or island.

It is not the whole story,
Nor can stand for such
As 'human relations' in little;
It is not so much
A paradigm as an interruption,
Not to be looked for in a day's travel.

And all these…!
Some 'civilized',
Some frenzied, some 'gravely moving',
But yours surprised,
Still dazzled in the roasted glade,
Astounded after long days in the forest.

Jacob's Ladder

It was agreed we would not mount by those
Platonic ladders planted on the heart,
Minds that abide the body and its throes,
Reluctantly, and only for a start.
But Jacob's is a ladder we ascend
Without our knowing any sense of strain,
To upland air that we need not expend
One gulp of carnal breathing to attain.
So here we are upon the heights, my love,
Although in habit's level pastures still.
We want, and yet we do not want, the skill
To scale the peaks that others tell us of,
Where breathing gets so difficult, and the will
Kicks back the ground it tries to rise above.

(1955)

A WINTER TALENT AND OTHER POEMS

Time Passing, Beloved

Time passing, and the memories of love
Coming back to me, carissima, no more mockingly
Than ever before; time passing, unslackening,
Unhastening, steadily; and no more
Bitterly, beloved, the memories of love
Coming into the shore.

How will it end? Time passing and our passages of love
As ever, beloved, blind
As ever before; time binding, unbinding
About us; and yet to remember
Never less chastening, nor the flame of love
Less like an ember.

What will become of us? Time
Passing, beloved, and we in a sealed
Assurance unassailed
By memory. How can it end,
This siege of a shore that no misgivings have steeled,
No doubts defend?

Dream Forest

These have I set up,
Types of ideal virtue,
To be authenticated
By no one's Life and Times,
But by a sculptor's logic

Of whom I have commanded,
To dignify my groves,
Busts in the antique manner,
Each in the space mown down
Under its own sway:

First, or to break the circle,
Brutus, imperious, curbed
Not much by the general will,
But by a will to be curbed,
A preference for limits;

Pushkin next, protean
Who recognized no checks
Yet brooked them all – a mind
Molten and thereby fluent,
Unforced, easily strict;

The next, less fortunate,
Went honourably mad,
The angry annalist
Of hearth and marriage bed,
Strindberg – a staring head.

Classic, romantic, realist,
These have I set up.
These have I set, and a few trees.
When will a grove grow over
This mile upon mile of moor?

Obiter Dicta

Trying to understand myself, I fetch
    My father's image to me. There he is, augmenting
    The treasury of his prudence with a clutch
Of those cold eggs, Great Truths – his scrivener's hand
    Confiding apopthegms to his pocket book.
    Does mine do more than snap the elastic band
Of rhyme about them? In an age that teaches
    How pearls of wisdom only look like eggs,
    The tide, afflatus, still piles up on the beaches
Pearls that he prizes, stones that he retrieves
    Misguidedly from poetry's undertow,
    Deaf to the harsh retraction that achieves
Its scuttering backwash, ironies. And yet,
    Recalling his garrulity, I see
    There's method in it. Seeming to forget

The point at issue, the palmer tells his beads,
    Strung by connections nonchalantly weak
    Upon the thread of argument he needs
To bring them through his fingers, round and round,
    Tasting of gristle, savoury; and he hears,
    Like rubbing stones, their dry conclusive sound.

Himself an actor (He can play the clown),
    He knows the poet's a man of parts; the sage
Is one of them, buffoonery like his own,
    Means to an end. So, if he loves the page
That grows sententious with a terse distinction,
    Yet lapidary moralists are dumb
About the precepts that he acts upon,
    Brown with tobacco from his rule of thumb.

'Not bread but a stone!' – the deep-sea fishermen
    Denounce our findings, father. Pebbles, beads,
    Perspicuous dicta, gems from Emerson,
Whatever stands when all about it slides,
    Whatever in the oceanic welter
    Puts period to unpunctuated tides,
These, that we like, they hate. And after all, for you,
    To take but with a pinch of salt to take
    The maxims of the sages is the true
Great Truth of all. To keep, as you would say,
    A sense of proportion, I should portion out
    The archipelago across the bay,
One island to so much sea. Assorted
    Poetic pleasures come in bundles then,
    Strapped up by rhyme, not otherwise supported?

Turning about his various gems to take
    Each other's lustre by a temperate rule,
He walks the graveyard where I have to make
    Not centos but inscriptions, and a whole
That's moved from inward, dancing. Yet I trace
    Among his shored-up epitaphs my own:
Art, as he hints, turns on a commonplace,
    And Death is a tune to dance to, cut in stone.

Mens Sana in Corpore Sano

Certainly, Lean-shanks, you have forced the pace –
In the bath your body shows it; and you have
The right, considering your shrunken hams,
To rock on that notorious see-saw, mind
And body. But you have forced the pace,
Not forced (take heart) that alternating tempo
To an inhuman standstill – forced the flesh
To some four-minute mile, or forced the mind
To play the ruffian pander to the blood.

Time's gradual and lenient castration
Unfilms the eye and stills the straying hand,
Unstops ear and nostril; and the tongue
Wags to expansive music, that could risk
(So loose it was till lately) only terse
And summary formulations. As for youth,
See where it throngs these garnished avenues
To deck a house under whose ageing beams
The blithe young tenant comes of age tomorrow.

You know the Stoic's one indulgence now,
The wrist that, opened, bleeds into the bath
Crimsoning Time's still water – yet with blood
(The Epicurean's boast) no violence
Has loosed upon yourself, beyond
That something less than suicidal forcing,
The acceleration of the chemistries
Of undeflected change. Prepare to open
All of the body's avenues but its veins.

At the Cradle of Genius

'Not the least enviable of your many gifts,
Being indeed (what seems unfair) implied
In that first bargain, genius, are two
Appurtenances or corollaries:
One which we hope you do not recognize
Or else it halves its value, one we hope you do
By the same token; and we mean
Charm in the first place, in the second
A narrowing of the choice of destinies.

For character may be fate, and yet vocation
(Differing from the casual gift, a flair)
Can so subsume the variants under types
That, all the issues coming clear,
The gift becomes of nothing else but freedom,
The only kind that you enjoy,
The recognition of a limitation
On idiosyncrasy, a choice
That, being narrow, can be seen as free.'

Thus your first fairy godmother, I suppose,
A learned, solemn, even a pedantic lady,
Edwardian resident of Bruges and Rome
Where she pursues her out-of-date researches
Into 'The Natural History' (save the mark)
'Of Genius'. Now I hear her sister,
The junior counsel but the cleverer,
Though in the plural, yet in other terms, address you
Not altogether to the same effect:

'The benefits that are at my discretion are
Particularizings of the general scope
This lady has endowed you with; and first,
Although a flair is of another order
Than what we give, yet as no spectacle
Is more to be pitied than of one who has
The genius, or to speak more properly
The temperament, and no aptitude, we give
Inalienable technical command.

Then, for your freedom: it is absolute.
Your law unto yourself is absolute
That you be lawless. Since you have no choice
(My colleague's paradox) you have
Absolute choice. Exceptionally fated
To break all rules, you are to find the rules
Of art and conduct waived. The moral law
Lapses before the selfless man, possessed
Of no one self, but of and by a style.'

'Not that you have,' the first impetuously
Resuming cried, 'no duty to be pure…'
'In heart', I fear she would have said; but here
The modern muse broke in on her with 'Pure,
Purged of all bearings on a human need,
The truest poem's at most a golden standish,
A tray to put your pens in.' Then a murmur
That swelled beneath the voices broke
Into a shout excluding all the muses.

It was the chorus of the acclamation lately
Accorded you as legendary hero,
Dilating on your prodigality,
Your arrogance, your abandonment, your art,
Though that seemed incidental. In the din
I caught by starts the sisters crying still,
And once the elder sounded menacing:
'Some have enjoyed what here I deny to you,
A self-betrayal not betrayed in art.'

The Mushroom Gatherers

After Mickiewicz

Strange walkers! See their processional
Perambulations under low boughs,
The birches white, and the green turf under.
These should be ghosts by moonlight wandering.

Their attitudes strange: the human tree
Slowly revolves on its bole. All around
Downcast looks; and the direct dreamer
Treads out in trance his lane, unwavering.

Strange decorum: so prodigal of bows,
Yet lost in thought and self-absorbed, they meet
Impassively, without acknowledgment.
A courteous nation, but unsociable.

Field full of folk, in their immunity
From human ills, crestfallen and serene.
Who would have thought these shades our lively friends?
Surely these acres are Elysian Fields.

The Wind at Penistone

The wind meets me at Penistone.
                                        A hill
Curves empty through the township, on a slope
Not cruel, and yet steep enough to be,
Were it protracted, cruel.
                                        In the street,
A plain-ness rather meagre than severe,
Affords, though quite unclassical, a vista
So bald as to be monumental.
                                        Here
A lean young housewife meets me with the glance
I like to think that I can recognize
As dour, not cross.
                                        And all the while the wind,
A royal catspaw, toying easily,
Flicks out of shadows from a tufted wrist,
Its mane, perhaps, this lemon-coloured sun.

The wind reserves, the hill reserves, the style
Of building houses on the hill reserves
A latent edge;
                        which we can do without
In Pennine gradients and the Pennine wind,
And never miss, or, missing it, applaud

The absence of the aquiline;
                              which in her
Whose style of living in the wind reserves
An edge to meet the wind's edge, we may miss
But without prejudice.
                       And yet in art
Where all is patent, and a latency
Is manifest or nothing, even I,
Liking to think I feel these sympathies,
Can hardly praise this clenched and muffled style.
For architecture asks a cleaner edge,
Is open-handed.
                 And close-fisted people
Are mostly vulgar; only in the best,
Who draw, inflexible, upon reserves,
Is there a stern game that they play with life,
In which the rule is not to show one's hand
Until compelled.
                  And then the lion's paw!
Art that is dour and leonine in the Alps
Grows kittenish, makes curios and clocks,
Giant at play.
                Here, nothing. So the wind
Meets me at Penistone, and, coming home,
The poet falls to special pleading, chilled
To find in Art no fellow but the wind.

Under St Paul's

Wren and Barry, Rennie and Mylne and Dance
    Under the flags, the men who stood for stone
    Lie in the stone. Carillons, pigeons once
Sluiced Ludgate's issues daily, and the dome
    Of stone-revetted crystal swung and hung
    Its wealth of waters. Wren had plugged it home
With a crypt at the nerve of London. Now the gull
    Circles the dry stone nozzles of the belfries,
    Each graceful City hydrant of the full
Eagerly brimming measure of agreement,
    Still to be tapped by any well-disposed
    Conversible man, still underneath the pavement

Purling and running, affable and in earnest,
    The conduit, Candour. Fattily urbane
    Under the great drum, pigeons foul their nest.

The whiter wing, Anger, and the gull's
Shearwater raucous over hunting hulls
Seek London's river. Rivers underground,
Under the crypt, return the sound
Of footfalls in the evening city. Out of wells,
Churchyards sunk behind Fleet Street, trickle smells
Of water where a calm conviction spoke
Now dank and standing. Leaves and our debris choke
The bell-note Candour that the pavior heard
Fluting and swelling like a crop-filled bird.

So sound the tides of love; yet man and woman
    May be my world's first movers, and the stream
    Still run no darker nowhere deeper than
Conviction's claim upon us, to deny
    Nothing that's undeniable. Light airs
    Are bent to the birds that couple as they fly
And slide and soar, yet answer to the flow
    Of this broad water under. There we ride
    Lent to the current, and convictions grow
In those they are meant for. As conviction's face
    Is darker than the speculative air,
    So and no darker is the place
For candour and love. What fowl lives underwater,
    Breeds in that dark? And hadn't a contriver
    Of alphabets, Cadmus, the gull for daughter?

Across the dark face of the waters
Flies the white bird. And the waters
Mount, mount, or should mount; we grow surer
Of what we know, if no surer
Of what we think. For on ageing
Labouring now and subsiding and nerveless wing
The gull sips the body of water, and the air
Packed at that level can hold up a minster in air.
Across the dark face of the water
Flies the white bird until nothing is left but the water.

Derbyshire Turf

That, true to the contours which round it
    Out and lie close,
The best beauty is barbarous, grounded
    On foreign bodies,
Flush to their angles, ungainly,
    Pawkily true –
Derbyshire turf, you tried vainly
    To point such a moral
When we, in our warmly remembered
    Youth, from the old
Armstrong Siddeley tourer descended
    Shouting upon you.

Then as now it was just where the boulder
    Lay scantily buried,
Or the gritstone poked up a shoulder,
    You sported your streaks
Of a specially sumptuous darkened
    Lush olive green –
Yet in those days none of us hearkened
    To this intimation
That where most intriguingly mounded
    Abrupt in its curves,
Beauty is richest and rounded
    Home on the truth.

Very well. Still we should wonder
    At farmers who loaded
Wagons with stones to lay under
    The grass of their pastures.
Much the same is the poet who prizing
    The shape of the truth
Studies to find some surprising
    Eccentric perception
To validate memory. Boys
    Are willing to guess
At the rock which lies under their joy's
    Elusiveness.

Dissentient Voice

1. *A Baptist Childhood*

When some were happy as the grass was green,
I was as happy as a glass was dark,
Chill eye beneath the chapel floor unseen
Most of the year, a mystery, the Ark.

Aboveboard rose the largely ethical
Glossy-with-graining pulpit; underground
The older Scriptures trembled for the Fall
And lapped at Adam with a sucking sound.

Grass-rooted goodness and a joy unmixed
Parch unbaptized inside a droughty head;
Arcadia's floor is not so firmly fixed
But it must tremble to a pastor's tread.

2. *Dissent. A Fable*

When Bradbury sang, 'The Roast Beef of Old England'
And Watts, 'How cloth the little busy bee',
Then Doddridge blessed the pikes of Cumberland
And plunging sapphics damned eternally.

Said Watts the fox: 'Your red meat is uncouth.
We'll keep the bleeding purchase out of sight.
Arminian honey for the age's tooth!
With so much sweetness, who will ask for light?'

Wolf Bradbury mauled the synod, but the fox
Declared that men were growing more refined;
And honey greased, where blood would rust, the locks
That clicked when Calvin trapped the open mind.

The wolves threw off sheep's clothing once or twice
(For Queen Anne dead, or the Pretender foiled).
But the fox knew that tastes were growing nice
And unction kept the hinge of dogma oiled.

Foxes however are their own worst foes;
And now their chapel door stands open wide,
Its hinge so clogged with wax it cannot close,
No fish so queer but he can swim inside.

The queerest fishes hunger for the trap
And wish the door would close on them, the rough
Jaws of Geneva and Old England snap:
They think their church not barbarous enough.

The fable seems extravagant, no doubt.
But Reynard ruled the roosts of heaven then,
And beastly pastors kept true shepherds out
While pike and barracuda fished for men.

3. *Portrait of the Artist as a Farmyard Fowl*

Pluming himself upon a sense of sin
     (Lice in his feathers' undersides)
He sported drab, the sooner Faith to win.
     Old zealots were such sobersides;
He felt their gooseflesh crawl upon his skin
     And hoped to feel their zeal besides.

Since then this would-be puritan has paced
     A cock unmatched although so spurred;
Purist who crowed at shadows, he debased
     The rate of evil and conferred
Its rights on squalor, out of sheer good taste.
     No hag would ride on such a bird.

Dark plumes, though puritanical in cut,
     Still clothe the cock of the studied walk;
A conscious carriage must become a strut;
     Fastidiousness can only stalk
And seem at last not even tasteful but
     A ruffled hen too apt to squawk.

4. *A Gathered Church*

In memoriam A.E.D. ob. 1939
Deacon, you are to recognize in this
The idlest of my avocations, fruit
Of some late casual studies and my need
(Not dire, nor much acknowledged as a claim
Upon your known munificence) for what
You as lay preacher loved and disavowed,
The mellow tang of eloquence – a food
I have some skill in rendering down from words
Suppose them choice and well matured. I heard
Such from your bee-mouth once. A tarnished sun
Swirling the motes which swarmed along its shaft
Mixed soot with spices, and with honey, dust;
And memories of that winning unction now
Must countenance this application. For
I see them tumbled in a frowzy beam,
The grains of dust or pollen from our past,
Our common stock in family and church,
Asking articulation. These affairs
Touched you no doubt more nearly; you are loath
To see them made a gaud of rhetoric. But, sir,
I will deal plainly with you. They are past,
Past hoping for as you had hoped for them
For sixty years or more the day you died,
And if I seem a fribble in this case
No matter. For I will be eloquent
And on these topics, having little choice.

You who were once an orator should know
How these things are decided, not by chance
Although to think so is our best recourse;
For we may pledge our faith that they are solved
In part by fervent feeling and in part
By strenuous intellection – so they are,
But by all these under the guise of chance,
Of happy yet exacting accident,
Out of whose bounty suddenly a word
Of no apparent pertinence or force
Will promise unaccountably to draw
The whole lax beam into a burning glass.

So here I take the husk of my research,
A form of words – the phrase, 'a gathered church',
A rallying cry of our communions once
For you perhaps still stirring, but for me
A picturesque locution, nothing more
Except for what it promises, a tang.
Here is the promise of the burning-glass;
Now turn it in the variegated light.

'A gathered church.' That posy, the elect,
Was gathered in, not into, garden-walls;
For God must out of sheer caprice resect
The jugular stalks of those He culls and calls.

Watts thought his church, though scant of privilege,
Walled in its own communion. In its walks
Some may have doubted if so sparse a hedge
Tempered the blast to blooms still on their stalks.

It was the rooted flower could be hurt:
The plucked that lived in living water felt
No more the stress of time, the tug of dirt.
Time lost for good the fragrance Heaven smelt.

When blossoms crowd into the waist of time,
Those cut and chosen for the eternal vase
Rot down to no kind humus, rather climb
And spend their charity upon the stars.

Abundant friction: not a deal of heat.
These are, you know, preliminary rites,
A form of invocation. So the glass
Is moved and dances, waterish, flashes out
Now on the wall, now on the floor... But now
Your face recalled swims up athwart the light,
The silken, heavy, iron-grey moustache
That reaffirms conciliatory smiles
Dispensing honey with a Dorset burr;
The hollow temples of a young man's brow;
The mild and beaming eye; the cheek still apple-hale.
Appealing gestures pregnantly curtailed
Conveyed impulsive courtesies, refined
The gross freak of your corpulence. That head

Was bowed beneath reproaches mostly mute
When 'Charity begins at home,' we said,
Feeling the pinch of your more public alms
Wise in our generations. And indeed
You thought so too; your home was somewhere else
And there you ran most fruitfully to seed.
Now all the churches gathered from the world
Through that most crucial bottleneck of Grace,
That more than hourglass, being waspish, waist
Where all the flutes of love are gathered in,
The girdle of Eternity, the strait
Too straitened for the sands and sons of Time,
More mean and private than the sticking-place
Of any partial loyalties – all these
In you, dear sir, are justified. Largesse,
Suppose it but of rhetoric, endears,
Disseminated quite at large to bless
The waste, superb profusion of the spheres.

The Priory of St Saviour, Glendalough

A carving on the jamb of an embrasure,
'Two birds affronted with a human head
Between their beaks' is said to be
'Uncertain in its significance but
A widely known design.' I'm not surprised.

For the guidebook cheats: the green road it advises
In fact misled; and a ring of trees
Screened in the end the level knoll on which
St Saviour's, like a ruin on a raft,
Surged through the silence.

I burst through brambles, apprehensively
Crossed an enormous meadow. I was there.
Could holy ground be such a foreign place?
I climbed the wall, and shivered. There flew out
Two birds affronted by my human face.

Samuel Beckett's Dublin

When it is cold it stinks, and not till then.
The seasonable or more rabid heats
Of love and summer in some other cities
Unseal the all too human: not in his.
When it is cold it stinks, but not before;

Smells to high heaven then most creaturely
When it is cold. It stinks, but not before
His freezing eye has done its best to maim,
To amputate limbs, livelihood and name,
Abstracting life beyond all likelihood.

When it is cold it stinks, and not till then
Can it be fragrant. On canal and street,
Colder and colder, Murphy to Molloy,
The weather hardens round the Idiot Boy,
The gleeful hero of the long retreat.

When he is cold he stinks, but not before,
This living corpse. The existential weather
Smells out in these abortive minims, men
Who barely living therefore altogether
Live till they die; and sweetly smell till then.

North Dublin

St George's, Hardwicke Street,
Is charming in the Church of Ireland fashion:
The best of Geneva, the best of Lambeth
Aesthetically speaking
In its sumptuously sober
Interior, meet.

A continuous gallery, clear glass in the windows,
An elegant conventicle
In the Ionian order –
What dissenter with taste
But would turn, on these terms
Episcopalian?

'Dissenter' and 'tasteful' are contradictions
In terms, perhaps, and my fathers
Would ride again to the Boyne
Or with scythes to Sedgemoor, or splinter
The charming fanlights in this charming slum
By their lights, rightly.

Corrib. An Emblem

Hairless and worse than leathery, the skin
Of the great ogre, Connemara, mounded
Silvery, fathoms thick. Within
The crook of tutelary arm that cradled
The Corrib's urn, the subcutaneous waters
In their still blue as bright as blood shone out,
By healed-up puckers where his pre-divinity
Was scored and trenched. To him suppose a Daphne
Pursued by art Palladian, picturesque,
Or else Hispanic through the Galway Lynches,
Merchant adventurers turning Medici,
Virtù in freight. Underneath his shoulder
Syrinx, the villa seen across the lough,
A reed now broken, flourished. In his hand
A nymph took root, and here and there a laurel.

The Wearing of the Green

Gold is not autumn's privilege;
A tawny ripening
In Meath in May burns ready in the hedge;
The yellow that will follow spring
Accentuates its wet and green array,
A sumptuous trill beneath
The shriller edge
Of Meath in May.

Green more entire must needs be evergreen,
Precluding autumn and this spring
Of Meath in May, its in-between
Of golds and yellows preluding
The liquid summer. Must the seasons stay
Their temperate career because
A flag is green
In Meath in May?

Imagination, Irish avatar,
Aches in the spring's heart and in mine, the stranger's,
In Meath in May. But to believe there are
Unchanging Springs endangers,
By that fast dye, the earth;
So blood-red green the season,
It never changes
In Meath in May.

Going to Italy

Though painters say Italian light does well
By natural features and by monuments,
Our eyes may not be fine enough to tell
Effects compounded of such elements.

And yet we trust our judgment as to fires
In their effects more subtle still, like love,
Which is a light that dwells about its squires
To tell the world what they are thinking of.

That fortunate climate is so apt for this,
As some aver, that not a thought can pass
Through spiritual natures, but it is
Seen in the air, like glitter in a glass.

If Rome should see us bathed in such a flue,
And all our even inward motions edged
Thus with the crispness of their follow-through,
I'd think not we but Rome was privileged.

Tuscan Morning

Presences are always said to brood;
And in the Boboli gardens just at noon
Toad-like Silenus squats inside a shade
While Michelangelo's giants cannot break
The curtain of their element, the haze.

But this is hardly Italy. At least
This is in Italy the hour and the place
That throw our Italy into high relief,
Which is italic cursive and alert
In early mornings and late afternoons.

High noon of the Renaissance was in Rome.
This was the Tuscan, Brunelleschi's morning,
The guidebooks say. What have renaissances
To do with noon? It is the edge of light
Goes cleaving, windless presence, like a ray.

Mr Sharp in Florence

'Mr Sharp from Sheffield, straight out of the knifebox.'

Americans are innocents abroad;
But Sharp from Sheffield is the cagey kind
And – out of the knifebox, bleeding – can't afford
To bring to Florence such an open mind.

Poor Mr Sharp! And happy transatlantic
Travellers, so ingenuous! But some
Are so alert they can finesse the trick,
So strong they know when to be overcome.

Now must he always fall between these stools?
Blind, being keen; dumb, so as not to shrill;
Grounded and ground in logic-chopping schools;
So apt in so inapposite a skill?

Beleaguered and unsleeping sentinel,
He learned the trick of it, before the end;
Saw a shape move, and could not see it well,
Yet did not challenge, but himself cried, 'Friend!'

Via Portello

'Nobody wants any more poems about... foreign cities.'
Mr Kingsley Amis

Rococo compositions of decay,
Each a still-life, the fruity garbage-heaps
Teem by themselves. A broad and cobbled way,
Tiepolo's and Byron's thoroughfare
Lies grand and empty in its sullied air,
And watches while the rest of Padua sleeps.

The conscious vista closed at either end,
Here by a palace, that way by a gate
At night pure Piranesi... Yes, my friend,
I know you have decided for your part
That poems on foreign cities and their art
Are the privileged classes' shorthand. You must wait;

Or, traversing the colonnaded mile
Of this decayed locality, extend
The warmth of your resentment to the style
Of Padua's poor. A civilization broken
Around them, theirs; and want, and no word spoken –
The conscious vista closed at either end.

The Tuscan Brutus

The Duke insists you stay; you could do worse.
You temporize, and promise him a fine
Head for his medal. As for the reverse,
That (now he jests) Lorenzo shall design.

That melancholy madman Lorenzino
De Medici, in sole attendance there,
Takes up the joke, agrees. The Duke should know
The risk he's running, but that's his affair.

There's more to this than meets your knowing eye,
Cellini, though we owe the tale to you:
You made one, but he made another die;
You were to strike the medal – he struck too.

He writes that his design is under way,
Claims that its greatness will be manifest
To later ages, and that night and day
He thinks of nothing else, and cannot rest.

A sad reverse it proved. Were you to know
Your lovely art had such a seamy side?
Amazed, you saw the spun coin fall to show
The antique motif of tyrannicide.

No end of tyrants – after Alessandro
Duke Cosimo... Oh you were right, of course:
For current coin his style would never do.
Yet for a medal yours was rather coarse.

The Pacer in the Fresco. John the Baptist

Already running, sprang from the womb; met,
Adored, inclined to, passed the Overtaker;
Fore-ran Him then around the course; and yet
Drew Him abreast, baptized Him into the lead
He need not challenge for – then in a stride
Took up the killing pace, and shook a bead
Of cool sweat on the Runner by his side.

Met from the first none could be waited for:
His father with a minatory gesture
Full of a blessing was fulfilled before
Much like a curse; his mother then, resigned,
Delivered still delivering – from whom
Departed running, he is first to find
The stadium packed and roaring with their doom.

Turns the last corner, round into the straight,
Into the last fierce panels of the fresco
Indomitably, the Pursuer's gait
Steady behind him and the easy breath
Fanning his cheek. He can afford to fall
Out of the running, when he sees his death,
Beating a foot, dance out along the wall;

Sees perjured judges clap the Victor in
After a lonelier circuit, and the headsman
Timekeeper plunge the stopwatch and begin
The ritual decollation of the flag
Ripe for its fall; and sees, at his command,
The pear-shaped classical canon start to sag
And sway down ripe, his ripeness come to hand.

We went to gape. But when the unflurried Athlete
Hove up behind, with high unhurried action,
Running so well within himself, His feet
Firm on the track, not flying, no one's eye
But left the lunging leader, though in profile
So aquiline, or knew him going by
Except as promise of a purer style.

The two-dimensional hero, moving fast,
Himself the movement, like the knife-edge angel
Of all annunciations, couldn't last:
He clove too cleanly ever to belong
In the close composition of the whole,
Himself too much the equilibrist for long
To tilt a saucer on the wading soul.

The Fountain

Feathers up fast, and steeples; then in clods
Thuds into its first basin; thence as surf
Smokes up and hangs; irregularly slops
Into its second, tattered like a shawl;
There, chill as rain, stipples a danker green,
Where urgent tritons lob their heavy jets.

For Berkeley this was human thought, that mounts
From bland assumptions to inquiring skies,
There glints with wit, fumes into fancies, plays
With its negations, and at last descends,
As by a law of nature, to its bowl
Of thus enlightened but still common sense.

We who have no such confidence must gaze
With all the more affection on these forms,
These spires, these plumes, these calm reflections, these
Similitudes of surf and turf and shawl,
Graceful returns upon acceptances.
We ask of fountains only that they play,

Though that was not what Berkeley meant at all.

Chrysanthemums

Chrysanthemums become a cult because
No Japanese interior is snug;
For even Fuji can be brought indoors
As lamps turn amber in an opal fog.

Here in the thick of opals, where the horn
Blurts from the seaward mountain through the pall,
Now fires are lit and the snug curtains drawn,
Shock-headed clusters warm the dripping wall.

A brazier or the perforated tin
Of watchmen huddled at a dockyard gate
Glows with such amber as the night draws in
As these bronze flowers, blossoming so late.

Chrysanthemum, cult of the Japanese,
You teach me no Penates can be lost
While men can draw together as they freeze
And make a domesticity of frost.

Yet bivouacs of Revolution throw
Threatening shadows and a scorching heat,
And embers of unequal summer glow
A hearth indeed, but in a looted street.

Cherry Ripe

On a Painting by Juan Gris

No ripening curve can be allowed to sag
On cubist's canvas or in sculptor's stone:
Informal fruit, that burgeons from the swag,
Would spoil the ripening that is art's alone.

This can be done with cherries. Other fruit
Have too much bloom of import, like the grape,
Whose opulence comes welling from a root
Struck far too deep to yield so pure a shape.

And Cherry ripe, indeed ripe, ripe, I cry.
Let orchards flourish in the poet's soul
And bear their feelings that are mastered by
Maturing rhythms, to compose a whole.

But how the shameful grapes and olives swell,
Excrescent from no cornucopia, tart,
Too near to oozing to be handled well:
Ripe, ripe, they cry, and perish in my heart.

Hearing Russian Spoken

Unsettled again and hearing Russian spoken
I think of brokenness perversely planned
By Dostoievsky's debauchees; recall
The 'visible brokenness' that is the token
Of the true believer; and connect it all
With speaking a language I cannot command.

If broken means unmusical I speak
Even in English brokenly, a man
Wretched enough, yet one who cannot borrow
Their hunger for indignity nor, weak,
Abet my weakness, drink to drown a sorrow
Or write in metres that I cannot scan.

Unsettled again at hearing Russian spoken,
'Abjure politic brokenness for good,'
I tell myself. 'Recall what menaces,
What self-loathings must be re-awoken:
This girl and that, and all your promises
Your pidgin that they too well understood.'

Not just in Russian but in any tongue
Abandonment, morality's soubrette
Of lyrical surrender and excess,
Knows the weak endings equal to the strong;
She trades on broken English with success
And, disenchanted, I'm enamoured yet.

Limited Achievement

(Piranesi, *Prisons,* Plate VI)

Seeing his stale vocabulary build
The same décor – observe this 'gloomy vault' –
We tire of this good fellow, highly skilled
No doubt, but pertinacious to a fault.

The same few dismal properties, the same
Oppressive air of justified unease,
Proclaim the practised hand from which they came,
Although these show a willingness to please.

Yes, some attempt undoubtedly was made
To lift the composition, and to pierce
The bald tympana – vainly, I'm afraid;
The effect remains, as ever, gaunt and fierce.

Those were his true proclivities? Perhaps.
Successful in his single narrow track,
He branches out, but only to collapse,
Imprisoned in his own unhappy knack,

Which, when unfailing, fails him most, perhaps.

A Winter Talent

Lighting a spill late in the afternoon,
I am that coal whose heat it should unfix;
Winter is come again, and none too soon
For meditation on its raft of sticks.

Some quick bright talents can dispense with coals
And burn their boats continually, command
An unreflecting brightness that unrolls
Out of whatever firings come to hand.

What though less sunny spirits never turn
The dry detritus of an August hill
To dangerous glory? Better still to burn
Upon that gloom where all have felt a chill.

Under a Skylight

Through a wide window all Somerset might look in
At the quiet act of love, but where we lie
Under a skylight in a double bed,
I cannot ignore the scrutinizing sky
Night's Peeping Tom. Could anyone turn his head,
However coarse in fibre, to begin
(With that mild aperture so wide above)
The tumultuous quiet of the act of love?

Skylight, that's heaven's light: an easy clue
For prurient exegetes supposing shame
Brazen on earth less bold in heaven's eye.
But down the dim shaft those slanted timbers frame,
Our four eyes glitter upwards at the sky
Like pussies in a well; and we pursue
Untouched by shame a feline interest
Compulsively, at nobody's behest.

No. Let's hear nothing of those notorious twins
Identical but different, Agape
And Eros, whom the mind
Like a celibate uncle pats uncertainly;
It puzzles me the more, though, why I find
An image for the married state that wins
My uncommitted heart, in these wide-eyed
Unsleeping bodies gazing side by side.

Gardens no Emblems

Man with a scythe: the torrent of his swing
Finds its own level; and is not hauled back
But gathers fluently, like water rising
Behind the watergates that close a lock.

The gardener eased his foot into a boot;
Which action like the mower's had its mould
Being itself a sort of taking root,
Feeling for lodgment in the leather's fold.

But forms of thought move in another plane
Whose matrices no natural forms afford
Unless subjected to prodigious strain:
Say, light proceeding edgewise, like a sword.

The Nonconformist

X, whom society's most mild command,
For instance evening dress, infuriates,
In art is seen confusingly to stand
For disciplined conformity, with Yeats.

Taxed to explain what this resentment is
He feels for small proprieties, it comes,
He likes to think, from old enormities
And keeps the faith with famous martyrdoms.

Yet it is likely, if indeed the crimes
His fathers suffered rankle in his blood,
That he finds least excusable the times
When they acceded, not when they withstood.

How else explain this bloody-minded bent
To kick against the prickings of the norm;
When to conform is easy, to dissent;
And when it is most difficult, conform?

Rejoinder to a Critic

You may be right: 'How can I dare to feel?'
May be the only question I can pose,
'And haply by abstruse research to steal
From my own nature all the natural man'
My sole resource. And I do not suppose
That others may not have a better plan.

And yet I'll quote again, and gloss it too
(You know by now my liking for collage):
Donne could be daring, but he never knew,
When he inquired, 'Who's injured by my love?'
Love's radio-active fall-out on a large
Expanse around the point it bursts above.

'Alas, alas, who's injured by my love?'
And recent history answers: Half Japan!
Not love, but hate? Well, both are versions of
The 'feeling' that you dare me to... Be dumb!
Appear concerned only to make it scan!
How dare we now be anything but numb?

Heigh-ho on a Winter Afternoon

There is a heigh-ho in these glowing coals
By which I sit wrapped in my overcoat
As if for a portrait by Whistler. And there is
A heigh-ho in the bird that noiselessly
Flew just now past my window, to alight
On winter's moulding, snow; and an alas,
A heigh-ho and a desultory chip,
Chip, chip on stone from somewhere down below.

Yes I have 'mellowed', as you said I would,
And that's a heigh-ho too for any man;
Heigh-ho that means we fall short of alas
Which sprigs the grave of higher hopes than ours.
Yet heigh-ho too has its own luxuries,
And salts with courage to be jocular
Disreputable sweets of wistfulness,
By deprecation made presentable.

What should we do to rate the long alas
But skeeter down a steeper gradient?
And then some falls are still more fortunate,
The meteors spent, the tragic heroes stunned
Who go out like a light. But here the chip,
Chip, chip will flake the stone by slow degrees,
For hour on hour the fire will gutter down,
The bird will call at longer intervals.

POEMS OF 1955–6

On Sutton Strand

I saw brown Corrib lean upon his urn,
　　And shawled Andromeda by the Atlantic sea;
I thought smooth eastern provinces would turn
　　To emblems of an equal suavity;
I thought that, nearer by a hundred miles
To Europe's heart, the Mediterranean styles
　　And milder forms of nature would agree.

But fables worked by what was fabulous.
　　It is the mildest proves intractable.
And here it is the sky that silences
　　The flutes of Greece and Sicily with the full
Chime of its equability. The bright
Items of colour glitter in a light
　　That makes men small and all their fables dull.

What in a seascape so entirely Dutch
　　Can Orpheus do but just believe his eyes?
No more the broad brush and the master's touch;
　　He has no choice now but to itemize
Bright fleck by fleck, and try by being neat
Where to command is hopeless, to compete
　　With an indifference equal to the sky's.

Aubade

I wish for you that when you wake
You emulate the leaf and bird;
That like them, touched with grace, you take
Note of the wind. You have not heard
Its low-voiced billows yet, nor seen
(Lost in your less elated rest)
The empty light upon the green,
The leaves and tumbling birds that gave
The wind its due, and then redressed
That small excess, each bounding spray
A boat that dances on the wave,
A whip that tingles in the day.

Dudwood

The roads getting emptier, air in a steadily purer
Stream flowing back past the old Armstrong Siddeley tourer;
Then, the next morning, at large in the boulderstrewn woodland –
What worlds away from our nest in the chimney of England!
The turf carpets laid for us, scroll-like or star-shaped or trefoiled,
Deep pile to the tread of the spring-heel Jack Sparrows of Sheffield.

The bluff before Birchover, fronting the valley and shaded
By rowan and pine where the outcrop capped the precipitous
Comber of meadow. That way, in search of Cos lettuce
Or pony-tailed carrots, the three of us often ascended
That very first morning – all ardent and plumed, all cockaded
With springing abandonments, lost now, barely remembered.

Dublin Georgian

A room designed by Orrery receives
The Roscius of the hour.
He bows and smiles and pauses by the door
Among less battered *putti*; but perceives
Advance towards him, borne upon a sea
Of smoke and noise,
The lady of a rival company
Whose progress West, the stuccodore, convoys
With birds and flutes. Now mutually entreating
By signs, they draw together; and one sees,
As exclamations punctuate their meeting,
The crisp swags droop a little on the frieze.

Were I to move among the talkers here,
I'd soon be disabused
About this artist, hearing him traduced
Wherever laughing malice has the ear
Of Irish wit. But I avert my gaze,
Refuse to know
His marxist and his mystagogic phase,
Or the connubial scandal years ago
Retailed around me. Every Irish master
Must learn to suffer, for the nation's sake,
The national proclivity for plaster,
Mouldings that chip, and pediments that flake.

The author of the genial comedies
From which this pair plucked fruit,
The edible stucco of their shared repute,
Has made no entrance; and yet there he is,
A brow that's broader than the marble mantel
There in the wall
Which thin heads nod in front of. Broad as well
Behind the brow, the soul. Broadness of soul –
What an inelegant and Russian notion!
It's more than Orrery could cater for.
His walls distend, the cornice is in motion…
Oliver Goldsmith! Samson heaves the floor.

Dublin Georgian (2)

A thin brown orphan in his washed-out blue
Opens the door a crack
Behind its sunblind and, subdued, peers through
At the wrecked street behind us. Standing back
He lets us into elegance preserved,
As he is, from the slum;
This orphanage, number twenty, that has served
Him as asylum, harbours also some
Few sedulous fragilities refined
On wall and ceiling. As we follow him
Beneath the famous plasterwork, I find
Art too (thus orphaned) vulnerably slim.

In rapt obscenities, the instructed taste
Admires the moulding, sighs
'Ah' at the staircase, and extols the chaste
Ceilings by Stapleton; occupies
(Thin shoulders raised, a flutter of bony hands)
The pure *gestalt*
Of the double arch; expatiates, understands
How architect and plasterer had felt
The underpinning of that virile beauty
In an age's order. Later, in the street,
He held forth to me how the artist's duty
Is mutiny, evasion, and retreat.

Eden

Adam had found what was not his to seek,
Command of motives; and the world grew heated,
The self extended and the will elated.
He can, he sees, make Eve again attractive
Almost at will, using this new technique
For rousing, as for quenching, an incentive.

A sin in gardens, where the shadows' play
Makes clarity a sin. So the attendant
Shows them the door. The garden was abandoned
To twilight, seasons, and the steady tread
Of natural wants that, once met, fell away,
Chill in the evenings, gratefully exhausted.

The Waterfall at Powerscourt

Looping off feline through the leisured air
    Water, a creature not at home in water,
Takes to the air. It comes down on its forepaws, changes
    Feet on the rockface and again extended
Bounds.   For it neither
    Pours nor is poured, but only here on its quarry
Falls at last, pours. No more the amphibious otter
    Than foundered ram can walk this water thrown
Catwalk across a further element.

Water itself is not at home in water
    But fails its creatures, as a fallen nature
Swerves from its course. And, less adaptable,
    Out of an element itself thrown out
The fallen creature cannot find itself
    Nor its own level, headlong.

Or else as a sealion, heavy and limber,
    Sedately slithers its short rock chute in the zoo
 (Foolish and haughty as, propped on a stock, the Prince Regent),
    And over the water it takes to
Shoots,   so the water
    Lobs itself, immerses in rock and, rebounding,
Surfaces smoothly backwards into space,
    Swimming the air as for freshwater miles offshore
The Orinoco dyes the ocean cold.

What end it answers, over the Sabine country
    Of Mrs Rafferty's Tusculum and Dublin's
Weekend hinterland, arching; or what use
    Insinuating underneath that ocean
Its chill of wit, who knows? The end it answers,
    The level it seeks, is its own.

THE FORESTS OF LITHUANIA

Foreword. Mickiewicz in England

Don John of Chesterton was riding to the wars
For Christendom and the Latin heritage
When Monica Gardner spoke of me. *Le coq*
Gaulois of Belloc crowed around the clock
'Too late, too late'; for Gorky held the stage
And 'Never a patch of plot,' said James, enthralled,
'To draw blood', in a story
By Turgenev.
     Scythians invest
Small perfect Europe, for whose sake
All Souls' High Table hears expressed
Dreams of 'Divide and rule'.

Did Belloc baulk, did Pound protest
When Saintsbury found Sienkeiwicz unlicked?
Who quoted Kochanowski, and to cap
What Latin tag? Who cared
That he was salvaged from Cyrillic script,
The Ronsard of Czarnólas?
       What orisons
Rose, modishly baroque,
       for our lady of Czenstochowa?
      Who could see
The Hun turn East? Who egged him on?
Who raged at Chamberlain for a guarantee
To Poland, honoured?
      Europe's paladin,
       the champion of the *civitas*,
He killed Cock Robin.

The man on the touchline sees most of the play
But may not know the rules. The Antipodean
Anti-Semite brilliantly alleges
The best of Europe's all around the edges,
The rest a ghetto, 'mittel-European'

His curse on Martin Buber.
                              In the white
Nights of the Neva, quays of Amsterdam
And lions of Venice violate a site
Stolen from quagmire and the Finn; an *urbs*
Not Augustinian yet not without
Pushkin's *urbanitas*.
                              Some work their passage
Home out of Kronstadt, through Crimean sonnets,
Or recognize in Florence with a start
The Piazza Demidoff. And Europe's heart
Is wherever community happens in any age.

I. *The Homestead*

White walls shone from far
White against green of poplars'
Windbreak against Autumn.
The house no great one, but the barn
Great, and with stacks beside it,
Gross country, full with foison.
Enter to these the youth
Beneath ancestral portraits,
Ancestral, and of heroes:
Kosciusko sworn and sworded
To drive three powers from Poland
Or fall upon that sword;
Rejtan, a Life of Cato
And the Phaedo before him,
These, and a knife turned inward;
Jasinski smiting the Russians
With Korsak, on the ravelin
Of Praga burning behind them.
Enter to these Tadéuez,
And to the grandfather clock
That plays Dombrowski's march,
And to his room when a boy ...

But this, so feminine?
Can this be the place? a piano,
Sheet-music upon it, books ...
And see, across a chair
The white gown freshly shaken.
Cross to the window. A brook
That ran through nettles once
Borders a garden plot
Of grass and mint. Those beds
Were lately rained upon:
The watering pot that stands
Half-full has felt
Just now her hand, the gate
Swings from her touch, on the sand
– Dry, white as snow – the print
Is light but clear of some
Unshod, unstockinged foot
That lately ran. His eyes
Rove, and as they rise
See her upon the wall
Balanced, in her white
And morning disarray
That will not screen,
Though crossed arms veil the breast,
Swan's throat and shoulders. Hair
In curling-papers rays
A small head, in the sun
Thus crowned, an ikon. Turning
From wall to turf, across
Stile and parterre, and up
A leaning plank, like a bird
Flying, and like a ray
Of moonlight darting through
The windowframe she gains
The very chamber. He
Blushes and bows, retires
And will not look, but hears
No one ... Half-wakened. When he looks
Cry as of a child

His uncle's house, the judge's,
Where he is entertained
In the stately manner: Assessor,
Seneschal, Notary,
Apparitor, in order,
Gaily but in order,
Not without heat discussing
Hounds and guns and tomorrow
A coursing-match; but his thoughts
Running on women, the girl
He has glimpsed already, women
And one place left at the board.

The Lithuanian judge
Offers by way of reproof
To the young Pan Tadéusz
Decorum, the difficult science,
No matter of graceful posture
Or ease at the affable counter,
But bearing of old Poland;
Courtesy, being extended
To all, not without distinction
But in the mode most proper
As to master with man, or to children
With parents, or each to each
In public husband and wife.
'Discourse in noble mansions
Was then a persistent history,
And talk among the gentry
The annals of their provinces;
Gentlemen watched their step,
Knowing such pains were taken
To judge of their deserving.
But neither name nor stock,
Associates nor achievements
Are now enquired after,
And each goes where he pleases
Short of the known informer
And the scrounger by profession.
Vespasian never questioned
Out of what hands his riches
Came to him, having decided
Money was "not to be sniffed at".

So men approve a title
By current estimates,
As if to strike up a friendship
Were also a transaction.
But a sense of personal worth
Is arrived at only by weighing;
The beam is only plumb
With a counterpoise in the pan,
A worthiness in another.'
To whom the Chamberlain speaks
From the place of honour: 'Recall
The pro-French element.
"All men are equal" – thus
In conversation one
Self-styled the marquis,
(Democrat later, later still
By dispensation
Of Bonaparte, *le baron).*
The doctrine doubtless ancient,
But the application ...? Worse
Than the Nogai tarters that
Frenchified generation,
Hating the faith of their fathers,
Foes to all precedent.
Ringworm in the great peruke!
Brochures and dissipation
Brought servile Lent. Far better
As now at last to earn
Glory from France, than learn
New fads as in the past.
Napoleon moves fast.
Valour bears glorious fruit,
Liberty from the laurel's root.'

And so to the legions!
So to news of the legions!
And yet not here, not now.
Who swam across the Niemen?
Gorecki, Pac, and Obuchowitz,
Piotrowski and the Mirzejewskis,
Brochocki and the Bernatowicz brothers,
Not here, not now. Perhaps
Later in private Robak

The Bernardine, the almoner
Of a foreign house, his bearing
So soldierly (and a sabre's
Cut on the brow), will take
A knife to scapulary. Now
Talk of the coursing, talk
Of the old dispute with the Count
With a foible for the Gothick
Who wants our ruined castle.
Tomorrow the folk may read
Their own gazette's citations
In the bearing of their betters
With pride, or brokenly. Or else
An old maimed beggar stands
Having his crust; and then
Out with it – Dombrowski
Assembling on the plains
Of Lombardy; Kniazewicz
Among the captured eagles
In Rome; or Jablonowski
His Danube Legion locked,
Among the sugar canes
And the pepper plants, with the blacks.

II. The Castle

Who does not remember his boyhood, gun on shoulder,
    Whistling through unobstructed fields?
Overstepping the bounds, yet offending no leaseholder
    Of Lithuania, where the chase was free?

There ocean-goer, unmarked ship, the hunter
    Ranged at large; as augur,
Read skies and clouds; or to townsmen occult, an enchanter,
    Heard the earth-whisper.

Look in vain for the landrail, as lost down the meadow calling
    As pike in the Niemen, and look
In vain overhead for the lark whose carillon falling
    Around us rings in the Spring.

There an eagle wing rustles, appalling the sparrows,
    A comet dismaying the stars. And a falcon,
Fluttering butterfly pinned, when a hare moves in the meadow
    Stoops like a meteor.

When will the Lord God have us return, inhabit
    Ancestral fields, bear arms
Against the birds, and only to ride down the rabbit
    Muster our horse?

    Breakfast the Judge
    Against the grain
    Admits alfresco:
    Sportsmen home again
    Move to and fro
    And serve the ladies, bear
    In Dresden ware
    Cups, capped in cream,
    Of coal-black, honey-thick
    Coffee, as aromatic
    As mocha, amber-clear
    On charming trays;
    Themselves the gentlemen
    Take as they may prefer
    Ham, goose or tongue,
    All cured in juniper,
    Or else stewed beef in gravy.

    As for the coursing match,
    Unsatisfactory:
    The dogs called off
    The hare in standing corn,
    The whole match off. And the Count:
    'They order these things better
    In Muscovy, respect the grain
    By ukase and decree
    As to time and place,
    "On a higher plane".' And thus
    Telimena, the lady of fashion,
    Installed in a summer villa
    Outside St Petersburg:

When fate must send
To live next door
Dog-loving dull *chinovnik,*
Alarming dogs conspire to rend
The night, and drive her frantic.
Worse is in store:
The lady swoons
To see her spaniel mangled
By cruel beagles, and before
Her eyes abruptly strangled.
The culprits brought to book,
The Czar's own hunting-master
Bends his tremendous look
On hound and master. 'What,
You coursed a doe?' 'Milord,
It was a dog.' 'Indeed,
So you prevaricate?
The hunting laws of Muscovy
Are meant to be obeyed.'
Four weeks detention cures
Suburban householders
Of hunting out of season;
Their dogs endure a summary
Death, for the same good reason.

Thus Telimena
To the room at large,
Thus, with composure:
Who'd not condone
The dubious note
In such a lovely cause?
Triumph of tone!
Her anecdote
Draws laughter and applause;
And now the swain
Forgets the maid
To court this ampler fair
Who sets in train
The ambuscade
Of love, and baits the snare;
Now she delays
The murmured phrase
Which he must stoop to catch;

Her gaze, his eyes,
His lips, her sighs
Mingle, and make the match.
Oh that a fly
Should come between
So close a tête-à-tête!
Pursuit, pass by
Nor intervene!
Domestic hygiene, wait!
Too late. The Seneschal
Has stalked his chosen fly
Too far. The blow must fall,
And fall it does. A start!
They jump apart,
Halves of a riven tree:
The lightning-stroke
Has cleft an oak
Of Love's own forestry.

Meanwhile by the castle wood
The Count as he rode to the coursing
Had checked at sight of the Keep
That rose from the morning mist
And seemed as tall again.
The roof of tin
Flashed in the sunlight over
Prismatic shards in the casements;
Mist hid in the lower stories
Jags and dilapidations.
Cries of the hunters from far
Windborne, returned by the walls,
For all the world from within
Sounded, as if the fog
With rapid restorations
Had pieced and peopled. The Count
Who aspired to be thought Romantic
Was reckoned an eccentric
Though honourable. Often,
Running the fox or the hare,
He would check and gaze at the sky
As mournfully as a cat
That sights a bird on a pinetree,
Or else as a motionless heron

Devouring fish through the eye.
And the horse he had turned from the road
Trod to the threshold. Alone
He sighed, gazed at the walls
That had once been his, and reached
For paper and pencil – yet started:
Twelve paces away another
Amateur of the picturesque
Counted the stones. Yet he knew him.
The ancient servitor
Of gentle birth, Gerwázy,
Who snatching his cap from a head
Bald and scored with the sabre
(A chopping block) recounted,
Conducting him through the courts,
Their sequestrated glories:

     'Here my old lord
     Sat, having dined,
     And here dispensed
     Rough justice. Jests
     And curious anecdotes
     Exchanged with guests
     Pleased his good humour, while
     In the court below
     Young men with staves
     Gave blow for blow
     Or else broke in
     His Turkish ponies.'
Entering the hall:
     'Less are the stones
     That pave this hall
     Than it saw tuns
     Of wine broached once
     At festival
     Diet or meet,
     When guests would haul
     By their belts cast
     Around them, from the vault
     Cask after cask.
     As wine went round
     Musicians played;
     A tucket's sound

Hailed Vivat first
The King, and then
The Archbishop, then the Queen,
And then all gentlemen;
Last the Republic – when,
The fifth glass drained,
The health is "Let us love
Each man his friend", a toast
While day remained
First drunk, but still proposed
As dawn came up
And coach and horse
Stood at the doors.'

Inflamed to re-achieve
His patrimony, stirred,
The impressionable Count
Wandered away. The scene
Round him, unseeing,
Changed slowly. Here the green
Tresses of carrot snared
Slim beans that stared
From a thousand eyes; the sage
And venerable cabbage,
That seemed to meditate
On vegetable fate,
Bared his bald head; the bold
And portly melon rolled
Far from his home, to wait
Upon the flushed estate
Of beetroots; while,
Drawn up in file
(Their leaf the snake, their scent
Repels the flies) the hemp
Screened every bed, and a girl
That was Zosia wandered.

Swimming knee deep, she trawled
The wrinkled waves and fronds
For vegetable fish;
Exploring feet directed
The hand's response,
To pick for a luncheon dish.

Her right hand raised
As if to pluck the air,
She dawdled down the rows.
Her eyes looked down, her bright
And straying hair
In the straw hat's shadow
Stirred as she went. The Count
Stood watch as a crane will stand
With neck outstretched outside
The feeding flock, one leg
Cranked up, clawing a stone
In its lean hand, that, falling,
With the shock will wake it.
A voice, and he turned, then looked
Once more. But she was gone.
Returning to quiet, a flood
Cut by a wing, the leaves
Rocked. The basket she bore
Rode the green swell alone,
Capsizing where she stood.

III. The Gathering of Mushrooms

Noon. And as from the hawk
Hanging under cloudbank,
Sighted in a hard eye skyward,
Of whom the alerted cock
Crows warning, in the rank
Barley, while the sky
Flashed fierce with summer, hens
And peacocks, geese
And even the pigeon caught
Out of reach of the eaves
Had sought the shade, to bathe
In sand, or on
The cropped turf pant. Among
These heads, rose children's heads,
The short hair white as flax
Bare upon bare shoulders. At their backs
A peacock, preening, spread
His spectral tail, a ground

Whose deep cerulean picked
The pale heads out. And lent
Light from that stellar wreath
Of all its eyes, the heads
(With one that was taller, Zosia's)
Shone where a diafan
Burned in transparency
Of aether that was gold
With maize, with mercury
Coraline, shot silver
By grasses, mallow-green.

Colours and forms in a screen
Of silver and gold grisaille
Plaited upon the air
Swam, a thrown veil. Above,
Nimbus or baldachin,
Hung butterflies, their bright
Cobweb and glass
And quadriparted wings
Stirring and not stirring
Whispered in air. In her hand
A grey whisk screened the heads
Against that golden rain
As with the other hand
To each in turn she proffered
A golden trumpet shape
Like Plenty's very horn.

Dulcinea to a Quixote
Out of the burdocks, who
Four beds away
Stood bowing. Like a lark
Skimming the leaves she'd have flown,
Had not the apparition
And her betrayed intention
Startled her charges. A spirit
Reluctantly hearing the magus,
She sat again and, soothing
The most distressed, she calmed
The small knee-hugging fledglings
Under her lee with 'Come,
That's rude. The gentleman

Will think you rude. For look,
It is no beggarman
But a guest of ours, and kind,
And look how pretty too.'
The pretty gentleman,
The Count, smiled pleasantly
To be so praised. She stopped.
Pretty he was, however;
Tall, and his face an oval,
Ruddy and fair, with mild
Blue eyes, and in his blonde
Hair worn long, the leaves
And grass, in his painful passage
Over the plots torn loose,
Showed green, a tattered wreath.
'O thou,' he hailed her, 'by
Whatever name I shall
Address thee, whether
Of nymph or goddess, speak,
Spirit or phantom. Was't
At thine own will thou cam'st
Hither, or hath some fell
Lord or harsh guardian chained
Thee by his spells within
This forest's pale?' And she:
'But
Excuse me
What are you doing in *our* garden?'

★

His soul like the earth after sundown
Darkened and chilled; his abstraction
Brought him bad dreams; he awakened
In anger that sought its occasion.
Much had he expected, much
Conjectured, as heart high
Head burning, he had wound
After his pastorella. Such
Charms as he'd projected! Now…
Pretty enough and slender
He'd found her. Yes, but how
Inelegant, and her face
So apt to colour

In an excessive, in
A vulgar transport. Clearly
Her mind still slumbering, and her heart
Inactive… And besides,
Oh the rusticity
Of those rejoinders! 'Come,
Why fool myself? Too late
I learn the truth, my nymph
A goosegirl.' The enchantment
Fled with the principal, those bands
Of lucent light and those
Thrown nets of silver and gold
Revealed as straw, he gazed,
Wringing his hands,
On cornflowers bound with grass,
The fly-switch he had thought
An ostrich plume. And gone
Down a child's throat the horn
Once Amalthea's, now
In short a carrot.

Meanwhile the judge had mustered
Mushroom-gatherers, whom,
Once more self-communing,
The Count mistook. For see!
Strange walkers these, in their
Processional parade
To and fro under low boughs,
Around them the birches white
And the turf green under.
These should be ghosts by moonlight.
Strange their attitudes: see
Slowly revolve on its bole
The human tree; all around
Downcast looks; and the dreamer
Direct in trance
Treading his lane
Undeviating. Strange
Decorum this that, prodigal
Of bows, will have them meet
Impassively, without
Acknowledgement, a nation
(So self-absorbed) polite

And yet unsociable.
Field full of folk, in their
Immunity from harm
Crestfallen and serene.
Who would have thought these shades
Our lively friends? Are these
Acres Elysian fields?
Mushrooms at any rate
In plenty: first
The *lísica* pursued
Rightly by swains if song
That marks the worm and fly
Abhor it, wisely prize
Its pallor as the badge
Of maidenhood; yet maids
Preferred *borówik,* slender
And ever under pines,
Called in the song
'The colonel'; all pursued
The smaller *rydz* as yet
Unfamed in song though sweetest
Of fungus kind, in winter
Salted, fresh in the Fall.
Alone the seneschal
Was to the flybane drawn,
Intoxicant toadstool. Some
As poor relations scorned
For ill effect or taste,
Yet deem not useless if
They shade flies, nourish beasts,
Enamel groves. The meadow's
Linen sustained the ware,
Stained yellow, red and silver,
Of *surojádki* lifting
To hold the various grape
Their crystals; like a cup
Inverted, swelled
The *kózlak* and, designed
For vintage of Champagne,
A kind called 'funnels'; white,
Shallow and broad, the cups
Of the *beliáki* proffered
The milk-laced mocha; while

The pepper-dredges
Of round *purcháwki* held
Their ebon dust.
                    Not these
Nor the succulent kinds engage
A lady's interests. Reared
Above the stream,
From Telimena's shoulders
A shawl's carnelian
Unwound, dropped to the turf.
As coral's amplitude
Might draw a winter swimmer
Reluctant, so the scarf's
Colour seemed to draw
Her stooping, who by stages
(Lilith upon a shawl)
Unwound, subsided. One
Palm to her temple, one
Elbow upon the turf,
She bent her head to a page
Of vellum's alabaster
Where her black ringlets wound,
Her ribbons coiled. The grass's
Smaragdine sheen, a shawl's
Carnelian, and a gown's
Fullness whose coral tint
Picked out the black of the shoes
The black of the hair, concurred
With flanking whitenesses
Of hose and linen,
The hand's and the brow's pallor –
So variously on distance
She crawled, a caterpillar
On a maple green.

Towards her Tadéusz first
Obliquely edged, as under
A movable hide
Slung between wheels, the sportsman
Approaches the bustard, or as
Out after plover, his gun
On the saddle or under
His horse's neck, he pretends

To be harrowing, riding the bounds,
His horse between him and the birds,
Thus Tadéusz; but straight to the mark,
A white-skirted smock in a flutter,
A kerchief tucked in a girdle,
A straw hat broad in the wind
Like a leaf of burdock, flapping
Back on his shoulders and forward
And over his eyes, in a hurry
The Judge arrived.
                              He began
A long tale too, and involved:
Of how Tadéusz,
Being the Judge's brother's
Son entrusted
To the Judge's care, should be married
To the Chamberlain's daughter. Protesting
'You want a hick?'
His kinswoman prescribed
Rather a course of polish
In the great world, perhaps
In Warsaw or, still better
With her in the coming winter
To gather in St Petersburg
An order or an office.

Young men, the Judge allowed,
Should see the world and learn
A certain poise. Himself
When young had been in Dubno
About the court and on his own affairs,
And once at least
In Warsaw. Not a little
He'd profited, as doubtless
His nephew should – though not
By job or decoration
From Moscow. What distinction
Of old or indeed today
Attached to such an office? Rank
In local affairs conferred
By suffrage of his fellows,
That was another matter.
                              'As you like',

Returned the lady.
                              Yet
This same elusive brother
Retained, it appeared, surveillance
Over his son, and sent
Robak the Bernardine
With a direction, thus:
Tadéusz to be wed
To Telimena's ward
Who, still a child, should now
Be groomed and move
Into society, in short
Why, Zosia.
                    And the storm
Broke, as the fair consultant
In what seemed panic spurned,
Hands flailing as if at midges,
His every word: 'For the boy
Let him be bailiff, serve
For all I care
Behind a bar! But Zosia,
That's my concern.' And the Judge,
Distressed and murmuring: 'If
They like each other, then ...?'

Out of the question, he was told. And yet
As tempers cooled, there was a sort of truce:
No one will use compulsion. It's agreed
The girl is young. And so the Judge departed.

IV. The Forest

'O happy skies of Italy!
Rose gardens of the Caesars!'
'Classic cascades of Tibur,
And Posilippo's crag ...'
Thus far that knight of the pencil,
The Count, and Telimena.

Yet round them even as they sigh
Lithuania's forests lie,

Currants wave their hop-crowned tresses,
Quickbeams blush like shepherdesses,
The hazel in a maenad's shape
Crowned with her nuts as with the grape
Twirls a green thyrsus, and below
The striplings of the forest grow –
The may, whom guelder-roses clip;
The blackberry, his ebon lip
Pressed to the raspberry's. Linking hands
(That's leaves) the trees and bushes stand
Like dancers, maid and man, around
The married pair in middle ground,
Two that for straightness, hue and height
Surpass their sylvan neighbours quite;
The silver birch, the well-loved bride,
Her man the hornbeam by her side.
Grave seniors sit some way apart
To watch their progeny disport,
Matronly poplar, hoary beech
Who gazing find no need of speech;
And a moss-bearded oak that bears
The weight of full five hundred years
Rests, as on tombstones overthrown,
On his own forebears turned to stone.

In the Botanical Garden at Wilno
Trees from eastward and southward
And the trees of Italy grow,
And which of them all is preferred
Before our trees? Is the aloe
Its stem like a lightning rod
Their match? Or will they show
The lemon of the lacquered leaf,
Strung about with its wealth like a widow
Short and ill-favoured but moneyed?
Or is it that emblem of grief
(Of boredom, some would have said)
The long lean much belauded
Cypress, that over the dead
Like a German flunkey is set,
Not daring to stir his head
So strict the etiquette?

Blue, that Italian sky
Clear, as is frozen water;
But in this country
As the wind or the storm passes,
What images, what actions
The sportive wrack composes;
Shower-logged, sluggish in Spring
Clouds like tortoises labour
Over a sky where tresses
Of the long rain sway earthward;
The bowling hailstorm crosses
The heavens by balloon
Blue, but with yellow flashes;
And then, what metamorphoses
Pursue the white quotidian
Clouds that like a gaggle
Of swans or geese the falcon
Wind hard presses;
Harried, they multiply
Prodigies, and crested
With sudden manes as serried
Legs bud beneath them, coursers
Over the steppes of the sky,
Necks arched, they gallop.

*

Does the great oak, Baublis, survive
In whose age-scooped bulk
As in a stout house
Twelve sat at table? The grove
Of Mendog, does it bloom
Still by the churchyard wall?
And in the Ukraine does it rise
Still on the banks of the Ros,
That linden, pride
Of the Holowínskis, spreading
So wide its leaves
Before their house that a hundred
Young men have danced
Beneath, with a hundred maidens?

Monuments of our fathers!
How many among you yearly
Fall to contractors' axes?
Will such officious vandals
Unhouse all forest-warblers,
Bird or bard, to whom
Your shade was grateful? One,
The linden of Czarnólas,
Jan Kochanowski's descant,
Is singing still, and singing
Though to the bard of the Cossack
Of marvels still. And I,
A wretched shot, escaping
My comrades' gibes, how many
Fancies have I not taken,
A nobler game,
Out of your quiet! Bearded
Mosses around me silver,
The berries crushed and blue-ish
Streaked them, as the tussocks
Of heather reddened, strung
With the huckleberry's coral,
Rosaries. Around
Darkness lay as, low
Green clouds, the branches
Hung over me. Above
That stable vault,
The wind was somewhere wailing
Roaring or howling – odd
And stunning noise, as if
A sea suspended
Over my head swung, tossing.

Below, the remains of cities
Oak overthrown;
Breached wall and shattered column;
And branching stumps,
Beams half-powdered
In a hedge of grass.

Looking within is fearful:
Lords of the woods,
Wild boar and wolf
And bear, dwell here;
Unwary guest,
Bones half-gnawed at the entry.

A double column of water
Behind the green grass
Rises – a pair of antlers,
Stag; and a sunbeam falling
Athwart the trees
Extinguished, a beast passing.

And again, quiet.

Rapping on the fir-tree, woodpecker,
In flight, there …!
Lost. And the rapping
Starting again,
The hidden child
Needing to be sought for.

Squirrel, a nut in its forepaws,
Cuirassier crested
With its own tail,
Fearful although so armoured,
Darting its eyes;
It flies the intruder;

Tree to tree, a dancer,
Like lightning flashes;
Into a fissure
Unnoticed in a tree-stump
Sidles, returning
To tree-form this Dryad.

And again, quiet.

Who has plumbed Lithuania's forest,
Pressed to the thicket's core?
As the sea-floor is known to the fisherman
Meagrely, even inshore,
So the hunter can know of the forest

Only the face of its waters
Never their bed. Of its centre
What fable and rumour have said
Has authority. Once past
The manageable tangles,
The rampart rises – logs,
Roots, stumps, which a quagmire defends –
And water, and nets
Of rank weeds and ant-hills, and knots
Of snakes, and the wasp's and the hornet's
Nests. And then small meres
Grass-choked yet unplumbable, thought
To harbour devils, hold water
Rust-spotted, emitting a thick
And stinking steam. In the fumes
The trees are bald and sicken,
Dwarfed, wormlike; bare
Of bark and leaves, they wear beards
Of filthy fungi, and a knot
Of bunched-up mosses – witches
Around their pot, the pool,
Thawed by a graveplot brew.

These pools no eye can pass,
Still less a foot; morasses
Here raise, miasmal, shrouding
The further reaches, clouds
That rumour says obscure
From view a purer air
And fruitful earth, where all is
As in the ark. Metropolis
Of beasts and plants, the region
Sees brutes forget their rages
And learn civility. The seed
Of every plant that seeded
Throughout the earth is there
Preserved; and the primal pair
Of every creature copulates
In pre-lapsarian state.

Tradition will allow
The ancient buffalo
The bison and the bear

Alone the right to wear
The purple. All around,
Treed that they may command
The land's approaches, wait
Their ministers of state
The lynx and wolverine;
Beside them where they reign
Fed on their broken meats
The two court favourites
Eagle and falcon skulk;
Boar, wolf and antlered elk
Each in suburban fief
Owe vassalage. The chief
And patriarchal pairs
Stay home among their peers
But send their progenies
Far out to colonize.

Themselves they know repose
Locked in their ancient ease
Never by cut or shot
To die, but of old age
In nature's course. They have
Likewise a place of graves
Wherein, when near to death,
Wildfowl bring home their feathers
And brutes their fur. The stag
Who barely moves his legs
Limps thither, and the bear
Who cannot chew, the hare
When his blood thickens, grey
Ravens and hawks that grow
Half-blind, and when cross-billed
So far as to withhold
The meat it craves, the old
Eagle. Inferior kinds
Whose bones no woodward finds
Within his walks, repair
When sick or hurt to expire
In that, their fatherland.

A polity well planned
Keeps order in the lair:

Meum nor *tuum* there
Embroil, and unaware
Of duelling or war
As once in Paradise
Keeping the peace, too wise
To butt or bite, the tame
And the wild consort. The same
Harmony would extend
Even to humankind;
Should ever human hunter
Although unarmed there enter,
Unhurt he'd pass between
The animals, and be seen
With that astonishment
Which their first fathers bent
On Adam when he first
Upon the sixth and last
Day of Creation ran
Through Eden. But to man
Death, Toil and Terror ban,
How luckily, access;
Nor can he ever press
To that secluded ground.
Only at times a hound
Fierce in pursuit may pass
Amid the pits and moss
And from what lies within
In terror run to whine,
Beneath his master's hand
Still quivering. Unscanned
By man, each ancient reach
Is called in hunter's speech
'Jungle'.

       Thou'dst little wit,
Bruin, in this haunt safe,
To venture out of it.
What didst so far from home?
Did ripe oats draw thee
Or the honeycomb
Along the open ride
Where trees grow sparsely
By the forest's side?

The ranger saw thee there
And sent his spies abroad
To learn from them the lair
Where thou o' nights hast slept
And where thou'st fed. And now
Thy foes have crept
To bar thee every road
Back to the jungle
And thine own abode.

The hunters strained their ears;
As to a curious discourse hearkening,
They heard the forest's silence
Play for them, where the dogs
As loons swim undersea
In and out flickered. Guns
Trained on the woodside, eyes
Covered the Seneschal
Kneeling, ear to the ground,
In whose face, as in the face
Of a physician Hope
And Terror read, they read
His diagnosis. And this,
Rising subdued, he delivered:
'They have struck the trail.'
                                        He had heard
What they would hear: a single
Yelp (now they heard it),
Two now, and now twenty,
Now the concerted whine
Scattered at first, and now
Closed up. Not this
The baying which announces
Fox, hare or deer,
But a constant sharp
And broken yelp – the hounds
In sight of the quarry. Yet
The cry ceased, as the pack
Closed with the beast. Unseen
The attack was launched. And the brute
Defended himself, for the cries
Were punctuated often now and often
With the long death howl.

Guns at the ready, bent
Like a bow, each huntsman's head
Pointed. And they could wait
No longer, but they broke
Station, the Seneschal
Shouting unheeded, and moved
Crowding, as from horseback
He promised them all,
Gentle and simple, the lash.
No help for it – they'd see
And all see first. Came three
Shots, then a volley, then
Above the volley, shocking
The woodland echoes, a dreadful
Sound where pain, despair
And fury mixed, the bear's
Tormented roar. And ragged
Behind it, yelps,
Cries, and the horns of beaters
All on the move, and all
Except the Seneschal
Exultant.
                    On the one side
They massed; but the beast turned back
To the open fields and the few
Who stayed, the Seneschal,
Tadéusz, the Count, with beaters
Where the wood thinned. A roaring
Within and the crackle of boughs
Came near and nearer.
                              Out
Burst like a thunderbolt
From cloud, the bear!
Torn, with terror
And the dogs upon him,
He stopped, turned, reared
Erect, and with a roar
Quelled his assailants; stooped
His forepaws scrabbling, tore
Roots from the earth and flung them
At dogs and men; uprooted
A tree he flailed like a club,
So turned and came on, rushing

Tadéusz and the Count,
Last of the line. Their muskets,
As lightning rods discharge
At a lowering cloud, discharged
And missed. Four hands together
Seize (the beast still bearing
Down on them) a pike
Planted between them,
Each way tugged at once.

So near to the bear
His double row of tusks
Gleamed on them from his red
Maw, and his claw descended
Upon them, thereupon turning
Through the sparse trees they doubled.

To claw the skull from their brains
As a hat uncovers a head,
The black paw reared. The Assessor
Appeared, and the Notary; Gerwazy
Showed up in front, and Robak
Behind him, running. As
At a command, together
Three shots rang out. Like a hare
Who, the hounds upon him, takes
To the air before them,
So leapt the bear,
Came down head foremost, hurled,
His four paws somersaulting,
His bloody bulk under the Count
And still would rise. The mastiffs
Each side closed upon him.

And now the Seneschal
Had seized his famous horn
That, mottled and involved,
Seemed a great snake. He bore it
To his lips, two-handed. His cheeks
Distended, and as his eyes
Were shot with blood, the lids
Half-veiled them. So he drew
From his pinched-in belly, breath,

And so expelled it. Cyclones
Of whirling air up-spiralled
To roll down and amaze the woods
With purity and volume. For he played
The original catch, the art
For which he was renowned
Of old through the forests: first
The morning call over the kennels,
Then yelps as the kennels were loosed,
The baying pack, and last
The volley sounded.

Here he broke off, but still
He held the horn;
It was the echo playing,
That seemed the Seneschal.

Again he sounded. You thought
The horn at his lips endured
Metamorphoses, swelling
And dwindling as it feigned
Now the bellow of bison
Cutting the wind; now, thickened,
The bear's throat roaring. It thinned
And a wolf's long howling
Came down wind.

Here he broke off, but still
He held the horn:
It was the echo playing,
That seemed the Seneschal.
Oaks to the oaks repeated it,
The beeches to the beeches.

Again he blew. The horn,
It was a hundred horns.
The wrath and terror
Of the men, the pack
And the quarry mingled. Last
The lifted horn pealed
Triumph skyward.

Here he broke off, but still
He held the horn:
It was the echo playing,
That seemed the Seneschal.
And all about the forest,
To every tree a horn.
Trees to the trees, as choirs
Take up from choirs, repeated
The note that broader, further
And fainter spread,
And in the extreme distance
At the sill of heaven expired.

But now his arms were thrown
Wide, and the horn
Fell, swung on a thong;
As, cruciform
And swollen-faced, his eyes
Lifted, still he tried
To catch the last and long
Long-drawn
Note from the skies,

As plaudits came to drown
The horn.

V. The Quarrel

Seneschal leaving the wood
Your hunt is over, but hers
In the empty house you return to
Hers is beginning.
Telimena sits without moving
Folding her arms; but her thoughts
Pursue from a view to a kill
At once, two quarries;
The Count, and Tadéusz.
(And so she gets up from the sofa.
Does she only seem to grow taller,
Parting her bodice, consulting
Sidelong the glass on the wall?)

'However their thoughts may wander
Young men are more constant at heart,
For conscience's sake, than their elders;
She who was first to impart
The sweets of love can expect
From their simple and maidenly feeling,
Long after, a grateful respect.
Youth welcomes and rises from love
As from a modestly planned
Meal that we eat with a friend,
Gaily. Consumed from within,
Only the old debauchee
Detests what he drowns himself in.'

Thus a woman of experience
Reflects on these matters,
Sensibly.

     But white,
In a long white gown,
Turning about as a fountain
Turns among flowers,
Zosia is feeding the fowl.
Over the wings and the heads
Pearl of a white hand, pearl
Of the hail of the barley
Scatters out, dense from the sieve.
Telimena, her guardian,
Summons. She deals them the rest,
Strikes on the sieve as a dancer
Will strike on a tabor, whirling
Striking a strict time. Swooping
Now she flies through the fowl
That scatter before her. Doves,
Doves go before her
As before Venus's car
As she goes, skimming.

Alas how unwise
To augment the advantage of girlhood
With a pitcher of water
Tipped into a basin of silver;
How much too indulgent

Unstoppering flasks from the Nevsky,
Pomade for corn-coloured hair
And scent too sweet for a rival;
Alas, and how rash
White open-work stockings from Warsaw
And white satin shoes,
And braids, the hair smooth on the temples.

In vain to importune a lover
Whose cheeks have paled for a youthful
Small head, once seen, now remembered;
In vain to attempt a diversion
And sharpen a jest on him standing,
Arm on a mantel,
Silent, apart, in a corner;
In vain, when all fail, to upbraid
Till he plunge, like a pike, for his freedom,
Dragging the iron and line.

His evil spirit has prompted;
He eavesdrops now on his rival
Engaging the diffident Zocia
With a private joke.
                              Digesti g
The bitterness into his soul
And as, full-fed upon poison,
A snake will coil
Death on a garden alley,
So full in the path of the talk
Tadéusz coils, envenomed;

And so resentfully
His eyes accuse
The nervous Telimena:
Those roses in her face
– Is he or she betrayed? –
Are false. And whether laid
Too thin a pane
Upon a coarse complexion,
Or scratched (and at his hand),
Or else by her returning
From the assignation mended
In too much haste,

The moth's wing dust of carmine
Blabs. And by his eyes,
Those secret agents, learning
A single piece of treason,
The newly instructed youth
Finds gap-tooth now, and freckle
And crowsfoot – nowhere, truth!

Alas, how unwise
To observe too closely a beauty!
Alas, how unworthy
To spy out the mole in a mistress!
Alas, how unwholesome
To change about in affection!
Yet the heart, who can constrain?
In vain, where love is deficient,
To call for injunctions on duty!
In vain by the flame of her glance
To thaw the ice of the soul!
In vain, if that glance, like a moon,
Throw a bright but heatless reflection
Over a frozen terrain.

VI. The Year 1812

Year well remembered! Happy who beheld thee!
The commons knew thee as the year of yield,
But as the year of war, the soldiery.

Rumours and skyward prodigies revealed
The poet's dream, the tale on old men's lips,
The spring when kine preferred the barren field.

Short of the acres green with growing tips
They halted lowing, chewed the winter's cud;
The men awaited an apocalypse.

Languid the farmer sought his livelihood
And checked his team and gazed, as if enquiring
What marvels gathered westward while he stood.

He asked the stork, whose white returning wing
Already spread above its native pine
Had raised the early standard of the Spring.

From swallows gathering frozen mud to line
Their tiny homes, or in loud regiments
Ranged over water, he implored a sign.

The thickets hear each night as dusk descends
The woodcock's call. The forests hear the geese
Honk, and go down. The crane's voice never ends.

What storms have whirled them from what shaken seas,
The watchers ask, that they should come so soon?
Or in the feathered world, what mutinies?

For now fresh migrants of a brighter plume
Than finch or plover gleam above the hills,
Impend, descend, and on our meadows loom.

Cavalry! Troop after troop it spills
With strange insignia, strangely armed,
As snow in a spring thaw fills

The valley roads. From the forests long
Bright bayonets issue, as brigades of foot
Debouch like ants, form up, and densely throng;

All heading north as if the bird, the scout,
Had led men here from halcyon lands, impelled
By instincts too imperative to doubt.

War! the war! – a meaning that transpires
To the remotest comer. In the wood
Beyond whose bounds no rustic mind enquiries,

Where in the sky the peasant understood
Only the wind's cry, and on earth the brute's
(And all his visitors the neighbourhood),

A sudden glare! A crash! A ball that shoots
Far from the field, makes its impeded way,
Rips through the branches and lays bare the roots.

The bearded bison trembles, and at bay
Heaves to his forelegs, ruffs his mane, and glares
At sudden sparks that glitter on the spray.

The stray bomb spins and hisses; as he stares,
Bursts. And the beast that never knew alarm
Blunders in panic to profounder lairs.

'Whither the battle?' – and the young men arm.
The women pray, 'God is Napoleon's shield,
Napoleon ours', as to the outcome calm.

Spring well remembered! Happy who saw thee then,
Spring of the war, Spring of the mighty yield,
That promised corn but ripened into men.

★

Out of the moist dark
Dawn without glow brings
Day without brightness.

Sunrise, a whiteness
In a thatch of mist,
Shows late to eastward.

Earth is as tardy;
Cows go to pasture,
Startle hares grazing.

Fog that had spared them
Dayspring's alarum
Dispels them with herds.

Groves where the damp birds
Brood are their havens
In the still woodland.

Storks clack from marshland;
Ravens on haycocks
Croak of wet weather.

Scythes ring together,
Clink of the sickle,
Hone, hammer, and dirge.

Fog at the field's verge
Strangles the echo
Of labour and song.

The bravery of its gentry,
The beauty of their women
Exalt Dobrzyn
Through Lithuania. Once
Six hundred gentry armed
Answered the summons,

The besom made of twigs;
But now no easy living
For gentry of Dobrzyn
In magnates' households,
In troops or at assemblies –
Like serfs they work their way,
Not clad like serfs, the men
In gowns black-striped on white,
In gloves their women spinning
Or leather-shod tending the herds.

All Bartlemies, Matthiases,
Of Polish stock,
Masovian still
In speech and usages,
Black-haired and aquiline,
Nicknamed to save confusion;
Their patriarch, Matthias,
'The Maciek of Macieks';
His house, although untended,
Their Capitol.

Mercury's vivid fringe,
Mullein and crocus bow
The thatch; and mosses tinge
The roof as green as tin.
The rabbit mines below
Windows where birds fly in.
Birdcage or warren now
The fortress of Dobrzyn.

Where once the gate would creak,
Swedes left a cannon ball.
Unhallowed crosses speak
Of sudden obsequies.
Specks swarm on every wall
And seem a rash of fleas;
In each there nests a ball
As in earth-burrows, bees.

Innocent every door
Of nail or hook or latch.
(The steel old swordsmen wore
Bit iron, and stood the test
Nor ever showed a notch.)
Above, Dobrzynski crests;
Cheeses the bearings smutch
And swallows blur with nests.

Four helms, once ornaments
Of martial brows, the dove,
Love's votary, frequents;
A corselet of chain mail
Hangs as a chute above
A horse's stall; a tail
Lopped from the charger of
The Ottoman cleans a pail.

Ceres has banished Mars;
Vertumnus and Pomona
And Flora heal the scars
On stable, house and barn.
Today shall they throw over
That distaff rule, and learn
Old habits to recover
To greet the god's return.

*

Fair weather, and the day breaking
Day of our Lady of Flowers;
The sky clear, hung over land
Like a sea curved forward and backward;
Pearls under its wave

Some few stars still, though paling;
White cloudlet alone
(Wing feathers fray out in the azure),
Spirit departing
Belated by prayers,
Fares fast to its heavenly fellows.

Pearls dim and go out in the deep.
Pallor on the sky's brow midmost
Spreads, and one temple is swarthy
Crumpled, pillowed on shadows,
The other ruddy. The distant
Horizon parts like a lid
On the white of an eye
Iris and pupil, and a ray circles
Dazzles, a gold shaft
Stuck through the heart of a cloud.

Fires cluster and dart
Cross over, light over light
Overarches the sky-round;
Drowsy, a broken
Light under lashes shaken
The eye of the sun rose up
Glittered, seven-tinted:
Sapphire by blood is to ruby
Ruby by yellow to topaz
Crystal, by lucent
To diamond, and by flame
Great moon or fitful star.
And the eye of the sun rose up
Alone across the unmeasured.

Strange manifestations expected
Bring piety in before sunrise;
Today come captains to worship.
Saints, the commanders of legions,
Gospel, the tale of their journeys,
Engagements, campaigns. A detachment
Thronged and surrounded convinces
The folk of their countrymen armed
Free, and on their lips Polish!

There, arm in a sling, stands
One who was lately a greenhorn,
A lancer now, Tadéusz;
And Zosia with him, explaining
Painfully how in his absence
Love was borne in on her,
Uncertainly recalling
The tear in his eye at parting,
Or, teased by her schoolfellows, finding
Her heart contract at his name.

Dombrowski said to Maciek:
'What about it, my friend?
Aren't you glad we're here?
What's on your mind?
Doesn't it do your heart good
To see the gold eagles and the silver eagles
And to hear the buglers
Sound Kosciusko's reveille?
Maciek, I thought you were more
Of a fighting man; if you won't
Take sabre and ride,
At least you will drink
Heartily, to
Napoleon and the hopes of Poland!'

'Aye,' said Maciek, 'I've heard
Of the set-up all right
And I see it, too. A pair
Of eagles, is it? They don't nest together.
The high and mighty ride
Piebald. And the Emperor's
A hero, is he? The Pulawskis,
Old mates of mine, they used to say
The hero Poland wants
Is a Pole, no
Frenchman nor Eyetie neither, a
Piast, a Jan or a Josef
Or a Maciek, maybe. The army ...
They call it Polish! All these
Grenadiers, engineers,
Cannoneers, fusiliers! I tell you
You hear more Jerry monikers in that crowd

Than ours, any day.
I reckon you've got Turks among you, Tartars,
Nonconformists, Christ knows what religion.
Haven't I seen them myself,
Setting on village women,
Beating up men in the street,
Mucking up churches?
The Emperor's off to Moscow!
It's a long haul that
For his most Imperial,
If he's got no God at his back.
And he don't hit it off
With the Padre, I understand …'

Thronged chapel spills into a meadow.
Lowered in worship the heads;
Field of ripe grain
The Lithuanian flaxen;
Girl's head with flowers adorned
Or as ribbons flow loose from a braid,
Cornflower in corn or a poppy;
And the heads sway down
As at a breath of the wind
Over the wheat ears
So to the bell on the wind.

Village girls brought to the altar
Spring's earliest tribute of green
Sheaves over altar and ikon
Belfry and galleries decked.
Zephyr of morning
Stirring out of the East
Throws down a garland
Fragrance as of a censer.

Epilogue

How many memories, what long sorrow
There where a man shall cleave to his master
As here no wife cleaves to her man;
There where a man grieves for loss of his weapons
Longer than here for who sired him;
And his tears fall more sincerely and faster
There for a hound than this people's for heroes.

My friends of those days made my speech come easy,
Each good for some singable idiom. Spring
Brought in the fable cranes of the wild island flying
Over the spellbound castle and the spellbound
Boy lamenting, who was loosed
By each pitying bird as it flew, one feather:
He flew out on those wings to his own people.

Against Confidences

Loose lips now
Call Candour friend
Whom Candour's brow,
When clear, contemned.

Candour can live
Within no shade
That our compulsive
Needs have made

On couches where
We sleep, confess,
Couple and share
A pleased distress.

Not to dispense
With privacies,
But reticence
His practice is;

Agreeing where
Is no denial,
Not to spare
One truth from trial,

But to respect
Conviction's plight
In Intellect's
Hard equal light.

Not to permit,
To shy belief
Too bleakly lit,
The shade's relief

Clouds Candour's brow,
But to indulge
These mouths that now
Divulge, divulge.

Nineteen-Seventeen

A glass in a Liverpool drawing room cracked across.
A telegram fell out of it for Rica.
Perfidious glass that would not mirror loss,
The omen had outstripped the telegram.

A glass in Roscoe's drawing room fell apart
And handed out a telegram from France.
Rica got up from winding bandages.

The gaze of the glass was frantic and averted.
A wet and severed wrist, a hand that shook
Came from the mirror and delivered death
To Liverpool and England in a look.

She reckoned there could not be long to wait.
A wedge of wrack was hunting in from sea
As stadiums spill spectators from a gate.
The thrumming bolt approached her from the blue.
Its piercing note already shattered glass.

A world of plush and leather came to pieces,
Mahogany was shivered into glass.
She smiled farewell to all their startled faces
And steadily outstripped the telegram.

To a Brother in the Mystery

Circa 1290

The world of God has turned its two stone faces
One my way, one yours. Yet we change places
A little, slowly. After we had halved
The work between us, those grotesques I carved
There in the first bays clockwise from the door,
That was such work as I got credit for
At York and Beverley: thorn-leaves twined and bent
To frame some small and human incident
Domestic or of venery. Each time I crossed
Since then, however, underneath the vast
Span of our Mansfield limestone, to appraise
How you cut stone, my emulous hard gaze
Has got to know you as I know the stone
Where none but chisels talk for us. I have grown
Of my own way of thinking yet of yours,
Seeing your leafage burgeon there by the doors
With a light that, flickering, trenches the voussoir's line;
Learning your pre-harmonies, design
Nourished by exuberance, and fine-drawn
Severity that is tenderness, I have thought,
Looking at these last stalls that I have wrought
This side of the chapter's octagon, I find
No hand but mine at work, yet mine refined
By yours, and all the difference: my motif
Of foliate form, your godliness in leaf.
And your last spandrel proves the debt incurred
Not all on the one side. There I see a bird
Pecks at your grapes, and after him a fowler,
A boy with a bow. Elsewhere, your leaves discover
Of late blank mask-like faces. We infect
Each other then, doubtless to good effect...
And yet, take care: this cordial knack bereaves
The mind of all its sympathy with leaves,
Even with stone. I would not take away
From your peculiar mastery, if I say
A sort of coldness is the core of it,
A sort of cruelty; that prerequisite
Perhaps I rob you of, and in exchange give
What? Vulgarity's prerogative,

Indulgence towards the frailties it indulges,
Humour called 'wryness' that acknowledges
Its own complicity. I can keep in mind
So much at all events, can always find
Fallen humanity enough, in stone,
Yes, in the medium; where we cannot own
Crispness, compactness, elegance, but the feature
Seals it and signs it work of human nature
And fallen though redeemable. You, I fear,
Will find you bought humanity too dear
At the price of some light leaves, if you begin
To find your handling of them growing thin,
Insensitive, brittle. For the common touch,
Though it warms, coarsens. Never care so much
For leaves or people, but you care for stone
A little more. The medium is its own
Thing, and not all a medium, but the stuff
Of mountains; cruel, obdurate, and rough.

Killala★

Forlorn indeed Hope on these shores,
White-breeched, under a tricorne, shouting orders
Into the wind in a European language
La gloire against the Atlantic.
                              And Enniscrone,
The unfocused village carefully grouped on absence...

Laden with Europe, toiling up out of the sea
With all the baggage of their own and Europe's
History barnacled, clammy with tawny jellies
And spotted silts, the wreck
Of unwashed hope is a more combustible flotsam
Than this more stranded,
More featureless than any conurbation.

★ *Killala:* where the French landed in Ireland in 1798.

Not memory (her lading) nor the vessel
– No, nor the vessel, for the *Téméraire*
Has been a dozen ships and all one venture –
But the venture persists. Such a temerity,
So bare a chance deserves a barer rock's
Less cluttered landfall. Nakedness
Is structural, asks a binnacle at sea;
By land, if not an oak, a standing stone
Hewn or unhewn in an open place, for the venture
To take a shape by. But the prudent Gael,
Disguised on the skyline as habitation tatters
A scarecrow coast, has blurred identity
By blurring shape, a flutter of rags in the wind.

Frenchman, the beacons flare across the Midlands.
Stopping the car and hating this ugly place,
Let this be as if I had lit the first of the beacons,
Of driftwood fetched from the shore,
Announcing your identity and presence:
Not an idea, abstract notion, quality
But a being only, able for life and action,
The same it was some time ago, in France.

With the Grain

1

Why, by an ingrained habit, deviate
    Into their own ideas
Activities like carpentry, become
    The metaphors of graining?
Gardening, the one word, tilth? Or thought,
    The idea of having ideas,
Resolved into images of tilth and graining?

An ingrained habit… This is fanciful:
    And there's the rub
Bristling, where the irritable block
    Screams underneath the blade
Of love's demand, or in crimped and gouged-out
    Shavings only, looses
Under a peeling logic its perceptions.

Language (mine, when wounding,
　　　Yours, back-biting) lacks
No whorl nor one-way shelving. It resists,
　　　Screams its remonstrance, planes
Reluctantly to a level. And the most
　　　Reasonable of settlements betrays
Unsmoothed resentment under the caress.

2

The purest hue, let only the light be sufficient
　　　Turns colour. And I was told
If painters frequent St Ives
　　　It is because the light
There, under the cliff, is merciful. I dream
　　　Of an equable light upon words
And as painters paint in St Ives, the poets speaking.

Under that cliff we should say, my dear,
　　　Not what we mean, but what
The words would mean. We should speak,
　　　As carpenters work,
With the grain of our words. We should utter
　　　Unceasingly the hue of love
Safe from the battery of changeable light.

(Love, a condition of such fixed colour,
　　　Cornwall indeed, or Wales
Might foster. Lovers in mauve,
　　　Like white-robed Druids
Or the Bards in blue, would need
　　　A magical philtre, no less,
Like Iseult's, to change partners.)

3

Such a fourth estate of the realm,
　　　Hieratic unwinking
Mauve or blue under skies steel-silver,
　　　Would chamfer away
A knot in the grain of a streaming light, the glitter,
　　　Off lances' points, that moved
A sluggish Froissart to aesthetic feeling.

And will the poet, carpenter of light,
    Work with the grain henceforward?
If glitterings won't fetch him
    Nor the refractory crystal,
Will he never again look into the source of light
    Aquiline, but fly
Always out of the sun, unseen till softly alighting?

Why, by an ingrained habit, elevate
    Into the light of ideas
The colourful trades, if not like Icarus
    To climb the beam? High lights
Are always white, but this ideal sun
    Dyes only more intensely, and we find
Enough cross-graining in the most abstract nature.

Red Rock of Utah

of golde and sylver they make commonly chaumber pottes, and
other vesselles, that serve for moste vile uses....
Furthermore of the same mettalles they make greate chaines,
fetters, and gieves wherein they tie their bondmen.
Finally whosoever for anye offense be inflamed, by their eares hang
rynges of golde, upon their fyngers they weare rynges of golde,
and aboute their neckes chaines of golde, and in conclusion their
heades be tied aboute with gold.

More's Utopia

Surely it has some virtue, having none,
Sighed to her bondman the Utopian lady
Telling the links of gold among his hair.
At wrist and ankle, fingers, head and neck
The unserviceable metal he must wear
In rings, chains, chainmail bonnets, riveted
Locked, knotted, wound on him whom her affection
Chose she conceived perversely; till she guessed
Its virtue was in helmeting that head,
A collar round the neck she hung upon.

What colour were Utopia's rocks?
Navajo red, the Mormon wives
Mutter, restless in drab smocks,
Would void the golden chamberpots
And strike off the golden gyves
In crimson Zion. Under the mesa's
Coronet, taken from such base uses,
Shall not red gold deck the wives of Utah?

'Convicting us, convict the Lord
Of barbarous inutilities:
What left His hand but a very gaud,
Red over canyon and mesa, good
For nothing but an artifice
To adorn His favoured? Little we ask
Who wintered for Him in Nebraska:
Red gold only, a little at wrist or ankle.'

'Has it then every virtue, having none?'
Sighs to the Lord in prayer the Mormon lady
And Nephi Johnson remonstrates, 'What good
The land, if not for cotton?' But the Lord,
Dear reverend pioneers, in His red blood
Sealed more than that hard promise of a sod
To turn in Zion. Planting such dubious
Capacities in your sons as might applaud
Gauds of gratuitous ornament in your God,
Your God depraved King Utopus himself.

Reflections on Deafness

For Kenneth and Margaret Millar

1

Making the best and most of a visitation,
The deaf can make it serve their purposes.
What else can any one use but his condition?
Is affliction turned to use the less affliction?

2

The voice called ours, played back to us on tape,
We hate at once, disown. The nerve of selfhood
Jumps at the drill of an achieved imposture.
The deaf cannot tell the King from the Pretender.

3

The blind have rights in that most delicate
And intimate of the senses, touch; the deaf
Lip-reader, in somnambulistic rape
On the act of sight, usurps the rights denied him.

Blindness can be rectified by reason,
Errors of calculation not in will
We tolerate; but wince to see the human,
Distinguishingly human act of speech contorted.

4

Yes, we are deaf to their condition, hear
All that we want to hear, the blind man's stick
Redeemably tap-tapping, but the voice
That cannot hear itself we cannot hear.

For an Age of Plastics

With the effect almost of carving the hillside
        They climb in their stiff terraces, these houses
Feed the returning eye with national pride
        In the 'built to last'. Approving elegance
Where there is only decency, the eye
        Applauds the air of nothing left to chance
Or brilliantly provisional. Not the fact
        But the air of it, the illusion, we observe;
Chance in the bomb sight kept these streets intact
        And razed whole districts. Nor was the lesson lost
On the rebuilt Plymouth, how an age of chance
        Is an age of plastics. In a style pre-cast
Pre-fabricated, and as if its site

Were the canyon's lip, it rises out of rubble
Sketchily massive, moulded in bakelite.

Annoyed to take a gloomy sort of pride
        In numbering our losses, I suppose
The ploughman ceased his carving of the hillside
        And all the coulters and the chisels broke
When he was young whom we come home to bury,
        A man like clay in the hands of his womenfolk.

A ploughman carved three harvests, each a son,
        Upon the flesh of Wales. And all were carried
Long since from those hillsides, yet this one
        Comes first to threshing. Nutriment and grain
For all the mashing of the interim
        Live in the load of him. Living again
His shipwright's years, the countryman's walks in the park,
        The scrape of a mattock in a too small garden,
The marriage to the capable matriarch,
        What would he change? Perhaps a stubbornness
That bristled sometimes, for the sensible hands
        To circumvent and gentle, would be less
Amenable to their shaping. But all told,
        His edged tools still would lie in the garden shed,
Still he would flow, himself, from mould to mould.

Whatever he showed of something in the rough,
        Sluggish in flow and unadaptable,
I liked him for; affecting to be gruff,
        An awkward customer – so much was due,
He seemed to think, to what a man was, once:
        Something to build with, take a chisel to.

The Life of Service

Service, or Latin *sorbus*, European
More especially English shadbush or small tree,
Asks all the shade the fancier can find
In a walled garden. This is no plebeian
Of cottage plots, though coarse in leaf and rind.

Planted, it is persistent, of a thick
Skin, and grows strong the more it's trodden on;
Or afterwards, as an established upas,
Thrives all the better by each welcomed nick
Of aggrieved knives wielded by interlopers.

By this indeed it knows itself. Self-thwarted,
It welcomes parasites, for playing host
To what insults and saps it is its virtue
And its fulfilment. Flourishing contorted,
All its long-suffering's overbearing too.

Some cultivators hold that it repays,
By its small edible fruit (in favoured species
Of a vinous taste), its culture. It does not;
All saner growth abhors it, and the Bays
Wither, affronted, in the poisoned plot.

The 'Sculpture' of Rhyme

Potter nor iron-founder
Nor caster of bronze will he cherish,
But the monumental mason;

As if his higher stake
Than the impregnable spiders
Of self-defended music

Procured him mandibles
To chisel honey from the saxifrage,
And a mouth to graze on feldspar.

A SEQUENCE FOR FRANCIS PARKMAN

The Jesuits in North America

Récollet friars and the very Huguenots were as often as Jesuits Champlain's companions on early investigations of the seaboard of Acadia and the estuary of the St Lawrence river. It was not at his instigation, though it was with his compliance, that the Canadian mission, big with a harvest of monstrous and astonishing martyrdoms, became a monopoly of the Society of Jesus.

Curé and pastor, dead at the one time
Buried in the one grave
To see would they lie peaceable together
Who never lived so on Acadia's coast;
And the Aeneas of a destined nation
Sees uses for recalcitrance,
No matter priest or pastor,
Sectarian zeal to rib the rock, Quebec.

Only the holy fathers were
Holy and resolute enough
To live in Huron lodges;
Only the wily fathers could
Only the holy fathers
Outwit the Iroquois.

Saguenay, Ohio, Colorado
Roll gloomy waters; and the Ottawa
Plunging, boiled. Shot spray from that concussion
Smoked out of Champlain's arquebuse
In Indian wars; he knew
A demon in the cataract. Tobacco
Disbursed on foam placates the Manitou.

Only the holy fathers were
Holy and resolute enough;
Devils and devildom
Incarnate, none but they,
The incarnate God's
Adepts and ministers,
Might recognize and slay.

Savages convert the savages.
Canoe that darted out upon the still
Bay of the Trinity, dark as Acheron,
Sanctuary of solitude and silence,
The soul of Champlain, dying, took such forms
As never a Jesuit of France could tell;
More shapes than one, since all were Canada.

At Sainte-Marie the fathers' mail from France
Accumulates unread. The holy fathers
Only the holy fathers
Were resolute for martyrdom. Apache,
Last suicidal chieftain in a column
Of blowing dust, a dry soil's levity
Too late affects the Roman.
Fatuity not cowardice undid
The Huron nation, and intractable
Indolence the Iroquois. But all
Had seen too many gods, as I have seen them
Too many, and too different. There is
No God but One and He is terrible
Dwells in the Huron lodges
Outwits the Iroquois.

Lasalle

Lasalle who, for no sordid end, pressing to the waters of the Mississippi, first by that watery highway attained to the Gulf of Mexico, was a spirit cold and stern.

His followers, who shared his perplexities and endured the effects of his perseverance, at most respected, always feared, and never loved him; a truth sufficiently attested by the circumstances of his obscure death at their mutinous hands in the deserts of Louisiana. In his letters written to his creditors and friends, he has confessed that the wilderness drew him not otherwise than as a theatre for his restless ambitions, where they would be less obstructed than in the palaces and faubourgs of Paris by a lack of that conversibility and address which alone, in a more civil society, can recommend and please.

Of this aspiring burgher who disdained
(Dumb in his pride of mortified reserve)
The usufruct of half a continent,
After the dark inexorable river
Delivers him the salt breath of the sea,
Still we complain: Dark it was not, until
He made it so, inexorable, nor fatal.

He loved solitude and he loved power
And Parkman loves him for it. Better love
Profit: if no principle nor faith
Move his lids' mountains, cannot Trade unsheet
The gathered waters of five inland oceans,
A prodigal Nature's parks and pleasure grounds,
Wild swans, wild turkeys, cranes and pelicans?

He never saw it, any of it: saw
The Mississippi that was bright, as dark,
Indifferent, as inexorable; saw
(As if in those accounts he never kept)
Digits and proxies, lean alternatives
To audiences with a Monseigneur
Where he had lacked complaisance and address.

He loved solitude and he loved power
And lonely as when born of chaos, bright
Voiceless, sail-less, without sign of life
The great Gulf opened, tossing – but what for?
Not for the Faith, for glory, or for France,
Whirled on the miry vortex of his need,
The light canoes of Indian nations foundered.

Frontenac

In what was wilderness as inviolate then as in the last century were the gorges of the High
Sierra when revealed to the astonished gaze of the intrepid John Muir, the Marquis of
Frontenac founded three hundred years ago the rude fortress of which the all but obliterated
site still, though uncertainly, preserves his name in the city of Kingston, Ontario. There,
however, a hundred will ask for Old Fort Henry, the surviving British edifice, for the one
curious traveller who enquires after the remains of Fort Frontenac.

The adjacent terrain is that which the pen of Fenimore Cooper has made interesting to
all amateurs of the sublime and romantic by the adventures of the immortal Chingachgook,
in romances which, if written in a manner no less orotund, reveal also a genius as copious
and spirited as the productions of the author of 'Waverley'. Yet however stirring and authentic
the narrative, it must inevitably fail in delineating scenes of which the impressive charm is
precisely that they were for so long untrodden, unless rarely by the moccasin of the savage and
solitary hunter, and celebrated only by the wind's pencil and the music of the cataract.

It was not by the force of arms, but by the framing of fraudulent contracts and the sale of
spirituous liquors, that these territories were wrested from their original dusky citizens.

Hearing from some how the Sierra answers
Even today, to John Muir's nails and rifle,
With human resonances,
I heard the long-tamed wilderness give back
Over the Lake and all too British Kingston
The one word, 'Frontenac.'
But after-echoes mocked: The rocky flanges
Of the Thousand Islands
Have more to do than take up challenges
From perfect strangers;
Agoraphobia among empty spaces,
The mountain ranges, the plains of corn,
Peoples the street at history's intersections
With famous faces.

Heart of Midlothian, the milky mother
(Sir Walter's Doric) of sane masterpieces
Fed at that flaccid udder, Walter Scott,
Great lax geometer, first plotted them,
Triangulations that explode
The architect's box of space, and by a torsion
As bland as violent sprain
Narrative time and the archives' single slot.

What's to be seen of old Fort Frontenac?
The British fortress, by a hundred years
More recent, but still Old
Fort Henry, draws the Buicks. Of the Frenchman
A mound remains by Kingston's waterfront
And a cadence out of Parkman: 'At Versailles
A portrait, beautiful and young, Minerva...'

Intervals in what never meets the eye
Meet the ear sooner, music's images
Not of Ontario's spaces but of spaces
Sketched by a gesture, virtual and French.

Alas for Caliban. The Thousand Islands
Were full of noises,
Landscape and history echoing back and forth
Under immense skies, till his master
Cabined his spaces in a folio
And Euclids of the tepee, leaning-to
Birch-pole isosceles in a glade of hemlocks,
Drank deafening whisky in a written treaty.

Montcalm

It is reported of General Wolfe that as he drifted by night to the secret assault of the Heights of Abraham he quoted to his companions some famous stanzas of the elegy of Grey.

The French and the British commander were alike destined to die on the morrow, and thus to illustrate the melancholy truth of the poet's reflections. Montcalm was himself a poet, and appended pious verses in French and Latin to a cross erected on his field of victory at Ticonderoga. He had the sentiments and inclinations of a country gentleman.

He died before he could learn which of his children had pre-deceased him.

In Candiac by Nîmes in Languedoc
He left a mill to grind his olives well
Who now must harvest laurels. Who had died
In Candiac? All Bougainville could tell
Was of a death. Mirète he thought had died
If it was Mirète. He never could decide
For whom the olives sighed in Languedoc.

To Candiac by Nîmes in Languedoc
A murmur reaches from the perjured wave
That floats surprise and France's great reverse:
At dawn, too late, the cliffs will answer back.
'The paths of glory lead but to the grave'
– Marmoreal verses, plumes to tuft a hearse
And scutcheons black for squires of Candiac.

From Candiac by Nîmes in Languedoc
Quoting Corneille – 'though, Christian! not Montcalm
Nor his sagacity nor up-ended trees
Nor men nor deeds checked England, but God's arm' –
Coming from this and homelier pieties
In Candiac by Nîmes in Languedoc
To earn the stucco tribute of a plaque,

Montcalm had met, if we should say his match,
We ought to mean his match in hardihood
Hardly in grace, James Wolfe, but most of all
His match in fate, his double. Did he catch
If not the low voice, still its tone, the mood?
The paths of glory led but to Quebec
From Candiac by Nîmes in Languedoc.

Both earned their stucco. Marble was reserved
To honour the intrepid, the serene
And the successful Amherst. But it served,
Pompous and frigid as it was, the phrase
'A martial glory': common ground between
The public lives, the private, Kent, Quebec,
And Candiac by Nîmes in Languedoc.

Pontiac

*Of all the savages of North America, history records none more eminent for great abilities
than Pontiac, a sachem of the Ottawas. He refused to acknowledge the capitulation of Canada.
Inflamed by him, a league of all the Western tribes invested the ceded forts, burned many,
and massacred the garrisons. At Detroit, the most considerable of these places, he was repulsed.
But not without justice does the modern metropolis recall, by the names she accords the prod-
ucts of her manufactories, not only her founder, Lamothe-Cadillac, but also him who would,
in the name of his violated nation, have razed her to the ground.*

Pontiac fires Detroit!
On Fort Duquesne afresh
The immaculate lilies! Turn,
Minavavana or
Le Grand Sauteur, and see
Behind the trader's knife
Plunging, *coureurs de bois*
Roll through the fired stockade
The unmentionable chapter –
Extermination of the Seminole,
Deportation of the Cherokee,
Transportation of the Saginaw...
A modern miracle of
Engineering fires
Detroit and Cadillac
Where, cast in steel
Or punched out of chrome
On a spinning wheel,
Freely may roam
This totem, this
Served, furbished car
With a name that's his,
Ranging so far:
Pontiac, Ottawa shade.

Bougainville

Lewis de Bougainville, lieutenant to the Marquis of Montcalm at the fall of Canada, later essayed to annex the Falkland Islands.

Baulked of this object by the more politic arrangements of His Most Christian Majesty, his next and most extraordinary venture for the glory of the French nation was a circumnavigation of the globe in the years 1766, 1767, 1768 and 1769.

See his narrative of this voyage, made into English by Mr Forster, and the later extension of this work by the celebrated Diderot, a supplement more ingenious than useful.

All the soft runs of it, the tin-white gashes
Over the muscled mesh and interaction
Of the South Seas tilt against him less unsteady
Than France had been, or a King who could destroy
Acadia sold, Montcalm betrayed by faction,
And all the meadows of the Illinois
Lost, the allies abandoned. Where the ashes
Still smoulder on the ceded Falklands, these
Islands and oceans he has failed already
Though he will navigate the seven seas.

The shame persists as scruple. The exact
Conscience of science chastens observations,
And the redaction of a log-book's soundings
Is scrupulously dry. Although the scent
Carries from Otaheite, can a nation's
Chagrin or honour weigh in the intent
Scrutiny of the sextant? Matter of fact
Dries the great deeps. And yet what tumults when
He marks the fathoms, what disorders, houndings
Of mortification, angers, drive the pen!

No accuracy there but testifies
To a concern behind it, to a feeling
In excess of its object, fact. Excesses
Of that concern (where God permits the pox
And a King is perjured) self-inflict their steeling
To this impassive dryness charting rocks,
Keys, and the set of tide-rips. Weather eyes
Whittled so blue by pains, exactitude
In the science, navigation, witnesses
To the heart's intentions answered, not eschewed.

Needing to know is always how to learn;
Needing to see brings sightings; steadiest readings
Are those that wishes father. In their ages
Of Eden's gold the archipelagos
Await his keel because he wants for Edens
Who held savannahs once and the Ohio's
Bison for France. The measure of concern
Measures the truth, and in the *philosophe*
A paradox of noble savages
Has met no need more urgent than to scoff.

A Letter to Curtis Bradford

Curtis, you've been American too long,
You don't know what it feels like. You belong,
Don't you, too entirely to divulge?
Indifferently therefore you indulge
My idle interests: Are there names perhaps
In Iowa still, to match the names on maps,
Burgundian or Picard voyageurs
Prowling the wilderness for France and furs
On the Des Moines river? And suppose there were
What would it prove? To whom would it occur
In Iowa that, suppose it so, New France
Not your New England has pre-eminence
If to belong means anything? Your smile
(Twisted) admits it doesn't. Steadily, while
You on the seaboard, they in Canada
Dribbled from floods of European war
Boiled in small pools, pressure built up behind
The dams of Europe. Dispossessed mankind,
Your destined countrymen, milled at dock-gates;
Emigrant schooners spilled aboard the States;
The dispossessed, the not to be possessed,
The alone and equal, peopled all the West.
And so what is it I am asking for,
Sipping at names? Dahcotah, Ottawa,
Horse Indian... Yes, but earlier (What is this
Need that I find to fill void centuries?)

Who first put up America to let?
You of the old stock paid him rent. And yet
Even so soon, crowds of another sort
Piled off the boats to take him by assault.
And a worse sort, the heroes. Who but they,
For whom the manifest was shadow-play
Of an all-absorbing inward war and plight,
Could so deny its presence and its right?
It was the given. But I only guess,
I guess at it out of my Englishness
And envy you out of England. Man with man
Is all our history; American,
You met with spirits. Neither white nor red
The melancholy, disinherited
Spirit of mid-America, but this,
The manifested copiousness, the bounties.

For Doreen. A Voice from the Garden

from *New Lines,* 2 (1963)

We have a lawn of moss.
The next house is called The Beeches.
A towering squirrel-haunted
Trellis of trees, across
Our matt and trefoil, reaches
Shade where our guests have sauntered.

Cars snap by in the road.
In a famous photographed village
The High Street is our address.
Our guests write from abroad
Delighted to envisage
Rose-arbour and wilderness.

They get them, and the lilacs.
Some frenzy in us discards
Lilacs and all. It will harden,
However England stacks
Her dear discoloured cards
Against us, us to her garden.

Anglophobia rises
In Brooklyn to hysteria
At some British verses.
British, one sympathizes.
Diesel-fumes cling to wisteria.
One conceives of worse reverses.

The sough of the power brake
Makes every man an island;
But we are the island race.
We must be mad to take
Offence at our poisoned land
And the gardens that pock her face.

Trumpington

EVENTS AND WISDOMS

Two Dedications

1. *Wide France*

Sunlight so blurred with clouds we couldn't tell
Light from shade, driving to Vézelay
Disgusted you that Northern day. You thought
Caressing weather started at Calais,

And I had thought, in Burgundy; and still,
When we had stolen guiltily from where
Mummy lay wretched in the loud hotel,
All we found was squall-dashed street and square.

Nothing to do but go to Vézelay
That afternoon. Both worried, and the seasons
Wrong as usual, winter in our bones,
We drove the ten miles for the worst of reasons.

Let me remind you. First there was a strong
High, famous church; and where the hillside falls
Away behind it, France was spread at our feet;
And at our back old streets and gates and walls.

Poor eight-year-old, but how could you remember?
So many, before and since; and such a fuss
As we always made, as if to convince ourselves.
And now you worry about the eleven-plus.

2. *Barnsley Cricket Club*

Now the heat comes, I am demoralized.
Important letters lie unanswered, dry
Shreds of tobacco spike the typewriter,
No undertaking but is ill-advised.

Unanswerable even the shortest missive,
Replies not sealed, or sealed without conviction.
Thumb-marks dry out, leaving the paper pouchy,
Tousled with effort, desperate, inconclusive.

'A thing worth doing is worth doing well,'
Says Shaw Lane Cricket Ground
Between the showers of a July evening,
As the catch is held and staid hand-clappings swell.

This almost vertical sun, this blur of heat,
All stinging furze and snagged unravelling,
Denies the axiom which has kept
My father's summers shadowy and sweet.

Remembering many times when he has laughed
Softly, and slapped his thigh, because the trap
So suavely set was consummately sprung,
I wish, to all I love, his love of craft.

Hard to instruct myself, and then my son,
That things which would be natural are done
After a style less consummate; that an art's
More noble office is to leave half-done.

How soon the shadows fall, how soon and long!
The score-board stretches to a grandson's feet.
This layabout July in another climate
Ought not to prove firm turf, well-tended, wrong.

Resolutions

Whenever I talk of my art
You turn away like strangers,
Whereas all I mean is the chart
I keep, of my own sea-changes.

It puzzles the wisest head
How anyone's good resolution
Can securely be implemented;
Art provides a solution.

This is the assessor whose word
Can always be relied on;
It tells you when has occurred
Any change you decide on.

More preciously still, it tells
Of growth not groped towards,
In the seaway a sound of bells
From a landfall not on the cards.

Life Encompassed

How often I have said,
'This will never do,'
Of ways of feeling that now
I trust in, and pursue!

Do traverses tramped in the past,
My own, cries-crossed as I forge
Across from another quarter
Speak of a life encompassed?

Well, life is not research.
No one asks you to map the terrain,
Only to get across it
In new ways, time and again.

How many such, even now,
I dismiss out of hand
As not to my purpose, not
Unknown, just unexamined.

Hornet

In lilac trained on the colonnade's archway, what
Must be a hornet volleys lethally back
And forth in the air, on the still not hot
But blindingly white Italian stone, blue-black.

I have seldom seen them in England, although once
Years ago the foul-mouthed, obligingly bowed
Rat-catcher of Cambridge made a just pretence
To a cup of tea, for a nest cleared in the road.

Those were wasp-coloured, surely; and this blue
Gun-metal blue, blue-black ominous ranger
Of Italy's air means an Italy stone all through,
Where every herb of holier thought's a stranger.

No call for such rage in our England of pierced shadows.
Stone's and the white sun's opposite, furious fly,
There no sun strides in a rapid creak of cicadas
And the green mould stains before the mortar is dry.

Housekeeping

From thirty years back my grandmother with us boys
Picking the ash-grimed blackberries, pint on pint, is
Housekeeping Yorkshire's thrift, and yet the noise
Is taken up from Somerset in the 'nineties.

From homestead Autumns in the vale of Chard
Translated in youth past any hope of returning,
She toiled, my father a baby, through the hard
Fellside winters, to Barnsley, soused in the Dearne.

How the sound carries! Whatever the dried-out, lank
Sticks of poor trees could say of the slow slag stealing
More berries than we did, I hear her still down the bank
Slide, knickers in evidence, laughing, modestly squealing.

And I hear not only how homestead to small home echoes
Persistence of historic habit. Berries
Ask to be plucked, and attar pleases the rose.
Contentment cries from the distance. How it carries!

Low Lands

I could not live here, though I must and do
Ungratefully inhabit the Cambridgeshire fens
And the low river delta we pass through
Is beautiful in the same uncertain sense.

Like a snake it is, its serpentine iridescence
Of slow light spilt and wheeling over calm
Inundations, and a snake's still menace
Hooding with bruised sky belfry and lonely farm.

The grasses wave on meadows fat with foison.
In granges, cellars, granaries, the rat
Runs sleek and lissom. Tedium, a poison,
Swells in the sac for the hillborn, dwelling in the flat.

How defenceless it is! How much it needs a protector
To keep its dykes! At what a price it commands
The delightful bizarre when it wears like a bus-conductor
Tickets of brown sails tucked into polders' hat-bands!

But a beauty there is, noble, dependent, unshrinking,
In being at somebody's mercy, wide and alone.
I imagine a hillborn sculptor suddenly thinking
One could live well in a country short of stone.

Green River

Green silk, or a shot silk, blue
Verging to green at the edges,
The river reflects the sky
Alas. I wish that its hue
Were the constant green of its sedges
Or the reeds it is floating by.

It reflects the entrances, dangers,
Exploits, vivid reversals
Of weather over the days.
But it learns to make these changes
By too many long rehearsals
Of overcasts and greys.

So let it take its station
Less mutably. Put it to school
Not to the sky but the land.
This endless transformation,
Because it is beautiful,
Let some of it somehow stand.

But seeing the streak of it quiver
There in the distance, my eye
Is astonished and unbelieving.
It exclaims to itself for ever:
This water is passing by!
It arrives, and it is leaving!

House-martin

I see the low black wherry
Under the alders rock,
As the ferryman strides from his ferry
And his child in its black frock

Into his powerful shadow
And out of it, skirmishing, passes
Time and again as they go
Up through the tall lush grasses.

The light of evening grieves
For the stout house of a father,
With martins under its eaves,
That cracks and sags in the weather.

Treviso, the Pescheria

Each of us has the time,
And both the times are wrong.
Our needs and likings chime
Sometimes, but not for long.

Your watch is often fast,
Mine usually slow.
And yet you cling to the past,
I laxly let it go.

You are like a ferryman's daughter,
And I the stream that blurred
Calls sent across that water,
Which loyally you have heard.

My lapsings I acknowledge.
And yet, on either hand
Combed green, the river's sedge
Sweetens the fish-wives' island.

The Prolific Spell

Day by day, such rewards,
Compassionate land!
Such things to say, and the words
And ways of saying to hand!

Bounties I cannot earn!
Nothing planned in advance!
Well, it is hard to learn,
This profiting by chance.

It is hard, learning to live
While looking the other way,
Bored and contemplative
Over a child at play.

Not everyone has a child.
All children grow away.
Sufferings drive us wild;
Not every mind can stray.

Nothing engendered, and so much
Constantly brought to birth!
This hand will lose its touch.
Profuse, illiberal earth!

Nothing could be planned
And so no credit accrues.
Ah compassionate land!
Such gain, and nothing to lose!

My utterance that turns
To always human use
Your brilliant mute concerns
Neither repays nor earns.

A Battlefield

Red mills and farms clumped soothingly here and there.
At a modest distance rose a plume of trees
On the green-bushed plain, and had from afar the air
Which poplars have in the pluck of a river breeze:

The crossing of the Piave! In what year
How many times, and by whose army, going
In which direction – none of this was clear;
With a sinking heart I felt it was not worth knowing.

A necropolis and a stand of cypress came
Predictably next, and all of it I knew
Was a peeling village with the curious name,
Victory, and fast traffic passing through.

The Cypress Avenue

My companion kept exclaiming
At fugitive aromas;
She was making a happy fuss
Of flower-naming;

And I, who had taken her there…
Not one scent could I name
In the resinous die-straight avenue's
Plume-irrigated air.

Her world was properly indexed:
The names were in my head
Familiar, double-columned, but
Hardly a page of text.

Just the swaying channel of shade;
The stippling everywhere
Of an otherwise dust-choked country;
The difference cypress made.

*

That night at the family sing-song
She had no repertoire;
Her ear was a true one, though
Her voice not very strong.

And that was an index too!
Hymns, shanties, popular numbers,
Ballads, rounds – how many
It turned out that we knew!

And what an encyclopaedia
Of smudged ill-printed feeling
They opened up, although to
Only a coarsened ear.

Humanly Speaking

After two months, already
My auspiciously begun
Adventure of blessing the world
Was turning woe-begone.

Still it might work out, I thought:
The hand-to-mouth way I live,
Not life itself, might be
What made me apprehensive.

But a truce to pieties!
I pull myself together
And get exasperated:
Damn this stupid weather!

So stupid, so uncreative…
I am rasped by a towel of wind
And boomed at by grey-green breakers
For seventy-two hours on end.

The weather invades me, throws
My every sense out of gear:
I cannot trust what I see
Or smell or taste or hear.

And because life itself
Is this one soured life I am leading,
And living it hand-to-mouth is
Natural, humanly speaking,

To swear at this barren fig-tree,
At seas uninventively breaking
In self-same pothers, becomes
A duty, humanly speaking.

But I, who had hoped no more
To have to point the finger,
Who had ventured on new feelings…
For me misgivings linger.

The Hill Field

Look there! What a wheaten
Half-loaf, halfway to bread,
A cornfield is, that is eaten
Away, and harvested:

How like a loaf, where the knife
Has cut and come again,
Jagged where the farmer's wife
Has served the farmer's men,

That steep field is, where the reaping
Has only just begun
On a wedge-shaped front, and the creeping
Steel edges glint in the sun.

See the cheese-like shape it is taking,
The sliced-off walls of the wheat
And the cheese-mite reapers making
Inroads there, in the heat?

It is Brueghel or Samuel Palmer,
Some painter, coming between
My eye and the truth of a farmer,
So massively sculpts the scene.

The sickles of poets dazzle
These eyes that were filmed from birth;
And the miller comes with an easel
To grind the fruits of earth.

The Feeders

Among the serviceable mills and
The galleries of riverside poplars,
In the holiday house, no hours
Were set aside for my writing;
It was less well-appointed than ours,
But Art found it inviting.

In that impelled present, a weight
Of water behind it, Art
And Life fed into each other:
Children who could not know
How uniquely their mother
Assisted, themselves did so,

On their long serpentine
Of that full river,
Simply by making demands.
Art liked that changeable weather.
I had only one pair of hands;
They held more, cupped together.

Now I must feed myself
On feelings fresh from their source,
Flashfloods tapped in the highlands
Under the glare of noon.
Still only one pair of hands,
And I have to hold the spoon.

In the uplands the stony beds
Chalk-white under vacant bridges…
My public has shrunk to one reader,
And that the most exacting
The hateful, insatiable feeder,
Art; and the rest, play-acting.

A Lily at Noon

Deep-sea frost, and
Lilies at noon…
Late leaves, late leaves
Toss every day.
The daymoon shines always for some.
In the marriage of a slow man
Eighteen years is soon.

Sun and moon, no
Dark between,
Foresight and hindsight
Halving the hours.
And now he collects his thoughts
Before it is too late.
But what can 'too late' mean?

Shielding with hands,
Binding to stakes...
Late leaves, late leaves
Toss every day,
The sun moves on from noon.
To freeze, to cup, to retard –
These measures terror takes.

Love and the Times

A knowledge of history fetches
Love out of its recesses,
Mapping its open stretches,
Its pits for trespassers.

Or it is staked out there,
For country airs to breathe
On seed-bed and parterre
Savour of field and heath.

Strange how we can imagine
Nothing else, although
We have no hope for the short run
That times can turn out so.

Across the Bay

A queer thing about those waters: there are no
Birds there, or hardly any.
I did not miss them, I do not remember
Missing them, or thinking it uncanny.

The beach so-called was a blinding splinter of limestone,
A quarry outraged by hulls.
We took pleasure in that: the emptiness, the hardness
Of the light, the silence, and the water's stillness.

But this was the setting for one of our murderous scenes.
This hurt, and goes on hurting:
The venomous soft jelly, the undersides.
We could stand the world if it were hard all over.

A Christening

What we do best is breed:
August Bank Holiday, whole
Populations explode

Across the wolds and in a slot
Of small cars pullulate
By couples. Millington Meadows

Flower with campstools. At
Beverley the font
Has a cover carved like a goblet.

The new baby is fed.
I stumble back to bed.
I hear the owls for a long time

Hunting. Or are they never
In the winter grey of before dawn,
Those pure long quavers,

Cries of love? I put my arms around you.
Small mice freeze among tussocks.
The baby wails in the next room.

Upstairs Mrs Ramsden
Dies, and the house
Is full of the cries of the newborn.

In red and smoky wood
A follower of Wren
Carved it at Beverley:

The generous womb that drops
Into the sanctified water immediate fruit.
What we do best is breed.

Agave in the West

I like the sidewalks of an American city,
Broad shadowed stone. I think of Agave,

Queen of the mænads, after incestuous fury
Shocked and quiescent, pleading for the cage:
Grids of a rectilinear plot, her cities.

Leaving the wilderness, she counts the loss
Of a world of signs – in algae, moss,
Guano, lichen, all the blooms of stone;
In cross-grained baulks and boles, in timber grown
Noble in groves or into monstrous shapes;
In rock-formations, cloud-formations, landscapes.
I like the sidewalks of an American city:

Sunstruck solitude of parking lots;
Taut vivid women, hair close-shaved from the armpit;
Glass walls run up, run out on the canyon's lip.
Barber my verses, pitiless vivid city.

In California

Chemicals ripen the citrus;
There are rattlesnakes in the mountains,
And on the shoreline
Hygiene, inhuman caution.

Beef in cellophane
Tall as giraffes,
The orange-rancher's daughters
Crop their own groves, mistrustful.

Perpetual summer seems
Precarious on the littoral. We drive
Inland to prove
The risk we sense. At once

Winter claps-to like a shutter
High over the Ojai valley, and discloses
A double crisis,
Winter and Drought.

Ranges on mountain-ranges,
Empty, unwatered, crumbling,
Hot colours come at the eye.
It is too cold

For picnics at the trestle-tables. Claypit
Yellow burns on the distance.
The phantom walks
Everywhere, of intolerable heat.

At Ventucopa, elevation
Two-eight-nine-six, the water hydrant frozen,
Deserted or broken settlements,
Gasoline stations closed and boarded.

By nightfall, to the snows;
And over the mile on tilted
Mile of the mountain park
The bright cars hazarded.

New York in August

(After Pasternak)

There came, for lack of sleep,
A crosspatch, drained-out look
On the old trees that keep
Scents of Schiedam and the Hook

In Flushing, as we picked out, past
Each memorized landmark,
Our route to a somnolent breakfast.
Later, to Central Park,

UNO, and the Empire State.
A haven from the heat
Was the Planetarium. We got back late,
Buffeted, dragging our feet.

Clammy, electric, torrid,
The nights bring no relief
At the latitude of Madrid.
Never the stir of a leaf.

Any night, as we went
Back, the children asleep,
To our bed in a loaned apartment,
Although I thought a deep

And savage cry from the park
Came once, as we flashed together
And the fan whirled in the dark,
For thunder, a break in the weather.

Viper-Man

Will it be one of those
Forever summers?
Will the terrace stone
Expand, unseal
Aromas, and let slip
Out of the cell of its granulations
Some mid-Victorian courtship?

Never a belle of that
Lavender century
But, though so stayed,
Basked in a settled spell;
And yet I guard
Against a change in the weather,
Snake whipped up in the yard.

In Chopin's Garden

I remember the scarlet setts
Of the little-frequented highway
From Warsaw to the West
And Chopin's house, one Sunday.

I remember outside the windows,
As the pianist plucked a ring
From her thin white finger, the rows
Of unanchored faces waiting,

And a climbing vapour, storm-wrack
Wreathing up, heavy with fruit,
Darkened the skies at their back
On the old invasion-route.

Masovia bows its birches
Resignedly. Again
A rapid army marches
Eastward over the plain,

And fast now it approaches.
Turbulence, agonies,
As the poised musician broaches
The polonaise, storm from the keys.

See them, ennobled by
The mass and passage, these
Faces stained with the sky,
Supple and fluid as trees.

Poreč

Pennies of sun's fire jazzing like silver foil,
In this off-shore pleasaunce of Croatia
Leased to the Sports Club of Munich,
Her blondeness under the swimsuit fits
That sunbrowned girl like a tunic,
And in falling light off the limestone island
Fishing boats groove water slick as oil.

Behind them is haze that is sea and sky at once.
In what was the wartime Germans'
Torpedo-boat haven in the Adriatic,
I erase the distinction between
Contemplative and athletic
As I swim, climb out, and smoke. This peacetime weather
Worries me, these seas with blurred horizons.

Stately and wide Croatia, how it shelves
To the waste of the sea, and shapes it!
The silent roadstead shimmers.
As under the narrowed eyes
Of English and German swimmers
Here in the shade, the file of the drifters passes,
We seem much pacified, seem so to ourselves.

Barnsley and District

Judy Sugden! Judy, I made you caper
With rage when I said that the British Fascist
Sheet your father sold was a jolly good paper

And you had agreed and I said, Yes, it holds
Vinegar, and everyone laughed and imagined
The feel of the fish and chips warm in its folds.

That was at Hood Green. Under our feet there shone
The modest view, its slagheaps amethyst
In distance and white walls the sunlight flashed on.

If your father's friends had succeeded, or if I
Had canvassed harder for the Peace Pledge Union,
A world of difference might have leapt to the eye

In a scene like this which shows in fact no change.
That must have been the summer of '39.
I go back sometimes, and find nothing strange –

Short-circuiting of politics engages
The Grammar School masters still. Their bright sixth-formers sport
Nuclear Disarmament badges.

And though at Stainborough no bird's-nesting boy
Nor trespasser from the town in a Sunday suit
Nor father twirling a stick can now enjoy

Meeting old Captain Wentworth, who in grey
And ancient tweeds, gun under arm, keen-eyed
And unemployable, would give a gruff Good-day,

His rhododendrons and his laurel hedge
And tussocked acres are no more unkempt
Now that the Hall is a Teachers' Training College.

The parish primary school where a mistress once
Had every little Dissenter stand on the bench
With hands on head, to make him out a dunce;

Black backs of flourmills, wafer-rusted railings
Where I ran and ran from colliers' boys in jerseys,
Wearing a blouse to show my finer feelings –

These still stand. And Bethel and Zion Baptist,
Sootblack on pavements foul with miners' spittle
And late-night spew and violence, persist.

George Arliss was on at the Star, and Janet Gaynor
Billed at the Alhambra, but the warmth
Was no more real then, nor the manners plainer.

And politics has no landscape. The Silesian
Seam crops out in prospects felt as deeply
As any of these, with as much or as little reason.

Right Wing Sympathies

France of the poujadiste!
France of the absurd
Citroëns, still on the roads
Of Marne and Doubs that summer:

Domestic and armoured,
Made out of sheets
Of corrugated iron,
They dive into the highway.

Travelling humps in the road,
Steel-snouted moles,
They gouge at each chug of their tired
Small engines a trench in the tarmac.

Walking is a perpetual
Falling down, and so is
Driving in these shovel-bills
Through the country of Jacques Tati.

Camel's head and hump
Of black rock, Briançon
Bulked not so large
But platypus must nose it

Out, and over ramp
On ramp of France
Snuffle and wheeze
Where Vauban and the Alps

Have framed the camel state,
Its ugly teeth
Yellowed at Italy,
In a geometer's heaven.

His exact nest
Of outwork polygons
Provided parking-lots
For Citroëns in bastion and embrasure

When I was there that summer,
Asking myself to explain
Myself to myself
By enrolling in a party of the Right.

In an old photograph
Dreyfus is falling down
Perpetually between
Two ranks of the backs of riflemen

For treason. But in court
The intellectual
Accuses the accusers. 'Shovel-bill!'
He tells them to their faces. 'Camel-tooth!'

So much I cannot face,
I sweat with those
Arraigned in his
Superb performances.

Hyphens

You remember Rossignano
Solvay, impossible hybrid,
Italian-Belgian? The hyphen
Was stretched to breaking.

Remember its streets, its piazzas?
The main line clove them, rammed
Through a truss of malodorous sidings
By the howling trench of the highway.

Black, smeared on the rocks
In the brilliant mornings,
Pontefract Cakes of naphtha
Stuck to the soles of swimmers.

Mazzimo, draughtsman
For Solvay chemicals,
Shrugging a bulky shoulder
At rigidity of Belgian blueprints,

Dived and hauled up
On the rocks an amphora,
Rough, plain and capacious,
Plucked from a foundered galley.

There too the hyphen stretched
In him to breaking, out of
Maremman cities where his Fiat spun
In week-end pieties

To the Ligurian polluted sea
And unpaved avenue
Which housed him, hardly less
A transient than his summer visitors.

Holding these halves together,
His Tuscan strove
For a coining of new compounds:
Firm-transient, chemical-civic.

A Meeting of Cultures

Iced with a vanilla
Of dead white stone, the Palace
Of Culture is a joke

Or better, a vast villa
In some unimaginable suburb
Of Perm or Minsk.

Ears wave and waggle
Over the poignant Vistula,
Horns of a papery stone,

Not a wedding-cake but its doily!
The Palace of Culture sacks
The centre, the dead centre

Of Europe's centre, Warsaw.
The old town,
Rebuilt, is a clockwork toy.

I walked abroad in it,
Charmed and waylaid
By a nursery joy:

Hansel's and Gretel's city!
Their house of gingerbread
That lately in

Horrific forest glooms
Of Germany
Bared its ferocity

Anew, resumes its gilt
For rocking-horse rooms
In Polish rococo.

Diseased imaginations
Extant in Warsaw's stone
Her air makes sanative.

How could a D.S.O.
Of the desert battles live,
If it were otherwise,

In his wooden cabin
In a country wood
In the heart of Warsaw

As the colonel did, who for
The sake of England took
Pains to be welcoming?

More jokes then. And the wasps humming
Into his lady's jam
That we ate with a spoon

Out in the long grass. Shades,
Russian shades out of old slow novels,
Lengthened the afternoon.

Metals

Behind the hills, from the city of an Etruscan gateway
To the city of a Sienese fortress
Through the metalliferous mountains,
If I had travelled to the age of bronze,
Of gold, the pierced axe-heads of archaic Greece,
This would have been my way.

For first we corkscrewed in a stink of borax
For climbing miles, then under the oakwoods
In unworked lodes lay poisonous zinc and copper.
With forty miles to go, the car bit gravel
Which spurted and hung in the air, and still no houses.

And I saw all stone as a weak concoction of powder,
The golden skin of the columns
Cemented as limply as a Rizla paper.
Rape may be worship. Where the sybil stands
In a pool of spent light at the heart of the mountain at Cumae,
The bowels of earth are of an unearthly weirdness.

Homage to John L. Stephens

There has to be a hero who is not
A predator but South
Of the Border down
Mexico way or wherever else she
Whispers, It's best not to linger.

Fever: bright starlight, and the sails
Flapping against the mast, the ocean
Glass, and the coastline dark,
Irregular, and portentous with volcanoes;
The Great Bear almost upon him, the North Star
Lower than ever, waning as he was waning,

And not that sort of hero, not
Conquistador Aeneas, but a tourist!
Uncoverer of the Maya, John L. Stephens,
Blest after all those beaks and prows and horses.

The Vindication of Jovan Babič

(Bosnia 1915)

Age is a pale bird, film of ice on the sea
Where I do not go, film of ice on the river
That I cross no longer after Sclavonian girls;
Cup, horse, kinsman, and the Sultan, the treasure-giver,
Gone from me now. And that old roan,
Lust, is a wryneck since my name was bandied
Among the Austrian matrons and the traders.
I pass for an old lecher since the pear-tree
Under the peeping Tom broke and betrayed us,
Me and my own house-wench. My neck is sprained
Where the boy fell on it. Now one
Of my own house can glory in collusion
With the butchers of Queen Draga, and the hysterical
Schoolboy of Sarajevo. It is a womanish time
That thinks the boudoir is historical,
Love an event. Ideal assignations
Discharge unnatural chastity in wars

Ideally total; virgins' consummations
Cannot be made except with bombs and sabres
And then are bloody. I foresee a time
When all of art and humane learning labours
To clench all history
In a child's fist at the nipple
Or straddle it with four bare legs in bed
And all in metaphor.
        My brutalities
Maimed less, for they were casual, unconsidered.
A flagging wing outsoars them, and the ice
Stiffens the pulse with a not unmanly shudder.

Bolyai, the Geometer

Arthur Allen, when he lived
In rooms beneath my rooms in Trinity,
Thought he had made a breakthrough that would turn
Mathematics inside out again,

As once geometry was spun around
Because the non-Euclidean emerged
Not out of nature, out of nothing extant
But simply as imaginable. Shade,

A flap of blackness folded back upon
Pillar and pediment that afternoon
Encroached upon the chapel portico
And there a wing whirled, flashing. So, I thought,

This turning inside-out is not so hard:
One looks across Front Square and there it is,
A wing that whirls white undersides, sustained
By what endangers it, the press of air.

And though his torque was different, not in nature,
And though my science is as pure as his,
Knowing no revolution more profound
Than that from black on white to white on black

(As though a shutter shot across the mind
One sees the lately formless as most formal,
The stanza most a unit when
Open at both ends, all transition) still

How pure is mathematics? Not enough
For Farkas Bolyai: 'Not geometry
Is altogether pure. This is a wound
Large and perpetual upon my soul.'

So with poetics: never a revolution
But has its mould. Look, in the overturning
Approaching comber, rolling inside out,
A roof of cream moves back through a mounting wall.

After an Accident

1

Smashed, and brought up against
Last things like pines'
Steep shadows and the purple
Hole in my darling's head,

I recall as an amulet
Against my shallowness
Uncalculated kindness
So much! Death, in my dream,

Half-length as in a portrait,
Cocks his eye, leads mine
Up a toothbrush ridge of pines
With an amused complicity

At seeing what is so
Beneath us as a mountain
Tower above us when
We have run out of road.

Death is about my age,
Smiling and dark, clean-shaven.
Behind him the valley-floor
Is ledged in a purple light.

Had I not sought the shade
Of what is so
Beneath us as chagrin,
I had not been afraid

Of his mountainous purple light,
Nor should I have run out
Of the soul of gratitude
Before I ran out of death.

2. *Between Dead and Alive*

For you to be thinking how
It was no bad place to lie in,
In this there was nothing morbid;
Nor was it too composed
In me, to think of your dying
As of an emigration.

This century one in five
On that hillside has emigrated,
And this is not melancholy,
Nor the spaciousness disconcerting:
Between the dead and alive
The ratio there is a just one.

And yet I would have sworn
Such thoughts as these were tricks
Of tearful literature;
That thoughts so unresentful
As mine were could not mix
With terror and compunction.

3. *The Heartland*

And so it is clear that this
Heartland has to be painted
In unrepresentative colours;

That the forests under the mountains
Live in an orange light
Without reference to sunset.

How clear it is, and how
Incapable of being
Foreseen or offered as solace.

That remorse without regret
Is a possible state of the soul,
Like grief without resentment.

4. *Windfall*

So Death is what one day
You have run out of, like
Luck or a bank-balance.
In that case, what is
Coming into it like?

Like coming into money!
The death we run out of is
Not the life we run out of;
The death that we may
With luck come into, is.

And without money, life
Is not worth living.
How did you manage
All these years,
Living and not living?

5. *Thanks*

You never did so much
As when you nearly died;
As if you nearly died
That I might show I lived.

That was no more your motive
Than it could have been my choice.
You cannot think I live
Just to give voice!

It was no poet's need you met,
And now survive,
But the need I had as a man
To know myself alive.

You never did so much
As when you nearly died;
You had to nearly die
For me to know I lived.

The Hardness of Light

'Via Portello,' I wrote,
'The fruity garbage-heaps…'
As if someone had read my poems,
Padua eight years later
Is so hot no one sleeps.

But this is a different quarter,
Just off the *autostrada,*
Touched by that wand of transit,
Californian, hopeful…
I grow older, harder.

I wake in the night, to rain.
All the old stench released
On the risen night wind carries
Coolness across the city,
Streaming from west to east.

The equivocal breath of change,
In a clatter of sudden slats
Across the room, disturbs me
More than ever, in new
Motels and blocks of flats.

What is this abomination
When a long hot spell is breaking?
Sour smell of my own relief?
The rankness of cooling-off?
Rottenness of forsaking?

I glare. In that renowned
Hard light of burning skies
Nothing grows durable
With age. It neither solves
Nor even simplifies.

POEMS OF 1962–1963

On Not Deserving

Worry hedges my days
Like a roil of thick mist at the edge of a covert
Fringing a tufted meadow. In that field
Monuments of art and sanctity
Arise in turn before
The clouded glass of my eye.
Last year the two churches of St Francis
Were piled up there, at the lowest verge of Assisi.

Autumn Imagined

The shuffle and shudder of Autumn
Are in our love.
Those last thin garments, come
Let's have them off!

Drop them about your knees.
The beech-tree rains its gold.
We are deciduous trees,
And our year grows old.

We cannot procrastinate.
Although we seem to delay
By having children late,
Our Autumn is today.

Indeed, give my body its due,
It read the signs aright
When it trembled at Autumn's hue
On our wedding night.

Hot Hands

'Warm hands, cold heart,' they say; and vice-versa.
 My hands are so hot always
That when they touch your coolness, they immerse
 Hissingly, charred and ablaze.

Folk-wisdom! For such old wives' sullen tales
 If natural law is thwarted,
If a rule of law, not rule of signs, prevails,
 Their sense is not inverted:

That hiss is the first breath I have sharply taken,
 Brought against you. Wrench
The text of the world as they will, they are mistaken.
 I am a brand you quench.

Where Depths are Surfaces

Where depths are surfaces
By the clear Tyrrhenian Sea,
I marvel at life that passes
So clearly over me.

Also I think of him,
The Englishman in me,
Whose skiffs can never skim
That deep, distrusted sea.

His trust is in the plummet.
And I seek equally.
Depths that the lead can come at,
Where all men sway with me.

But boats I would not trust
On the golden skin of the sea
Shadow those waters, thrust
Their ghostly prows at me.

For tides we need not sound through
Flow in the human sea,
Whereas the lead goes down to
Depths, depths endlessly.

Vying

Vying is our trouble;
And a devious vice it is
When we vie in abnegations,
Services, sacrifices.

Not to be devious now
(For perhaps I should not begin
Taking the blame for winning
If this were not how to win),

I assert that such is the case:
I seem to have more resources;
I thrive on enforcing the more
The less naked the force is.

Mutinies, sulks, reprisals
All play into my hand;
To be injured and forgiving
Was one of the roles I planned.

Married to me, you take
The station I command,
As if in a peopled graveyard
Deserted in an upland.

There I, the sexton, battle
Earth that will overturn
Headstones, and rifle tombs,
And spill the tilted urn.

from THE POEMS OF DOCTOR ZHIVAGO

March

The sun works up to a lather,
To a thresh in stupefied lowlands.
Like the chores of a strapping cow-girl,
Spring's busy-ness seethes through the hands.

Snow sinks, anaemia saps it
Along weak, blue, twig-like veins.
But life smokes up from the cowhouse;
Hale, it darts out from the tines of pitchforks.

All these nights, these days and nights!
Thud of the thaw at noon, the spatter
Of icicles dripping from roof-tops,
The sleepless culverts' chatter ...

Open it all lies, stable and cowshed.
Pigeons peck oat-ears out of snow.
Off the all-blameable, all-engendering
Dunghill the air blows freshly.

Fairy Story

In days of old
Through a fabled land
Rode he amain
Over hill and hollow.

He sped to the fray.
On the dusty plain
Rose up afar
A dark wood in the way.

A keen pang
At the heart griped him:
'Ware of the well-water,
Draw the girth tighter.

Nothing list the rider
But made his steed to bound
And flew he amain
To the woody mound.

Turned he at the barrow,
Came into the dry fosse,
Passed he through the glade
And the mount he has crossed.

And strayed by the hollow dell
Come by the dark way
Found he the beasts' trace
And water of the well.

And deaf to the summons sent
No heed to ill bode,
Down to the brink he rode,
Gave to his horse to drink.

★

By the stream a cave's mouth,
Before the cave a ford.
As it were brimstone burning
Flamed in the opening.

Smoke billowed dun-red
His gaze baffled:
With a cry far sped
Sounded the forest.

Thereat upon the cleft
The horseman, ware,
Stepped soft-foot straightly
To whence the voice calling.

Saw then the horseman,
Tightened his lance-hold,
Head of the dragon,
Scales, and the tail coiled.

Ardent from maw spilt
Light showed plain
Three boughtes a damsel round
Wound he her spine.

Body of the serpent
As a whip's lash folds her,
His swayed the neck there
On hers the shoulder.

By that land's usage
Was paid in fee
To the monster of the wood
A captive comely.

Folk of the land
Huts that were theirs
Ransomed by rent paid
Thus to the serpent.

Serpent it was that bound
Hands fast, enwound her,
Took into throes of
The scapegoat the offering.

Looked in supplication
To high heaven the horseman.
Couched for altercation
Clasped he the lance then.

*

Sealed close the eye's lids.
Heights. And the cloud's climb.
Rivers. River-fords. Waters.
The years, the spans of time …

Rider, the helm brast,
Brought down in combat,
True steed with hoof-spurn
Tramples the serpent.

Charger next dragon's corse
Heaped on the sandbar,
In a swound the rider,
The damsel stounded.

Sheen of the noon's arch
Azure, dulcet.
What's she? A tsar's child?
Slip of earth? Earl's blood?

Abounding gladness
Flows now in tripled tears,
Now to a dead trance
Lie they in durance.

Charged to new hardihood
Now, and now listless,
Life in the spent blood,
Unstrung the sinews.

Beat still the hearts of them.
Dame first, then man
Strives against cumber,
Fails into slumber.

Sealed close the eye's lids.
Heights. And the cloud's climb.
Rivers. River-fords. Waters.
The years, the spans of time …

The Miracle

He fared from Bethany to Jerusalem,
Foreshadowings of affliction weighing on him.

Burrs of brushwood scorched on the steep bluffs' oven,
Over the hovel nearby no blown smoke stirred;
Hot breath of the air, and the reedbeds there unmoving,
And on the Dead Sea repose immovably anchored.

With sourness at heart that vied with the sour sea-water
He fared, while behind a few clouds raggedly followed,
Along the dust-choked road to some man's shelter,
Fared to the town, where some He instructed gathered.

And so far sank He, self-absorbed and brooding,
A wormwood smell came up as the field saddened.
All stilled. Alone He midway along was standing,
And the terrain stretched, sheeted in unfeeling.
All swam and merged: the balmy air and the barrens,
The lizards, the gushing springs, the waters running.

A fig-tree rising no great distance off,
Utterly bare of fruit, nothing but leaves and wood,
He said to it: 'Do you do me any good?
Is your stockstillness anything to be glad of?'

'I hunger and thirst, and you – you barrenly flower.
Encountering you is comfortless as granite.
What a trial you are, and how devoid of talent!
Stay as you are to the world's last hour.'

Throughout the tree ran the quake of condemnation,
As the levin-flash along a lightning-rod
Flashed on the fig-tree sudden incineration.

Had leaf and branch and root and stem been granted
One moment's freedom, then the laws of Nature
Had made all haste, and doom been intercepted.
But a miracle is a miracle, a miracle is God.
When we are all at odds it comes upon us
Instantaneous, and when least expected.

Magdalene

People spruce themselves for a party.
Keeping clear of this lot,
I wash down with balm from a bucket
Your feet without spot.

I can't even find the sandals.
Crying, I can't see.
My hair's come down, hanks of it
Hanging over my eyes caul me.

I've clutched your legs into my skirt,
I've sluiced them with tears, and there
I've the beads from my neck for a cord around them, Jesus.
I've smothered them in a burnous of hair.

I see what happens now, each item of it
As if you'd had the whole thing grind to a stop.
Just now I'm so good at predictions
I can see through things, I'm a sybil.

Tomorrow the screen comes down in the temple,
We shall be bunched together at one side
And the earth wavers under our feet.
I've a sense that it's sorry for me.

The escort will form up again in column.
They'll make a start to the movement away of horses.
Like a waterspout in a cyclone, over our heads
The sky will be torn open, round that cross.

I'll hurtle to the ground at the foot of the crucifixion.
I'll be out of my mind, I'll gnaw my lips.
You'd clasp too many, hands that on the cross's
Arms stretch out to the tips.

Who is it for in the world, so much bounty,
So much hurt, such a capacity?
Is there so much of being and life in the world?
So much of colony, of river-run and spinney?

But they'll wear by, three times sun-up to sundown,
And ram such vacancy that through
All that terrific intermission
It's Resurrection I'll be thriving to.

ESSEX POEMS

Rodez

Northward I came, and knocked in the coated wall
At the door of a low inn scaled like a urinal
With greenish tiles. The door gave, and I came

Home to the stone north, every wynd and snicket
Known to me wherever the flattened cat
Squirmed home to a hole between housewall and paving.

Known! And in the turns of it, no welcome,
No flattery of the beckoned lighted eye
From a Rose of the rose-brick alleys of Toulouse.

Those more than tinsel garlands, more than masks,
Unfading wreaths of ancient summers, I
Sternly cast off. A stern eye is the graceless

Bulk and bruise that at the steep uphill
Confronts me with its drained-of-colour sandstone
Implacably. The Church. It is Good Friday.

Goodbye to the Middle Ages! Although some
Think that I enter them, those centuries
Of monkish superstition, here I leave them

With their true garlands, and their honest masks,
Every fresh flower cast on the porch and trodden,
Raked by the wind at the Church door on this Friday.

Goodbye to all the centuries. There is
No home in them, much as the dip and turn
Of an honest alley charmingly deceive us.

And yet not quite goodbye. Instead almost
Welcome, I said. Bleak equal centuries
Crowded the porch to be deflowered, crowned.

The North Sea

North Sea, Protestant sea,
I have come to live on your shore
In the low countries of England.
　　A shallow gulf north-westward
Into the Isle of Ely
And the Soke of Peterborough
Is one long arm of the cold vexed sea of the North.

Having come to this point, I dare say
That every sea of the world
Has its own ambient meaning:
The Mediterranean, archaic, pagan;
The South Atlantic, the Roman Catholic sea.

But somewhere in mid-America
All of this grows tiresome,
The needles waver and point wildly

And then they settle and point
Somewhere on the ridge of the Andes
And the Rocky Mountains
True to the end of the world.

Pacific is the end of the world,
Pacific, peaceful.

And I do not know whether to fear
More in myself my bent to that end or
The vast polyp rising and beckoning,
Christ, grey-green, deep in the sea off Friesland.

July, 1964

I smell a smell of death.
Roethke, who died last year
with whom I drank in London,
wrote the book I am reading;
a friend, of a firm mind,
has died or is dying now,
a telegram informs me;
the wife of a neighbour died
in three quick months of cancer.

Love and art I practise;
they seem to be worth no more
and no less than they were.
The firm mind practised neither.
It practised charity
vocationally and
yet for the most part truly.
Roethke, who practised both,
was slack in his art by the end.

The practice of an art
is to convert all terms
into the terms of art.
By the end of the third stanza
death is a smell no longer;
it is a problem of style.
A man who ought to know me
wrote in a review
my emotional life was meagre.

The Blank of the Wall

after St-J. Perse

The blank of the wall is over against you; which
Is the conjuration into a circle
Of reveries. The image none the less
Emits its cry. An aftertaste of rich
Fats and sauces furs
The teeth your tongue explores
Inside the uneasy head which you have set
Upon the lived with, the familiar
Upholstery of a greasy chair; and yet
You think how clouds move purely on your island,
The green dawn growing lucid on the breast
Of the mysterious waters. And it is
The sweat of exiled juices and
There on the hearth the snapping spar,
Split from how cheap a crate, secretes
The resinous stands of all of Canada.
The need is lived with, that this answers to.

Out of East Anglia

Pacific: in Russian as
In our language
Peaceful is the word
For that last sea at the edge;
And nearer than the Americas'
Awesome, vertical falls
Into the Western Ocean
The imperceptible, tempting
Declivity, inanition!

Sometimes when all this side
Of England seems to hang
Suspenseful on that slide,
How peace might be is near.

January

Arable acres heave
Mud and a few bare trees
Behind St Michael's
Kirby le Soken, where
The pew I share
Promises the vicinity I leave.

Diatribe and
Denunciation, where
I spend my days,
Populous townships, sink
Into the haze that lowers
Over my neighbours' land.

Resignation, oh winter tree
At peace, at peace…
Read it what way you will,
A wish that fathers. In a field between
The Sokens, Thorpe and Kirby, stands
A bare Epiphany.

Pietà

Snow–white ray
coal–black earth will
swallow now.
The heaven glows
when twilight has
kissed it, but
your white face
which I kiss now does
not. Be still
acacia boughs,
I talk with my
dead one. We speak
softly. Be still.

The sky is blind
with white
cloud behind
the swooping birds. The
garden lies
round us and
birds in the dead
tree's bare
boughs shut
and open themselves. Be
still, or be
your unstill selves,
birds in the tree.

The wind is
grievous to the willow. The
underside of its
leaves as the wind
compels them is
ashen. Bow
never, nor dance
willow. How can
you bear it? My
head goes back on
my neck fighting
the pain off. Willow
in the wind, share it.

I have to learn
how time can be
passed in public
gardens. There my
dead lies idle. Much
bereaved and sitting
under a sunny wall
old women stare
through me. I
come too soon and
yet at last to
fixity, being alone and
with a crone's pastimes.
In memoriam Douglas Brown

Sunburst

The light wheels and comes in
over the seawall
and the bitten turf
that not only wind has scathed but
all this wheeling and flashing, this
sunburst comes across us.

At Holland on Sea
at an angle from here and
some miles distant
a fisherman reels back blinded,
a walker is sliced in two.
The silver disc came at them
edgewise, seconds ago.

Light that robes us, does it?
Limply, as robes do, moulded
to the frame of Nature? It
has no furious virtue?

The God of Details

after Pasternak

Come rain down words as does
The garden its dried-peel, amber,
Distractedly, profusely,
Yet sparsely, and yet sparsely.
No need to gloss the reason
Why thus punctiliously
In madder and in lemon
Leafage precipitates;

Nor who has moistened quills
And gushed across bare staves
Music on to bookshelves
Sluicing through window-slats;
Who got the rug at the door
Pencilled with small craters,
Sackcloth latticed through with
Poignant, italic tremors.

You ask, who stablishes
That August be a power?
To whom no thing is bauble,
Who goes about to staple
Light leaves to the maple,
And since Ecclesiastes
Has never left his station
Working the alabaster?

You ask, who stablishes
That asters taste, and peonies,
Agonies come September?
That the meagre leaf of the broom
From grey of caryatids
Come down upon dank flags of
Infirmaries of the fall?
You ask, who stablishes?

The omnipotent God of details,
The omnipotent God of love,
Whose sexual spark has lit
And fuelled dynasties.
I do not know the riddle
Of the pitch dark past the tomb,
But Life is, as the autumn's
Hush is, a minuteness.

Ezra Pound in Pisa

Excellence is sparse.
I am made of a Japanese mind
Concerning excellence:
However sparred or fierce
The furzy elements,
Let them be but few
And spaciously dispersed,
And excellence appears.

Not beauty. As for beauty,
That is a special thing.
Excellence is what
A man who treads a path
In a prison-yard might string
Together, day by day,
From straws blown in his path
And bits of remembering.

Sun moves, and the shadow moves,
In spare and excellent order;
I too would once repair
Most afternoons to a pierced
Shadow on gravelly ground,
Write at a flaked, green-painted
Table, and scrape my chair
As sun and shade moved round.

Tunstall Forest

Stillness! Down the dripping ride,
    The firebreak avenue
Of Tunstall Forest, at the side
    Of which we sought for you,
You did not come. The soft rain dropped,
    And quiet indeed we found:
No cars but ours, and ours was stopped,
    Rainfall the only sound.

And quiet is a lovely essence;
    Silence is of the tomb,
Austere though happy; but the tense
    Stillness did not come,
The deer did not, although they fed
    Perhaps nearby that day,
The liquid eye and elegant head
    No more than a mile away.

Orford

after Pasternak

With the actual the illusory
With the vegetable growth the granite.

As it might be in Spring on the day of the Annunciation
It is announced to us out of charity
By earth in every fissure of the stone
By a growth of grass from under every wall.

By the thrivings of life and verdure,
By the vestiges of antiquity,
By earth in every minute cranny,
By a growth of grass from under every wall;

By earth in every pockmark of the stone
By grass grown up in the warp of every floorboard;

By fragrant thick convolvulus
Through centuries twined over bushes
Twined over greatness gone
And what is to come of beauty;

By the lilac double-hued,
The purple spray and the white,
The various mixed with the steadfast,
Loose sift over the stronghold.

Where people are kin to the elements.
Elements neighbourly to people,
Earth in every hollow of the stone,
Grass growing in advance of every doorway.

Thanks to Industrial Essex

Thanks to industrial Essex,
I have spun on the greasy axis
Of business and sociometrics;
I have come to know the structures
Of public service
As well as I know the doves
Crop-full in mildewed haycocks.
I know that what they merit
Is not scorn, sometimes scorn
And hatred, but sadness really.

Italic on chalky tussocks,
The devious lovely weasel
Snakes through a privileged annex,
An enclave of directors.
Landscapes of supertax
Record a deathful failure
As clearly as the lack
Of a grand or expansively human
Scale to the buildings of Ilford.

The scale of that deprivation
Goes down in no statistics.

Expecting Silence

Whatever is said to be so
Is so, if the saying is
Of an agreeable strictness.

Unutterable until
That way uttered is
What we have lived through lately.

The confidence with which
A man goes off by himself,
Reconciled to a longish silence,

Is not for married people.
Seeds of calamity rain
On our strangulated partings.

Our forebodings say
Much about who we are,
Nothing about the future.

A Winter Landscape near Ely

It is not life being short,
Death certain, that is making
Those faintly coffee-coloured
Gridiron marks on the snow
Or that row of trees heart-breaking.

What stirs us when a curtain
Of ice-hail dashes the window?
It is the wasteness of space
That a man drives wagons into
Or plants his windbreak in.

Spaces stop time from hurting.
Over verst on verst of Russia
Are lime-tree avenues.

A Death in the West

May's, whose mouth was
Open under the gauze.
She lay like a child in her coffin.
Often in that front parlour,
Excessively peremptory,
She struggled to belie
Her timorous nature.

Her sisters found the funds
She lacked, of confidence
To train her for a trade.
Her profession was children's nurse.
Children of conspicuous parents
Grew up under her care
To figure in divorce-scandals.

She and her sister sat
Plumb on grey sands in Cornwall
One day, the two most planted
And stubborn tubs in Nature.
Vivid in pastel sweaters,
We walked along by the cliffs
Over the eye-bright shingle.

She deluded us after all.
If she could not be forceful,
Could she be stolid? She
Liked to sit on the sands,
Looking at wide wet beaches,
Scud over Cornish seas, and
Bright shirts under the cliff.

If one of her ancient charges
Had come in a beach-wrap, stalking,
His tired eyes fierce with gin
From foreign embassies,
Her eyes had been equipped
By so much seaside watching
To know him for Ulysses.

From the New World

for Paul Russell-Gebbett

Old Glory at halfmast
For Adlai Stevenson
Drooped under PepsiCola
Flashing all night on Lima.

There, smiling and contained
And lawless through
The boardrooms of New Spain
Don Felix passed;

Smiling and contained
And lawless through
The boardrooms of New Spain,
He ushered us, and was

One of us. His son
Is at Downside,
His English flawless and
His manners too.

British is what we are.
Once an imperial nation,
Our hands are clean now, empty.
Cause for congratulation.

Plaintive the airs
With sorrows when, sails set
Against miscegenation,
Our keels leaned in from Europe.

Freight of Atlantic airs
When doxies lined the rail;
Songs of the Cavaliers
Twanged on the tainted gales;

The English fever-ships,
Though hopes re-painted, fetched
Up on the Carolinas
To wailing strings.

Rubber-faced Uncle Sam!
Unhappy Adlai,
Dipping in on the clipper to
The heritable blame,

The melancholy strains
No one alive has lived with:
England's historic guilt,
France's, or Spain's.

'What,' said our diplomat,
'Sort of nation is
This that I represent
In South America?' I said:

'A nation of theatre-people,
Purveyors, not creators,
Adaptable cyphers, stylists,
Educators, dandies.'

Rubber-faced Uncle Sam!
Unhappy Adlai,
A name that is of Zion…
British is what I am.

Zion, a park in Utah.
So many available styles!
Heavens, the New is New
Still, to us quizzical monsters!

Stratford on Avon

I look a long way back
To a house near Stratford.
You had come out of our black
Barnsley, a girl, to Oxford.

Beautiful, boys pursued you.
In dusk and the overgrown
Garden I, as you knew,
Watched you sitting alone

On the creosoted stair
To the girls' dormitory.
No one else was there.
You slept on the first storey.

Lanes crept by the riverside.
We had said Goodnight too soon,
Strange to that countryside
Famous under the moon.

And yet within the echo
Of our lame exchanges
No grasses ceased to grow,
No apple pair turned strangers.

And that was the summer of nineteen
Forty, the war still slack.
Twentyfive summers since then.
I look a long way back.

Barnsley, 1966

Wind-claps of soot and snow
Beat on the Railway Hotel's
Tall round-headed window;
I envy loquacious Wales.

Taciturn is the toast
Hereabouts. Were this Wales,
My father had ruled this roost,
Word-spinner, teller of tales.

If he missed his niche
I am glad of it today.
I should not have liked him rich,
Post-prandial, confident, bawdy.

He was rinsed with this town's dirt
For seventy wind-whipped years,
Chapped lips smiling at hurt,
Eyes running with dirty tears.

A Conditioned Air

A wind I know blows dirt
In and out of the town that I was born in,
The same wind blowing the same dirt in and out,
Coal-dirt, grit. No odorous cloud-cleaving
Typhoon of Crusoe grew upon the West
To satisfy your hunger for afflatus,
Masters of the last
Century, attending
A plaint in the mouth of the hearth, a night of
Wind. The wind
Was a draught in the flue of England. I attend
How the electric motor
Gulps and recovers and
The image on the television screen
Contracts and distends like a reptilian eye,
As somewhere the high wind slaps at a power-line
Out in the country. In the howling quick
Of the bud the branches suffer
Retardations much as you did. I,
Before an empty hearth
In an unfocused house,
Behind me the quietly blasting
Hot-air grille, attend
The delicate movements of
Conditioned airs
I learn to love, as small
As that is, and as prompt
In its dispersed and shaking service. My
Storm-window's foggy polythene claps and billows.

Sylvae

Not deerpark, royal chase,
Forest of Dean, of Windsor,
Not Cranborne, Savernake
Nor Sherwood nor that old
Plantation we can call
New, nor be, it is
So old, misunderstood;
But the primordial oak-wood.

This it is our hedgerows
Preserve from the pre-Saxon:
Not the perennial pastures;
Not Hanoverian georgics;
But a prodigious dapple
Of once uninterrupted
Cover we at best
Subvert by calling 'forest'.

Sprung of this cultured landscape
The fiction-makers of
My race have so completely
Made over that it hardly
Smells of that shaggier love,
I radicalize reversion:
I think of Robin Hood,
The flecked man in my blood.

I think how the tractable Nature
Of the cultivator has
Before now, at the hand
Of many a bookish writer,
Burgeoned in garden-crops
By seasons, and he has
Made homage of them for
Patron or paramour.

But I have kept no gardens,
Am of that vanquished sort,
The gatherers, the most
Primitive of woodland cultures;
I have to offer her
To whom I most would make
Offer, no more than nuts,
Berries, and dubious roots.

Amazonian

Riparian origins… did you know
The hammock was an invention
Of Amazonian Indians? Ours
Hangs from a cricket-bat willow
To the hedgerow stump where a wasps' nest sang
Last summer. Out of hands
That could not afford to be feckless it has passed
To us who are
Improvident as primitives. Retted cordage
Rots beaded in
Green light on our overcast garden,
As it might be in Hemingford Abbotts
Beside the sliding Ouse.

Intervals in a Busy Life

'Room for manœuvre,' I say,
'I ask for an undertaking.'
Manœuvring, king-making…

Only when death happens
Do I see the tops of the trees
Out of my attic window,

And they are always there:
They have looked on the death of my friend
And on my father's death.

They are the deathly markers;
And thereby, even when leafless,
Green; ungrudging sources

At which, as at holy springs,
One does not drink
Habitually nor lightly.

Filling the intervals
Without propriety
Itself is reverential.

Iowa

The blanched tree livid behind
The smaller conifer
Looks to be entangled with it.

Dutch elm disease is in town,
Carried by worms from the eastern seaboard
Twelve hundred miles.

Gesticulating down
And around, emaciated,
This is the many-armed,

This is the elephant-headed
Ganesh of good beginnings,
God of the Hindu, gone sick.

Tomorrow, if the night is warmer,
The snow will be gone in patches
From the clay-spoil hillock.

White on white, a white
Framehouse amid the snow
Is a peculiar beauty.

The tree is an ivory colour.
In a white world there are
So many kinds of white.

They leak into black shadows
Draining them blue. I shall be
Sorry when the world goes piebald.

Red on red was a good chequer,
The red man dead in his blood;
And black on black, the weighed bough swinging

In a night of Alabama. White on white
Is a man of my colour, sick,
Falling down in the snow.

Back of Affluence

That time of the early year
When the sun has a head of hair
Crisp but growing out,
When already the long nights have
Stirred away southward, when
The engraver frost still makes
Likenesses of his sister
Snow, but with a nib
That will not hold its point,

Then the Iowan farmer,
His fodder low, looked out
And saw the prairie white.

He threw up a heavy arm,
He stamped in the house at a loss.
His wife rose lame and stiff.
His children snarled like dogs.

Then he came back with the team;
She into her best dress
Wrinkled at waist and shoulder.
No farming, a day on the town!
Rail depot through to horsepond
And lumberyard, one street.
She with a child in arms;
No place to go from the wind.

Some one has said that it
Brutalized. It did,
That poverty. And what she
Could have seen, she had not
The ease of heart to see:
The sun like a Chinese brush
Writing in delicate shadow
'Tree' on a framehouse front;
The handsomely carpentered boards
Fanned across, splayed over
With a serene springing.

Or, Solitude

A farm boy lost in the snow
Rides his good horse, madrone,
Through Iowan snows for ever
And is called 'alone'.

Because gone from the land
Are the boys who knew it best
Or best expressed it, gone
To Boston or Out West,

And the breed of the horse madrone,
With its bronco strain, is strange
To the broken sod of Iowa
That used to be its range,

The metaphysicality
Of poetry, how I need it!
And yet it was for years
What I refused to credit.

MORE ESSEX POEMS

My Father's Honour

Dim in the glimmering room
Over against my bed...
Astonished awake, I held
My breath to see my dead,
My green-eyed, talkative
Dead father come.

That look he has! A rare one
In a vivacious man.
I grasp at the uncommon
Identifiable look,
Reproach. The charge it levels
Is no unfair one.

Hold to that guise, reproach,
Cat's eyes! Eerily glow,
Green, prominent, liquid;
Level the charge, although
I could not have done other,
And this you know.

Hold there, green eyes! But no,
Upon the nebulous ground
His merciful nature cuts
From shot to genial shot,
Indulgent now, as if
In honour bound.

Rain on South-East England

This place is so much
Mauled, I have to think
Others besides these Dutch
And low green counties drink
The summer rains, before
I hold it in my mind
What a soft rain is for:
To ease, flush through, unbind.
Tightly starred, on the flat
Marred ground once, with a thin
Unambitious mat
I mended England's ruin.
Growth these last years works
My roots into the air;
Aspiring on long stalks,
My blooms digest no fare
Coarser than light. The strain
Of self-enhancement frees:
I take no care for the rain,
Soured soil, and shattered trees.

Pentecost

Up and down stairs of the inner ear,
Its ivory chambers, stray
The stumbling, the moving voices;
The self-communers; of whom
It seems hardly to matter
Whether we say that they are
Not at home in our language
Or they are too much at home.

What faculties we are lacking!
We have eyes to see, and we see
Not, sometimes; ears to hear and
Sometimes we hear. But they have
Faculties without organs;
They see and hear with the thorax,
They are eloquent in pidgin.

Our sons and our daughters shall
Prophesy? That gift of tongues
To the Beat and post-Beat poets,
The illiterate apostles,
Is what, if I should cherish
Much or mourn my lack of
Or ape their stammerings,
I must betray myself.

Winter Landscapes

Danger, danger of dying
Gives life in its shadow such riches.
Once I saw or I dreamed
A sunless and urbanized fenland
One Sunday, and swans flying
Among electric cables.

There are so many of us,
Men and swans, in places
Congested with new dangers.
It hurts that we are mortal
Less there, for we remember
Mortal is what the race is.

Swans in unimpeded
Flight above bare hawthorn
Ask, as a more austere
Occasion, a taste for the sparse
That likes its landscapes Northern,
Serener, and more hurtful.

Behind the North Wind

'the Arctic Ocean was open during glacial stages and its
margins would have been habitable for man'

Envisage it: the Atlantic
Cold and silent, ice-sheets
Drawn to the chin of the land-mass
Far southward, but a buzz
Round the rim of the living Arctic.

I fondled a kitten once
Where a blue lake locked in the hills
Winked like cottagers' delph
Behind a forgotten Front
Of 1942.

Empty the iron hills
And the dirt-road to Murmansk,
A cat's nine lives ago;
A rinsing wind from the west
Blew over the firth from Finland.

Will oceanographers set
The Yenisei on fire?
And though a hyperborean
Thesis is revived,
Will the Ob flow backward?

More than ever I need
Places where nothing happened,
Where history is silent,
No Tartar ponies checked, and
Endurance earns repose.

Pages of an atheist journal,
The 'AntiReligioznik',
Scurried on one bald hill-top;
Even the Front up there
Had never moved in years.

Revulsion

Angry and ashamed at
Having not to look,
I have lived constricted
Among occasions
Of nausea, like this book
That I carefully leave on the train.

My strongest feeling all
My life has been,
I recognize, revulsion
From the obscene;
That more than anything
My life-consuming passion.

That so much more reaction
Than action should have swayed
My life and rhymes
Must be the heaviest charge
That can be brought against
Me, or my times.

Oak Openings

The 'I have' poem
(Have been, seen, done)
Is followed by the 'What about it?' poem.
There is plenty new under the sun,
This poem says, but what's
So new about the new?

It is not as if the attention
Steadily encroaches
Upon the encircling dark;
The circle about the torch is
Moving, it opens new
Glades by obscuring old ones.

Twigs crack under foot, as the tread
Changes. The forge-ahead style
Of our earliest ventures flags;
It becomes, as mile follows mile
Inexhaustibly, an exhausted
Wavering trudge, the explorer's.

New Year Wishes for the English

Beware the ball-point lens:
Lord Thomson and Lord Snowden be
Far from your door.

May the girl with the questionnaire
Meet only the neighbourhood zanies;
May she calibrate obsessions.

May the humanitarian
Blackmail be paid no longer;
Instead may you work a little.

May you have, against the incessant
Rain of the new, the all-new,
Indifference as an umbrella.

May you be quiet, may you
Not be hectored by me,
But left alone for a little.

May you recognize that these
Are wishes for the inception
Of a long recuperation;

That they are not what a poet
Would wish you if he could,
But the most he dares to hope for.

(1966)

Preoccupation's Gift

When all my hours are mine,
I husband them with care;
Pre-empted hours are those
    I have to spare.
Step by step, one
Calculated stage
After another, writing
    A laboured page –
Give me my freedom back
And this is how I live,
Frugally, for lack of
    Anything to give
Short of my freedom. Thrift
Gives nothing it gives up;
But absent-minded pourings
    Brim every cup.
The provocations so
Prodigal, and the response
Parsimony? No,
    No vigilance!

The North Sea, in a Snowstorm

Dark ages, calm and merry
Beside the sea of my boyhood
Sparkled on a Whitby
Of cricketers in August.

Blockhouses of 1940
In the undercliff at Walton,
The Roman Empire dying,
A Count of the Saxon Shore
Far from the sparkling synod,
I walk by a sea that is
A concave opal.

Up from its deep, its submarine, sub-zero
Unimaginable furnace,
Rigour arises where it steams and burns
With a superior cold.

Transparencies, and shivers of running greens!

To Certain English Poets

My dears, don't I know? I esteem you more than you think
    you modest and quietly spoken, you stubborn and unpersuaded.
    Your civil dislikes hum over a base that others
    shudder at, as at some infernal cold.
But pits full of smoky flame are sunk in the English Gehenna,
    where suffering souls like ours are bound and planted
    now in the one hot spot, now in another.
The operator is an imagination of Dante
    that plucks us out of the one and plugs us at once in another
    with an obedient pip-pip-pip at the switchboard.
Like you I look with astonished fear and revulsion
    at the gross and bearded, articulate and good-humoured
    Franco-American torso, pinned across
    the plane of human action, twitching and roaring.
Yet a restlessness less than divine comes over us, doesn't it, sometimes,
    to string our whole frames, ours also, in scintillant items,
    with an unabashed crackle of intercom and static?
Or will you, contained, still burn with that surly pluck?

Democrats

Four close but several trees, each green, none equal.
They are the glory of this countryside:
Sequestered households of the field and hedge,
Not copses and not spinneys and not groves.

Green and uncertain in the early summer;
Patient endurers down the depth of winter,
Immobile dancers. In these fields the axe
Of the leveller Tarquin trembles, and advances.

Epistle. To Enrique Caracciolo Trejo

(Essex)

A shrunken world
Stares from my pages.
What a pellet the authentic is!
My world of poetry,
Enrique, is not large.
Day by day it is smaller.
These poems that you have
Given me, I might
Have made them English once.

Now they are inessential.
The English that I feel in
Fears the inauthentic
Which invades it on all sides
Mortally. The style may die of it,
Die of the fear of it,
Confounding authenticity with essence.

Death, an authentic subject,
Jaime Sabinès has
Dressed with the yew-trees of funereal trope.
It cannot be his fault
If the English that I feel in
Feels itself too poor
Spirited to plant a single cypress.
It is afraid of showing, at the grave-side,
Its incapacity to venerate
Life, or the going of it. These are deaths,
These qualms and horrors shade the ancestral ground.

Sabinès in another
Poem comes down
To the sound of pigeons on a neighbour's tiles,
A manifest of gladness.
Such a descent on clapping wings the English
Contrives to trust
No longer. My own garden
Crawls with a kind of obese
Pigeon from Belgium; they burst through cracking branches
Like frigate-birds.

Still in infested gardens
The year goes round,
A smiling landscape greets returning Spring.
To see what can be said for it, on what
Secure if shallow ground
Of feeling England stands
Unshaken for
Her measure to be taken
Has taken four bad years
Of my life here. And now
I know the ground:
Humiliation, corporate and private,
Not chastens but chastises
This English and this verse.

I cannot abide the new
Absurdities day by day,
The new adulterations.
I relish your condition,
Expatriate! though it be among
A people whose constricted idiom
Cannot embrace the poets you thought to bring them.

Cold Spring in Essex

Small boy in a black hat walks among streaky shadows
Under my window, and I am at ease this morning.
This day reminds me of Budapest. All over
Europe is the North and Protestantism has conquered.

The Roman Catholic North in the black-oak cabinet of Antwerp
Is an irreplaceable grace-note, as at Sawston
The manorial chapel of the Huddlestons for the pilgrims.
'Which of them will make a good death?' my friend in Antwerp
Wondered through the plateglass over beer and coffee
Looking to the end.
                         But I am happy this morning,
Looking into my garden, seeing the cold light standing
Oblique to the grey-green tree-trunks and the grasses,
All over my illimitable future.

LOS ANGELES POEMS

To Helen Keller

Yours was the original freak-out: Samuel Beckett's
mutilated prodigies, for whose
sake these last years we bought so many tickets
and read so many books, were hotter news
when your and Anne Sullivan Macy's iron will,
back in the 'twenties, stooped to vaudeville.

One will, two persons... yes, let campus-rebels
account for education at that level,
that give, that take. I wonder if it troubles
our modish masters of sardonic revel
that you, who seemed typecast for it, were not
conscious of Black Comedy in the plot.

You were by force of circumstance, by force
of your afflictions, I suppose, the most
literary person ever was.
No sight nor sound for you was more than a ghost;
and yet because you called each phantom's name,
tame to your paddock chords and colours came.

This too, at this, the mind of our time is appalled.
The Gutenberg era, the era of rhyme, is over.
It's an end to the word-smith now, an end to the Skald,
an end to the erudite, elated rover
threading a fiord of words. Four-letter expletives
are all of that ocean's plankton that still lives.

You, who had not foreseen it, you endured it:
a life that is stripped, stripped down to the naked,
asking what ground it has, what has ensured it.
Your answer was: the language, for whose sake it
seemed worthwhile in Tuscumbia, Alabama,
month after month to grope and croak and stammer.

Christmas Syllabics for a Wife

When I think of you
dying before or
after me, I am
ashamed how little
there is for either
one of us to look
back upon as done
wholly in concert.

We have spent our lives
arming for them. Now
we see they begin
to be over, and
now is it too late
to profit by what
seems to have been a
long preparation?

The certainty that
many have scaped scot–
free or even praised
sets the adrenalin
anger flushing up
through me as often
before, but can we
wait now for justice?

Horace says, Be wise
broach the ripe wine and
carefully decant
it. Now is the time
to measure wishes
by what life has to
give. Not much. So be
from now on greedy.

Idyll

after Giorgio Bassani

As a horn of the high moon veers in clear skies over Main Street
And inflames with a fugitive heat the sea-green pavements,
Out of the town cloaked horsemen ride across sleep
On lukewarm roads that founder halfway in hayfields.

Quiet the night, and clear, and from the moist
Low meadows comes up lightly a milk that billows
In gusts of the wind, and a sound comes of distant trains
Aimed, blindly anxious, at packed market-places.

But you, a god who smiles at the gain and the loss,
Bless your black adepts all the way with spells,
All the good way past fields whose green is here!

The woman who keeps the inn, unbar her window,
Call down to the door the maids from their odorous beds,
Shine in the wine, light rapturous eyes in the shadows!

Brantôme

Burly, provincial France,
Your rarefied, severe
Renaissance is
Material and four-square
Here, in a stout arrangement
Of water, stone and grass
Where the unlettered can
Come and read in the clear
Air of a weeping April
Thus rendered, the austere
Theorems of the jurist
Or fierce geometer.

I walk your foreign turf.
My native tongue was leased
Fawningly, long ago,
To the too long appeased
Long pitied vulgar. I
Speak to myself in French,
Thinking myself in a place
Where a lettered man's remorse
For intellectual pride
And ruthlessness of the mind
May be accepted, not
Pounced on and misapplied.

Looking out from Ferrara

after Giorgio Bassani

It needs there to be no one
Left in the piazza,
Only a boy on his own,
For the thunderhead that shelves
Its far slateblue over small
Lit farms in the plain, to be dealt with
Smilingly. Nor is there
Need of more than his hand
Sketching a smudged goodbye,
Before the thunder edges
Clear of the pinkish mild
Immensity of acres.
And then there is spread abroad
About the roads the darkling
Shade of an old and humble
Townland of that locale,
With, passing across it, the long
Wind of the Spring that will make
Promises some time soon
In whispers, and the drowse
Of boyhood is borne off the meadows
Freighted as high as the evening;
Warm in the wagons the dusky
Grasses, the acrid poppies.

An Oriental Visitor

To a bell in Lincoln Cathedral
A butterfly out of the fens
Of Lindsey has ascended
Up labouring steeps of air
And there, exhausted, it sleeps
Furrily clinging. In
Lincolnshire are no
Fireflies, more's the pity!

Had one of them climbed there, what
Delirious ringing
Over the railway yards
And the level-crossing
And the factories making tractors,
And the minicars at the mini-
Intersections! What
Swing of a coppery rim
To carve off episodes!

To the thunderhead it calls
'Avanti!' – the long high narrow
Pole-pennant carried in rain-squalls.

The spearmen are gone. And for those
With tufted lances, only
The tossing pampas-grass.

The tomb of Atsumori, and
Not one cherry-tree
To stand against it!

When she bites at the acrid
Persimmons of Japan,
It is then that from the oldest
Wooden building in the world
A bell begins to clang.

Cloud-treader, breather of mist...
A skylark goes up
Into its element, singing.

And as for singing, the
School of the skylark and
The school of the frog dispute.

Meanwhile the one
Pure ring in the world, the moon,
And the numberless stars dispute
The dark green of the heavens.

And the clouds pile
White canvas southward
From where we stand,

And the artery of the town is
A slow-flowing stream between alders,
Though quartering wires cries-cross it.

And though the wintry river
Receives the abandoned dog's
Stiffening cadaver,

Moon-rise at evening; and
An ancient plum-tree drops
This year's first blossom on
A foreign girl's guitar.

'Abbeyforde'

Thirty years unremembered,
Monkey-faced black-bead-silken
Great-aunt I sat across from,
Gaping and apprehensive,
The thought of you suddenly fits.
Across great distances
Clement time brings in its
Amnesties, Aunt Em.

'Abbeyforde': the name
Decyphered stood for Ford
Abbey, in Somerset. There
Your brother's sweetheart Nell,
My grandmother, drew him to her,
Whom later he pitchforked North.
Such dissolutions, Em!
Such fatal distances!

'Keep still feast for ever...'
A glow comes up off the page
In which I read of a paschal
Feast of the diaspora
In Italy, in a bad
Time for the Jews, and it is
As if in that tender and sad
Light your face were illumined.

England

1

Eight hours between us, eight
hours by the clock between us,
eleven hours flying time.

Chill and slack as you are,
the torrid is what you affect;
the slipway of greasy Anne
at Shottery launched more keels,
you think, than cleanly Helen.
Although this has to be proved.

A staring world that Engels
never underwrote:
as, of the '45 –
'some few thousand serfs
variously bludgeoned
and misled into fighting
against a few thousand proles'.
The March of the '45...
Confound it, the theme exacted
a certain elevation!

And if there is corruption
in every detail
(notably, of language)
and bed is a display-case
(coloured lights come on:
psychedelic), how
long can the civil servant
at the Ministry of Pensions
remain, as a rule, uncorrupted?

★

Heroic fuzz has been
your unparliamentary choice
all over again, I notice.
Hotspur is playing John Ball
all over again. A neutral
tone was (Note the passive
voice) preferred by no one
really, no one at all.

Entranced, my thoughts of you
climb no mountains, enter
no bowels but their track
is outward always and over
a curve of the earth, the night's
selva oscura approaching
and fleeting away beneath me
as I fly over the flattened
Pole or by some other
Great Circle route to London.

History entrances
as on the Great North Road
at Newark for instance, those
bowels we have entered;
but it is less than
visionary, whether
we enter the Edwardian boom
in Balham or Palmer's Green
about the turn of the last
century, or contend for
where Queen Eleanor slept.

Lower to lower-middle
to middle, or else downwards...
The drift of any English
conversation or memoir
is less than continental.
I dwell, intensely dwell
on my flying shadow
over the Canadian barrens,
and come to nothing else:
land migrates, and ice,
and Eskimo, and from
his social station my
father in an early
narrative by Wells.

★

Historical time is not
the dimension of these reproaches.
Unkindness is the reproach.
An emptied rectitude
in his cockaded topee
as Governor of the Islands;
a cause of much uncertain
hilarity in 'the Loyals',
in the disloyals, of hatred.
Faithful, knowing the first,
he will not prefer the second.
Unkindness is the reproach.

Sharp? Yes, you are sharp.
The heavy footfall, each
stretch, each stoop an achievement.
Suddenly, disportings!
The younger trees encircle
the thick bole's blossoming autumn.
In the polemical light
between the grey trunks, each
mushy core upheld
still by its cortical
armature of sunlight,
curved knives are out and take it.

I know a man who knows you
so well, so inside-out,
he is appalled by the knowledge;
you must not be seen to be
dishonoured, he thinks, and so he
lowers the threshold of honour;
for your sake he will revise
the entire inheritance downwards.

You are more lovely and
more temperate than you take
any pride in supposing.

Beknighted actors, youth
in tall hats, trailing feathers,
society a congeries of roles...
Napoleon was right:
a nation of purveyors.
Now we purvey ourselves.

The amused blade: 'Talk of the gods...
you have seen them?'
                         'I have not seen them.'

                         2

And this is a poem not about you
but FOR you, for
your delectation, lady;

and turning for now on certain
characters (not heroes,
half my friends are whelmed
in deeper gulphs) who are
dislikeable: Scots on the make
who gave their names to forts
on the Coppermine River or
headlands in Arctic seas.
Donald Smith of Forres
finished up Lord Strathcona
(strath of the coffee-machine?
Glen of Conan); and
the Bonaparte of Lachine
(Cathay in French), the bastard

able diminutive George
Simpson was later Sir George,
a small inflexible pin
on which the unwieldy engine
of the Hudson's Bay Company turned,
having eaten his words and worse
for the Proprietors' sakes.

A holy terror. What
a bastard from Loch Broom,
Ross-shire; caught up on McLoughlin
20 days start from York
at River la Biche
July the 26th,
1824
at 7 in the morning. 'Shameful
mismanagement' (forks of Spokane) …
'scene of the most wasteful
extravagance… high time …
ample Field for reform…'
'Having performed the voyage
from Hudson's Bay across
to the Northern Pacific Ocean
in 84 days, thereby
gaining 20 days
on any Craft that ever
preceded us.' What a bastard!

Fascist, we have to face it.
No, but I mean, precisely;
not the mere four-letter
objurgation but
a caribou at that
stage of the class-migration.

Nothing to pay, said his kinsman
Thomas, the explorer,
contemptuously sordid,
explaining why distance was
held of little account
'in the North American wilds',
who paid, paid with his blood
for driving his *voyageurs*
cruelly over distance.

George has been blamed for that
implausibly, but still
it gives his quality as
it was discerned. He was thought
ready at need to kill
his kindred if they should
thwart the Company's will.

Or as J.H. Lefroy described him
in 1843:
'the toughest looking old
fellow I ever saw;
on the Egyptian model,
height two diameters or
one of those short square massy
pillars in a country church'.

>   (Lefroy, an Army man:
>   Victorian rectitude.
>   Governor of Tasmania
>   later, with the cockaded
>   topee and full-dress blues.)

Prizeman of Aberdeen
University, Thomas
Simpson had pretensions:
'The practice of mothers casting
away their female children,
common in Madagascar,
Hindostan, China, and other
countries more blest by nature
than the Mackenzie River...';
and sends us to read in Gibbon,
being immune however
from irony. The candid
inquirer, says Thomas, will
also do well to reflect...
On what? On there being never
again enough space for our children?
Or are these deeper gulphs
than any with boats or sledges
plumbed by the Romantic
admirer of 'dear Sir Walter',

in 1838
on Great Bear Lake
reading Gibbon and Hume,
Robertson, Shakespeare, Smollett,
Plutarch and dear Sir Walter?

This is the country we fly
over, over the Pole
from Los Angeles to London
or Leningrad. This is where
the Hare Indian squaw or whatever
co-ed from Oregon in
Haight-Ashbury dumps her baby.

Yes, but the driving, the king-
pin, does it have to be Lenin
on whom the unwieldy engine
turns? Is there no arranging
for Thomas Simpson, though
young and vaporous (he
was dead at 32)
to act, but through committee?

driving his crews past Boat
Extreme, Point Turnagain,
and Franklin's farthest?

3

The professor is emphatic
when we speak of 'the last eccentrics'.
Bluff stuff. 'Plenty about still!'
He's working at it.
Or there's the unco' guid with
a brutal difference. 'My
father was in the Asquith
tradition, and pro-Boer.
Which is a pity because
                    I wish they'd killed the lot.'
Scotswoman on the make
at 70 plus, where the make
now is, with the teen-age newsmen:
'The qualities she most

values are curiosity,
courage and kindness.' KINDNESS!
Tergiversations of the Left.

The bluff stuff. Double bluff when
back from the Dardanelles
with lead in your lung, Ted Hughes
runs you for a long
still running season, rats
behind the industrial arras
of Mexborough, the pasteboard
Barnsley of grime and phlegm
hawked up, thrillingly mined with
rats and stoical killers.
The bluff stuff. Double bluff.
Brutal manners, brutal
simplifications as
we drag it all down.

Twenty years ago
the gloaming Hamoaze
and the Fal above Penryn
harboured the mothball fleet.
And that seems like the best
time, the point of rest,
an entr'acte of exhaustion
before the impudent flourish
of kettledrum and cornet.
Now some one has said it at last:
Defection! The renegade rats
on a ship not sinking however
but sold downriver to Long Beach,
a floating stage off Long Beach
for What the Butler Saw.

'Display,' said Lawrence, 'of
nothingness. Still, display.
Display! Display! Display!'
Nothing is left of the play
but the character-parts, the charade.

... children's voices singing
rou-cou under the drum
of language where the dung-fed
pigeon rhymes with love...
When I read the British
contemporaries I
admire, I am abashed
by the levelness of their tone.
They are saying how all children
are, whenever they are
flustered, unkind, however
mild and soaring their voices
under the drum. I have
a reading knowledge of English.

Et ô ces voix d'enfants...
those children were as little
children like my own
as doves, doves, are like pigeons!
The words of this age are spoken
from and on a stage.
The speakers are as little
children like my own...

Curtain. *Coup de théâtre!*

The stage however is larger
than a floating pier off Long Beach.
It is larger than any one can
occupy. Language envelopes.
It forestalls us always.

Connie Chatterley lives,
or did two years ago.
She asks herself (and gives
an irritated *moue):*
In this extravagant scene
of towering Queens and Queers,
just what is a girl to do?
Or who has whom by the ears
now nothing is overheard?
And what is there left to be seen
by Tom the butler now

we couple like dogs in the yard?

Display! Display! Display!

*

4

England: a Rosciad.
A poem about or for
a superannuated
England, sapped and distracted
by vying rhetorics and
impeccably evenly-toned
social comedies and
Swadlincote, 'so ugly
it made you laugh';
                        and for
Geoff Bond, who came from Sheffield
who died the other day
at 48 and was
ironically bewildered.

(On a Sunday morning he died,
of a pain in his chest he died
within the hour, who had
lowered the threshold of honour
'Why *shouldn't* they swing the lead?' –
to save your honour, England.)

Stromness in Orkney, no,
never; Lyness I knew
in 1942,
PQ 17 assembling,
the famous fated convoy.
And I was in the old
'Iron Duke', Beatty's flagship
bottomed in concrete, anchored
for good in Scapa Flow;
and never knew, no more
than Stripey hauled back drunk
from runs ashore, whatever
Athabascan sighs

circle like gulls about
that catchment of recruits
for the traditional routes
through the Canadian wilds:
Knee Lake, Hayes River,
                              Lost
(the historians cannot be trusted)
that long Scandinavian saga.
Sinclairs were of Stromness
or of Pomona; William
Sinclair died at York
Factory, 1818.

In 1831
'Robertson brought his bit
of Brown with him
to the Settlement this spring…'
That is to say, his squaw.
And that was Governor Simpson,
got Betsy Sinclair with child,
whose mother had been a Swampy
Cree. The permafrost
spins out a skein of wings
that sting to a sexy heat;
but not Sir Alexander
Mackenzie, whose
buffaloes were attended
by their young, whose elks
would soon exhibit the same
'enlivening circumstance',
who saw Peace River as
'this theatre of nature'.
This is what we pay for:
the language that forestalled them.

The bronze that the poet, naming
his moribund friends, lays claim to
is harder to believe in
now than the Christian heaven.

★

Lay-er of the ocean-cables
from Hampshire, the Anglo-Cuban,
the Anglo-Brazilian, Anglo-
Argentine, none of us young,
in a Manxman's ship on the slant
through the South Atlantic to 'home',
Our Bonny was over the ocean
We sang, not one of us Scottish.

Henry Mackenzie's Athens
of the North… My English father's
breeks and glengarry, his
Forth and Holyrood Palace,
Castle and Prince's Street
and Portobello since
1915! Arthur's
Seat swirled in a reek
of sentiment, and along
wynds of his conversation
a Burns's turbid feeling
eddied, a Carlyle's
blurred at the edge.
      Thom Gunn
played in the overgrown
gardens of Hampstead when
already I wrote a letter
(unpublished) to *Time & Tide*
enthusiastic for
Mihajlovič, that Serb,
Bonny already over
the edge.
    Browning, Millais,
Huxley, Arnold, Spencer
on the occasion of
Victoria's jubilee had
no tickets for the Abbey;
an eminent actor had,
Thomas Hardy says,
25 tickets sent him.

Shortbread tartans, a voice
for the voiceless and lachrymose English,
our kings implausibly kilted,
we all came out of the author
of *Waverley*. 'Sir Walter
Scott is no more,' wrote George
Simpson, who had not envisaged
a teen-age culture. 'Our
universally admired,
respected fellow-
countryman is gone.'
Gone, gone as the combo
starts in digging the beat
and the girls from the nearest College
of Further Education
spread their excited thighs.

And there shall be no more cakes
nor choruses nor Drambuie
under the Southern Cross.

Envoi

The plane makes travel nothing,
Ann Stanford says, not I.
Thank God it's second nature
Nowadays to fly.
Thank God that 'aviator'
Is now a queer old word,
And every passenger watches
As calmly as a bird,
Seeing the pioneer
Has played his grease-paint role,
Los Angeles to Moscow
By Fairbanks and the Pole.
Thank God to be alive,
Now we can look and learn
Geography through the eye,
And see the cosmos turn
Or the Mackenzie's fingers
Hook out on either hand
To pluck away a mountain

And pucker the anxious land.
Thank God those devil-masks
Of goggles and flaps are gone,
Gone with Hubert Wilkins
And Amy Mollison.
Thank God the histrionic
Temperament must seek
Some other job than flying
To London twice a week.
And we? We can look down
And see, or think we see,
The eider's shank shed feathers
Over the Barents Sea,
And a bewildered freighter
Bound out of Bergen crack
Under the pressure of ice,
Ribs fast-gripped to the smoke-stack.
When in all points like the North,
Lady, unmarked I arise
Across the unwinking ice,
Swilling the seals' blind eyes
With the dome of midnight, think:
I am a rimed unbudging
Mast surveyed by winter;
A sea-mark, yours at last.

Certainly air comes near it;
The idea of air does come
Near to whatever might
Now assuage the spirit.
Air, not the conquest of air
But air, a dimension we have
Polluted of course but that was
Assured by our going there.
(We smell, and leave smells behind us
And poisons, but what do we think
We are, that we should resent
Trailing our noisome remainders?)
Air, the musical crystal...
Look, we are buoyed upon it!
As if the Scottish down
Should steer back to the thistle,
Or clouds of pollen come

Intently homing in on
Indigenous British Sea
Starwort or Michaelmas Daisy.

Emigrant, to the Receding Shore

for the shade of Herbert Read

The weather of living in an island
That is not an island in the ocean
Crackles in the hallway. What is salt
And ancient in us dries
To an inland heat. The Atlantic
Is a pond sunk in a garden,
A concrete mole has sealed the Aleutian vents
Browned already; only beside New Zealand
Perhaps do sobs refresh
A walled-up bind of waters.

Alfred in Athelney, Hereward in the Isle
Of Ely, learn to go mounted.

Tooling through second-growth Sherwood
In an Armstrong-Siddeley tourer,
Percheron of the 'twenties,
My grandfather unmeaning
Anything but well
Discharged his quiverful:
Aridity, and levels.

The anti-cyclone regions
Of population pressure,
Respondent to the pulse of
Asia, Arabia, Kansas,
Send out their motorized
Hordes, the freely breeding.

And the Age of Chivalry prinks
Pygmy-size to my daughter's
Gymkhana, though the Godolphin
Arabian has invaded
The forested, painfully cleared
Lands of the Clydesdale, the Suffolk
And the Shire horse, the old black English.
The great trees sail the oceans,
Spill acorns on Pitcairn Island.
And all of this is over.

The Break

after Pasternak

Break it off? Listen! we have left a jagged edge,
The whole place is infected.
Sad like this, one might as well be a leper.

Angel, my angel
Of double-talk, don't pretend:
Nobody dies of it. More like
A sort of eczema of the heart, a skin sore as
Your present at parting. What was that for? Why
Unconscionably do you
Kiss as the drops of rain do, and as time
Laughingly kills, for the lot of us, here, before us?

I am so ashamed, it is a weight upon me!
I know, I know, I tell myself, this break
(I made it too soon) it is tangled with illusory hopes.
I was man enough one day, nearly; except I was mixed
With lips and the hollows of your temples and
Eyes, cheeks, shoulders, the palms of your hands.

If I had only, then,
With the whistle of a strophe,
The sign that it makes, and the cry of it, and
That constant thing, my needing you, that young thing, had I only
Thrown in all these, they asked only to be committed,
I might have beaten you out of it there and then.
Such a disgrace to me as you are!

Take and block me, see if you cannot. Come
                              move in upon me, clamp
Down on this bout of my pain
                    that crepitates today
                              like mercury in Torricelli's tube.
Move in, move in – warm to it, come, harder!

I want to weave together
This choppy welter:
Chill elbows and the magisterial, satin,
Slack palms of your hands, my lady...
Bear down on them, arranger
Of regattas! Fast, and take them!
Masts in the ancient forests
In this furious follow give voice,
Fast-gorged with hallooing echoes
In Calydon, where Atalanta
Hounded like a fallow deer
The oblivious Actaeon gladeward;
Where in the illimitable
Blues there was a loving
That whistled in the ears of horses;
A kissing, the insistent
Ululation of the hunt;
And a caress, the trolling of the horn
To the crackle of the trees, of hooves and talons!

You thought you could count on distress, with her distended
Pupils, and tears, to be invincible?
In the Mass the murals were going to flake from the vault,
Jolted by some Horatio's lips performing?

This is a drag.
A flagellant is wanting the whip.
Your weeping capes, they might have clawed me home.

Amiable, moderate, my own, oh just as, just as at night,
                    in mid-passage by air from Bergen to the Pole,
Drifts, lofted and soft, the down
                    from the eider's shank lapping like snow,
I swear, my temperate friend, I swear I am nothing loath
When I say to you, 'Forget and fall asleep, my lovely.'

When like the ribs, fast-gripped to the very smoke-stack
                    of a lost barque out of Norway,
Her rimed unbudging masts surveyed by winter,
I rise before your boreal eyes
With jokey talk of 'Sleep, be comforted,'
All in good time, my dear, it will scab over.
                    Be calm then, and no tears.

When in all points like the North
                    past the ultimate habitations,
Unmarked across the Arctic and unwinking ice
With the dome of midnight swilling the seals' blind eyes
I speak up,
          do not rub them. Sleep, forget:
                    It is a nonsense really.

                    ★

Night falls when your head nods.
Everything lies down 'under thy sovran shoulders'.
Switch off the world's light. We have forced the isthmus,

Hand-spanned it, not in flakings! This will do:
The barque in the ice is fixed, the bright privation grips.

Pilate

The chief of the civil administration
                    of the occupying power reflects
in the forty-five minutes he allows himself each morning
over a cigarette for the world to
                    re-achieve its third dimension daily
(Saving shadows and memories
                    vine on his nerves' snapped trellis):

'Between the judicial and
                    the nervously judicious
the best of Rome bleeds
                    into the sands of Judaea.'

The best? Ho-hum. The keeping up of standards
(The right ones, Roman), how it sustained him once!

The harm it does him,
                    the practice of severity
which someone has to do, he
                    knows. He knows it. He is bad at it
in his own estimation, but
some one has to and
                    whether in good faith
is no problem:
                    You keep yourself busy,
too many cases in too little time and such
scruple as there is time for.

Aggressive-pusillanimous, the harm it
did him, and perhaps it does
                    any one is known to him, wherein
virtue perhaps. He has
nothing to show to be proud of
                    from his H.Q. years but rare
acts of intellectual
                    brutality: 'This is no good...'
'No, I will not...'
                    His
skills were not of that order
                    but being of no account
until perverted, they

                    patiently were perverted:
skills to the end of inspiring
emulation, that
                    ingenious artifice
called 'leadership' (and what
an orator he might have been, a
poet even) were
                    perverted to other ends,
to the end of sitting in judgement.

It is the lion of Judah is all claws.
Caiaphas has the style of the officer-class.

Skills to the end of finding
out short-circuited
                    in finding fault, he
knows. He knows it. He is bad at it.

But if it is all he finds with
certainty? The *pax*
Romana is worth something. His
                    wish to be lenient mimes
a charity he dare not
                    not respect but knows he
cannot profess.
                    He does not
in any event perceive
that for these responsible scruples
                    the *soi-disant* King of the Jews
has very much more forbearance
than His accusers.

Trevenen

1
His Return (Christmas, 1780)

Winds from Cook's Strait cannot blow
Hard enough to lift the snow
Already comfortably deep
Where Roseveare and Treyarnon sleep;

Knit to the centre from the far
Fastness of their peninsula,
The Cornish dream that distance can
Deliver their young gentleman
Unaltered to his mother's arms,
To be in rectories and farms,
Assembly-rooms and markets, shown
As the great Cook's and yet their own.
    Camborne's as certain as St James
That vocabulary tames
The most outlandish latitude;
That, at a pinch, to speak of rude
Hardihood will meet the case
And teach a Bligh to know his place;
And 'gallant' and 'ingenious' will
Confine their irrepressible
Midshipman who murders sleep,
Sprung from the London coach to heap
His hero-worship of the dead
Hero on each doting head.
    It would be years before he knew
Himself what it had brought him to;
What it had meant, his profiting
By the good offices of King
And Bligh, the mote-dance in the air
Of their vacated cabins where
Sea-glitters pulsed above his head
Bent to his books. And loving dread
Of his commander's furies taught
Lessons of another sort
If he could trust to having seen
How far from rational and serene
Command might be. When, at the oar
Under Cook's marginally more
Indulgent but still beetling eye,
He clawed a cutter round the high
Northwestern overhang, it meant
The profile of a continent.
So much he knew, and knew with pride;
And yet he was not satisfied,
Not now, nor later. But for now
He chatters to his mother how
Captain King he can instate

As the dead Cook's surrogate:
King, with his connections; King
In Ireland now and finishing
The narrative of the fatal cruise
(Awaited, though no longer news);
King, and his kindness (Bligh, the spurned,
Unconnected patron, burned
With a jealousy that seared
King's account, when it appeared,
With marginalia…); King, whose eyes
Smiled on skill and enterprise
Such as young Trevenen knew
He could boast, and ardour too;
Sweet James King, whom more than one
Hawaiian wanted for a son;
King, then (and so the plaudits end)
At once a mentor and a friend,
Rare composite of gall and balm,
Skilful to command and charm.

     Thus, mixed with talk of azimuth
And quadrant, to confound Redruth,
Trevenen, merrily enough,
Talks of how it merits love,
Some men's authority; and some
Clerical auditors keep mum,
Shocked to know how near they come
To greeting (so enthralled they are)
With an impious 'huzzah'
Such a sublime condition as
They've pressed on their parishioners
As more than human. 'Well, but no,'
They tell themselves, 'the boy don't know
How near he grazes Gospel-truth.
Brave spirit of ingenuous youth!'
And so they huff and puff it home
With (to their wives) 'Come, madam, come!'
Their wives and daughters half aware
Dear Papa has an absent air.

     It troubles him, as well it might,
To see in such resplendent light
Mortal redeemers crowd upon
A stage that should be cleared for One,
That One, Divine. There was some doubt

Whether Cook had been devout;
Though as to that one could not feel
Happy with excess of zeal,
Remembering saintly Wesley whose
Vexatiousness had emptied pews
Down all the stolid Duchy, packed
Gwennap Pit, and loosed in fact
Who knew what furies in deluded
Tin-mine Messiahs? So he brooded,
The honest rector. As for that,
He thought, there's worse to wonder at:
Wrong principles inflame and spread
When they aureole a head
Rank has exalted more than those
Who merely by their talents rose.
Thus, nothing's more alarming than
That too warm Christian gentleman,
Lord George Gordon, the inspired
And loved authority that fired
Prison and church, and did not spare
Lord Mansfield's house in Bloomsbury Square...
'Bah!' he thought, 'what has all this
To do with young men's loyalties?'

2

Life and Contacts (1784–7)

The poet Crabbe, with whom he shared
Burke as patron, never cared
(It appears) to throw a frame
Round the poems that made his fame.
There, as if through window-glass,
Men like James Trevenen pass
Plain and unflattered. Never mind
Asking what poetic kind
Crabbe's tales belong to; they escape
Any predetermined shape,
Comic, heroic, or whatever.
Pointing morals was, however,
Crabbe's substitute. Subtitled 'Or
Hero-worship', would a more
Rationally pleasing piece,
With less of oddity and caprice

In the conduct of it, come
Of this that we're embarked upon?
Hardly: morals underlined
Outrage our taste. Besides, my mind
Is far from made up in this case
About what moral we should trace
In a story that is more
Painful than I've prepared you for.
– First, the untimely death of King.
His malady was lingering,
And yet it did not take very long
Once it attacked the second lung.
Then, the death of brother Matt
At twenty-three, beleaguered at
Okehampton in the inn, who trolled,
'Unlike the ladies of the old
Times', his song; 'their hue unfaded
That needed no calash to shade it…'
The light young tenor 'of the old
Times, the old ancient ladies' told,
Echoing in a brother's head
Cracked gaiety, the singer dead.
       A man, thus severally bereaved,
Labours not to be deceived
By smiling seas of Life, nor Art's
Flattering pledge to furnish charts.
And no such suave commitment mars
Crabbe, the realist *sans phrase*…
Perhaps had Johnson lived, whose pen
Tinkered with *The Village,* then
Some one had upheld the claims
Of spectacles defined by frames,
Or songs like Matthew's, set to airs
Traditional at country fairs;
But Johnson died, unwept by most,
And left, to rule the sprawling roost,
Crabbe's earnest, just, unfocussed page
As prolix model to an age
Which, fed on ornament, would brook
Pindaric Odes to Captain Cook
And, stretched on Ossian, did not shirk
Orations paced by Fox and Burke:
Splendid, sublime and fervent, strong

In argument, but long, but long.
    Apart from that, it can be shown
To have been an age much like our own;
As lax, as vulgar, as confused;
Its freedoms just as much abused;
Where tattle stole a hero's thunder,
His death a thrill, and nine days' wonder;
Where personalities were made,
And makers of them plied a trade
Profitable and esteemed;
Where that which was and that which seemed
Were priced the same; where men were duped
And knew they were, and felt recouped
By being town-talk for a day,
Their Gothic follies on display;
Where (and here the parallel
Comes home, I hope, and hurts as well)
Few things met with such success
As indignant righteousness.
    Burke's the paradigm of this,
Hissing at enormities
In India, at Westminster-hall
(Holy debauch, a free-for-all);
A man of principle, not able
(Like Fox, who had the gaming-table
To share his heart with politics)
To guard against the squalid tricks
That Tender Conscience and Just Rage
Play, when on a public stage;
Not keeping, in his fevered heart,
Passion and Principle apart;
But purchasing his never too
Much honoured sense of what was due
To private merit and indeed
Domestic virtue, by a need
To compensate for his serene
Privacies by public spleen…
    To King, the friend of Irish friends,
Burke gives a bed, and Jane Burke tends
His hopeless case. And King's release
Comes in that same year, in Nice,
Whither Trevenen had, with one
Other, conveyed him, to the sun.

The Burkes had sent him; and he rode
Back to them, slowly, overshadowed
Thenceforward, always, by a sense
Of human life's inconsequence.
    No man more worthy of his trust,
It might be thought – nor, if he must
Still worship, of his worship – than
The great, good Anglo-Irishman,
Edmund Burke. Secure within
That circle, guest of Inchiquin
At Cliefden, or else entertained
At Gregories itself, he gained
Dubious information how
Iniquitous were Pitt and Howe;
How unregarded was the merit
Of Cook, of King; how to inherit
Their mantle meant he must not hope
For advancement of much scope.
At other times the conversation
Was a liberal education
In men and manners; how Lord George
Gordon, once again at large
(Though, some years before, expelled
From this circle) was impelled
By honour when for the disbanded
Mariners he had demanded,
The year before, some action such
As could have shipped them for the Dutch;
How Cowper, in *The Task,* confessed
To remaining unimpressed
By the reasons given for
Incursions on Tahiti's shore;
How fractious Barry must be borne with,
Painting lineaments of myth
For all his tantrums, the antique
Burning his style down to the Greek;
How Nollekens had little sense
Of decency, yet could dispense
With it, to mould a *busto;* how
Cagliostro made his bow;
How civil good Sir Joshua was,
And Admiral Saunders; how, across
A field from where they sat, was found

The plot of venerable ground
Where slippery Waller lay; and how
Illiberal was Pitt, was Howe...
　　　Small wonder if his head was turned,
If a renewed resentment burned
In him to sell his rusting sword
Wherever sovereigns could afford
Ensigns announcing to the gale
Citizens of the world in sail.
Bligh gets the *Bounty,* and not he;
He's pledged himself to Muscovy.

3

His End (The Battle of Viborg, 21 June 1790)

Long, splendid shadows! Cornwall, lit
Bronze in the evening, levels it
Off, and pays all; the yea or nay
Of switched allegiance, as the day
Dies on the old church-tower, seems
A dilemma of our dreams
Which, however urgent once,
Awake we need not countenance.
The gilding beams that reconcile
This antique issue, can for mile
On cloud-racked mile slant on, to reach
Amber on a Baltic beach...
Apollonian, reconciling
Art, that is drenched in tears, yet smiling!
Persuading us to think all's one,
Lit by a declining sun.
　　　Not for George Crabbe! His it is
To give untinged veracities;
And, though it's Christian, this indeed
Our baffled heroes seem to need,
Moving to their wasteful ends,
Betrayed by principles and friends –

　　　Cold and pain in the breast,
　　　Fatigue drives him to rest.
　　　Rising, 'to open a new
　　　Source of comfort to you'
　　　(Writing to his wife

The last night of his life),
Captain Trevenen, sick,
Wears on no other tack,
Aware man's born to err,
Inclined to bear and forbear.
Pretence to more is vain.
Chastened have they been.
Hope was the tempter, hope.
Ambition has its scope
(Vast: the world's esteem);
Hope is a sickly dream.
And seeking, while they live,
Happiness positive
Is sinful. Virtue alone –
This they have always known –
Is happiness below.
Therefore, she is to know,
Whatever is, is right.
That solid, serious light
Shall reconcile her to
Candidacy below
For where his sails are furled,
Far from fame and the world.

Camborne's rector would have seen
Comfort in the ghastly scene,
There in the British burial-ground
In summery Kronstadt, had he found
His son so firm, and yet so meek.
So truly Christian, truly bleak
The sentiments a man should speak,
Meeting his Maker! In our eyes
A man we cannot recognize
As Burke's or King's accomplished friend,
Cowed mumbler from the sealed-off end
Of Celtic England, glares and points;
And this raw difference disjoints
Our and Elegy's specious frame,
Framing all our deaths the same
(Our loves, our worships, levelled in
The eyes of Art, that Jacobin).
　　Lord George Gordon! he was found
Worshipful, the country round,

Some years before. Now no one hears
His civilly enounced ideas
Without reserve. But when, as host,
He gives his Radicals their toast,
'Mr Burke! who has afforded
Grounds for discussion', he's applauded.
And, sure enough, we may well find
Burke and the Jacobins of one mind,
One self-same ruinous frame, unless
We recollect that Burke could bless
Those death-bed words from one whose head
He may have turned, whom he misled:
  'Though Will finds worldly scope,
   We have no earthly hope.'
Edmund Burke had cried, 'Amen!'
And James King, and most other men.

Vancouver

Nobody's hero, George Vancouver, ever;
Never a woman in his life, and never
Given a thing but money. Out of luck
Out of mind, he saw no medal struck
To celebrate a second Captain Cook
Come home, in him. The only way he gained
Some jeering notice was by being caned
Publicly, off Piccadilly. Yes,
Some mystery there… biographers suppress
The incident as best they can. All told
No, no Cook. Who loved him, who extolled,
Who even liked him? An enduring glory
For Riou, Trevenen… that's another story;
Fierce Welshman, David Samwell made that claim.
And yet Vancouver's shouldered them out of fame.
  It seems he was not likeable; he made
What friends he had by a prudential trade
Of courtesies across interpreters
With his Peruvian or Andorran betters
In Spanish-speaking California, when
He warmed to Quadra or to Lasuèn.
True, he spoke of Hergest as a friend,

Whom he had known with Cook. But Hergest's end
(One of the band, Trevenen's friend and Riou's)
Lifts the record of Vancouver's cruise
Almost to myth; it makes Vancouver look
More than ever like a ghost of Cook,
Weird revenant to North Pacific air,
A presence, and yet humanly not there.
  Oahu saw poor Hergest re-enact
A play that he had sat through once. Attacked
No one knows why, and clubbed to death, he suffered
Cook's fate in duplicate. Only the island differed,
Hawaii killed them both, as if it meant
To kill the one man twice; and then a spent
Bloodless simulacrum called Vancouver,
That went through resolute motions, was left over,
A living corpse with mortal sickness on it.
(So it proved.) The double duty done it,
Freed or placated, some one's spirit fled
The expedition and its ailing head
When Hergest died.
     What nonsense! Still, it's queer,
The way the thing repeats itself; a mere
Re-run, let's say, as if Time struck a groove,
Stuck there, and rhymed, and then began to move
Clack-clack, and jerkily.
      It's less than just,
This, to Vancouver. His persistent thrust
Was crucial, and to come; the dying man
Drove, and would drive, his boat-crews, and a plan
To its fulfilment on the charts. Moreover
The drive comes though, the ruthlessness. Vancouver
Was harsh, and human; rage, tongue-lashings… Thus,
Just thus however, Cook *redivivus*
Would run a taut ship – on his third and last,
His fatal cruise, not many weeks went past
Without Cook's raging. Thus it might be shown
Even Vancouver's faults were not his own.
  The only difference was, Cook never came
Home to be caned in Conduit Street? Ill-fame,
A savage dog called Gillray, only bayed
Meat on the hoof? Not quite. He was afraid,
He must have been, Vancouver, riding home
Goitred and stiff. He knew it had to come,

Caning, or something like it. He'd transgressed
The cardinal unwritten law of caste,
Flogged the young gentleman – it was more than Cook
Had done, or dared. And, to be brought to book
For the transgression, he'd compounded it
By flogging, of all midshipmen, a Pitt,
The dangerous puppy, Camelford! There it is:
The mystery. For these audacities
What rhyme or reason? Say he was a sadist
(Which no one says), why should that nasty twist
Have sought its objects among officers
And settled on milord? The emphasis
Is obvious, and suicidal. True,
The man had been at sea for twenty-two
Years of his forty… out of touch, and yet
Not just, it's plain, an old-style martinet
Of his own quarterdeck, but some one more
Conscious of what he gambled, and what for.

      What for, if not authority? High play,
With that at stake, was common in that day:
Camelford himself, in English Bay,
Antigua, in seventeen-ninety-eight
Shot a man dead, to vindicate
His dubious seniority; and for
Mutineers of Spithead and the Nore
Courts-martial daily, hangings. This in fact
Must have saved Vancouver, when attacked
By and over Camelford. Command,
The sanctity of it, had to seem to stand,
Where possible, that year. So, in disgrace
And made to feel it, he can save his face,
And Camelford is interceded with,
Bought off, or cowed. A shabby end to myth
And to a life: no trumpets, but the sly
Susurrus of accommodations by
Pitt and his placemen – Dundas, Wedderburn –
Makes hugger mugger of a chief's return.

      Theirs was the authority he wanted,
The white whip-hands. I venture he resented,
As certainly Trevenen did, the way
Cook and his services were filed away,
And by the Pitts, the Wedderburns. No doubt
The stolid Dutchman never worked it out

(He named a creek for Wedderburn), and yet
Cook was the model he would not forget,
He'd sworn as much. Thus, loyalty to Cook
Could have been what impelled him, when he took
The whip to Camelford, and challenged Pitt
And gauged the outcome, and raged through with it.

If this is special pleading, let's admit
Vancouver needs the benefit, and may claim it;
We put the best construction that we can
On an unfriendly and a friendless man.

Commodore Barry

When Owen Roe
O'Sullivan sang Ho
For the hearts of oak
Of broken Thomond, though
Weevils and buggery should
Have wormed the wooden walls
More than De Grasse's cannon,
The sweetest of the masters
Of Gaelic verse in his time,
Lame rhymester in English, served
And laurelled Rodney's gun.

Available as ever
Implausibly, the Stuart
Claimed from the Roman stews
His sovereignty *de jure;*
But Paddy, in the packed
Orlop, the *de facto*
Sovereignty of ordure,
King George's, had to hedge
His bet upon a press
Of white legitimist sail
Off Kinsale, some morning.

A flurry of whitecaps off
The capes of the Delaware!
Barry, the Irish stud,
Has fathered the entire
American navy! Tories
Ashore pore over the stud-book,
Looking in vain for the mare,
Sovran, whom Jolly Roger
Of Wexford or Kildare
Claims in unnatural congress
He has made big with frigates.

Loyalists rate John
Paul Jones and Barry, traitors;
One Scotch, one Irish, pirate.
In Catherine the Great's
Navy, her British captains
Years later refused to sail with
The Scot-free renegade. Jones
And Barry took the plunge
Right, when the sovereigns spun;
Plenty of Irish pluck
Called wrong, was not so lucky.

'*My* sovereign,' said saucy
Jack Barry, meaning Congress;
And yes, it's true, outside
The untried, unstable recess
Of the classroom, every one has one:
A sovereign – general issue,
Like the identity-disc,
The prophylactic, the iron
Rations. Irony fails us,
Butters no parsnips, brails
No sail on a ship of the line.

Lady Cochrane

Before the House of Lords, 24 July 1862

That honoured name!
       Hero of a hundred fights!
A man who could have ruled
the world upon the sea…
       She cannot bear
       to be sitting there
to vindicate the name
for ages and for ages
'has run the World with his deeds'.

Once too often he had fenced
With the Commons, when, incensed,
       Coldly they saw depart
       Their pocket Bonaparte.
Nor would their chiefs, though too obtuse
To recognize in him a loose
       Bold travesty upon
       Cast down Napoleon
(Their fiercer Cromwell, now immured
On St Helena, and secured
       By sloop and spyglass), grieve
       To see rash Cochrane leave.

'Hero of a hundred fights!
I have stood upon the battledeck.
I have seen men fall. I have raised them.
I have fired a gun to save a man.
For the honour of my husband, I would do it again.'

So liberated Chile bought
The impenitent class-traitor out:
       The stormy petrel planes
       Again the ocean-lanes!

'Yes, I did assent
to accompany him to Scotland.'
– What time did you leave London? –
'The evening of the sixth of August
eighteen hundred and twelve.'

– How did you travel? It is
unimportant? –
                        'Yes, it is unimportant.'
– With great speed, with four horses? –
'Sometimes, sometimes with two
as we could, night and day.
He named Carlisle and several other towns.
I was tired, worn. I was young.'

Demonic syren–voices choired
From St Helena, as the hired
        Condottiere sailed
        Past impetus that failed.
O'Higgins then, and San Martin
Await him, in the Alpine, keen
        Air they have burned through, all
        Singed by an Empire's fall.

'A sort of pet name of his own
he had for me, and he said:
"It is all right, Mouse.
Mouse, we are over the Border."
He said: "You are mine for ever."
He snapped his fingers the way
that Scotchmen do
when they are pleased. I arrived
at Annan on the evening of the eighth,
and when I arrived at the Queensberry Arms
he was very joyous; I suppose
men in love are. He said:
"It is all right, it is all right."
He sat himself down as any gentleman might:
"I came here, Dick, to be married
and this is my wife," turning to me; and he bowed.'

Look! Abashed, the Portuguese
Are scoured in one year from the seas:
        So much one man can do
        That does, and knows not how.
Brazil, a Lusitanian mouth,
Can best acclaim, and will, the South
        American Lafayette,
        And pay at last her debt;

And shall she weakly countermand,
To one grown stiffer in command,
      His licence to hold sway
      Who will, at will, obey?
Does genius not inscribe and fill
Time's empty page with eagle's quill?
      So, when the albatross
      Has fished, and sailed across
One mast and tossing ensign, will
The flag direct him where to kill
      Next, in the self-sought, clear
      Taut arc of his career?

'After the paper was signed
and the servants gone, he began
to dance the Sailor's Hornpipe.
He put his hands up, so,
and "Now you are mine," he said.
– You marry like this in Scotland? –
"Oh yes," he said, "you are mine.
I have no time to spare, I have no time to lose.'
He kissed me, he did not go
into my room, and he went off as he came.'

– I understand your ladyship
to say it was in order
not to displease his Uncle,
from whom he had expectations,
he kept his marriage a secret? –
'Entirely so. By a secret
marriage he would avoid
this fortune going away.'

Still voluble, still undeterred,
Our Cochranes keep their cloudy word:
      The same arts that did gain
      Them power, their power maintain,
Though thou, the war's and Fortune's son,
Terse Napoleon, bend upon
      Play-acting pitched so high
      A veiled, sardonic eye.

'The old lady there, in the house
spoke a very broad Scotch. I never
heard Scotch before. I said
(I was but young you know,
perhaps a little pert)…
I said: "What kind of place
do you call this?"
                        She said:
"The Queensberry Arms at Annan.

'I have stood on the battledeck…
I would do it again…' the voice
defensive and defiant.

OTHER POEMS OF THE 1960s

England, for Ezra Pound

'Chesterton's England of has-been and why-not'
(Ezra Pound, *Canto LXXX*)

Aquitaine, England's loss,
Maurice Hewlett drove across
That Christmas. It was Pound
Saw the English underground
Angevin. Yellow grain
From the bone springs again
This summer, in defaced
Surrey, and Hampshire's waste.

Whose land this is, is there none of these parts
To say, and call him suzerain?

Southampton to Carlisle
Hugh Casson found the style
Uniform, England's boast
Common from coast to coast;
Plate glass and frosted glass,
Caving grange, poisoned fosse;
Green holly and the dancers
Far as the fields of France.

Grain in grange shall no men's hearts
Swell, but the dead of those parts.

The light for Grosseteste
Corporeally pressed
England; and everywhere
Motes in the thickened air.
Constable's summers spiced
A loaf of honey sliced
By minsters' towers. Where
Now the gold and the vair?

Where now should a Bishop of Lincoln
Through the smoke learn light's behaviour?

T.S. Eliot (1928)

'Peut-être qu'une fois de plus la couronne d'or nous serait présentée comme elle le fut à César.'
(Maurras, *L'avenir de l'intelligence*)

L'avenir de l'intelligence
Was where? Was in whose head? Jefferson's?
Has Calvin Coolidge heard of it? We go back
To the second President, his term aborted,
President Adams whom the young Republic
Put out of office when he would have taught
Uses for emulation. It is Spring.
Beyond the Mississippi the snow melts
At last, and at the edges of small towns
As the chill sun westers in the silence, streets
Are streets of lake-pavillions, where the shadows
In the long yards are water or else like water.

And that would have been the time for it, before
The open door and the squalid openings westward
Postponed, dissolved, and obviated. Spring!
When the Atlantic states were all the states,
Their Cincinnatus, Washington. When Adams
Writes of the laticlave, augusticlave
And praetext; and the chairs of ivory;
Also the civil and the mural crowns
Of gold; of ivory; of flowers; of
Herbs; of laurel branches; and of oak leaves,
Adams and Washington are the names of streets
Where one rides by, his eyes indifferent, watchful ...
'He that has power to hurt and will do none.'

John Adams quoted Shakespeare, and that's much.
One gropes to a theory of the potentate
As cynosure. The dog's tail wags the dog
'Whose worth's unknown although his height be taken.'

Was ever better use made of the passion
For consideration than the Romans made?
Adams asked, thinking of stone and bronze.
Consideration (or to be of note)
Is it a passion? Adams said it was,
And universal. Not in England. There
To be distinguished is a kind of horror
For the many whose strength is union.

And whose hand shot McKinley? If the realm
Is all a spectacle, the North Star even
(Called 'cynosure', that's 'dog's tail', in the Greek),
Assassin is a civic dignity.

Columbian Minerva! See the purchased
Scholars and wits of the Old World perform
Gladiatorial for your famished young!
In a Republic no one knows his place.

Cowper's 'Yardley Oak': A Continuation

for Raymond Williams

            'History, not wanted yet,
Lean'd on her elbow, watching Time, whose course,
Eventful, should supply her with a theme; –'

Nor wanted now. Space and Geography
Call the disoriented Briton out
From History's disabling truth, lost acres,
And her disabling fiction, a lost virtue.

Whether with Cook or in the mind, as once
Th'improvident first gatherers, clad in bark,
Were over-arch'd and sponsored by their oaks,
So with a new unthrift Crusoe casts off,
Bound for who knows what waiting, watching headland!

Midsummer's Eve

Now I am afraid for a child,
Embowered and my own,
Running ahead, alone,
Through night-shade rank and wild;

And, seeing the evening shade
That gathers in Turpin's Lane
Is John Clare come again
To England, I am afraid.

A boy who gashed his shin
Mowing in Russia before
The Revolution, swore
A voice drove the scythe-blade in;

And I have feared all along
The clear voice suddenly raised
In a waveringly phrased
Archaic reapers' song.

August, 1968

I discover in myself
To my own surprise, conviction;
I would not die for it
Naturally, but
Unnaturally I find
To my gratification I would
Lose friends and comrades for it.

History is not
A Nietzschean poet, and
Posterity, its creature,
Will never reprimand
Dubcek or Mayor Daley
For not having embraced
Wholeheartedly and gaily
The roles that History gave them.

But Destiny is. And that
Discredited tribunal
Takes as no sign of grace
A dubious, a lowering
Or apprehensive gaze
Turned upon events.
It seeks its own: a stony,
Unmoved, inflexible face.

Why I should be depressed
To think that we shall stand
Before no other bar
Than History's faded eyes,
I do not understand;
Thinking somewhere a higher
Court is in session both
Contents and terrifies.

In San Francisco where
Through the Golden Gate is shipped
Daily a people-burning
Preparation, the Christian
Church, as is said 'that great
Harlot', is passing away,
So Czeslaw Milosz says.
And I have no quarrel with that.

But I would call it God,
That court in perpetual session.
(And where's the harm?) It must
Be of impartial stone,
But wrinkle a little or sweat
At certain kinds of crime.
For, please, it has to suffer
With us, from time to time.

Energies

Night frost glitter glazes
Under the moon the firs.
Junipers creak with it,
The jet hills rife with bears.

Night long a high canal
Launches the overspill
Cascades a cobbled hill
At thudding intervals.

Vapours veil a cave.
A head with a cock's comb wags
Across the aperture.
It gropes for milk and eggs.

The votive mass recruits
Deity's spent force,
King Cobra's, that can sprint
Fast as a running horse.

A match of motions comes
Clean in ancient scores;
Old men with gong, bronze bell
And flute yoke snake with horse.

The fiddle is hired to play
Emphatic jovial airs.
Against a wedding day
Winds rock the house all night.

Boyhood Misremembered

It needs there to be no one
Left on Market Hill
But a boy, for out by Smithies
The thunderhead that shelves
Its far slateblue over small
Lit farms in the east, to be dealt with
Smilingly; nor is there
Need of more than his hand
Sketching a smudged goodbye,
For the towering weather to edge
Clear of the pinkish mild
Expanse of the smoky acres.

It was by Hoylandswaine
Or making towards Ingbirchworth
Not Thurgoland, as I had it,
We came to the ancient shippon.
Fancy my forgetting!
I had remembered or
Fancied I had remembered
Leading the hay, the smell
Of poppies. Yes. So far then
Oblivion extends
Its slateblue ledge, so soon it
Shafts its unearthly russets.

Fatherhood

Though love is the word a mother
Has earned the monopoly of,
A man with a twenty-year-old
Son has the right to say
In a grandmother's idiom, harshly:
'All children grow away.'

For a child grown is a child lost;
Grown up is grown away.
'Christopher Waddams is dying,'
You wrote to me today.
He was a bird-like bachelor,
Fellow of my college.

A sad thing, dying childless.
And yet a father of three,
Though the three have kept in touch
And given him cause for pride,
Dies as alone as ever
A Cambridge bachelor died.

Reticence

Provided for! Provided for,
All of it, the horns
Drawn in, the drinking habits
Perfected, years ago;
In the expensive dawns,
The afterpleasure of
With difficulty rising and
Over his toast to know
This was provided for!

His devious compensations
Paying off, his pride
Force-fed to make the gross
Savouries of his silence;
Provisions made and made
Over the years, he comes
Into his own with an iron
Regimen over his drams:
Anger, malice, and tears.

SIX EPISTLES TO EVA HESSE

First Epistle

Not, I keep being told, the Time
That gets to me in one straight line
But (I knew this had to come)
A Space-cum-Time continuum;
A field of (wouldn't you know it?) force,
Not that dumb clockwork Time of course –
This and not that I should be writing,
Every one tells me. It's exciting
Stuff, all right (this Time, I mean),
A sort of poet's plasticine;
We get a date wrong – what's the odds?
We're not historians but gods.
Yet some of it seems resistant stuff
Still, and linear enough.
Trade routes like so much knotted string
Stretch out across the charts, and bring
John Jacob Astor, La Pérouse
And Captain Cook into the news
'That stays news', poetry; in fact
Into geography, the intact
Oregon of their future where
Now in our past they haunt the air,
Faint and limp from long ago.
But although some one says we grow,
If we are poets, like a tree
Through ring on ring of history
Back into our past, instead
Of getting sun to get ahead,
Still, string or insulated wire,
Conducting trade, conducting fire,
Has a sort of truth that brings
Electric saws to redwood rings.
Oilmen and their bankers stage
This very day in Anchorage
Alaska something that no doubt
Time to come will level out…

Another string, another knot...
It looks like meaning, but it's not.
Instead it's news, and it will stay,
Though not so long as poems may.
Transcending's fine, but then we might
As well get what's transcended right;
No one is going to mount a stair
Planted in what isn't there.
No, Madam, Pound's a splendid poet
But a sucker, and we know it.

Given a set of random pegs –
Five fingers, or a chair's four legs –
You can do a lot with string,
And turn it into anything:
A double helix, say (and that
We know we have to goggle at);
A Manxman's three free-wheeling legs,
Although that asks a lot of pegs;
A swastika; a hammer and
Sickle; or an ampersand.
Come, given fingers deft as Madam's,
I'll outmatch Del Mar or Brooks Adams.

No, look! Unravel it, the thing,
When all is said and done, is string.
Can it, to take an instance, be
Any help, remembering three
Incentives from the Polar North,
The Northmen's three adventures forth
(I'm paraphrasing Olson now)
In the tenth century, and how
His three legs (Manxman, take a bow)
Went West, East, South – can this, I say
Help with that best of Hudson's Bay
Arctic travellers, John Rae?
Norseman from Orkney, was his fate
To come eight centuries too late?
For sanity's sake, what can it mean,
Skipping the centuries between?
Confound it, history... we transcend it
Not when we agree to bend it
To this cat's cradle or that theme

But when, I take it, we redeem
This man or that one. La Pérouse
Lives when he's no longer news.

Moreover (it's an obvious point)
Strings webbed from every fingerjoint
Mean hands that cannot grasp at all.
('Enslave''s the meaning of 'enthrall!'.)

Thinking along these lines (You see?
We're trapped in linearity),
I'm in a bind, hung up between
The Aesthete and the Philistine.
Now, bind is what cat's-cradlers do
And cradles are suspended too,
And when the wind blows the cradle will fall
And down will come baby, bathwater and all,
And therefore it appears to me
The question has some urgency.
Mum who muttered, 'This place looks
Like Troy-town', didn't know the books
That tell what troy-towns are, nor had
She found it in the *Iliad*.
Contented in her heedlessness,
All she meant was, 'It's a mess';
And that's a sense to which we come
Sooner from 'ruined Ilium'
Than from the eighty-year-old *opus*
Die Trojaburgen Nordeuropas,
Which says the troy-town was a maze
Or labyrinthine dancing-place,
A spiralling of little fosses
Copied in Somerset from Knossos,
Where feet upon the Blackdown Hills
Practised Daedalian rites and skills…
– A pretty picture, but suppose
Woodhenge and Stonehenge framed on those,
As nowadays it's thought they may be,
Will that cat's-cradle hold our baby?
I mean, for instance, this Byronic
Writing keeps architectonic
Principles entirely other
Than those so sadly missed by Mother;

Woefully linear, not to say
Rambling. Now, is this a way
To write, from now on quite uncouth,
Not qualified to tell the truth?
Henceforward must a poem twist
Back on itself, or be dismissed?
Or has it as much to do with us,
Constructing towns and epics thus
By spirals round themselves as, say,
Eirik Bloodaxe with John Rae?

Of course it may be said, and should,
That there is no more likelihood
Of worthy characters like Mother
Reading the one poem than the other,
With not much time for either. So
Why not write for those who know
What troy-towns are, and can rehearse
How Woodhenge breathes Projective Verse?
True. And yet one might insist:
What of the biophysicist?
The Muse has better things to do,
We may suppose, than bridge the Two
Cultures, but it wouldn't hurt her
To make her Araby less Deserta.
Will Crick cry, having read Christine
Brooke-Rose, 'Why, this is where I've been!
My new-found-land! Arabia felix!
This poem is a double helix'?
Will Watson, spurning from his desk
Anything that's Audenesque,
Exclaim, 'At last I'm catered for!
I like *Piers Plowman* more and more'?

No, but seriously, though
Spirals may make the whole thing go,
The way we got so fast so far
(Boring I know, but there we are)
Must be a linear affair;
Like any track from here to there,
Evolution is a thing
We picture as a length of string.

What irks me, if I have to pin it
Down is, There are no knots in it;
Everything's news, so nothing's news,
And that's bad news for La Pérouse,
Rae, Cook, or any name you choose.
I'm saying, I suppose, that Man
Leaves me cold, though Sid and Stan,
Distinguished individuals, awe me.
(Jonathan Swift said this before me.)
Yet if we hold in one equation,
As types of human adaptation,
The *polis* of Byzantium
And the distinctly separate thumb
(Expedients both to grasp and shape
Experience, beyond the ape);
I mean, if Evolution's not
Over when Man begins to plot
His emergence from his past
(A linear scheme still, first and last);
If, too, it is not Man but some
Named men by whom the breakthroughs come –
Why, then Biology makes shift
To come to terms with me and Swift.
(News, even so, is all we've got;
It looks like meaning, but it's not.)

Teleology, an upright
Darwinian, gave the Church a fright
By saying Nature works towards ends;
'It is *as if* she did,' contends
Teleonomy, his cliff-
Hanging cousin. And 'as if'
(That smart young cousin knows the score!)
Gives us the break we'd waited for.
Thus Comedy – which is all I'm after,
I want to raise no Cain but laughter –
Has raising laughter for its aim,
But aim and end are not the same.
A laying peacefully to rest
Is how one critic has expressed
The end of comedy. (If it's true,
This should be happening to you.)
But 'end', as Aristotle saw,

Implies some things that go before;
Beginnings, middles… and those are
Inextricably linear.

Therefore (for now these laughs may tend
Towards their term, if not their end)
I give you meaning, and not news:
Jean François, Comte de la Pérouse,
A person singularly winning.
And to begin with his beginning,
It was in Albi, where a square
(I first made his acquaintance there)
Holds him in effigy. For his
Youth, see the French biographies.
Take him in 1782:
That year his sails lift into view
In Hudson's Bay at Churchill Fort,
Which place he takes – an exploit fraught
(And here see History's comic sense)
With no long-lasting consequence;
But worth remembering, none the less,
For something we may call *finesse,*
And that not least in how he treated,
Civilly, those he had defeated.
To prove the civilizing role
Of France, he next, in 'La Boussole'
With 'L'Astrolabe', sets sail from Brest
To vie with Cook in searching West.
He rounds the Horn and gets his fix
(This is in 1786)
Upon Hawaii. Thence the Count
Makes headway north as far as Mount
St Elias, Alaska; reaches
After that, by pine-fringed beaches
On French leave southwards to survey
The coast as far as Monterey.
After that, Macao and
Manila draw him out, as planned.
A strait is named for him, between
Hokkaido and Sakhalin.
Kamchatka then, Samoa, Tonga,
Botany Bay. And then no longer
The grizzled admiral stems the seas.
He's lost off the New Hebrides.

There, I propose, we let him sleep,
Rocked in the cradle of the deep
Compassionate and comic Muse
Who, smiling, makes for La Pérouse
Friendlier lullabies than sing
Round epic cradles made of string.

Second Epistle

I'm going on with this affair;
Enough of comedy and to spare
In the history of the North
Western fur-trade and so forth...
Oh, but you've got there, Olson! Wait,
Miss Hesse, I must interpolate...
Olson in a magazine
Explains what his cat's-cradles mean;
Each is, he says, a *trampoline*
'Trampolines, nets or mattings we
Stand in...' It makes sense to me;
His knots in history he intends
That we should take as means towards ends.
The strings of Time are to be plaited
Like woven canvas, bound or matted
Into (these are Olson's glosses)
A vibrant standing-place to toss us
Into who knows what upper air?
(Thus elated, who would care?)
How he bounces! Look how high!
Olson, you're the Malachi
Stilt-jack of our times, all right,
On stilts that spring you out of sight!

Oh yes, I like that. And it's time
I used a Yankee paradigm.
Shall I, I ask myself, desert
Frenchmen and such and, to avert
Any chauvinistic odium,
Lead Charles Olson to the podium?

No. 'Hero' is, however meant,

A title too ambivalent
To give a man whom in the end
I would rather call a friend.
Brief holdings after years of hope…
Heroes come dear to those who cope
With the aftermath of crisis
Or shock that follows their demises.
Still I confess I have them, clutch
At some I recognize as such…
Moreover I'm prepared to find
Their peers in regions of the mind;
Although here too I must confess a
Preference for the adroit successor
Or stout lieutenant over such
Minds as originate too much.
And Comedy suits this predilection;
Plainly, a quizzical inflection
Is always to be heard when she
Presents 'Our hero' to your scrutiny.
So with the man I have in mind;
Protagonist of a modest kind.
And if this paladin I choose
Seems to be French, like La Pérouse,
Why, History upon my plan
Is always a comedian;
And what's more comic than a scene
Where never Frenchman might have been
To plant a fort or write a sonnet,
For all the mark he's left upon it,
Place-names the one persisting, slim
And unpronounceable sign of him?
(I speak of places further South
Than the St Lawrence or its mouth.)
Anyhow, though you'll think this man
French, he is Italian.
Let me present, my verse still jaunty,
Gallicized, Henri de Tonty;
Who earned a fate I cannot choose
But think much worse than La Pérouse
In that, true mate and faithful friend,
He made too late too mild an end
Too quietly. For, like the priest,
The Muse, the Epic Muse at least,

Hopes for an edifying death
And hangs upon our last-drawn breath.
And even Comedy, it's certain,
Likes to ring down a strong last curtain.
(Though Horace taught her she must laud
A Sabine farm, in fact she's bored
With solid worth and modest ease,
Can't see the Bloody Wood for trees;
For we must make it very plain
The Comic Muse is no Plain Jane
And, never quite at home in Boston,
She wasn't always called Jane Austen.)
Moreover – here I interpose
What, like much else, is really prose –
Tonty was, I must relate,
Peculiarly unfortunate:
Geography could not abide him,
Her memorials were denied him.
Backed as he was by the Prince de Conti,
Lake Erie should have been Lac Tonty,
And Fort Niagara was a name
Supplanting on the rolls of fame
Fort Tonty. Thus we see that maps
Fool us as History does, perhaps.
Or else, Geography is more
Sinister than we took her for,
Less the comedian than her sister.
Poets, if they're wise assist her
By calling place (all places) holy,
Because it seems she may be slowly
Mustering her enormous forces
To blast her own, and our, resources,
Giving pollution for pollution.
A nice twist, that, to Evolution!
(What's nice about her, to be sure, is
Just that she has such vengeful furies,
Or so a poet may think who fears,
Yet wants, a Justice that inheres.
What will you do, he wants to ask her,
About the gang-rape of Alaska?)

However, Tonty's sun was setting
Some time ago. I keep forgetting.

Turn back the clock, and take the man
Now, at his meridian:
Observe him. Getting little joy
Out of the frozen Illinois,
His vigilance does not abate; he
Winters here in 1680
For his visionary chief,
La Salle, gone East, not for relief
But for the needful to equip
There, on the stocks, the half-built ship
That Tonty in that queer dockyard,
The wilderness, is left to guard.
Comes Spring, comes no La Salle. Instead,
Of the gang that Tonty led
(In theory), most decide to skip.
Though landlocked, they abandon ship,
Abandon Tonty, writing thus:
'We're savages, each one of us.'
(A sentiment reverberated
Through Badmen not yet generated,
Who were to take odd satisfaction
In savage pleas for savage action;
A practice copied by their betters –
It has its counterpart in Letters.)
Meanwhile the loyal remnant sought
Refuge and lodging in the fort
Of the assembling Illinois
Indians, whom the Iroquois
(Bless those rhyming Indian nations!
And curst be the exterminations
Of later, more enlightened times
That killed off tribes, and with them rhymes…)
Whom, I say, the Iroquois
Decided that they must destroy,
And for good reason, inasmuch
As furs the English and the Dutch
Would pay good guilders for might all
Be sent direct to Montreal,
Should Tonty or La Salle persuade
The Western tribes to ply that trade;
After which brief genuflection
In the economists' direction,
I give you Tonty, some time later,

Trying to play the mediator
Between these rival parties and
In equal peril from each band,
From both of which, to keep his head,
Wounded by one of them, he fled;
And met, in 1681
With no companions but one
Reaching Michilimackinac,
La Salle, on one more journey back.

Now, where Fidelity is the plot,
Comedy, we know, is not
Conspicuously enthusiastic;
She likes her things a bit more drastic
So she can smooth them out at last,
Lothario's peccadilloes past.
Her view is, we are all too human
And stand in need of her *dénouements,*
As by and large we do of course.
It follows Comedy perforce,
When we tell her that we've got
A mystic bond, a true-love knot,
Because her business is untying,
Supposes that we must be lying.
The point is, though, 'Auguste, his friend'
Must get some credit in the end;
And Tragedy and Epic, sold
So totally upon the bold
Unbalanced hero, are askew,
Quite hopeless from this point of view.
So we must make the Comic Muse,
If reluctantly, infuse
The homelier, more homespun virtues
With some quality of *éclat,*
A *Je ne sais* (exactly) *quoi.*
The more so, since we see anew
How History's bits of string won't do;
La Salle's French colony in Texas
Was knotted into no cash-nexus;
Nor did Tonty long enjoy
St Louis of the Illinois,
A place that Kings and History meant
Never should be permanent.

It really seems we'll have to whistle
For a hero, this epistle.
For human virtues cannot earn
The marble plinth, the sculpted urn;
And being trusty, being true,
As Tonty was, will never do.
Like La Pérouse, he had to make
History in a hero's wake,
And drudging on the track of those
Blazers of archipelagos
Means discovering *déjà vu*
Whatever strait one ventures through;
No coral isle, no sea-girt rocks
Not disfigured by the pox.
So, in the speculative seas
That wash up into libraries,
Taint on the breezes of the mind
Points to each Pitcairn that we find.
Thus, as for love of Letters and
Of Arts, it comes, we understand,
From mere debility, a state
That it can only aggravate,
Though suffering's so severe in some
Cases that it has become
Needful, to prevent expiry,
They persist in their enquiry.
(Thus said, as I suppose you know,
The insupportable Rousseau,
In the history of thought
A hero of the direst sort.)

True, there are provinces of Letters
Where these troubles don't beset us;
Regions that Rousseau never knew,
Scrub in his time, now ploughed anew.
Olson hereabouts is found,
Bounding on archaic ground;
And Pound and David Jones are planting
Glyphs with crucial pieces wanting.
Here making a distinction is
Nearly the worst of felonies,
Only exceeded, it appears,
By entertaining clear ideas.

('Cartesian', this crime is called;
A charge at which to stand appalled.)
Here no one's fooled by talk of Hector;
Troy was unspooled, Achilles wrecked her
By running counterclockwise round
The spindle of her Sacred Mound.
Here the surreal is the true,
And hashish may be good for you.
And sure enough, this province is
The nicest of dependencies.
Only, to finance it all
Depends upon the capital
Truth, not soon accumulated:
That zanies should be tolerated.
Now, I concur with those who fear
Truths like this, not crystal-clear
(For crystals take the light, and burn
With furious colours, as they turn)
But plateglass-clear, a sort of glare
Scorching our purchase on despair;
Despair, the bight that we can never
Let Enlightenment dissever,
Considering to what we tend –
The certain term, the dubious end.
And thinking of the poet's (Olson's)
Elastic traverse of the Oceans
And Epochs, how inert appears,
Beside such feats, whatever years
Of sprightly exile taught to Bayle!
That nothing be beyond the pale,
The best enforcement we can find
Is generosity of mind,
Not Toleration's equal haze
Of *plus ça change*... (or some such phrase).
Plainly the human lot is bettered
When deviant thinkers go unfettered;
But no one feels exhilarated
At being merely tolerated.
And yet some lump of English clay
Grounds me, and makes me grudge the play
Of mind, the freedom of it. Lean
Limbs upon a trampoline
Of zany theories, crazy rhyme,

Crossings of syncopated Time,
Leap into language. Why I should
Need to distrust such hardihood
Is a question I can face
Best by falling back on race:
How English, trying to make peace,
Reasonably, with Caprice!
(Mercurial Byron was – I'm not
Sure that it helps – of course a Scot,
Where Knox and Calvin keep the screws on
Taut nerves to bounce the Comic Muse on
As rhyming Beppo did. If Byron's
Vulgar pungency should fire one's
Emulation in this way,
One ought to know just what's in play
– Instead of Tolerance and Reason
And all things being good in season,
Byron found, as I find, handy
Rather liberal draughts of brandy.)
And Bayle knew this much: though to diddle
Both sides is easiest from the middle,
Holding the middle ground is harder
And asks more judgement, no less ardour,
Than to espouse exclusive themes
And fly to one of two extremes.
This must be part of what we mean
By talking of a trampoline
Where, yes, no bounce would have a sequel
If tension both ends were not equal.
Therefore the place I should maintain is,
So it seems, among the zanies;
And yet, I don't know how it is,
Tonty and his fidelities…
Some more common sense position
Is needed, for their recognition.

So, to resume… But why rehearse
What Parkman has, though not in verse,
Recounted nobly? Why go on
About La Salle, son of Rouen,
Or Tonty, his most faithful creature
Whose birthplace was, they say, Gaeta?
Some narrative, and then a moral…

With the latter you can quarrel,
And if the former you could spare,
It only comes in here and there.
Tonty should adorn a tale;
If not, it must be I who fail.
But as for pointing morals, why,
The one he prompts is rather dry:
That, pledges being given for keeps,
Whatever just reproach one heaps
(Or might) on fast-cemented love,
Its bargain, though repented of,
Is not aborted by that token;
One's word, once given, 's not unspoken.

Third Epistle

Heroic comedy, I suggest,
Fits American history best;
A charming mode not wholly lost to
Poetry since Ariosto
But, with us, rare. Since being glum
Has failed to bring millennium
At all decypherably to
The New World (or to me and you),
Let's see what being merry can
Do for the American.
Are we downhearted? Yes, we are.
But this is not peculiar;
All of us have been more or less
Bemused by our own wretchedness
Much of the time, it seems to me,
Throughout recorded history.
To raise our moan or raise a laugh,
To blubber or resort to chaff,
Are both all right, so long as we
Can do our thing inventively.
Though gay hysteria in a nation
Seems a wrong sort of adaptation
(This cap fits England, and she'll wear it
With a grin – her 'Grin and bear it'
Is a bore and lacks invention),

Still Comedy, it's my contention,
Can be magnanimous, in the sense
Of showing proper deference
To the pathfinders of our kind,
While soft on those they leave behind.
Indeed, to pay respects while smiling
Is more than usually beguiling,
It may be thought. And now's the time
To venture a Defence of Rhyme;
Rhyme, of all the tricks that are
In the Muse's repertoire
The most irrational, a mere
Foolish indulgence of the ear.
Zaniest of phenomenons,
It makes the rhymed forms open ones –
Open enough to see at once
Tonty the doughty and the dunce,
Or, while revering common sense,
Do it with jokes at her expense.
Is it prejudice to treasure
A zaniness that I can measure
(Sixteen syllables, more or less,
Is the frequency, Miss Hesse)
To random lunacies a man
May feel, but cannot learn to scan?
Total freedom in the fiction
Is of all the worst constriction,
For every licence to surprise
Turns out, in your reader's eyes,
To constitute just one more norm
To which he asks that you conform.
Thus rules we keep and rules we flout
Change places and turn inside out.
And so with rhyme: the Hudibrastic
Form of it's the least elastic,
And what was built as Liberty Hall
Allows few liberties at all.
The licences it thought to profit
By are soon demanded of it;
Surprise! Surprise! our readers cry
And, missing it, lay the volume by.
But rhyme in less licentious mode
Ensures a wavering switchback road

Which, I aver, I trust much more
Than five-lane free-verse highways for
Egotists to roar along
In self-enclosed unmeasured song.
Theirs are the closed forms, theirs the flat
Fiat of synopsis that
Makes every goddess the Great Mother
And women types of one another,
And Hathor, Circe, Aphrodite
One pair of breasts inside one nightie.
That closed-in Kosmos served by myth
Is just what Rhyme must quarrel with.

So, Muse, abandoning these loose
And heated pantheons, peruse
More frigid histories. Tune your rhymes
To Queen Victoria's costive times
When a man could come a cropper
From being in the least improper.
Sing, moreover, in hushed tones,
That most erogenous of zones,
The Arctic, where lascivious day
Whines, summer-long, on Hudson's Bay
And the months-long winters keep
Men abed who cannot sleep.
Thence stiff James Hargrave, terrified
Of waking with a squaw for bride,
Fled, for honour and dear life,
To Bonny Scotland for a wife;
And found one neither he nor I
Would ever want to deify,
For whom I none the less will claim
A sombre record, if not fame –
Letitia, of the Clan Mactavish!
Nature wasnae unco' lavish
Endowing her; not hers the face
Launched ships for Troy or any place,
Though Orkney sailors were to bend
A hawser for her at Gravesend.
Therefore, though less than heavensent,
A suitor was convenient.
So Hargrave comes, and Hargrave woos,
Is liked, and is too good to lose.

This solid man she settles for
Is sixteen years her senior.
And what a settlement it is!
Backed up against immensities
Of muskeg barrens… Theirs henceforth
The Pontine marshes of the North,
Where the swamps and foggy air
Rack the unlucky loyal pair
Through eleven years that see
A due access of progeny;
Five births, one death – one little boy
Sent home, bewildered, to enjoy
The benefits (past computation)
Of Caledonian education.
Her letters home survive, and bore.
Never an item in them for
Revolving Time to trifle with;
Domestic news, too trite for myth,
All on one cheerful-cheerless note –
The baby's colic, her sore throat;
Never a thing that can be pried
Free of the times she lived inside,
The nineteenth century's fifth decade.
Weep, Comedy, to see displayed
The short unsimple annals of
The poor in health: his qualms, his cough,
Her constipation, her confinements,
Her headaches… and of all assignments
The Company makes, its northernmost,
Busiest, least salubrious post
Year after year. Who sings the quiet
Martyrs to inappropriate diet,
To wrong and rigid hygiene, and
Dyspepsia in Prince Rupert's Land?
Who ever does can bear to see,
Dry-eyed, the tame small tragedy:
There, on the post they'd waited for,
Snug by Lake Superior,
The cholera descends, and makes
A widower upon the Lake's
Abruptly desolated shore;
She dies in 1854.

Poor child! She comes through as a sort
Of foundling waif, an awed, untaught,
Casually adopted charge
On family estates too large
For more than transient regret
When stewards' households are upset.
Baffled at best, at worst unnerved
By the culture that she served
(The legendary 'Boz', she had
Heard it rumoured, must be mad;
And flagging interest revives
In Shakespeare's romp, 'The Merry Wives
Of Windsor', only when she can
Observe that gentlemanly man,
Prince Albert, showing much good sense
And shyness, in the audience),
How many since have I not seen,
Like her, stand quivering for the Queen
With guilelessness that is construed,
The more the argument's pursued,
As stiff-necked prejudice? Alas,
God Save the Queen from thee, my lass!
God help England, and defend us
All from such obtuse befrienders
As warm Letitia… Oh, a cool
Comedian makes her look a fool
Out of her own mouth, soon enough.
Shakespeare, Dickens and such stuff
Possessed, in her days as in these,
Nothing to instruct or please
A hemmed-in way of life like hers;
And yet that way of life recurs
Each generation, with the need
We feel, or think we feel, to breed.

Mothers of the pioneers,
Patching and mending through the years,
Might come to *Lear* or *Little Dorrit,*
Some hallowed text, conceiving for it
Gratitude, as their children had
Proved loyal, or had turned out bad.
But she, who never lived to raise
One of her children, could she praise

Sincerely either version of
The rendings of parental love?
With little meaning and less news
In the record, can the Muse
Even of Comedy maintain
Hers was a life not lived in vain?
Mythographers who can elide
Centuries are not satisfied
Such mournful limits can be placed
On the exercise of taste.
For them, we notice with a shock,
An early death's no stumbling-block;
The racial memory will see
To it, the short-lived can be
Initiate of each mystery
As surely as we others who
Are spared to see the drama through.

Believing that, we might as well
Go the whole hog to Heaven and Hell,
For if blind faith's in order, why,
A crustier pie in clearer sky
Is cooked by an established Church,
Less apt to leave one in the lurch;
As indeed Letitia knew
Who lived and died with Heaven in view.
Sorrowing for her, I begin
Thinking there's some virtue in
A place where prepossessions are
Less confidently saecular
Than where the exegetes romp through
Millennia in an hour or two;
A place where Mrs Hargrave might
Have heard debate she'd think was right
About child-care and sanitation,
Paid holidays and compensation...
My native land! secure, humane,
Where no one works (I mean, for gain),
Where, though the rule is Man the Measure,
The module man shall have no leisure
More than an ailing housewife with
Five small children. What price myth
In such a world? What price the lives

Lived there, where computation thrives
To breed the social engineers
Who have the nation by the ears?
Tickets for *Lear* are not much prized
Where all's been de-mythologized,
Nor much of merriment survives
In Windsor's bright unhappy wives
Financing, out of foreign loans,
Welfare and the Rolling Stones.

No, England, if I have to choose,
There are some myths too good to lose;
And if my choice must lie between
Barbara Castle and Christine
Brooke-Rose, I have no wish to flatter
In plumping firmly for the latter.
To be more positive; I bless
All such girls as you, Miss Hesse.
Among the men, too, I prefer
Often the mythographer;
A good companion, erudite
And witty far into the night.
And yet James Hargrave might be more
Welcome as a son-in-law,
Who surely more sincerely grieved
Than livelier men, the more bereaved
In that he was resourceless in
His stolid pain, and could not spin
Tales to himself of passionate
Divorce and death, to cushion it.
I'm glad to leave that thought alone;
It comes, and cuts, too near the bone.

So Comedy, once more our saviour,
Quash such unreserved behaviour.
Do what you can (it isn't much)
To save Letitia from the touch
Of levelling and defiling time;
Cripple the measure, wrench the rhyme!

Fourth Epistle

Sparkle sparkle, little verse,
Not poetry, nor yet discourse…
Let a nation's honour be
Billed as brittle comedy;
Waste and Oblivion stalk the scene
Of *The London Magazine*
And a sickness at the heart
Talk trenchantly of Life and Art.

So, once again… But how begin?
Hero I lack, and heroine.
Perhaps a poet… Is it time
For self-congratulating rhyme
To honour as established fact
The value of the artefact?
Stoutly to trumpet Art is all
We have, or need, to disenthrall
Any of us from the chains
History loads us with? Such strains,
Wafted on the foetid air,
Are found emollient everywhere
The poet or the painter goes
Except inside the studios
Or garrets that they work in, where,
Though too preoccupied to care,
All of them notice at least two
Sides to the dubious thing they do.
      Savage Landor – there's a poet
Spurned England, and took pains to show it.
Not his the slack, impetuous style
I improvise in all this while;
Headstrong, not headlong, was his case,
Consumed with contumely of race
And insolence of rank, whose sweet
Self-love makes Como seem effete.
      Savage, all too savage Landor,
Less England's Cato than her pander,
Pimp to her appetite, then as now,
For thinking, 'Holier than thou'.
(Florence was insolent indeed
Not to know the bulldog breed

More than Ghibelline or Guelph
Was a law unto itself.)
No surprise, then, if he's found
In the pantheon of Pound
Who, similarly unabashed,
Was the very thing he lashed:
Ole Uncle Ez, the crustiest sort
Of Yankee at King Arthur's Court.
Both poets, relishing the state
Of mortified expatriate,
Through blunder after patent blunder,
Scrape after scrape, found face to thunder
At home-grown mischiefs, and expose
Fools or knaves, in verse and prose.
    Such doubleness is on the cards
Too plainly, for self-banished bards
Who never lack for occupation,
Each hectoring his relinquished nation
Even as they exemplify
The prepossessions they decry.

Besides, we've reached rock-bottom now;
Byronic skiff and Crabbe-like scow
And Landor's lovely craft alike,
Forced upon the shoreline, strike.
They fill before they feel the shock,
In such small print it is; the rock
Of the obituaries, on whose
Shallow ubiquity the Muse
Time and again has struck and foundered.
The insignificant! The unsounded
Reaches of the trite! We grind
The lakebed gravels of the mind.
A stilted posy on the grave
Is all that Art can do to save
Poetry's and a Nation's honour:
'Canada's soil lie light upon her...'
As upon so many others,
Sickly brides, benighted mothers,
French explorers. Only places,
Patches of earth by the good graces
Of local polymaths sometimes
Name, to make exotic rhymes,

Small successes or near-failures:
Ill-bred wives, unlucky sailors.

Thus New Zealanders maintain
The name of Marion du Fresne
Who, Skye-ward navigating, tore a
Princely botanist from his Flora
Once upon a time; who now
Knows better than to make his bow
To a no longer Young Pretender.
Instead he dwells in modest splendour
On a colonial estate
Secured in 1768
In l'Île de France (which is to say
Mauritius, at the present day).

And yet he rushes on his doom,
Sets all at risk, and will resume
Nautical life. He sinks behind
The south-east skyline, there to find
Some paltry islands, of which one
Commemorates him: Marion
His mark, his sea-mark. (And this matters:
Astringent comedy never flatters
The ruinous Quixotes of their day,
John Franklin or Wolfe Tone or Che,
Too virginal to wed Success,
Intact in ineffectiveness.)
Not Carthaginian Hanno nor
Odysseus, prudently inshore,
Their crude technologies unripe
For the deep waters, is his type;
The mythological parallel
As usual works out far from well
As soon as we imagine how
Things really were. Take notice now,
For instance, that the second ship,
Manœuvred with poor seamanship,
Hereabouts with some commotion
Collides with his one in mid-ocean;
The culprit turning out to be
A sprig of the nobility,
The mishap cannot help but seem
Due to the *ancien régime,*
A far from mythical condition

Through which he limps upon his mission,
Hurrying now, and making for
Tasmania's vaguely charted shore
There to recoup, refit. But no,
Van Diemen Land cannot bestow
Wood, nor water, nor much ease
Not vexed by aborigines.
  In March of 1772,
Accordingly, he ploughs the blue
Waters of the Tasman Sea
Helped by a strong south-westerly,
Makes land and, weathering new mischances,
Declares New Zealand thenceforth France's.
North Island's earth lie light upon
The breast *etcetera* of one
Whose bones, outlandish treasure-trove,
Enrich Assassination Cove.
(That is to say, his bones at least;
His meat had made a Maori feast.
Comedy goes for jokes like these;
Her humour's black, like Cruelty's.
Unamiable! None the less,
Noteworthy for straightforwardness:
If in such rites she shows us how
To be as crude as Chairman Mao,
Cruelty's what she had in mind;
She won't be cruel to be kind
Nor, anthropophagous, pretend
Doing it serves some higher end.)
  From Utopian projectors
Caustic Comedy protect us!
Under whose corrosive shield
I re-affirm we ought to yield
Firm pre-eminence of status
Among projections, to Mercator's;
Trusting the lie of lands and seas
Before such lies as History's.
  Between his stanchions I can sling
My own small lattices of string,
Slack hammocks where I can compose
Into a somnolent repose
The harrowing abbreviations
Of lives endured, inured to patience

Or insensate, flailing round
Some misappropriated ground
Of pride or Polynesia or
That atoll not worth sailing for,
National honour. Lulled upon
The loll of reverie, even one
That time was at no pains to ravish –
Letitia Hargrave, born Mactavish,
Raped in her own and History's sleep –
Is comforted and learns to keep
Good company in the Isle of Skye,
The Bay of Islands and Versailles.
The dancing clews, the bulk and sway
Of slipping shadows web the day
Between decks to the music of
Strains and chafings, suave enough
To help us orchestrate a mood
By latitude and longitude;
Parameters our captains must
Abstractedly pursue and trust,
And by their grid upon the chart
Mesh fluid Nature into Art,
But which, in truth, will barely serve
To plot our conquest of the curve
Of oceanic earth. Instead
We can weave a swinging bed
(Too lax to make a trampoline)
Of the surprising, unforeseen
Conjunctions human beings prove
The more the rule, the more they move.

Most poets sail another tack:
To the Piraeus, and then back.
Browning's anxiously despairing
Enquiry, 'What's become of Waring?'
Asked of one who took his chance
In poor Marion's Austral France,
Still touchingly pursues us where
We've emigrated to, by air.
And Landor, Pound and Browning are
All in this sense too insular
To help us much, who need to probe
A way to humanize the globe

By which (upon this point I yield)
Space and Time inscribe one field,
But (and here I give no quarter)
Space is the long side, Time the shorter.

Still, older poets had the sense
At least to run a staked-out fence
Around their fields. And those fields are
Better than rectilinear;
The curve of earth takes care of that,
Unless of course you think it's flat
As apparently those do
Whose pastures melt into the blue
Unfenced Beyond of the sublime,
The mythopoeic waste of Time.
     True, the power of myth engages
Some of the old masters' pages.
(They know things are not what they seem;
That in the Polynesian scheme
Of things it may be Marion died,
A case of ritual deicide.)
But La Pérouse's rigid page
Is icy with contempt and rage,
Telling the not dissimilar end
Of his own too trusting friend,
De Langle, butchered out of reach
Of help on a Samoan beach;
Unfair it may be, but I fear
(Miss Hesse or any other dear
Reader) those bluff sailors thought
Ill of people of our sort
Whose surveys, something less than global,
Had declared the savage, noble,
Thereby fashioning a myth
Their shipmates could be murdered with.

Fifth Epistle

A thesis, though sincerely meant
Is in the end impertinent,
Comedy says. In her sharp praxis

There's no place for grinding axes;
Thesis, antithesis, the same,
A more or less convenient frame
For weaving on. The web is tattered;
Mending it's all that ever mattered.
　　All the same, an axe is ground
So gratingly, on that renowned
Marmoreal paragon, Captain Cook,
Its squeak is hard to overlook.
Was it presumption when he trod
Hawaii, an acknowledged god?
Did, when he died, the Age of Reason
Learn the irrational was in season?
There, on the black sand, hacked, dismembered
Worshipfully, he remembered,
Did he, that last instant, how
A man-god could not disavow
In Gethsemane the weight
Of divinity, and fate?
Or did he, dying blindly, still
Think that, given mind and will,
Something there was a man could do
To exorcize a myth come true?

A worse hypothesis will fit him:
That he never knew what hit him.
Navigator through and through,
Hydrographer with a job to do,
Was that James Cook? The very first
(So Coleridge was to say) that burst
Into that silent sickening sea –
Professional speciality?
– A mask, perhaps; the shy, self-made
Provincial hides behind his trade.
If so, it works: the self-respecting
Yorkshireman there's no detecting.
In the Ridings we admire
The man with expertise for hire,
Who by his code austerely sells
Fierce competence, and nothing else.
Wilfrid Rhodes and Maurice Leyland
And Hedley Verity… I stand
Dwarfed by Father as we clap,

And surly Leyland tugs his cap
And (No, this *isn't* out of books)
Black as Lucifer he looks,
Coming with a racing stride
And booted thunder, past our side
Up the pavilion steps, to gain
His private dark. Aye, Bramall Lane
Will never see his like again...
And just as well – it was a poor
Cramped nobility, to be sure,
That disdainful dourness which
Had the globe for cricket-pitch
Once – which now, if it survives
At all, informs the sullen lives
Of Yorkshire bards who take perverse
Pride in writing metred verse,
All their hopes invested in
One patent, brilliant discipline.

Well, we can hardly pick and choose:
Not much to gain, but much to lose,
We find nobility where we can,
Even in a Yorkshireman.
But that is neither here nor there;
Nobility's not comic fare.
Nor are cowards – which puts paid
To the horribly afraid
Lieutenant Williamson. Nor is
The brave and brutal Bligh, whose story's
Never been told with justice, such
A theme as Thalia's light touch
Does justice to. And so we might
Scan all whom History's brought to light
Out of the muster of Cook's two
Ships and, having conned them through,
Rule the lot of them out of court.
(Our Muse is choosier than we thought.)
Instead, as you'll have guessed, there's one
Case that I've chosen – Corporal John
Ledyard.
        He's been much maligned,
Ledyard has, by those who find
Any disrespect for Cook

A hanging matter, in their book.
(Whereas, for Cook's own sake, in fact
Blemishes is what we've lacked
All this while, and any stain
Of fallibility's sheer gain.)
And Ledyard, on the other hand,
Though seldom in his native land
Remembered, was a curious man,
Authentic and American.
In 1787 he strode
Along his own untravelled road
In winter, carrying all he had,
From Stockholm round to Petrograd,
1200 miles on foot in eight
Weeks... But I anticipate:
Some years before, with Cook, he'd been
A less accomplished peregrine;
As witness his account of it,
Where passages of exquisite
Silliness reveal a man
Whose role, not yet pedestrian,
Is never to be much surprised
When sudden gusts of bowdlerized
Laurence Sterne (from whom he's stealing)
Type him as the Man of Feeling.
(Words! Insidious avengers!
Time, that brings in its revenges,
Has too keen, too true an ear:
It's not enough to be sincere,
You have to seem so. History smiles,
Custodian of exploded styles.)
'Mystic sheer distance was in thine
Eye,' wrote Olson's friend and mine,
Ed Dorn, addressing Ledyard. And
'Mystic' is right. It was the land,
Dorn's land and his, made manifest
In him its destiny, heading West
The long way round if need be, by
Tomsk and Kachuga. 'In thine eye',
Ledyard, all America smiles
Already, ribboning through miles
Of trailers, and the pent air slaps
Whick-whick against us through the gaps

Between the parked cars, as we prove
The way to live is on the move.

To wrest from Russia the distinction
Of slaughtering into extinction
Such animals as Steller's sea-
Cow and the sea-otter, he
(So the accepted version goes)
Had the prescience to propose
America dispute the ground
The Russians had, from Nootka Sound,
And thus imperiously invade
The fortune-making peltry trade
That desolated Arctic seas
To warm the backs of Cantonese.
And there's his greatness! What a man
It took, to frame so gross a plan!
What a Napoleon of crime,
Born not before, but of, his time!
Thus the historians, lost in awe
As soon as Nature's rule of law
Is breached on a sufficient scale.
Cachalot and walrus quail.
Prayed after from Connecticut,
Dissolute grave whalers gut
Leviathan's cows, and under Cape
Brett in the Bay of Islands rape
Maori women on the sands
Mauled by Marion's dying hands.

Luckily, none of this is true:
Any nation's flag would do
To plant upon the unexplored,
Unbestowable seaboard
That beckoned Ledyard like a dream,
Unprofitable and extreme.
America and Freedom earn,
It's true, apostrophes *à la* Sterne
Still, in the desultory pages
That trace him by Siberian stages
Eastward; but after John Paul Jones
And Jefferson fail to raise the loans
He'd hoped to touch them for, occurs

No mention of the trade in furs.
A pretext that had failed to raise
The wind, he might as well erase
(And did) from the aspiring mind
That thought to benefit mankind...
Travelling as sheer condition!
Exploring *that* was the commission,
Self-bestowed, on which he went
Walking through a continent.
Thus was History outwitted!
He wore the motley till it fitted;
The reach-me-down of silly phrases,
Exclamation marks, self-praises,
Points and frills, falls into shape.
Can mere farrago thus escape
The times' and Comedy's clutching hands?
Yes. When Catherine countermands
Her passe-partout, and by her order
He's dumped across the Polish border,
No one has the heart to smile
At the pretensions of his style.
Deluded, verminous, alone,
The rhetoric he'd made his own
Comes true, at last his situation
Demands the note of desperation.
His fever-pitch was queered before
The Empress pushed him out the door.
Febrile, excitable, effusive
He chose to be, and chose to live
Up to what that style demands,
Grasping his fate with shaking hands.

And so he fades from us, you see...
A figure, once, of comedy,
Now asking for some other kind
Of honorarium, gone to find
Death in Cairo in the very
Year that saw his plans miscarry
Of following a Yankee star
Through the dominions of the Czar.
(I'm sorry, by the way – and yet
It's fitting, when you think of it –
That I couldn't follow through

The life of Ledyard with the due
Observance of successive time
That Comedy exacts of rhyme;
I trust that none the less you've pieced
Together, bit by bit, at least
A general notion where he went
First and last, and in the event
With what success.) There still remains
One awkward truth: for all the pains
We take at Comedy's behest
To be poised and unimpressed
And keep our heads, we cannot guard
Against, nor take account of, hard
Gamblers of the do-or-die
Variety, who make the sky
Their limit, and provoke their fate
By being disproportionate.
Comedy just cannot brook
A Ledyard, nor perhaps a Cook…
So, dear Miss Hesse, if I were you
And you were found to be the true
Empress Eva of all Russia,
Faced with a Ledyard, I should usher
Him out across my frontier fast;
Heroes are safest in the past.

Sixth Epistle

The impetus, awesome!
The imperial momentum
Flogs still: 'Among the first
And farthest…' The unslakeable thirst
Still logs its marches. If it is
Late for these intensities,
If it's too late (or else too soon)
For landing parties on the moon,
Then ponder an alternative:
That fever, easier to forgive,
When a Ruskin's narrowed eyes
Crimp to the nicer enterprise,
'Not place, but the expression on

The face of it.' The light is gone
Over the lake and off it, while
Autumn, the amber of a style,
Dyes it his in whom his own
Time and year's time mix a tone
Mellowed for it. And for this
Meshing of uncertainties
Not too late? The space for it
Is narrowed on the face of it,
Branded with a coming doom
Wreaked or suffered. Little room
Left to articulate the fine
Crowsfoot and serif, scroll and line,
When Nature's indeterminate face
Frowns, or fawns with craven grace
On her despoiler. Still, it is
An honourable emphasis –
On the refining mutual shock
When ravisher and patient lock
Looks in one haggardness that hones
Weasel and rabbit to thin bones,
To one bleached gossamer. The tension
Of a mortal apprehension
Steadies the web to such a fine
Reticule, the debile line
Parts at the pressure of a gnat.
No cradle here, to swing a cat!

Says Romance: 'You need some rope.
Put away your microscope,
Set your manikin in motion
Across what continent or what ocean
All you need's a general notion.'
Insufferable! If it's true
There's virtue in a bird's eye view,
Some better reason must be found,
Still valid when we're on the ground.
It might be this: that there is one
Abstracted potent lexicon
Of place, which helps us understand
Where, in some ultimate sense, we stand;
That heath and strand and wood and cape
Make up a grid we can't escape,

However manifestly these
Vary with localities.
And being English helps with this.
My emblem of all barrens is
The Langsett moors, and the Great Wood
Is tiny Hugsett, where we would
Cull bluebells forty years ago:
Great Wood, Great Barrens, though we know
Better, or worse. Thus 'great' and 'far',
'Remote' and 'wild' and 'trackless' are
Nomenclature that cannot fail
To stay authentic and in scale,
Being as felt. We made our claim
To them, for instance, with the name
'North America' for the last
Ruined homestead that we passed
Breasting the moor. Domesticated
Little England is, and fated
To get much more so; none the less
This way she'll march with Lyonnesse
For us, for good. And Lyonnesse
Or Tryermaine is wilderness,
Bewildering, and not lightly entered,
Where if we travel (as demented
Aberrant Ledyard punned) we are
In error. There, the near is far,
The old home unfamiliar,
The little, great. But all the same
Great this, great that, advance a claim
By authors of an island-nation
That demands substantiation,
For instance, as to climate. Why
Should we suppose a scudding sky
And chill damp airs delineate
More truly than less temperate
Weathers do, our mortal state?
Moreover, 'manikin' may do
For hobbits or an elf or two
Or for myself when, still a child,
I took for emblem of the wild
And waste, a meadow rank with clover
And vetches, long ago built over.
But Geography's too great

And fierce a power to tolerate
Being, through a Tolkien's eyes,
Toyed with, and cut down to size.
        It may well be that any scene
On land or water, whether seen
Up close or from a long way off,
Presents us with at best a rough
Approximation to the true.
And yet the snail's, the bird's eye view
Both serve us better, we may hope,
Than turning round the telescope
Until what's insular and near
Seems crisp, definitive and clear
As in Romance. Romance, though charming.
Seeming gratuitous and disarming,
Has in fact an end in view
Not always good for me or you.

Therefore, like others we've applauded,
Our final actor's a recorded
Personage – the most renowned
Hero in fact I've so far found:
Thomas Jefferson!
                    My reader,
Though he's British, shouldn't need a
Résumé of *that* career.
But every one will think it queer
If I propose him as a prime
Example, in his place and time,
Of the comic. So he seems,
However, if the several themes
I've tried to tease out in this poem
Have any rhyme or reason to 'em.
Indulgent friends, like you, Miss Hesse,
Will take my drift. Let others, less
Persuaded or amused, reflect
That Comedy is circumspect;
So statesmanlike that a Romantic
Pathos winces at each antic
She performs upon the stage
Of Jefferson's or any age.
Comedy always keeps her cool
When other Muses play the fool.

The curtain rises! There, before us,
Stands a patron of explorers:
Ledyard and Meriwether Lewis.
Difficult deciding who is
The crazier of that couple. He
Sincere in his civility,
Dispatches to their destinations
Both of them, their aberrations
Noted, allowed for. When they die,
Both violently, in his eye
Brightens a pained, regretful smile
As he, in one unruffled style
(Too humane a style to break,
Too inclusive to mistake
For mischance, logic) with entire
Justice, in the steady fire
Of rational prudence immolates
Both in one memoir. In their fates
He reads excess, and so impales
The pair of them. He never fails.
... As does, for instance (I regret
Digging a little deeper yet
Into Americana) his
One-time foil in rivalries
For President, the first John Adams.
The only rhyme to that is 'madam's'
As Yeats discovered; so it's yours,
Miss Hesse, who will recall of course
Among the Adamses, that Brooks
Whose wayward, dazzling history-books
Are monotonously found
Scriptural, by Ezra Pound.
And, reader, this is no digression:
Brooks comes of John, by due succession,
And Henry too... in all we see
Men mesmerized by History.
Set Jefferson against his peer,
Adams, and the issue's clear –
The one, successful and serene;
Behind him mountains; and between
His sanguine forehead and the rim
Of the medal struck for him,
Stretching savannahs: but behind

The other's angry head, designed
By an engraver in the pay
Of secret party, some *mêlée*
Or massacre or mob-unrest,
A tumult of crossed interest,
Crowding the middle ground inside
The milled edge of resentful pride.

Of course we know which one we like:
Betrayed, traduced, and with the strike
Against him always, Adams. Yet
It's Jefferson we can't forget
Who, though he never went there, hung
All Oregon upon a young
And urgent nation's parlour-wall.
Our hearts go out to those who fall,
Success is vulgar. None the less
A breakthrough into spaciousness,
New reaches charted for the mind,
Is solid service to mankind.

THE SHIRES

Bedfordshire

Bunyan, of course. But Potton it was, or Sandy,
Threaded on the Cambridge road, that showed
Dissenting nineteenth-century demureness
In a brick chapel. I have never known
What to do with this that I am heir to.

My daughter-in-law has studied for her thesis
The Protestant Right in France between the wars,
l'Association Sully. Bedfordshire
Might nurse an English counterpart of that:

Our swords for Calvin and the Winter Queen,
The ancient frail collaborating Marshal!

Berkshire

for Michael Hamburger

Don't care for it.
                    We talked of syntax and
synecdoche, the various avant-gardes,
their potencies, their puerilities.
And, Michael, one we knew
in Reading, he approved such conversations;
crippled and dying he contrived occasions
when they could come about. And yet he
felt (we knew) not scepticism, rather...
oh certainly not scepticism, rather
an eager, a too eager warmth in him
starved for a lack of body in that talk.

In his last months I stood him up for supper.
That night I should have stayed with him I stayed
talking with Christopher Middleton in town.

So nowadays as the biscuit-factory flies
past the train-window and announces Reading,
I keep my head down.

Buckinghamshire

A thin green salient aimed at the heart of London,
The trains run in and out of Baker Street.

Chalfont St Giles, Chalfont St Peter, Fenny
And Stony Stratford breathe again. The old
A6, the clamorous ditch we edge along,
Ribbons in evening sunlight south to Bletchley.

To west and east the motorways draw off
Poisons that dogged this artery. Abandoned
Transport-cafés blink at the weedy asphalt;
An old white inn by a copse-side yawns and stretches.

Cambridgeshire

'An air that kills' – Housman

Housman came, savage recluse,
Lover of boys. 'To be sure,
That also I endure,
    yet not from there
Blows into Whewell's Court
    an air that kills.'

Came wincing Gray: 'Why that
Libertine over the way,
Smart of Pembroke, should
    have had the luck
    of running mad
Is more than I can say.'

Smart stares at William Blake:
'Mad? Mad as a refuge
   merely from Locke?
Shame on the subterfuge!
   Let the wind pluck
Your wits astray, *then* talk!'

And Blake: 'I accept the reproof.
Better be sane like Housman
Than under Bedlam's roof,
Self-soiled, wind-plucked. And yet
   I think it's not
   an airless place?'

Smart, Gray, all of them, look:
The face of Harold Monro!
'An air that kills? At all
   events an air!'
Tuneless, he growls from Caius
   in his despair.

Cheshire

A lift to the spirit, when everything fell into place!
So that was what those ruined towers remained from:
Engine-houses, mills. Our Pennine crests
Had not been always mere unfettered space.

Not quite the crests, just under them. The high
Cloughs, I learned in the history-lesson, had
Belted the earliest mills, they had connived
With history then, then history passed them by.

His savage brunt and impetus, one survives it?
Finding it all unchanged and the windowless mill
Between Wincle and Congleton silent and staring, I found
The widow's weeds restorative and fit.

And Mr Auden, whom I never knew,
Is dead in Vienna. A post-industrial landscape
He celebrated often, and expounded
How it can bleakly solace. And that's true.

Cornwall

(Treasure Island)

Cornwall, the unreality
of Cornwall:

hull down, the mobile homes
are shelling the Bristol Channel

which fights right back! Storm-lanterns
swing in the black
wind, and tomorrow
perspex and fibre-glass
will slosh about in the eddies.

Cornwall, the fabulous wreckers
of Cornwall: novelists.

A county in Bermuda,
that unreality also.
It was a literary Empire.

Black Jack Pendennis has
been out again. To a lonely
inn upon Bodmin Moor
etcetera, on a wild
October night
etcetera.

Different for the Cornish,
it must be. But for us
Lancashire and Yorkshire
interlopers who
run curio-shops on the quay
it has, as an arena
for growing old in, one
desolate advantage:
it cannot be believed in.

Black patches on both eyes...

Cumberland

I tend to suppose the part I know least
Of England is the north-west.

A honeymoon in the Lake District
Is conventional matter-of-fact;

And ours was the winter of '45!
On ghyll and yew-tree grove

And packhorse-bridge, the blowtorch air
Was singeing the nostril-hair;

Snow that had lain deep for weeks
Fantasticated our walks;

And Rydal Water to our tread
Rang, till Helvellyn heard.

Exalted by love, in wintry rigours
Unlikely Cumberland rages

Thus in my memories. North-west,
I know you least, or best?

Derbyshire

We never made it. Time and time again
Sublimity went unexamined when
We turned back home through Winster, lacking heart
For walking further. Yet the Romantic part
Of Via Gellia, where it dives through chasms
To Ashbourne, is historic; there, short spasms
Of horror once in many a heaving breast
Gave Derbyshire a dreadful interest.

And I too was Romantic when I strode
Manfully, aged 12, the upland road.
Only the name of 'Via Gellia' jarred;
It seemed to mean a classical boulevard
With belvederes at intervals. I swelled
My little chest disdainfully, I 'rebelled'!

Devonshire

Discharged upon the body of the world
    Drake, Hawkins, all that semen
    Has left no stain! Instead
    The disblitzed Plymouth: first
Violin to squeal the eunuch's part
    Well-planned, a work of art.

We run through a maze of tunnels for our meat
    As rats might; underpass,
    Walkway, crash-barrier lead
    Our willing steps, as does
The questionnaire that we shall be so kind
    As to complete (unsigned)

Between North Road and Paddington. Drake's Circus
    Proffers the hoops the trained
    Corpulent animals are
    Glad to jump through. Drake,
This is the freedom that you sailed from shore
    To save us for?

Dorset

John Fowles's book, *The French Lieutenant's Woman*:
'A grand ebullient portrait certainly'
Of Thomas Hardy's country, where however
I would not strike such sparkles. Slow and vocal
Amber of a burring baritone
My grandad's voice, not Hardy's, is what stays
Inside me as a slumbrous apogee,
Meridional altitude upon
Pastoral England's longest summer day.

O golden age! Bee-mouth, and honeyed singer!

County Durham

Driving up from Tees-side
The first and only time,
I had been there before;
I might have been in Goldthorpe.

My cousin kept a shop
For baby-linen in Goldthorpe;
Doing the same in Brighouse
An aunt went out of her mind.

But mostly, visible beauty
Intruded on a coal-field
So little, one was not
Unsettled by its absence.

Coal-field! A term like tundra,
Rain-forest, *karst,* savannah;
A humanly created
Topographical constant.

Indelible! Let rosebay
Willow herb, fiery emblem,
Push as it will, let the pits
Close, there will still be Goldthorpe.

I am told at the miners' gala
They bear green boughs and, Prince-
Bishop, a Lord of Misrule
Preaches in your cathedral.

And I am supposed to be
Delighted by that survival?
My Lord, your Lord of Misrule
Ruled, and rules, in Goldthorpe.

Essex

Names and things named don't match
Ever. This is not
A plethora of language,
But language's condition;

Sooner or later the whole
Cloth of the language peels off
As wallpaper peels from a wall,
However it 'hangs together'.

With Essex moreover the case is
Especially grievous: hope,
Disappointment, fatuous shocks
And surprises pattern the fabric.

Constable's country merits
Better than I can give it
Who have unfinished business
There, with my own failures.

Gloucestershire

for Charles and Brenda

Not architecture, not
(Good heavens!) city-planning,
But a native gift for townscape
Appears to have distinguished
The pre-industrial English.

Parochialism therefore,
Though of a Tuscan kind,
Discovers in the practice
Of this one homely art
The measure of *civiltà*.

A laudable Little England
Grounded on this conviction
Would fortify the Cotswolds,
Adopting as its tribal
Metropolis Chipping Camden.

Hampshire

'Our argute voices vied among the bracken.'
    My sixth-form prize from the North
Was Ronald Bottrall's *Festivals of Fire,*
    My own precocious choice.

A chaste young sailor (one thing I was not
    Precocious at was sex),
Abruptly, two years later, I pronounced
    This verse to a willowy Wren.

An educated girl, she recognized
    The bracken where we stood
Alone together in a woodland ride,
    And took 'argute' on trust.

Past that same wood near Wickham, that same year,
    My nineteenth autumn, I
Rode the country bus from Winchester
    To 'Collingwood' at Fareham.

Alone I'd spent my week-end's leave upon
    St Catherine's Hill, upon
Wolvesey Castle, the Cathedral Close;
    Seen the Round Table, doubtful.

All the South Country that I knew from books!
    Joining the Navy meant
My first time south to London, south from there
    Into my element:

Verses and books, 'argute' and Camelot.
I could correct that Hampshire, but shall not.

Herefordshire

At Hay, or near it, 1944
on winter leave, and walking through the moonlight
the country roads with Gavin Wright, I sealed
with a prompt fear the classical commonplace:
'As one who walks alone at night and fears
each brigand bush, each clump a nest of spears...'
I read that later, out of Juvenal.

A classical region, then? I think so, yes.
Though those were the Welsh Marches, it was not
classical Europe that we beat the bounds of;
barbarians indeed were at our doors
but not round there where, in a world at war,
with atavistic Englishness I saw
the black Black Mountains menacing our acres.

Hertfordshire

Was it, I wondered, some freak
of earth or just bad technique
    on the builder's part that made
    the pavement blocks before
    our friends' house hump and crack?
Could we, as our city shoes slipped
think Hertfordshire equipped,
    as Kent and Surrey were not,
    thus to resist the encroaching
    concrete apron of London?
No hope of that, alas!
An aspiring middle-class
    could however, we saw,
    make a humanly touching thing
    out of a suburb. It was
not wholly anonymous ground
on which they moved around,
    if it could mutiny thus
    in an Anglo-Jewish enclave
    between Finchley and Barnet.
Displacement and decay
provided for, brought into play
    by a prudent builder ensure
    that, suddenly dying, we leave
    our friends with something to say.

Huntingdonshire

Italian prisoners of war still haunted
    The Huntingdon we quartered
For flats to rent, untimely family
    A student's grant supported.

Many such families, then. The shaking frames
    Of a shared memory feature
A man from Pembroke with his Serbian bride,
    A sexless rawboned creature.

They lived, they said, in a jacked, abandoned bus.
    We wondered: Could they suckle,
Those flattened breasts? And the fingers! Labour Camps
    Had broken every knuckle.

What has become of them? Foolish to ask. But to couples
    We sometimes meet, we assign a
Not dissimilar past: our Roman host
    Has a Polish wife with *angina*.

Huntingdon's bard, androgynous William Cowper,
    Announced it to us all:
That Simoïs and Mincio, like Ouse,
    Sucked down his garden-wall.

Kent

Chatham was my depot,
Chatty Chatham, 'chatty'
Meaning squalid. So it
Was, the little town
One trundled to out of London
As to a dead-end England.

Of course I knew this was
To get things upside-down;
Still, so it proved for some
Soon after, in E-Boat Alley.

Lancashire

My father was born in Horton
In Ribblesdale – the highest
Signal-box in England
He'd say, but he was biased.

Though Horton is in Yorkshire,
The Ribble flows to the west.
I have imagined that river
With awful interest:

Dark gullies, sobbing alders
Must surely mark its course;
It rolls and rounds its boulders
With more than natural force.

For down that sombre valley
(I knew, without being told)
The famous Lancashire witches
Had long ago taken hold,

And a troop of Catholic gentry
Mustered from manors near
Rode hopelessly to Preston
To join the Chevalier.

Liverpool, Manchester, Salford
I've seen, and felt oppressed;
But Clitheroe's haunted river
I've never put to the test.

Should anyone taunt me with this,
The sneer's well merited.
But I pray you, remember my father –
The fault's inherited.

Leicestershire

From a view to a kill in pursuit
Of what can't fill the belly
May do for hunting the fox;
But I.A. Richards on Shelley
Was an obfuscating splendour.

Equally there in Leicester
I listened to the aureate
Archaic tongue of Blunden,
Who through his spell as laureate
Of Oxford smiled and was speechless.

Perhaps the Leicester Poetry
Society is still calling
Its week-end schools together;
It's my fault if I've fallen
Out of touch with its sponsors.

At Loughborough, I remember,
A man too little regarded
(Dead since), V.C. Clinton-
Baddeley afforded
Several views of Yeats.

Lincolnshire

for Kathleen Wilson

Simpering sideways under a picture-hat
Gainsborough Lady, every Odeon
Or Gaumont of the 'thirties knew her well.

Those British films she regally inclined
To sponsor were, I see now, laying claim
To suavities like Gainsborough the painter's.

Tricked by the name, though, I for years envisaged
Milady at her town in Lincolnshire;
Gainsborough, a sort of Tunbridge Wells.

Beau Nash was there, Beau Brummel took the waters.
If films were shot there (not the ones we saw
Oddly enough), they were demure and tasteful.

The place to go to see the Gainsborough Lady,
As I remember, was the Globe in New Street.
Cousin Kathleen, did you ever go there?

I think you may have done, going or coming
From grandmother's in Day Street. If you did,
Were you, like me, seduced by the genteel?

Easy to see you might be. There were rough
Diamonds all about us; Barnsley-born,
In us some mincing was forgivable.

In Louth that Tory stronghold, in the trilled
Late light on the wolds, a false refinement irks
As not in grimy Gainsborough or Scunthorpe.

Middlesex

Germans, she said, were sometimes independent;
Her countrymen were all for package-tours,

A girl from Wembley Stadium serving beers
In a Greek bar. A maxiskirt from Bristol
Hawked prints on the Acropolis; from Chepstow
Another served us in a coffee-bar.
Our age-group is dependent, but not theirs.

Temporary drop-outs or true wives
To young and struggling Greeks, they do us more
Credit than we deserve, their timid parents.

The longer loop their Odysseys, the more
Warmly exact the Ithakas they remember:
Thus, home she said was Middlesex, though Wembley
I should have named, indifferently, as 'London'.

Monmouthshire

for Doreen

The colonist's 'they' that needs no antecedent;
And as self-evident for the colonized –
Both mouths remorseless. For the Silurist
Self-styled, for Henry Vaughan, both
    Unthinking pronouns missed
The peaceful point three hundred years ago.

Anglo-Welsh: that mixture took and held
Through centuries. My dear wife, we endorsed it:
Our sons are a quarter Welsh if they care to think so.
Our brother-in-law was happy, when the Sappers'
    Reunion was in Chepstow,
To gossip with old comrades of Cawnpore.

Norfolk

An arbitrary roll-call
Of worthies: Nelson, Paine,
Vancouver, Robert Walpole.

Vancouver, stolid Dutchman
Born at Lynn, forgotten;
Too much the flogging captain.

Walpole: heaven-high smell of
Whitewash on tainted beef,
Piquant in learning's nostril.

(Unprincipled, vindictive,
All that Pope said, and worse
Confirmed, and spelt as virtue.)

But Nelson and mysterious
Tom Paine, baleful in Thetford,
Napoleonic portents...

Who answers for the double
Aspect of genius, arcing
From Corsica or Norfolk?

Northamptonshire

King's Cliffe, in the evening: that Northampton stone
As fine as Cotswold, and more masculine...

Turpin on wheels, my long-lost self that rode
Southward the Great North Road, and had

This bourne in mind, that night was disconcerted:
Youth hostel, yes; also a sort of shrine.

To William Law! Well, later on I learned
To gut that author for my purposes.

Questions remain, however. William Law,
Saint of the English Church... And what is sainthood?

Some leading questions must be answered soon,
Lead where they will, scared schoolboy, where they will!

Northumberland

'I hear Aneurin number the dead' – *(Brigg Flatts)*

Johnson's pentameters, nailed by the solid *ictus;*
'Felt percussion of the marching legions.'

Late excavations on the Wall report
The garrisons lived there in their excrement;

Centurions with their centuries, some thousands
– A decimal system drills to a count of ten –
Barked to a halt when Aneurin numbered the dead.

The laboured mole dilapidates, surmounted
By barrel-chests, Aegean or Cymric metres.

Nottinghamshire

Rosebay willow herb pushing
through patches of old slag
in the curtains of driving rain
obscured the Major Oak.

Or else (our steam was blurring
the windows of the Hillman)
it was our being hounded
out of doors that felled
the last tall stands of Sherwood.

Robin of Locksley, Guy
of Gisborne, and the Sheriff
of Nottingham had been dapples
under my mother's smiles
all down the glades of boyhood.

But now she could take no more
of us, and of our baby.

In the country of *Sons and Lovers*
we think we know all too much
about the love of mothers.

Angry and defiant,
rash on industrial waste,
the rosebay willow herb
is, of all the flowers
she taught me, one I remember.

Oxfordshire

'Start such a fire in England, Master Ridley,
As shall not be put out' – the coupled martyrs
That Oxford steers by in its Morris Minors
Fried for a quibble in Scripture or Canon Law!

Saints we remember, must we remember martyrs?
Baptists though we were, I knew from childhood
Latimer's words, and knew the fire he meant:
Godly work, the pious Reformation.

Crucifixions! Hideousness of burning,
Sizzle of fats, the hideous martyrdoms:
Palach consumed in Prague, a human torch;
A Saigon Buddhist, robe a more lambent saffron;

Dead for a country, dead for a Constitution
(Allende, in his mouth the emptied chamber
Of prompt and fluent deputies), were these
Crucifixions? They were suicides.

'Martyrs may seek their death, but may not seize it...'
Fine scruples, fine distinctions! Can there be
Any too fine for fine-toned Oxford, in
The smell of roast meat and the glare of torches?

Rutland

for George Dekker

Joke county, smallest in England.
But I remember distinctly, more than once,
Swinging the car at the bend by the railway yards
In Oakham, Rutland's county town. The last
Time was to see – I think you remember, George,
For your own reasons – paintings by my old
Friend, Bill Partridge. Dead now. Had you noticed?

How heavy that weighs, how wide the narrowest shire!

Shropshire

This has to be for my school-chum Billy Greaves
Who surfaced out of the past two years ago,
Breaking his journey to Fiji off one of his leaves;
He spoke to me by phone from San Francisco.

If we had met (we agreed upon 'next time'),
Would reminiscences have turned to Clun,
Clungunford, Clunbury, and Housman's rhyme?
('Quietest places,' he called them, 'under the sun.')

Possibly not; though once we wore out brake-blocks
Coasting from Wenlock Edge. And days gone by
Furnish a line of talk that's orthodox
For chance-met class-mates under a foreign sky.

Things change. Gone now the troublesome chores of Empire
That might earn such indulgences. We've seen,
Billy and I, our fractious nation tire
Too soon of holding Suva for the Queen.

Our parents at their tennis-club… A high
Lob in the last light hangs like Nemesis
On 1912! Deceived, my father's eye
Foresees the easy smash that he will miss.

Still, I'd quite like it, Billy, if you could
Recall for me above what gravelly flats
In what fly-haunted stream it was, we stood
In the weak light, pyjama-ed, swiping at bats.

Somerset

Antennae of the race,
'the damned and despised *literati*…'

Just how, she wanted to know
(swinging a shopping-bag
from Bridgewater), could
William Pitt have depended
for his intelligence on
a coterie in Racedown:
Coleridge and Southey, Wordsworth?

Big as a mule, a stag
through hedgerows down from Exmoor,
wall-eyed, nostrils flaring,
could not intrude more rudely
upon an *avant-garde*
seminar in the Quantocks.

Staffordshire

The jaunty style of Arnold Bennett's 'Card'…

From years ago I call to mind my father,
flushed and uncertain, stalling time after time
a borrowed car in Newcastle-under-Lyme,

who had sung as a young man, 'I was one of the knuts'.

Suffolk

Something gone, something gone out with Nelson,
With him or by him. Something in its place:
A Dynamo! Broke of the Shannon takes,
Crippled in his retirement, a sedate
Pride in totting up the butcher's bills
Of single-ship engagements, finds his own
(His head still singing from an American cutlass)
The bloodiest yet. Audacity of Nelson
Sired Broke and calloused him; Jane Austen's hero,
Honourable, monogamous and sober,
Gunnery-expert, servant of the State,
His small estate was somewhere here, in Suffolk.
A better image should be found for it.

My education gave me this bad habit
Of reading history for a hidden plot
And finding it; invariably the same one,
Its fraudulent title always, 'Something Gone'.

Gainsborough might have painted him, with his
Wife and children and a sleek retriever
(Thomas Gainsborough, born at Sudbury)
In a less glaring light, a truer one.

Surrey

'In yonder grave a Druid lies' – ('Ode on the Death of Thomson')

Who now reads Thomson or Collins?

'Conifer country of Surrey,'
wrote Betjeman, 'approached through
remarkable wrought-iron gates.'

No missing the affection
there, nor the observation.

But on the Thames at Richmond
less tenderly, an eye for
the general more than the pungent
had lifted it to grandeur:

'Suspend the dashing oar.'

Sussex

Chiddingly, pronounced
Chiddinglye: the oast-house
Received us with warm brick,
A croquet-lawn, and squirrels.

And like the transatlantic
Visitors we were,
Our self-congratulations
And charmed response were fervent.

The most poeticized
Of English counties, and
An alien poet's eye,
Mine, there to endorse it.

We had to pinch ourselves
To know we knew the rules
Of cricket played on the green.
Our boy will never learn them.

'Brain-drain' one hears no more of,
And there's no loss. There is
Another emigration:
Draining away of love.

Warwickshire

for Roy Fisher

Eye on the object, eye on the congeries
of objects, eye on the scene
with figures of course, eye on the scene with figures,
delivers us Birmingham. Who is to say it squints?

And yet Spaghetti Junction on the M
6 is, shall we say,
a comparable alternative solution
(to a problem of traffic-flow
in several ways at once on several levels)
to the Piazza d'Aracoeli. Shall we
say that much or in
the Shakespeare country can we? If the tongue
writhes on the foreign syllables, it shows
small relish for your balder registrations,

intent, monocular, faithful.

Westmorland

Kendal... Shap Fell! Is that in Westmorland?
For one who espouses the North,
I am hazy about it, frankly. It's a chosen
North of the mind I take my bearings by,
A stripped style and a wintry;

As on Shap Fell, the only time I was there,
Wind cutting over and snowflakes beginning to sail
Slantwise across, on haulage vans clashing their gears
And me who had walked from Glasgow.

An end-of-October taste, a shade too late
For the right full ripeness. The style is decadent almost,
Emaciated, flayed. One knows such shapes,
Such minds, such people, always in need of a touch
Of frost, not to go pulpy.

Wiltshire

A brutally sheared-off cliff
Walling a cutting between
Barnsley and Doncaster is
The Railway Age in essence.

More cliffs, the hanging gardens
Of gossamer soot as the train
Creeps into Liverpool Street –
This too is in keeping.

But also consider the bugle
And stage-coach clatter silenced;
The beep and vroom of the Daimler
Unheard, and on the chalk

The human beetle rising
And falling for hours in the silence,
The distance: Jude the Obscure
Approaching, on Salisbury Plain.

Worcestershire

for Doreen

The best way in (not that I've checked the map)
Might be from West by North, as once we came
After a drive through spooky Radnor Forest
Where you had sat upon a picnic rug
And wept and wept. I laboured into verse
My sense of that, and made no sense at all.

Maria Theresa, I addressed you as,
Imperial sorrow. God knows what I meant
By that, or thought I meant. If I could not
Make you Fair Austria then, I shall not now;
But spin you down, down by whatever stages
Wise maps might tell me, into the blossoming plains.

Feed you with apples, stay you with flagons, Empress!
Acre on acre of orchards of Worcester Pearmains!

Yorkshire

Of Graces

The graces, yes – and the airs! To airs and graces
Equally the West Riding gave no houseroom
When I was young. Ballooning and mincing airs
Put on in the 'down there' of England! I was
Already out of place in the heraldic
Cities of the Midlands – Warwick, Leicester, the South …

    – And therefore it is a strain, thinking of Brough
    And Appleby gone from King John to a Frenchman
    For dirty work done on the roads of Poitou.

This helps me – not to pipe like your reed, Bunting,
Master of Northern stops – but to remember,
Never quite well enough, Kirkby Stephen
By Aisgill on to Hawes, to Aysgarth, Askrigg,
The narrow dale past a hump of broken stones.
Slant light out of Lancashire burnished the fell.

Alix, Kate, Eleanor, Anne – Angevin names –
You were not my hopscotch-mates; but Rhoda,
Thelma and Mona. Enormous their mottled
Fore-arms drove flat-irons later, strove with sheets
In old steam-laundries. There the Saxons queened it
No less – the Elfridas, Enids, many Hildas.

Ladies, ladies! Shirley or Diane or…
Which of you girls will be mine? Which of you all
In my dishonourable dreams sits smiling
Alone, at dusk, and knowledgeably sidelong,
Perched on a heap of stones, where 'Dangerous' says
The leaning board, on a green hill south of Brough?

Where is the elf-queen? Where the beldam Belle Dame?
Feyness of the North, kelpie of some small beck
In a swale of marble swirls over Durham,
Irrigates Elmet, combs the peat in Ewden.
And I have no faith in that: *le fay* thinned out
Into a pulse in the grass, St Winifred.

Eleanor rather, Alix, ladies of Latins,
I call you down. (And Mary, Mother of Heaven?)
Justice and Prudence (Prue, a name not given
North of the Trent), Courage, and Temperance were
Your erudite names, mothers of Latin earth.
What *royaume* of earth, elf-queen, did you sway ever?

Charites or *Gratiae,* the Graces,
Lemprière says, 'presided over kindness',
Each dam in her own kind fructive. Only two.
(Three came later.) Two: *Hegemone,* the Queen,
And *Auxo*, Increase. Queen of Elfland, in what
Assize did you sit, what increase ever foster?

Now every girl has this elvish admixture.
Thomas of Ercildoune, what you dreamed of once
Fogs every brae-side: lank black the hair hangs down,
The curves of the cheek are hollow and ravaged.
Their womanhood a problematic burden
To them and their castrated mates, they go past.

I have a Grace. Whether or no the Muses
Patronize me, I have a Grace in my house
And no elf-lady. Queen she is called, and Increase,
Though late-come, straitened, of a Northern Province.

IN THE STOPPING TRAIN
AND OTHER POEMS

Father, the Cavalier

I have a photograph here
    In California where
You never were, of yourself
    Riding a white horse. And
The horse and you are dead
    Years ago, although
Still you are more alive
    To me than anyone living.

As for the horse: an ugly
    Wall-eyed brute, apparently
Biddable though, for I cannot
    Believe you were ever much of
A horseman. That all came late:
    Suddenly, in your forties,
Learning to ride! A surrogate
    Virility, perhaps...

For me to think so could not
    Make you any more
Alive than you have been here,
    Open-necked cricket-shirt
And narrow head, behind
    The pricked ungainly ears
Of your white steed – all these
    Years, unnoticed mostly.

The Harrow

Unimaginable beings –
Our own dead friends, the dead
Notabilities, mourned and mourning,
Hallam and Tennyson... is it
Our loss of them that harrows?

Or is it not rather
Our loss of images for them?
The continued being of Claude
Simpson can be imagined.
We cannot imagine its mode.

Us too in this He harrows. It is not
Only on Easter Saturday
That it is harrowing
To think of Mother dead,
To think, and not to imagine.

He descended into –
Not into Hell but
Into the field of the dead
Where he roughs them up like a tractor
Dragging its tray of links.

Up and down the field, a tender bruising,
A rolling rug of iron, for the dead
Them also, the Virtuous Pagans
And others, He came, He comes
On Easter Saturday and

Not only then He comes
Harrowing them – that they,
In case they doubted it, may
Quicken and in more
Than our stale memories stir.

The Departed

They see his face!

Live in the light of...

Such shadows as they must
cast, sharp-edged;
the whole floor, said to be crystal,
barry with them. And long!

Spokes that reach even to us,
Pinned as we are to the rim.

Rousseau in his Day

So many nights the solitary lamp had burned;
So many nights his lone mind, slowing down
Deliberately, had questioned, as it turned
Mooning upon its drying stem, what arc
Over a lifetime day had moved him through.

Always he hoped he might deserve a Plutarch,
Not to be one posterity forgot.
Nor have we. He has left his mark: one tight
Inched-around circuit of the screw of light,
As glowing shadows track the life of roses
Over unchosen soil-crumbs. It was not
What he'd expected or the world supposes.

After the Calamitous Convoy (July 1942)

An island cast
its shadow across
the water. Where
they sat upon
the Arctic shore
it shadowed them.

The mainland rose
tawny before
their eyes and closed
round them in capes
the island must
have slid from, once.

Under one horn
of land not quite
naked, above
the anchorage
white masonry
massed round a square.

From there one gained
the waterfront
by, they perceived,
a wooden stair
that wound down through
workshops and godowns.

Admiringly
their eyes explored
make-do-and-mend:
arrangements that
the earth lent – stairs,
cabins on struts,

stages of raised
catwalks between
stair and railed stair,
staked angles, ramps
and landings in
the open air.

Roof of the world,
not ceiling. One
hung to it not
as flies do but
as steeplejacks
move over rungs.

Survivors off
the Russian run,
years later they
believed the one
stable terrain
that Arctic one.

Depravity: Two Sermons

1. *Americans: for their Bicentennial*

The best, who could, went back – because they nursed
A need to find depravity less dispersed,
Less, as it seemed, diluted by crass hope.
So back went Henry James to evil Europe,
Unjust, unequal, cruel. Localized,
The universal could be realized
In words and not in words; not by the Press
Nor the theatrical Pulpit. Prefaces
Delineate the exquisite pains he took
To bottle up a bad smell in a book.
Inordinate pains! For Paris, London, Rome
Were not much less disorderly than back home;
There too, already, what he sought was traced
Upon no maps, but must be found by Taste,
A nostril lifted to the tainted gale
Of words, of words – all shop-soiled, all for sale.
Each year that he survived, things fell apart
Till H.G. Wells was 'Life', and he was 'Art'.
'Life'! Is it something else than life, to live
On the scent always of that faint, pervasive
Smell that alone explains what we've become?
What ought to be, and once was, axiom?

2. *St Paul's Revisited*

'The change of Philomel, by the barbarous king,
So rudely forced'.
*[In the myth, Philomela became a nightingale, and
Tereus, her ravisher, a hoopoe.]*

Anger, a white wing? No, a hoopoe's wing,
King Tereus, Hatred. Crested ravisher,
The motley lapwing whoops and whoops it up
Greek Street and Fleet Street till the gutters run
Their serial feature. Liquid, yellow, thick,
It pools here, fed from the Antipodes,
The Antilles... For the seven seas run with bile
To the Pool of London, sink where the ordure, talent
At home in this world, gathers. And it pools
Not only there but in whatever head
Recalls with rage the choir of Christ and Wren.

Horned and self-soiling, not the barbarous king
Of Thrace and the anthologies, nor a brute,
A plain quick killer, but degenerate,
The rapist lapwings sideways through our heads
And finds no exit. There's a place it might:
The A-to-Z preserves no record of it
Though Strype or any antique gazetteer
Describes it well enough, a Thames-side borough
Decayed already, called Depravity.
If we could find it now, our hoopoes might
Hop from inside our heads, and Thames run cleaner.

Anger won't do it. Ire! Its hooked bill gouges
The chicken-livers of its young. Irate,
We are depraved, and by that token. Gulls
Cry, and they skeeter on a candid wing
Down slopes of air, but not for anger's sake.
Spite, malice, arrogance and 'Fuck you, Jack',
Birds in the gables of Depravity
Twitter and cheep, but most inside my head
And can be lived with. But the hoopoe whoops
Always inside, and rancorous. Rancour! Rancour!
Oh patriotic and indignant bird!

Seeing Her Leave

'gardens bare and Greek' – Yvor Winters

This West! this ocean! The bare
Beaches, the stony creek
That no human affair
Has soiled… Yes, it is Greek,

What she saw as the plane
Lifted from San Jose.
Under the shadow of Wren
She walks her ward today;

Once more my tall young woman
Has nerved herself to abandon
This Greece for the Graeco-Roman
Peristyles of London,

Where the archaic, the heated,
Dishevelled and frantic Greek
Has been planed and bevelled, fitted
To the civic, the moralistic.

And that has been noble, I think,
In her and others. Such
Centuries, sweat, and ink
Spent to achieve that much!

Lloyds of London, some
Indemnity for our daughters!
Those who trust the dome
Of St Paul's to the waters…

So much of the price is missed
In the tally of toil, ink, years;
Count, neo-classicist,
The choking back of tears.

(California)

Mandelstam, on Dante

1

Russian Jew, for you
    To re-think Dante, dissolve
Into fluids that four-square slab
    Of Christendom, meant a resolve

(So it must seem) to taunt
    And tempt the unsteadied Gentile,
As it might be me, to act
    In nettled Stalin's style.

Dangerous, those corrosives
    You handle. First and last
Powder the graven image!
    'Jew' means 'iconoclast'.

Can we believe the impulse
    Consciously suicidal?
Or was the play of mind
    Lordly, the interest idle?

2

About the skies, you went wrong somewhere. Let
Some nearer neighbour of theirs make the corrections.
For them it was easier, them the nine Olympic
Dantescan discuses, to clang directions!

You are not to be thought of apart from the life you lived
And what Life intends is at once to kill and caress
That thus the distress which beat in on your ears, on your eyes
And the sockets of your eyes, be Florentine.

Let us not then assign to you, no, let us not fit about your
Hollowed-out temples that bittersweet prickle, the laurel –
Better in your case if we should split your
Heart into blue and clamorous bits of ocean.

For when you died, having served out your time,
You in your time friend to all lifetime-livers,
Yes, there transpired a broader, a loftier chime
Sent from the skies in your entire chest's heavings.

3 (Voronezh, 1937)

'About the skies, I went wrong somewhere. Let
Some nearer neighbour of theirs make the corrections.
For you it was easier, you the nine Olympic
Dantescan discuses, to clang directions,
Be out of breath, get black and blue contusions…

But Thou, if Thou art not the heretofore's
Nothing-accomplishing hero, if Thou art bent
Standing over me now, wine-steward, to proffer the cup,
Pour me the strong wine, not the ephemeral ferment
To drink of, to pledge the vertiginous, towering, straight-up
Insane blue-azure's hand-to-hand engagement.

Dovecotes, black holes, starlings' nesting-boxes,
Blue of the bluest, case of the key at its keenest,
Ice of the heretofore, high ice! – ice of the Spring…
Clouds, look – the clouds, against soft collusions embattled…
Quiet now! Storm-clouds, see where they lead them out, bridled.'

4

Rhyme, you once said, only
   Points it up, tags it, the blue
Cabinet-making of Heaven
   And Earth, the elegant joints
All of them flush as given!

Symmetries in this blue
   Cabinet, the small
Rooms of stanzas – in this
   No woe, you said, but the happy
Chances of mathematics.

Clouds come and go like a French
   Polisher's breath on walnut,
Protean, fluid… And you
   A lordly squandering playboy!
No bequest but you blue it!

At home in the Empyrean...
    Yes, but one joint had sprung
Long, long ago. The woe
    Came, and was Florentine?
As well say: Galilean.

Death of a Painter

in memoriam William Partridge

Behind the grid, the radiant
planes and translucent ledges
of colour,

the constructions,

feelingful but extreme
distortions, as my eye found them,

three or four trees and a Norman
church-tower in Leicestershire? Well
yes, if you say so.
You painted always from nature.
That mattered, you always said.

Hard to see why, unless

among these cobalts and
pale yellows, these
increments and crumblings,

in that or another churchyard
we are permitted to speak
to a Divine Distorter
these lines that you occasion.

Portland

after Pasternak

Portland, the Isle of Portland – how I love
Not the place, its name! It is as if
These names were your name, and the cliff, the breaking
Of waves along a reach of tumbled stone
Were a configuration of your own
Firm slopes and curves – your clavicles, your shoulder.
A glimpse of that can set the hallway shaking.

And I am a night sky that is tired of shining,
Tired of its own hard brilliance, and I sink.

Tomorrow morning, grateful, I shall seem
Keen, but be less clear-headed than I think;
A brightness more than clarity will sail
Off lips that vapour formulations, make
Clear sound, full rhyme, and rational order take
Account of a dream, a sighing cry, a moan.

Like foam on all three sides at midnight lighting
Up, far off, a seaward jut of stone.

Orpheus

named them
and they danced
they danced: the rocks, stones, trees.

What had possessed them,
or him? How did it help?

What had got into those stones,
throwing up puffs
of yellow dust as they bounced, and could he
hear them, an irregular percussion
there in the blinding sunlight
like a discotheque at a distance?

No, I'm afraid not: weightless.
For them to dance
they had to be light as air,
as the puff of air that named them.

Thistledown rocks! Who needs them?

Well but, they danced for joy,
his holy joy
in stones, in there being stones
there, that stones should be,
and boulders too, and trees...

Is that how it was? One hopes so.

Ars Poetica

in memoriam Michael Ayrton, sculptor

Walk quietly around in
A space cleared for the purpose.

Most poems, or the best,
Describe their own birth, and this
Is what they are – a space
Cleared to walk around in.

Their various symmetries are
Guarantees that the space has
Boundaries, and beyond them
The turbulence it was cleared from.

Small clearances, small poems;
Unlikely now the enormous
Louring, resonant spaces
Carved out by a Virgil.

The old man likes to sit
Here, in his black-tiled *loggia*
A patch of sun, and to muse
On Pasternak, Michael Ayrton.

Ayrton, he remembers.
Soon after reading his
Obituary, behold!
A vision of him:

The bearded, heavy-shouldered
London clubman, smiling
Against a *quattrocento*
View of the upper Arno.

This was in answer to prayer:
A pledge, a sufficient solace.
Poor rhyme, and are you there?
Bless Michael with your promise.

The old man likes to look
Out on his tiny *cortile,*
A flask of 'Yosemite Road'
Cheap Chablis at his elbow.
                    (California)

In the Stopping Train

★

I have got into the slow train
again. I made the mistake
knowing what I was doing,
knowing who had to be punished.

I know who has to be punished:
the man going mad inside me;
whether I am fleeing
from him or towards him.

This journey will punish the bastard:
he'll have his flowering gardens
to stare at through the hot window;
words like 'laurel' won't help.

He abhors his fellows,
especially children; let there
not for pity's sake
be a crying child in the carriage.

So much for pity's sake.
The rest for the sake of justice:
torment him with his hatreds
and love of fictions.

The punishing slow pace
punishes also places along the line
for having, some of them, Norman
or Hanoverian stone-work:

his old familiars, his
exclusive prophylactics.
He'll stare his fill at their
emptiness on this journey.

Jonquil is a sweet word.
Is it a flowering bush?
Let him helplessly wonder
for hours if perhaps he's seen it.

Has it a white and yellow
flower, the jonquil? Has it
a perfume? Oh his art could
always pretend it had.

He never needed to see,
not with his art to help him.
He never needed to use his
nose, except for language.

Torment him with his hatreds,
torment him with his false
loves. Torment him with time
that has disclosed their falsehood.

Time, the exquisite torment!
His future is a slow
and stopping train through places
whose names used to have virtue.

A stopping train, I thought,
was a train that was going to stop.
Why board it then, in the first place?

Oh no, they explained, it is stopping
and starting, stopping and starting.

How could it, they reasoned gently,
be always stopping unless
also it was always starting?

I saw the logic of that;
grown-ups were good at explaining.

Going to stop was the same
as stopping to go. What madness!
It made a sort of sense, though.

It's not, I explained, that I mind
getting to the end of the line.
Expresses have to do that.

No, they said. We see…
But do you? I said. It's not
the last stop that is bad…

No, they said, it's the last
start, the little one; yes,
the one that doesn't last.

Well, they said, you'll learn
all about that when you're older.

Of course they learned it first.
Oh naturally, yes.

★

The man in the stopping train
sees them along the highway
with a recklessness like breeding
passing and re-passing:
dormobile, Vauxhall, Volvo.

He is shrieking silently: 'Rabbits!'
He abhors his fellows.
Yet even the meagre arts
of television can
restore them to him sometimes,

when the man in uniform faces
the unrelenting camera
with a bewildered fierceness
beside the burnt-out Simca.

★

What's all this about flowers?
They have an importance he can't
explain, or else their names have.

Spring, he says, 'stirs'. It is what
he has learned to say, he can say
nothing but what he has learned.

And Spring, he knows, means flowers.
Already he observes this.
Some people claim to love them.

Love *them?* Love flowers? Love,
love… the word is hopeless;
gratitude, maybe, pity…

Pitiful, the flowers.
He turns that around in his head:
what on earth can it mean?

Flowers, it seems, are important.
And he can name them all,
identify hardly any.

★

Judith Wright, Australian

'… has become,' I said, 'the voice
of her unhappy nation.'
O wistfully I said it.

Unhappier than it knows,
her nation. And though she will tell it,
it cannot understand:

with its terrible future before it,
glaring at its terrible past;

its disequilibrium, its
cancers in bud and growing;

all its enormous sadness
still taking off, still arcing

over the unhistoried
Pacific, humming to Chile.

Stone heads of Easter Island!
Spoiled archipelagos!

How they have suffered already
on Australia's account

and England's. They will suffer
no more on England's.

Judith Wright, Australian,
'has become,' I said,

'the voice of her unhappy,
still-to-be-guilty nation.'

Wistfully I said it,
there in the stopping train.

*

The things he has been spared...
'Gross egotist!' Why don't
his wife, his daughter, shrill
that in his face?

Love and pity seem
the likeliest explanations;
another occurs to him –
despair too would be quiet.

★

Time and again he gave battle,
furious, mostly effective;
nobody counts the wear
and tear of rebuttal.

Time and again he rose
to the flagrantly offered occasion;
nobody's hanged for a slow
murder by provocation.

Time and again he applauded
the stand he had taken; how much
it mattered, or to what
assize, is not recorded.

Time and again he hardened
his heart and his perceptions;
nobody knows just how
truths turn into deceptions.

Time and again, oh time and
that stopping train!
Who knows when it comes to a stand,
and will not start again?

★   (Son et Lumière)

I have travelled with him many times
now. Already we nod,
we are almost on speaking terms.

Once I thought that he sketched
an apologetic gesture
at what we turned away from.

Apologies won't help him:
his spectacles flared like paired
lamps as he turned his head.

I knew they had been ranging,
paired eyes like mine,
igniting and occluding

coppice and crisp château,
thatched corner, spray of leaf,
curved street, a swell of furrows,

where still the irrelevant vales
were flowering, and the still
silver rivers slid west.

★

The dance of words
is a circling prison, thought
the passenger staring through
the hot unmoving pane
of boredom. It is not
thank God a dancing pain,
he thought, though it starts to jig
now. (The train is moving.) 'This',
he thought in rising panic
(Sit down! Sit down!)
'this much I can command,
exclude. Dulled words, keep still!
Be the inadequate, cloddish
despair of me!' No good:
they danced, as the smiling land
fled past the pane, the pun's
galvanized *tarantelle*.

★

'A shared humanity…' He
pummels his temples. 'Surely,
surely that means something.'

He knew too few in love,
too few in love.

That sort of foolish beard
masks an uncertain mouth.
And so it proved: he took
some weird girl off to a weird
commune, clutching at youth.

Dear reader, this is not
our chap, but another.
Catch our clean-shaven hero
tied up in such a knot?
A cause of so much bother?

He knew too few in love.

His Themes

(after reading Edmond Jabès)

His themes? Ah yes he had themes.
It was what we all liked about him.
Especially I liked it.
One knew, nearly always one knew
what he was talking about, and he talked
in such a ringing voice.

What did he talk about? What,
just what were his themes?
Oh, of the most important!

Loss was one of his themes;
he told us, as any bard should,
>   the story of our people
>   (tribe), he had memorized
>   chronologies, genealogies,
>   the names and deeds of heroes,
>   the succession of our kings,
>   our priests, the sept of our pipers,
>   the mediations... and this
>   while, young and old,
>   we extolled the immediate, meaning
>   the unremembering. *Yes,*
>   *and what was his theme? His theme, you said, was... ?*
Loss. Loss was his theme.

And duty. He taught us our duty;
he taught us, as any
legislator should,
>   the rules of hygiene, the clean
>   and the unclean meats, the times and
>   the means of fumigation,
>   the strewing and spreading, of fires,
>   and what to do with the old
>   and how to dispose of the dead
>   and how to live with our losses
>   uncomplaining... and this
>   while, young and old,
>   we did our best to be free,
>   meaning unruly. *Yes,*
>   *and what was his theme? What did you say his theme was?*

Duty. His theme was duty.

Fear also. Fear was a theme;
he taught us, as all seers must,
continual apprehension:
>   of one another, of
>   our womenfolk and our
>   male children, of
>   the next clan over the mountains
>   and of the mountains, also
>   the waters, the heavenly bodies
>   wheeling and colliding,
>   of the wild beasts both large

and infinitesimal, of
revenants and of the future,
and of the structure of matter
and of the unknown… and all this
while, young and old,
we tried to keep our nerve,
meaning, to be heedless. *Yes,*
and what was the theme, did you say, of this voice both hollow and
ringing?

Fear. Fear was the theme.

We like to be told these things.
We need to be reminded.

He sounds like a sort of priest.
What was your priesthood doing?

Nonsensical things, like spinning
a shallow great bowl of words
poised on the stick of a question,
pointing it this way and that
for an answering flash, as the bend
of a river may come in a flash
over miles and miles
from a fold in the hills, over miles.

We paid them no attention.

To Thom Gunn in Los Altos, California

Conquistador! Live dangerously, my Byron,
In this metropolis
Of Finistère. Drop off
The edge repeatedly, and come
Back to tell us! Dogs and cherry-trees
Are not your element, although
You like them well enough when, cast
Ashore and briefly beached, our Commodore,
You take a turn among them, your cigar
Fragrant along a sunny garden wall,
Home between voyages, with your aunts in Kent.

Home… Is that home? Is even Land's End 'home'?
You shrug and say we are mid-Atlantic people,
You and I. I'd say for you
The mid-Pacific rather: somewhere out
On the International Dateline, so far out
Midsummer Oregon and midwinter Chile
Are equidistant, and 'the slow
Pacific swell' you generate lifts and crunches
Under the opalescent high fog with as much
Patience in one hemisphere as the other,
An exhalation from the depths you sound to.

The plesiosaur! Your lead-line has gone down to
The Age of Reptiles, even as
Over your head the flying lizard
Sprung from its Lompoc silo, Vandenberg Airforce Base,
Tracks high across mid-ocean to its target.
Ignore it, though a tidal wave will rage
From where it plunges, flood Japan
And poison Asia. This is the pacific
Ocean, the peacemaker. Nothing rhymes with this
Lethal indifference that you plumbed to even
Once in a bath-house in Sonoma County.

This is the end of the world. At the end, at the edge
We live among those for whom
As is natural enough
The edge is the navel of earth, and the end, the beginning.
Hope springs not eternal nor everywhere – does it
Spring in Kent? For these our friends, however,
It springs, it springs. Have we a share in it?
This is the Garden of Eden, the serpent coiled
Inside it is sleepy, reposeful. It need not flex
A muscle to take us. What are we doing here?
What am I doing, I who am scared of edges?

Seur, near Blois

That a toss of wheat-ears lapping
Church-walls should placate us
Is easy to understand
In the abstract. That in fact
The instance of seeing also
A well with its wrought-iron stanchion,
Of feeling a balmy coolness,
Of hearing a Sunday noon silence,
Of smelling the six ragged lime-trees,
A church-door avenue, should
Placate, compose, is as much
As to say that the eye and the nose,
Also the ear and the very
Surface of one's skin is
An ethical organ; and further,
If indeed it is further
Or even other, a learned
Historian of man's culture.

Gemona-del-Friuli, 1961–1976

We have written to Giulia, saying
'Are you still alive?'
And no reply comes.
This is a bad look out.

What sort of a life this is
I thought I knew, or I learned,
Some 15 years ago
Precisely in Giulia's country:

Gemona, the heartland, the forests
Living in an orange light
After calamity. That one!
That was the place;

Where a calamity, not
In any case undeserved,
Chastened, I thought, and instructed
Gravely, biddable me

As to the proper proportions
Of the dead to the living, of death
To life, and out of all
Proportion, love ... Now this!

Earthquake! And the entire
Small city of Gemona
Flat in one enormous
Stir of that rock-ribbed earth

Which had not in 700
Years – for some of Gemona
Had stood that long – not stirred
Like that in 700 years.

What colour of justification,
What nice, austere proportion
Now can be put on the mountains?
At whose hand this chastisement?

An Apparition

Gina, I saw you walk
Suddenly, in white
Brassière and panties under
A fish-net wrap; your sallow skin,

Firm and sullen to fire,
Inflamed the Panamanian
Day to exceptional ardours
In Tehuantepec Bay

As our Edwardian prow
Ploughed southward, and decrepit
Bodies basked in renewed
Delusory bronze and vigour.

The posh ships, P. & O.,
Trace in phosphorescent
Peppermint-fire on the oceans
An after-image of Empire.

The sun stooped down to take you,
Stiff on your bed in Boulder,
Colorado, Gina;
You will never grow older,

Nor will your empire ever,
Italo-American girl,
Crumble in Eritrea,
Dear wraith, raped by Apollo.

Horae Canonicae

Prime

New every morning is the love
Our wakening and uprising prove,
Bond it in warranty a hundred proof.
Giving his thanks for roof, for bed and board,
Mr Saint Keble, meek and lowly,
White with rite, and clean with holy,
Wordplays to the morning's Lord.

Terce

New every morning is the power
That activates us, active though we are…
At 9 o'clock, the scriptural 3rd hour,
Mr Saint William Law is eating his
Sweet humble pie: 'We have no more
Power of our own to move a hand or stir
A foot, than to stop clouds, or move the sun.'

Sext

'Filling us with such bowels of
Compassion as when' (Come, Mr Law, we are furnished
With bowels, and they are full, or they are not;
What room for other organs?), glimpsing her
Appallingly in Cambridge Circus, tracing
The faceless angel who mounted her once and vanished,
'We see the miseries of an hospital.'

Nones

At 3 o'clock in the afternoon,
Loggy with gin, with wine, with Mexican beer,
Resignation to the will of God
Comes easy. That it should be 'hardly worth
Living in a world so full of changes
And revolutions' – ah, how wrong! Yet dozing,
Fanned in a garden-chair, is hardly 'prayer'.

Vespers

This one for the telling of sins. And for
The original horror, the victimization, no problem.
But for our own, our particular own, in the sorry
Unrollings, where was the harm? Not nowhere, but
Where? In prayer, no place for 'all-over-the-place',
It comes to seem… My instructors' awful calm
Tell-tales the stink: half spunk, half frightened sweat.

Compline

Now I lay me down to sleep
Perhaps not to wake, and I am alone in the house!
How much alone in whatever house of bone,
Suddenly I love my fellow creatures
So much, though for that the hour was Sext, was noon.
I tell you over feverishly, my loved ones.
You are my own, you are? My own! My own?

Morning

Rose late: the jarring and whining
Of the parked cars under my windows, their batteries drained,
Somehow was spared. When I let out our schoolboy
Into the street, it was light: the place was alive and scented.

Spared too, for the most part, the puzzling tremulousness
That afflicts me often, these mornings. (I think
Either I need, so early, the day's first drink or
This is what a sense of sin amounts to:
Aghast incredulity at the continued success
Of an impersonation, the front put on to the world,
The responsibilities...)
                              Let all that go:
Better things throng these nondescript, barged-through streets
(The sun! The February sun, so happily far and hazy...)
Than a mill of ideas.
                          Sin, I will say, comes awake
With all the other energies, even at last the spark
Leaps on the sluggard battery, and one should have
Prosopopoeia everywhere: Stout Labour
Gets up with his pipe in his mouth or lighting
The day's first *Gauloise-filtre;* then stout
Caffein like a fierce masseur
Rams him abreast of the day; stout Sin
Is properly a-tremble; stout
Vociferous Electricity chokes and chokes,
Stumbles at last into coughings, and will soon
Come to the door with a telegram – 'Operation
Some Day This Week'; and stout
Love gets up out of rumpled sheets and goes singing
Under his breath to the supermarket, the classroom,
The briskly unhooded
Bureaucratic typewriter. See how
Sol winks upon its clever keys, and Flora
In a northern winter, far underground,
Feels herself sore at nubs and nipples.

And that mob of ideas? Don't knock them. The sick pell-mell
Goes by the handsome Olympian name of Reason.

To a Teacher of French

Sir, you were a credit to whatever
Ungrateful slate-blue skies west of the Severn
Hounded you out to us. With white, cropped head,
Small and composed, and clean as a Descartes
From as it might be Dowlais, 'Fiery' Evans
We knew you as. You drilled and tightly lipped
Le futur parfait dans le passé like
The Welsh Guards in St James's, your pretence
Of smouldering rage an able sergeant-major's.

We jumped to it all right whenever each
Taut smiling question fixed us. Then it came:
Crash! The ferrule smashed down on the first
Desk of the file. You whispered: *Quelle bêtise!*
Ecoutez, s'il vous plait, de quelle bêtise
on est capable!   Yet you never spoke
To us of poetry; it was purely language,
The lovely logic of its tenses and
Its accidence that, mutilated, moved you
To rage or outrage that I think was not
At all times simulated. It would never
Do in our days, dominie, to lose
Or seem to lose your temper. And besides
Grammarians are a dying kind, the day
Of histrionic pedagogy's over.

You never taught me Ronsard, no one did,
But you gave me his language. He addressed
The man who taught him Greek as *Toi qui dores*
(His name was Jean Dorat) *la France de l'or.*
I couldn't turn a phrase like that on 'Evans';
And yet you gild or burnish something as,
At fifty in the humidity of Touraine,
Time and again I profit by your angers.

Widowers

'i segni dell' antica fiamma'

Atheist, Laodicean or
Whatever name our hand-to-mouth evasions
Earn for us, all of us have the thought
That states of soul in some uncertain sort
Survive us – sealed, it could be, in locations:
A yard, a coomb, an inn, a Cornish tor.

These leak their fragrances. To tap the fount
Of consolation calls on us for no
Dexterity at first; it isn't hard
To bruise a hip by falling in that yard
Or on that hillside. Hurt is all we know,
Stout alpenstock as we begin to mount

The purgatorial steeps, the terraces
Kicked back behind us. Then we sweat, we stink,
We fear that we forget. Our ancient haunts
Glow far above us, and the glimmer taunts
Our coming numbness. There she dwells, we think…
She does, although our need to think so passes.

Some Shires Revisited

1. *Norfolk*

The scroll is defaced; the worm
Is in the roof; and the flaking
Inscription may be cleared
Of ivy but, if it is read,
It must be on the firm
Presumption it is mistaken.

Reading from haunted air
Certain great (which is not to say, good)
Historical presences – Walpole,
Nelson, landmarks in Norfolk –
I had readers who thought that I could
Never in fact have been there.

2. *Devonshire*

'Into Spooner's, looking for remnants,'
Said Mrs John; and her face was wistful
As if the town she recalled, the tenements
Burnt in the blitz, the streets like tunnels
Turning and twisting at cliff-like corners
Under the web of the wires, were a haven
Unspeakably lovely and calm. The destroyers
Had threatened her future; the young rebuilders
Tore down that future perfect in the past
Of a new-planned Plymouth, 1951.

3. *Leicestershire*

Clinton-Baddeley, Richards,
Blunden... these I have blessed:
Three good men named, and as many
Of those who invited them there
Unnamed, their equals or betters,
Upholders of what they professed
To care for, the world of letters
In the not quite wholly benighted
Midlands of England. In these
Worthies I have delighted
With a droll rhyme or two;
Leicestershire, when it housed them,
Did better than it knew.

4. *Staffordshire*
for Charles Tomlinson

'As once on Thracian Hebrus side' (to use
Your own Etrurian idiom, jasper-ware)

'The tree-enchanter Orpheus fell
By Bacchanalians torn',

So I have seen you – gasping, bloodied – fall
Time and again over twenty-five years, and the Maenads

Quite honestly astonished: 'But we surely
(Serenely, suavely) always gave him his due?'

Your love of our country has not been returned, and won't be.

5. *Bedfordshire*

Crop-headed nonconformists,
  Cromwell's Ironsides, sprang
Out of this clay. But not all
  The sour battalions rang
With benedictions when
  The sage dictator willed
  A king was to be killed.

Redbrick, round-windowed chapels,
  Squat on these gravels, rose,
And yet not all their broadcloth,
  When the time came, chose
The Red Flag as the only
  Colours to march to. Some
  Never came back from the Somme.

Born one of them, I think
  How it might be to be French;
How Protestants might man
  Pétain's untenable trench
And, rendering unto Caesar
  What's due to Caesar, might
  Die fighting the wrong good fight.

Grudging Respect

As when a ruined face
Lifted among those crowding
For the young squire's largesse
Perceives him recognize
Her and she grabs, not for any
Languidly lofted penny
They scrabble for, but for his eyes
And pockets them, their clouding
That instant; and the abruptness
With which his obliging is checked,
His suddenly leaving the place…

Just so may a grudging respect
Be, from a despised one,
Not just better than none
At all, but sweeter than any.

A Spring Song

'stooped to truth and moralized his song'

Spring pricks a little. I get out the maps.
Time to demoralize my song, high time.
Vernal a little. *Primavera*. First
Green, first truth and last.
High time, high time.

A high old time we had of it last summer?
I overstate. But getting out the maps...
Look! Up the valley of the Brenne,
Louise de la Vallière... Syntax collapses.
High time for that, high time.

To Château-Renault, the tannery town whose marquis
Rooke and James Butler whipped in Vigo Bay
Or so the song says, an amoral song
Like Ronsard's where we go today
Perhaps, perhaps tomorrow.

Tomorrow and tomorrow and... Get well!
Philip's black-sailed familiar, avaunt
Or some word as ridiculous, the whole
Diction kit begins to fall apart.
High time it did, high time.

High time and a long time yet, my love!
Get out that blessed map.
Ageing, you take your glasses off to read it.
Stooping to truth, we potter to Montoire.
High time, my love. High time and a long time yet.

Townend, 1976

When does a town become a city? This
That ends where I begin it, at Townend
With Wright the Chemist (one of the few not changed),
Grows cityfied, though still my drab old friend.

Thanks therefore for the practical piety
Of E.G. Tasker, antiquarian;
His *Barnsley Streets*. Unshed, my tears hang heavy
Upon the high-gloss pages where I scan

What else, though, but remembered homely squalor?
Generations of it! Eldon Street
Smells of bad drains of forty years ago
Ah sweetly. But should penury smell sweet?

An end to it then. An end to that town. Townend.
A Tetley's house, the Wheatsheaf, holds its station
Since 1853, where Dodworth Road
Stars into five streets, 'major intersection'.

Portentous words! Hoist up to suit South Yorkshire's
Administrative centre, such perforce
This town must live with, must live up or down to:
'Intersection'; 'shopping precinct'; 'concourse'...

And not to be sneered nor sniffed at. This is not,
It never was, Blackheath or Tunbridge Wells;
No buildings 'listed', nor deserving it,
Press to be saved as civic ardour swells.

Of cities much is written. Even Scripture
Has much to say of them, though mostly under
The inauspicious name of 'Babylon'.
What a town is, one is left to wonder.

Is homely squalor, then, its sign and function?
Is it a swollen village? If it is,
Are swellings lanced? Have towns a size or shape
More than villages and less than cities?

I think of the Irish, or perhaps the Celtic
'Townland'. (Also, 'township' might provoke us.)
'Townland', so my Irish years persuade me,
Means never a star of roads, never a focus.

Never! By no means! There's a lead at last:
Focus, a hearth. The English circumstance
In town or village draws to a hearth, a fug:
Townend, the up-draught up five flues at once!

Whatever meets that need, it's certain 'concourse',
'Complex' nor 'intersection' ever could.
Upon their hunkers, 'carring' (cowering) down
By a spent flame, the colliers of my boyhood...

That was in the 'thirties, 'the Depression';
Outside whatever pub it is in Kingstone,
Unwanted in the open, nipping air,
All the one class, a hardship town, all one.

Something, I take it, not to be found in cities;
No, nor in villages, what with parson, squire,
Farmer and farm-hand. (Just as well: the once
And ever martyred stoke a sullen fire.)

Up above Glossop, weeping cloud at Woodhead;
Up again after, over the last high hogsback,
The clean black waters shine up steel, not silver,
The peat is black, the lowering skies are black.

Millicent Dillon, if you ever visit
This town as you say you will, this is the way:
Ashbourne to Buxton, Buxton to Glossop, over
To an ash-boled England and a Baltic day.

For this is under us now, as we come down:
The Silkstone seam, where woods compacted lay
Shade upon shade, multiplication of blackness
That seeps up through: *'black* Barnsley', we would say.

The sneer of it – black Barnsley, that my mother
Indignantly thought corrupted out of 'bleak',
'Bleak Barnsley'. Who else cared? Corruption in
All that we do, decay in all we speak.

Ireland, America, the Atlantic writ
Here runs no longer. Out of the sunset shires,
Ireland, and Wales, they called us; and we shut
Behind us the West that beckons, that aspires.

Westward, the moors: shield more than barrier, closing
Utopias off. We were not to be tricked:
Depravity stalked the streets with us. A city
Needs, on the contrary, a red-light district.

Barracks, industrial barracks: 'town'
In that late sense. Sensational the feat,
Making a city of the regimental
Lines, as you might say: Day Street, Peel Street, Pitt Street!

Well, it has started; air is let in, and light,
All to the good. And now what will befall?
Concourse and complex, underpass and precinct,
The scale not human but angelical:

Squalor on that scale; homeliness as 'home'
Might be for Rebel Angels, or their hordes,
Machinists of 'machines for living in';
No fug upon the windy drawing-boards!

Some things get better: not *in situ*, in
Stone (that gets worse), or steel; but in
Our knowing, though our architect were Wren,
We live in Babylon, we aspire in sin.

The end of a town – however mean, however
Much of a byword – marks the end of an age,
An age of worn humility. Hereafter,
The Prince of Darkness and his equipage!

OTHER POEMS OF THE 1970s

Mandelstam in the Crimea

Symmetries, harmonies,
Stanzas! This is no woe,
This is the joy of it, beautiful
Chances of mathematics.

And rhyme that tags it, rhyme
Points up the cabinet-making
Of Heaven and Earth, the elegant
Joints all flush as given!

Oh this is the deep-blue cabinet
Wherein we walk and live.
Forgiveness! The need for forgiveness
For sharing in this, unthankful …

Such regularities
Outside us, without us, extant!
Poems stand around. They stand
Without our exclamations.

Robinson Jeffers at Point Sur

Nature? No, not Nature.
What did she ever make
Here, but an artless moan
Of ecstasy some feature
Of coast must, for the sake
Of Art, blush for, and own?

So much is lacking! So
Much (O pioneers)
A waggon-train's supplies
Won't run to. There is no
Substitute, it appears:
A long past fructifies.

So much is lacking! So
Much that we have is a mess:
Joaquin Miller, Bret
Harte and — years ago —
Alfred Noyes in distress
Lest (Kipling's) we forget

The Mission bells! Not that,
Not that at all events!
Colonialist mistakes,
Well-meant, pound into fat
Kiwanis' prose our sense
For what, here, builds and makes.

Berryman

1

New surprises? No. No new surprises:
The course my life takes has begun to bore
Me, as to interest others. Berryman's
Cross-talk, however, now he is safely dead …?
Ah but forget it! Palpitations and
Palpitations of the ego … My good friend
Amboise survives its builder, Shakespeare's sonnets
Silly Will Shakespeare. (Emendation: 'sully'?
By no means.) Count them: halfway into nine,
Or ten now, lines of verse. This looks like being
A sonnet, then. Trust me, trust Robert Lowell:
That's how the thing resolves itself, the problem
Of form? There is no problem. There's the problem
Of how to write down anything at all.

Not that we lack for certainties. Of those
We've had enough since time began, and more
(As muddled, wretched Berryman recognized)
Since Calvary. No, no, we have enough
Of things worth saying; but it's how to say them ...
How, with such bite, such necessarily vulgar
Acridity as may etch them on to such
Pliant plates we hardly can call them 'minds',
Flit as they do, as they are meant to do ...
Well, here's a stab at it: in Harvey Road,
In Cambridge, England, some one recalling then
And there the remembered, imperturbably armoured
Berryman of Clare.
                              His polished, empty
Poems of those years I carried off under my arm.

Replying to Reviewers

'Collapse of a civil privacy of manner
as any way of coping any longer ...'
He's right, you know; prognosis none too good.

The Silent Service, ironclad constraint,
still pumps its shells into a continent.
But who can live for twenty years on anger?

Like such-a-one, the firebrand of the Left
in 1930s Oxford, long since come
to a patrician Whiggism and the Church;

like such-and-such, provincial on the make
who made it in the 1950s, now
striking his right-wing attitudes like clockwork;

like such another, lifted from the pop-charts
in 1960, sold the vicious pup,
a cut-price culture savaging its master ...;

'like (dare one say it?) Muggeridge ...' One dare,
because he has. Don't answer your reviewers.
Proud Brian Patten didn't, there's my boy.

THREE FOR WATER-MUSIC

The Fountain of Cyanë

1

Her father's brother rapes her!
                              In the bright
Ovidian colours all is for delight,
The inadmissible minglings are recounted
With such finesse: the beery ram that mounted
His niece and, hissing 'Belt up', had her, is
Hell's grizzly monarch gaunt in tapestries;
The thrashing pallid skirry under him
A vegetation myth; the stinking slum
Is Enna's field where Phoebus ne'er invades
The tufted fences, nor offends the shades;
And her guffawing Ma assumes the land,
Coarsely divine, cacophonous, gin in hand.
Sky-blue, dark-blue, sea-green, cerulean dyes
Dye into fables what we hoped were lies
And feared were truths. A happy turn, a word,
Says they are both, and nothing untoward.
Coloured by rhetoric, to die of grief
Becomes as graceful as a falling leaf;
No chokings, retchings, not the same as dying
Starved and worn out because you can't stop crying.
Cyanë's fable, that one; how she wept
Herself away, shocked for her girl-friend raped –
'Her varied members to a fluid melt,
A pliant softness in her bones is felt…'
Sweet lapse, sweet lapse… 'till only now remains
Within the channel of her purple veins
A silver liquor…' Ah, the master's touch
So suave, mere word-play, that can do so much!
And now at last imperious, in bad taste:
'Nothing to fill love's grasp; her husband chaste
Bathes in that bosom he before embrac'd.'
The spring-fed pool that is Cyanë may

Be visited in Sicily today;
And what's to be made of that? Or how excuse
Our intent loitering outside Syracuse?

2

Modesty, I kept saying,
Temperate, temperate... Yes,
The papyrus were swaying
Hardly at all, and late,
Late in the season the rings
Widened upon the reedy
Pool, and the beady-eyed frogs
Volleyed out after mayfly.

Fountain? No jet, no spume,
Spew nor spurt... Was this
Where Pluto's chariot hurtled
Up out of 'gloomy Dis'?
Male contumely for that
First most seminal rape,
Proserpine's, prescribes
Some more vertiginous landscape.

Late, late in that season...
Easy, easy the lap
And rustle of blue waters...
Wholly a female occasion
This, as Demeter launches
One fish in a silver arc
To signalize her daughter's
Re-entry to the dark.

3

The balked, the aborted vision
Permits of the greater finesse;
The achieved one is fugitive, slighter,
One might almost say, 'loose'.

And yet the oceanic
Swells of an unencumbered
Metric jiggle the planes
Epiphanies must glow from.

So, though one might almost say 'loose',
One mustn't. They like the closed-off
Precincts all right, but never
When those exult in their closures.

The shrine is enclosed from the bare
Fields and, three miles away
Clearly in sight, the high-rise
Shimmering haze of the city.

But the fence is of wire; the warped
Palings give easy access;
No turnstile; and at the pool
Of Cyanë, nothing to pay;

No veil to be rent, no grille,
No holy of holies. The Greek
World, one is made to remember,
Was Christianized quite early.

Epiphanies all around us
Always perhaps. And some
Who missed the flash of a fin
Were keeping their eyes on rhyme-schemes.

4

And so with stanzas... moving
From room to room is a habit adapted to winter,
Warm and warming, worship Sunday by Sunday,
And one is glad of it. But when
Now and again I turn the knob and enter
The special chill where my precarious Springs
Hang water-beaded in still air, I hear
A voice announce: 'And this is the
Conservatory!' Greenish misted panes
Of mystifying memory conserve
In an unnatural silence nymph and pool;
It is an outside room, at the end of a range of rooms
But still a room, accounted for or even
Entered upon the impatient plans in my
Infidel youth. At that time no
Nymph, and no pool: still, it appears,

Room left for them – and yet
Rooms should have an outside door, I think;
I wilt for lack of it, though my plants do not.

5

Yet there was enough in this –
And it was nothing, nothing at all
'Happened' – enough in this
Non-happening to cap
What Scripture says of the Fall

Which, though it equally may
Not in that sense have happened, is
A postulate day by day
Called for, to explain
Our joys, our miseries.

A fish jumped, silver; small
Frogs took the mayfly; papyrus
In the Sicilian fall
Of the leaf was bowing. How
That weightless weighed with us!

Why, when an unheard air
Stirred in the fronds, did we assume
An occidental care
For proximate cause? Egyptian
Stems abased their plume.

So inattentive we are
We think ourselves unfallen. This
Pool, when Pluto's car
Whirled up, was wept by Cyanë
For her abducted mistress.

One could go round and round
This single and Sicilian less
Than happening, and ground
Therein what might suffuse
Our lives with happiness.

Wild Boar Clough

1

A poet's lie!
        The boarhound and the boar
Do not pursue their pattern as before.
What English eyes since Dryden's thought to scan
Our spinneys for the Presbyterian,
The tusked, the native beast inflamed to find
And rend the spotted or the milk-white hind,
The true Church, or the half-true? Long ago
Where once were tusks, neat fangs began to grow;
Citizen of the World and Friend to Man,
The presbyter's humanitarian.
The poor pig learned to flute: the brute was moved
By plaudits of a conscience self-approved;
'Self in benevolence absorb'd and lost'
Absorbed a ruinous Redemption's cost.

This too a lie; a newer zealot's, worse
Than any poet's in or out of verse.
These were the hunting-calls, and this the hound,
Harried the last brave pig from English ground;
Now ermine, whited weasel, sinks his tooth
Deeper than wolf or boar into the Truth.
Extinct, the English boar; he leaves a lack.
Hearts of the disinherited grow black.

2

When he grew up
in the England of silver
cigarette cases and
Baptist chapel on Sundays,

long white flannels were still
worn, and the Mission Fields
ripe for the scything Gospel
cost him a weekly penny.

The missionary box!
It rattled as he knocked it,
crouching near the wireless:
deuce, Fred Perry serving...

Doggedly he applies
himself to the exhumations:
these pre-war amateurs,
that missionary martyr.

As gone as Cincinnatus!
Still tongue-in-cheek revered, as
Republican virtue by
a silver-tongued florid Empire,

tired of that even, lately.

3

To Loughwood Meeting House,
Redeemed since and re-faced,
Once persecuted Baptists
Came across sixty miles
Of Devon. Now we ask
Our own good wincing taste
To show the way to Heaven.

But if under clear-glassed windows,
The clear day looking in,
We should be always at worship
And trusting in His merits
Who saves us from the pathos
Of history, and our fears
Of natural disasters,

What antiquarian ferrets
We have been! As idle
An excrescence as Ionic
Pilasters would be, or
Surely the Puritan poet:
Burning, redundant candle,
Invisible at noon.

We are, in our way, at worship;
Though in the long-deflowered
Dissenting chapel that
England is, the slim
Flame of imagination,
Asymmetrical, wavers,
Starving for dim rose-windows.

4

And so he raged exceedingly,
excessively indeed, he raged excessively
and is said to have been drunk, as certainly
in some sense and as usual he was;
lacking as usual, and in some
exorbitant measure, charity,
candour in an old sense. How
a black heart learns white-heartedness, you tell me!

Raged, and beshrewed his audience of one
without much or at all
intending it, having his eyes not on
her but on the thing to be hunted down;
or so he will excuse himself, without
much confidence. The rapist's plea:
not her but womankind. He has
the oddest wish for some way to disgrace himself.

How else can a pharisee clear the accounts, and live?

5

Wild Boar Clough... known to his later boyhood
    As the last gruelling stage before,
Feet and collar-bones raw, the tarmacadam
    Past unbelievable spa-hotels
Burned to the train at Buxton. Julian Symons,
    His poems, *Confessions of X,* reviewed
In *Poetry London,* bought on Buxton Station...

A nut-brown maid whom he cannot remember
    Sold him herb beer, a farmhouse brew,
One day above Wild Boar Clough, whose peat-sieved brown
    Waters were flecked below them. Legs
Were strong then, heart was light, was white, his swart
    Limbs where the old glad Adam in him,
Lissom and slim, exulted, carried him.

Somewhere that boy still swings to the trudging rhythm,
    In some brown pool that girl still reaches
A lazy arm. The harm that history does us
    Is grievous but not final. As
The wild boar still in our imaginations
    Snouts in the bracken, outward is
One steep direction gleefully always open.

So Lud's Church hides in Cheshire thereabouts
    Cleft in the moor. The slaughtered saints
Cut down of a Sunday morning by dragoons
    Grounded the English Covenant
In ling and peat-moss. Sound of singing drifts
    Tossed up like spume, persistently
Pulsing through history and out of it.

The Fountain of Arethusa

1

A boy turned to a newt!
        A chuffy lad
Who dared be sly when Demeter ran mad
At loss, at rapine, or to find her rule
Of nature crossed to make a girl a pool.
A filmy scarf of water... and that first
Apparition liquefied, dispersed.
None of us but has indulged the same
Insanity, holding Sicily to blame
For tendering first the lovely benefit
Rushed at and clasped, and then retracting it.
But loss of love has nothing to do with place.
Time ticks, a flaw flies on the water's face

But that is not it either. Remonstrate
As Arethusa may, expatriate
From Elis, threading underseas, who found
Vent for Greek waters on Sicilian ground,
It cannot help. The loves that we have lost
Are not, like her, translated or transposed,
Somewhere intact. Who ever read, for these
Poor palliatives, the *Metamorphoses?*

2

'Arethusa arose
From her couch of snows
In the Akrokeraunian mountains...'
More thrilling today
My mother's way
With Shelley, than this fountain's
Circus of grey
Mullet, or sway
Of papyrus-fronds. Pulsations
Still rill it through;
What once she knew
Of crags, reverberations,
Couches of snows,
The nymph still knows,
Still pushing her liquid lever
Up and out,
As when it brought
Greeks once in a choleric fever
To Syracuse.
Mother, my Muse,
There are the springs that matter:
Small thrills sustain
The source, not vain
Glories, nor consonants' clatter
Down a moraine
In Shelley's brain
But smaller vaunts. One day
In a parlour-game,
Required to name
Mountains beginning with A,
Proudly, aged ten,
I pronounced it then;

The Akrokeraunian Mountains!
   Grown-ups demurred;
   But sand-grains stirred
Then, as now, in those fountains!

3

   To have failed to
   measure up
   not to myth, but to
   the need for gratitude…

   In a desert of
   ingratitude, this was one
   small triumph, one
   spout of a filial spring.

4

At Syracuse the blue pool,
Dragonflies, leaping silver.
But here, at Naxos…
Trouble.
   In the cafés
Of Taormina the black
American sailors, and the white
Sat at separate tables, and an old
Anglo-Sicilian made
Trouble; and 'Attaboy, Yank'
Was the best I could do for
Those beardless boys,
Not themselves enamoured
Of Europe, but enacting
Their hope against its hopelessness, like any
American *inamorato,* like the type
Of all of them, the pontifical Henry James.

They had made the Naxos passage, and their old
Destroyer lay for a day and two nights offshore
In a spill of dangerous late-October light
Over the shoulder of Etna, watery, weak
And inconstant as any American's sense of Europe.
And we had been to Naxos, had descended

The gradient of millennia, and met
Trouble: the male will splayed across its Honda
Wristily revving, and the motor-coaches,
Though out of season, nosing the Holiday Inn.

So when we made it at last
To the Cyclopean wall
And the sacred mound
Sheer from the shingle where the exhausted galleys
Lay beached once, blocked
Now from the sea by a tall and later wall,
Stillness there was, a profusion of late blossoms
In the leafy place, and we were grateful, lingered
For the trouble to settle, settle. But the god
Awaited in vain indignantly the lunge
Of a silver fin in our thinned-out devotions,
The blue burn of the dragonfly, living ingot,
Flaw in the too late amber of our season.

5

The one in the poem is not
The one that you will visit.
Syracuse you may visit,
The poem also – one
Casts no light on the other.

Through the one there strays
One and one only walker.
The city has its claim
Upon this one who can
Meet it in curious ways:

By brilliant turn of phrase?
No. For it is the past
Is brilliant, Pasternak says;
The debt we owe it, only
More modest coin repays.

So in the padlocked, man-walled
Fountain of Arethusa
Papyrus wave, but of course
Cigarette-packets float
Above Ortygia.

Not a hard lesson to learn
That this is proper, since
History has to happen;
In this case at least it seems
A not unwarranted freedom.

And so in the verdant, man-made
Latomìa, a grotto
Loud with seepage houses
No lonely inscrutable Tristan
And Iseult, but a rope-walk!

Ropemakers gone from under
Mottled impendings, still
Their hempen gossamers ran
Taut and knee-high through the shafted
Light and the cavernous air.

Gratitude, Need, and Gladness –
These are the names of the walker,
These are the strands of the hemp:
Gladness at meeting the need
The gratitude imposes.

This is our walker's scope.
You think he makes too bold?
To make this visit, think
Of how to test a rope:
Swing on it, trust it to hold.

A gimcrack drum with spikes,
Knee-high, the T-shaped stretchers...
This is the phrase he will use:
Warm honesties of makeshift
Transvalue Syracuse.

THE BATTERED WIFE
AND OTHER POEMS

The Battered Wife

She thinks she was hurt this summer
More than ever before,
Beyond what there is cure for.

He has failed her once too often:
Once, it turns out, more
Than she had bargained for

In a bargain that of course
Nobody ever struck!
Oh, she had trusted her luck

Not once too often, but
All along the line:
And even this last time,

This summer, when reduced
To surely the bone her hope

Was just to live it through, his
Incalculable enmity
Rose up and struck. That he

Could no more calculate
Nor understand it than
She can, absolves the man

For the first time no longer. He
Will come back, she knows. She dreads it yet
Hopes for it, his coming back. A planet

Or else a meteor curves at the extreme
Bend of its vector, vehicle of
Prodigy and plague, and hopeless love.

G.M.B.

(10.7.77)

Old oak, old timber, sunk and rooted
    In the organic cancer
Of Devon soil, the need she had
    You could not answer.

Old wash and wump, the narrow seas
    Mindlessly breaking
She scanned lifelong; and yet the tide
    There's no mistaking

She mistook. She never thought,
    It seems, that the soft thunder
She heard nearby, the pluck and slide,
    Might tow her under.

I have as much to do with the dead
    And dying, as with the living
Nowadays; and failing them is
    Past forgiving.

As soon be absolved for that, as if
    A tree, or a sea, should be shriven;
And yet the truth is, fail we must
    And be forgiven.

Short Run to Camborne

The hideousness of the inland spine of Cornwall!
Redeemed (for of course in the long run all,
All is redeemed), but Wesley's chapels and all
In the slipstream of our short run rock rock to their fall.

And we surge on for Camborne, cheapness cheapened
By our going by as, with wreaths to honour the end
Of one who endured this cheapness, with our reeking
Put-put exhaust we exhaust the peace we are seeking.

Cheapness of granite-chips on the oil-starred road above Looe;
Our wandering from the Wesleys and (it's true)
Dear-bought though they were, heaven-sent, their wanderings too …
Surge, surge we may but stray is all we do.

The spinelessness of the rock-ribbed once! The riven
Granite of Wesley's gospel that all are forgiven
Since all are redeemed… The loose shale slides and shelves
As we forgive each other and ourselves.

All are forgiven, or may be. But we owe
This much to our dead sister (at Polperro
Pixies and trivia …): humanly we know
Some things are unforgivable, even so.

Livingshayes

(A tradition of Silverton, Devon)

'Live-in-ease', and then to wash
    Their sins in Lily Lake
On Corpus Christi, for their own
    And their Redeemer's sake.

Easy living, with that clear
    And running stream below;
First contract the harm, and then
    Wash it white as snow.

Not altogether. Chris Cross first,
    'The top of a high hill.'
Living it up and easy needs
    Him hung and bleeding still.

The Admiral to his Lady

With you to Bideford,
Too old for stomaching
Rebuffs, not soon deterred
Nor often crossed of late,
I boomed along not brooking
      The sky's mandate.

Habits of testy command
Forgot to say 'weather permitting'.
Though gales had rocked the land
And us, early and late,
There I was, squalls intermitting,
      Still hectoring fate.

Yet rained on, shoulders bowed,
Colour too high, too florid
In manner, voice too loud,
I felt like a youngster with you
That day, as wet winds flurried
      Torridge askew.

Wrecked body, barque of your wrecked
Hopes, or some of them – bitter
Reflections?… Harbours reflect
The changefulness of skies;
Bideford's waters glitter
      Like your hurt eyes.

Still, as the afterskirts
Of one black patch streel over
I brew up the next. It hurts
Each time a little less;
To cope with a demon lover
      Learn carelessness.

That rocking, jaunty way
You have, like Torridge's waters
Dancing into the bay…
You know what serves your turn;
You have, of all Eve's daughters,
      The least to learn!

Screech-owl

I had to assure myself:
What it seemed I heard…
Was it my own stale self
Exhaled, or was it a bird?

Therefore with pride and relief,
Half-awake, coughing in bed,
I assure myself that screech
Came from outside my head.

Not the disgusting pipe of
Mucus lees that are
Replenishing the soon
Choked chambers of catarrh,

Not snore I heard, nor wheeze,
But something out of phase
With all of me: an owl
Out over Livingshayes.

In fact the birdcalls I
Can name are precious few.
Nightingales sang to me
Once, and I never knew.

Woodpigeon, meadowlark
With coo and trill augment
A gamut that remains
Indubitably scant.

And if, now I remember,
I lifted my head out of books
Enough to know one other
Call out of England: rooks…

Is it not crows I mean
Or, what I am told is rare,
The death-conveying raven's
Croak through leaden air?

Bowels, adenoids,
Bald logic, brazen tongue…
Where is the other song the
Blackcap and wren have sung?

Cuckoo, plover, and owl:
A perilously confined
Aviary of sound for
One bedridden, or blind.

Fare Thee Well

Bideford! Nothing will do
To make the place ring true
To its after-rain luminous presence
That day last summer, so
Precipitous, tempest-whipped
As that summer was to us two,
And as Bideford was also
That day we were there,

But embarkations: faces
Cheese-white in lamplight; lights
Dancing on blackness as
They rock away; oars are shipped,
'Ahoy!' and an answering growl,
And they climb aboard, and the wicker
Basket and bird-cage are
Hoist in; and the anchor is tripped.

Make what you will of the figure
Of outward, I cannot afford
To let you go, to unloose you
To that all-levelling
Hardship of ocean. See!
Some one has cast a hawser,
Some one has caught it. Wrapped
On a bollard, it checks, it is gripped.

Oh it is you I would check.
When it comes to the outward bound,
You are to be outstripped:
Farewell! I am far down the Sound,
Dwindled, my moorings slipped.
Somewhere by Barnstaple Bay
I have embraced you, I turn
Seaward. 'Farewell,' I say.

Because in the event
The hawser will not be bent
Nor gripped so handily, and
Goodbyes will be untoward
In some more sterilized place
Than Bideford, accept
This easy rehearsal: that when
The time comes, we be equipped.

Grace in the Fore Street

for Roy Gottfried

You saw the sunlight ripen upon the wall,
Inching daily as the year wore full.

Behind you as you worked at Shakespeare rose,
Slovenly shelved, the job-lot of my books

An image of my randomness. Across them
A bush in the yard on a fine cold morning throws

Calendared shadows wavering over Bishop
Wilson's Maxims, and Calvin excerpted in French:

One late lunge after piety; and one
Long ago at face-saving erudition.

Which motive, or what other one, procured
The Psalms of David in Arthur Golding's version

I wish I knew, and knew what price to put on
'The fear of the Lord is clean, and endureth for ever.'

I imagine you or another American friend
Explaining of me, when dead: 'Now in his day

As an Englishman...' But not my Englishness
Nor anything else about me ever ripened.

The English year revolves and brings to leaf
Great ancient oaks which then unleaf themselves;

In which there is no consolation nor,
The scale at best but saecular, grounds for hope.

A better hope let me from my unkempt
Bruised library bestow on you. It goes:

    'Who can understand his faults?
    Cleanse me from my secret faults...'

Unearned composures have been known to enter
A place of unfirm purpose and fleet shadows.

Some Future Moon

after Pasternak

Before me a far-off time arises
Far in the future. You,
Whoever you are, are mine;
This is to say I know you.

The sodium street-lights beam
On to a stonescape as
Remote from the Plymouth I know
As mine from Frobisher's.

You are a girl or a boy;
All the same, one of the few.
Whoever you are, you are mine;
This is to say I claim you.

This which I need to tell you
Quietly is none
Other than what the Tamar
Shines to the Eddystone.

Listen! For the lisp of
The waters at Admiral's Hard
Decayed in my day already
Now can scarcely be heard.

They neither shine nor sound
Unless in a little tune
I name both them and you
And set you under the moon.

Watch with me how the moon
Sinks on Mount Edgecumbe. Think
How many lovers' joys
With that moon rose, and sink.

And yet think also how,
Whatever your war-machines
And your machine-made songs,
These are unchanging scenes:

Because I say so, Mount
Edgecumbe's shelving ground
Crowds to the dropping down
Of warships outward bound;

Because I say so, you
Unknown sit with me here,
Your eyes a-shine because
I will it so, my dear.

You have this world no man
Nor man's machine can take
Away from you because
I made it for your sake.

Ox-bow

The time is at an end.
        The river swirled
Into an ox-bow bend, but now
        It shudders and re-unites:
        Adversary! Friend!

Adverse currents drove
        This pair apart.
A twin tormented throe embraced,
        Enisled between them, one
        Quadrant of earth, one grove.

Now for each other they yearn
        Across the eyot
That the peculiar flow of each
        Carved out, determined. Now,
        Now to each other they turn.

And it is past belief
        That once they forked;
Or that, upstream and bypassed, trees
        Mirrored in mid-reach still
        Break into annual leaf.

A Late Anniversary

Constant the waterman
Skims the red water
Of sunset river,
Singing to Marian
The miller's daughter.

Wharf nor weir on this
Stretch of river, it pours
Mournful and nebulous, Time's
Unseizable accomplice.

Sing to her, waterman.
Woo her unfaltering,
Constant as best you can,
Self-same by altering.

Your traffic is yourself:
The sidelong pour off a shelf
Or the popple about a stone.
It is what she would wish,
You have to think.

No Epitaph

No moss nor mottle stains
My parents' unmarked grave;
My word on them remains
Stouter than stone, you told me.

'Martyred to words', you have thought,
Should be your epitaph;
At other times you fought
My self-reproaches down.

Though bitterly once or twice
You have reproached me with how
Everything ended in words,
We both know better now:

You understand, I shall not
If I survive you care
To raise a headstone for
You I have carved on air.

Utterings

(Bird)   To flex in the upper airs
To the unseen but known
Velocity of change
That both prevails and gives –
If anything that lives
That is able to know it, knows
Better to bend to the press
Of need, and so command it,
Him I envy, his
So much more strait duress.

(Salmon)   Pressures, pressures of water,
Of running water, because
As needs must downward driving,
Define imperatives.
If anything that lives
That is able to know it, knows
Better than I do the spine
Set taut against the grab
Of gravity, that thing knows
More happiness than mine.

(Man)   Making your own mistakes
And living the blame of them, making
The same ones time after time,
Which nobody forgives –
If anything that lives
That is able to know it, knows
A better happiness than
This – and he is Legion
That thinks he does – he is
Disranked from the branch of Man.

(Angel)   On us no pressures, none.
Adoration is
Not required, but what
Each one desirously gives.
If anything that lives
That is able to know it, knows
A better happiness, then
The frame of the world is askew;

I share the happiness
Of salmon, birds, and men.

(Sheepdog/   Knowing your own business,
Artist)   And such a delicate business;
Uttering it with the promptness
That such a knowledge gives –
If anything that lives
That is able to know it, knows
A better happiness
In his dog's life than this,
He is welcome to it; most,
I apprehend, know less.

Skelpick

sub galea pastor iunctis pice cantat avenis,
proque lupo pavidae bella verentur oves
                (Ovid, Tristia)

Below us all day, a mile away, in a flashing
Bend of the river a manikin is for manly
Sport not sustenance casting after and gaffing
The innocent salmon while over us all the clouds
Choir the incessant the variously lovely
Descants of shadows up and across the valley.

This is their glen, the Mackays of Strathnaver who
Were Hanoverian in the '45, who
Furnished the thin red line at Balaclava,
Whose sole exploit in earlier centuries was,
On a tribal foray against the Morays of Dornoch,
The spoliation of Scotland's prime cathedral.

Our childish companion, thinking excrement
Though it be of sheep is hilarious, is shouting
With laughter at me as I kick away sheep-shit
From the green knoll our rented cottage stands on,
Grease on the toe of my boot, me silently cursing
The mindless machines that they are, cropping and cropping.

Yet this is the one who, heaving himself from the small
Citroen he has required should stop, Good Shepherd
Labouring stiff-legged, cradles a possibly crippled
And certainly dam-spurned lamb, and then transports what
If it survives, survives only for slaughter
To a more sheltered dimple in the bracken.

One is not – I hope one is not – escaping the blood
Of the lamb, the excrement, the unsteady gait
After the dug that is always withdrawn, or the holy
Gaffed and gasping fish, the stinking fishwife
Raped beside the Dornoch Firth, by calling
For air, for air, for a distance, calling on

Tristia, the threads of a destiny woven
From a black fleece when a poet was born in Sulmona;
Tristia, the pipe pitch-bonded played
From under a war-bonnet over the shuddering flock;
Tristia, the beldam black Chaldeans'
Disastrous flocking torrent through the birch-trees.

Strathnaver

Dear language, English, whose
'Loyal' means the thing
A cairn by the road records
In clearwater green Strathnaver.

It honours the 83rd
Sutherland Highlanders, of
A Presbyterian clan,
Mustered in 1800.

Their sons and daughters were
Prised out to populate,
Far from the lonely shieling,
Canada and New Zealand.

And under Ben Loyal by
The ruined Clearances village
Of Scrabster Sutherland can
Heal me with space and silence.

A temporary remission,
Sour in any case. Hour
On hour of loyal service
Thus to be rewarded!

Spare from your frenzied mutters
Of 'Fool, fool, fool!' the men
Of the earliest 83rd,
Their cornfields gone to sheepwalks.

Winter's Talents

for Peter Scupham and Robert Wells

Nebulous, freezingly moist,
The need for a feelingful voice
Moves athwart and away
And upon us again, as we move
Northwest. The silvery stripes
Of mist come in and recede.
Past Hereford, each tree,
Grass-stalk and hedge stands dressed in
The need, a fur of rime.

Dee-side and Mersey-side
Lie up ahead, blocked off
In freezing fog. To them
The voice must speak. The rime
Dies off in the chemical reek.
Whose swag, whose chiselled cadence
Crusts, or whose coral, in
Garston, Halewood, Speke?
The voice, though, needs must speak.

Nor will it be content
With the abrupt sweet carol
Peeled against April brick,
The lyric; no, nor the dry
Incontestably true
Chirrup of pathos. New
Poets move across England.
Islanded, I salute them:
Elaborate talents of winter.

Marooned as I am in my own
Undoubtedly misread season
(Smoky noons I remember
In Liverpool), I salute the
Articulators of winter
Wonderlands. Delamere Forest's
Ramifications extort
Arpeggio and cadenza,
Too ornate for the *scouse*.

The need for a feelingful voice
Thwarts me, moves away,
Moves back. The bands of clear,
Then claustral weather gather
And then disperse. Rehearse,
Voices not mine, in England's
Interminable winter:
Sycamore, Tarporley, all
Intricate, cavernous splendour!

To Londoners

I get, surprisingly, a sense of space:
As on the rush-hour underground, when in fact
Every one touches, still in his own place
Every one rises above the smirch of contact,
Resolute to assert his self-containment;
A charged field cordons every sovereign will.

The City empty on a July evening,
All the jam-packed commuters gone, and all
The Wren and Hawksmoor spires and steeples shining
In a honeyed light... But also mental spaces
As I see now, all energies withdrawn
To hold the frontiers each day menaces.

Trying to hold my own place just inside
The emptied space round Hawksmoor's drawing-board,
I shoulder, I am rancorous, I have tried
Too long, with too much vigour and the wrong
Sort of patience. On the District Line
Budge up a little, tell me I belong!

Gallant baritones whom nothing soured
Between the wars, still hooked on Rupert Brooke
Who adumbrated for the earlier war
A wide and windy Iliad in the embowered
Old garden of the Vicarage, Grantchester...
Is that the bugle-note you listen for?

Given a voice thus confident, thus confiding,
As intimate as a commuter's week
And yet as sweeping as imperial war
Or global peace, how spaciously I could
Bind in one *sostenuto* Temple Bar
With Turnham Green, St Paul's with Chorleywood!

But now or later you will have to say
I am one of yours. Do you not hear the cramp
Of overpopulation, of *mêlée*
In this too tamped-down, pounded-together ramp
Of phrases I manhandle towards what yawning
Yard of what temple, what too void arena?

A Liverpool Epistle

to J.A. Steers, Esq, author of 'The Coastline of England and Wales'

Alfred, this couple here –
My son, your daughter – are
Can we deny it? strangers
To both of us. Ageing, I
Find I take many a leaf
Out of the useful book
Of your behaviour. 'Prof.',
Your title for years, becomes
Me, or meets my need;
Mask for what heartaches, what
Uncertain, instantaneous
(Panicky sometimes)
Judgements how to behave in
This net we seem to have woven
Between us, or been caught in.

Under a rusty gown not
Actual but conjured
By our behaviour, what
In some diminished sense
Compromising situations we
Either escape, or handle! Still,
Today I was found at a loss,
Confronted with the local
University's stalwarts
Of a past age: Bernard Pares,
Oliver Elton, George
Sampson, Fitzmaurice-Kelly...
Not that they did not deserve
Attention, there in their daubed
Likenesses; but how?
What was required of 'the Prof.'?

In the event I managed
Well enough by my
Lenient expectations, but
I had such a sense of how
Tragical, one might say,
Our occupation is
Or may be. How
Beset it is, after all,
How very far from 'secluded',
This life of the scholar my son
And your daughter have followed us into!

It was explained to me,
For instance, there was one
Liverpool professor
Had had to be painted out
Of the group-portrait: Kuno
Meyer, Professor of German,
Whose notable devotion
To Ancient Irish took,
Come 1914, rather
A different colour. He
Declared himself for his Kaiser
Belligerently. And I
Must admit I am baffled:
Passion also has its

Claims upon us, surely;
Even the sort that is called
Smirkingly, 'patriotic' .

Kenneth Allott, a poet
I think you will not have read,
Gave us ('I give you', he wrote)
'The riotous gulls and the men
Crumpled, hat-clutching, in the wind's
Rages, and the shifting river',
Giving us Liverpool. Here
Anyone must be prompted
To solemn reflections in
A wind that must seem like the wind
Of history, blowing the chemical
Reek out of Runcorn over
The eerily unfrequented,
Once so populous, Mersey.

Cold hearth of empire, whose
Rasping cinders bring
Our erudite concerns
Home to us, with such
Asperity! This is
Liverpool, one enormous
Image of dereliction
Where yet our children warm themselves
And so warm us. We too
Are netted into it – you
Known as the protector
Of England's coastline, and
I, supposedly
Custodian of that other
Line around England: verse.

This turns, of course. Yes, one
Verse-line turns into the next
As Rodney Street into a slum, or
Philologists into Prussians;
Turnings in time as your
Headlands and bays are turnings
In space. A bittersweet pleasure
At best one takes in these

Revolutions, reversals,
Verses, whereas
The veerings of a coastline
(Seen from a lowflying aircraft,
A coastal road or, best,
A coasting ship) must be
Experienced, I think, as
A solemn sweetness always.

As prose at its saddest is less
Sorrowful than verse is
Necessarily, so
Geography, I have long
Thought, must be a sweeter
Study than history; sweeter
Because less cordial, less
Of heartbreak in it. More
Human warmth, it follows,
Is possible or common
In Liverpool than in
Some spick-and-span, intact,
Still affluent city. So
The warmth of our children's household
For the time being persuades me.

Well-found Poem

'Of tried goodness, merit, or value – 1887' (O.E.D.)

'We last of Yugo-Slav
Air Force. Please tell Alex.
we coming.' Signal received
21st April 1941 by
H.M.S. Chekla, towing,
somewhere south of Crete:

      'the

port quarter fairlead was
used, because *Desmoulea*
would be sheering
violently to starboard, and
if the fairlead should collapse, the

wire would bring up against
the portside of the steering-engine house
against which it was hoped
to hold it by a heavy
shackle (around the wire)
on a chain, with a tackle rove
to bowse it against the house.'

These are zones of language, zones
of the affecting universe
of Pepys's English prose and Dryden's verse.

The use of the slip-hook made it
impossible to
'freshen the nip'
of the towing wire
through the fairlead, but

so they managed that ship

★

At Ostend's
evacuation, 'one
lady who threatened to go
into labour unless she sailed
in a destroyer'. This
'pleasure she was accorded but
without result'.
                    By which
he means presumably
labour was not averted;
the lady was delivered
safely of a nine-
or eight-and-a-half pound fruit
of pleasure once accorded:
sturdy destroyer, male.

★

'To re-establish tactics and
the skills of command...'

precision–guided missiles
favour it; so far from
'push-button warfare', the problem
is, with them,
no longer to
'hit early and keep on hitting'
but knowing what it is
you hit, and what happens to it;

as for instance Mr
Wilson, Commissioned Gunner,
'had his face blown away';
'unable to move him', nor
'had I the time',
'left him covered with a blanket'.

★

We last of Yugo-Slav
Air Force. Please tell
Alexandria,
Athens, Rome
in a violet light

we coming. Oberleutnant
Prell is coming, and
Commissioned Gunner Wilson
is coming, and

tactics and the skills
of command are coming and

these are zones of language and

we would not have it otherwise. The cities
form and re-form in the violet light, and

his face had been blown away and
we would not have it otherwise, destroyers

male, and tell Alex. We
coming, we always coming:

'... these brave men...'

Artifex in Extremis

In memoriam Howard Warshaw

Let him rehearse the gifts reserved for age
  Much as the poet Eliot did, but more
  Than thirty-five years after: ... Rending rage
Discountenanced by his Church, the rent and sore
  Patient nods under gin or seconal
  Or his small fame, such drugs. His visitor,
The one and only in this hospital,
  Is nurse and woman. Time and time again
  She brings her numbing serum, whom to call
A button's by his bed. He calls her when,
  Ashamed, he feels his practised self-control
  Slipping a notch. Hotly he asks her then:
'Is there no choice? Am I to sell my soul
  Short, or fake it, for my nearest kin
  Forever; till I die?' Prompt on the whole
She brings her priceless needleful of guilt,
  Oblivion, and equality; his rôle
  Is possum, playing possum to the hilt.

The hilt, though, is a long way down and in;
  The whole blade is before it, going deep
  Bleeding and shearing. Though the mottled skin
Knits up and shines, the legless cries in his sleep
  For pain in the limb aborted. There was once,
  Torturing to remember, in that steep
Slope off to nowhere, stamping-ground and stance,
  Foothold, some hard earth under. He discerns
  Still many a cherished, hard-earned eminence
Loom from his past, on all of which by turns
  He took his stand. No need to specify.
  There is not one of them that now he spurns;
On all that ring of hills his drowsing eye
  Sees his young self still model rectitude
  Erect and certain. Clear against the sky
Above his drug-dimmed but still savage mood,
  Seen but by him, the things that he has held by
  Unchangeably enforce his solitude.

His arrogance is terrible to no one
    More than to him. It is incurable.
    The enormity of it ramrods bone on bone
When he stands up for anything at all,
    Rending both it and him. No palliation
    In trusting to posterity, at call
No longer for belated vindication;
    The future, if it comes (as he is not
    Sure that it will), will in his estimation
Be more obtuse, not less. His work is what
    Stands, but as if on Easter Island, rude
    And enigmatic effigies, a lot
Unsold at history's auction. When of crude
    Unlettered clergy Thomas Cranmer's prose
    Demands too much, what but desuetude
Attends one's best? This being what he knows,
    His own sick say-so and presumption can
    Alone sustain the artificer in the man.

Then why, he asks himself (his self-contempt
    Half self-pity), of late these reams on reams
    Addressed to a young kinsman? To attempt,
Having no heirs, to write one's will – it seems
    The enforced sell-out: exegetes pre-empt
    Prophecies, polemics serve for dreams,
And pedagogue supplants protagonist,
    As rhetoric, action. Always in the event
    One must, despite the lacerating twist
Of disbelief, limp to a testament
    Too shrill for dignity. Of late he's missed
    That most – the dignity. A low sun lent
Once or twice, his monumental forms
    Upon the hill-tops just the effect he meant:
    Scrutable, yet unfathomable. Norms
Of expectation (anxious, confident,
    His kinsman's face …) obscure them; one performs
    Simply such things, intent, without intent.

For the most part now he drifts, his conduct as
    Considerate as has come to be expected,
    Querulous seldom. His *superbia* has
Been at such pains to savage undetected
    (And swelled the more) that now he practises

Unthinkingly the long ago perfected
Deceit of warming to the common touch,
    Much-loved, attentive. That too he has made
    A point of, staunchly – not to ask, for such
As he is, special licences. Betrayed
    By that pretence of unpretension, much
    As now he may regret the terms of trade
He fixed himself, he has to acquiesce
    When he perceives his own dear things are weighed
    And shelved at market-prices. To confess
The work that would, he thought, speak for itself
    Has not, comes hard. Benumbed, he stands himself,
    With all his other pieces, on the shelf.

'A good life,' he will tell me, 'though I wish...'
    And so on – much what anyone might say.
    Blind to his own case? Or this queerer fish
That terrifies me, reading him today
    Into myself tomorrow – which one thumbs
    The bedside button, and no woman comes?

The Bent

Thinking how it is
    too late to undertake
        one more dutiful office
against my bent ('the grain',
    I called it once), too late
        to make as much as can
be made of Paul Celan or
    Zukofsky's 'A', and
        recalling how I met
the latter, reluctantly though
    rewardingly in the event,
        and how he is dead, I am left
with the conjecture poets
    have treated me with as much
        compassionate gentleness as
we might ascribe to centaurs
    finding within their troop
        either a man or a horse.

When I consider these
whose operations are
not beyond me but
as it were beside me
in an alternative cosmos
I do not envy them.

Catullus on Friendship

'Cancel, Catullus, the expectancies of friendship
Cancel the kindnesses deemed to accrue there…'
(tr. Peter Whigham)

It must make a great difference, having friends.
Yeats had Pound and Pound had Yeats, and Frost
Had, briefly, Edward Thomas. It must make
A world of difference, having trusted friends
And trustworthy – eh, my Lampadius?

It must make all the difference, having friends
To be dealt with cleanly, honestly – must it not,
Busy Lampadius? Friends who are not too busy
To recognize the claims one has on them,
The vise one has them in – that too of course.

A world, a world of difference, my
Never quite trusted and yet far too trusted
Friend, Lampadius… One must rub along.
Just so, just so; the debts of friendship must,
Given the state of the market, be adjusted.

Lampadius, you're a poet; a busy one,
And not half bad. Whichever god you sing
Or speak to, it's a lonely business; if
To no god but a friend, it's lonelier;
But loneliest when there's no one there but 'readers'.

What puzzles or intrigues me, then, is how
Your busy-ness refuels. In our youth
Mere self-advancement is a sufficient target:
The sort of fame that's 'being talked about'.
What kept you going when you'd tired of that?

A secret, and you'll keep it. I don't know
   Whether or not to envy you the possession
Of such pure fuel as it seems I never
   Had, or have lost. My name for it was 'friendship';
Which can't be right, I think when I think of you.

'Kindred souls' – a prettily old-fashioned
   Extravagant name for what we had and have,
A competition between siblings. Such
   Olympian squabbles as that phrase clears up,
Which exercised the ancestors so direly!

Cleared up, acknowledged, cleared away... And yet
   The gods help friendship, since the life-force holds
No stake in it. Lampadius, what I
   Mean to say is I can't sing or speak
When friends and kindred can be sold downriver.

Two from Ireland

1. *1969, Ireland of the Bombers*

Blackbird of Derrycairn,
Sing no more for me.
Wet fields of Dromahair
No more I'll see

Nor, Manorhamilton,
Break through a hazelwood
In tufted Leitrim ever.
That's gone for good.

Dublin, young manhood's ground,
Never more I'll roam;
Stiffly I call my strayed
Affections home.

Blackbird of Derrycairn,
Irish song, farewell.
Bombed innocents could not
Sing half so well.

Green Leinster, do not weep
For me, smce we must part;
Dry eyes I pledge to thee,
And empty heart.

2. *1977, Near Mullingar*

for Augustine Martin

'Green Leinster, never weep
    For me, since we must part.
Dry eyes I pledge to thee,
    And empty heart.'

Travelling by train
    – For I am a traveling man –
Across fields that I laid
    Under this private ban,

I thought: a travelling man
    Will come and go, here now
And gone tomorrow, and
    He cannot keep a vow.

Forsworn, coming to Sligo
    To mend my battered past,
I thought: It must be true;
    The solder cannot last.

But, dear friends, I could weep.
    Is it the bombs have made
Old lesions knit, old chills
    Warm, and old ghosts be laid?

Atrociously, such changes!
    The winning gentleness
Gentler still, and even
    The poets not so reckless.

Twenty-five years at least
    Higher up the slope
That England plunges down:
    That much grounds for hope.

Easy pronouncements from
    The stranger, as he leaves!
The truth is, he was home
    – Or so he half-believes.

Penelope

And so, the retraction.
Time for it: after much
Effusion, undertow.

And all right, so;
The year wears, and the worn
Capacities, coarsening,

Honour the thing
Beyond them, the transaction
Clinched lately, clinched no more.

Charity for
A while; then, grace withdrawn;
The flow, and then the ebb.

What wove the web
Now frays it, with as much
Devotion in each breath.

Long-absent Death
Veers in the offing; nears
And goes off, to-and-fro.

And all right, so;
This being out of touch
Alone tests constancy.

It is to be
A prey to hopes and fears;
Fears mostly, as is right.

In landfall light
The faithless absentee,
Death, assays our loves.

Though nothing removes
The weight of it, when the year's
Circuit spells: 'dry',

Not asking why
But blessing it, is to see
At last impunity.

Devil on Ice

Called out on Christmas Eve for a working-party,
Barging and cursing, carting the wardroom's gin
To save us all from sin and shame, through snow,
The night unclear, the temperature sub-zero,
        Oh I was a bombardier
        For anyone's Angry Brigade
That Christmas more than thirty years ago!

Later, among us bawling beasts was born
The holy babe, and lordling Lucifer
With him alas, that blessed morn. And so
Easy it was, I recognize and know
        Myself the mutineer
        Whose own stale bawdry helped
Salute the happy morn, those years ago.

Red Army Faction could have had me then;
Not an intrepid operative, but glib,
A character-assassin primed to go,
Ripe for the irreplaceable though low
        Office of pamphleteer.
        Father of lies, I knew
My plausible sire, those Christmases ago.

For years now I have been amenable,
Equable, a friend of law and order,
Devil on ice. Comes Christmas Eve... and lo!
A babe we laud in baby-talk. His foe
        And ours, not quite his peer
        But his antagonist,
Hisses and walks on ice, as long ago.

Advent

Some I perceive, content
And stable in themselves
And in their place, on whom
One that I know casts doubt;
Knowing himself of those
No sooner settled in
Than itching to get out.

I hear and partly know
Of others, fearless and
Flinging out, whom one
I know tries to despise;
Knowing himself of those
No sooner loosed than they
Weeping sue for the leash.

Some I see live snug,
Embosomed. One I know
Maunders, is mutinous,
Is never loved enough;
Being of those who are
No sooner safely lodged
They chafe at cherishing.

Some I know who seem
Always in keeping, whom
One I know better blusters
He will not emulate;
Being of those who keep
At Advent, Whitsuntide,
And Harvest Home in Lent.

Some who are his kin
Have strewn the expectant floor
With rushes, long before
The striding shadow grows
And grows above them; he,
The deeper the hush settles,
Bustles about more business.

The eclipse draws near as he
Scuttles from patch to shrinking
Patch of the wintry light,
Chattering, gnashing, not
Oh not to be forced to his knees
By One who, turned to, brings
All quietness and ease.

Self-contradictions, I
Have heard, do not bewilder
That providential care.
Switch and reverse as he
Will, this one I know,
One whose need meets his
Prevents him everywhere.

Having No Ear

Having no ear, I hear
And do not hear the piano-tuner ping,
Ping, ping one string beneath me here, where I
Ping-ping one string of Caroline English to
Tell if Edward Taylor tells
The truth, or no.

Dear God, such gratitude
As I owe thee for giving, in default
Of a true ear or of true holiness,
This trained and special gift of knowing when
Religious poets speak themselves to God,
And when, to men.

The preternatural! I know it when
This perfect stranger – angel-artisan –
Knows how to edge our English Upright through
Approximations back to rectitude,
Wooing it back through quarter-tone
On quarter-tone, to true.

Mystical? I abjure the word, for if
Such faculty is known and recognized
As may tell sharp from flat, and both from true,
And I lack that capacity, why should I
Think Paradise by other light than day
Sparkled in Taylor's eye?

Siloam

for Clyde Binfield

'By cool Siloam's shady rill' (Heber)

Arkansaw's westernmost county
Is dry; we nip back over
The out-of-town stateline for
Liquor in Oklahoma.

In the next one, 'wet', a drive-in
Announces 'Kinky Ladies';
A shack says 'Modern Massage',
Not open yet for trading.

A titter: 'This is what
Free Churchmen mean by a *felt
Religion* ? We are, are we not,
At the heart of the Bible Belt?

We are. This is Siloam
Springs. Once off the highway,
We walk in the 1930s,
Provincial yesterday:

The two or three blocks we walk
Of dark-brick downtown, sparsely
Frequented, could be almost
How I remember Barnsley,

Except for this river, whatever
River it is, scarved round
The whole small so-called 'city',
Flowing without a sound.

Green, deep-bushed green, the waters
And weir under the hill;
A little park by cool
Siloam's shady rill

Recalls in bronze the appalling
Highest the waters rose
Once, and the devastation –
By God's will, we suppose.

Imagine a deacon of
Drowned bottomlands, his brows
Sternly, despairingly knitted,
In the next county's whorehouse

Drowning himself! This country
Was lately and not completely
Humanized; here the dooms
Come suddenly and stately.

It is thus I perceive this lady,
Hatted and gloved, advancing,
Two grandchildren in tow,
Her eyes on us bright and dancing.

And this is on the bridge
Under the hanging wood,
Feeling precarious over
Siloam's fateful flood.

A Christian Hero

(J.H. Lefroy, Canada, 1843–44)

'Not the action of rowing:
Intentness, intelligent will
In the crewmen of the canoes,
Facing the way they go in...'

Who is this candid traveller, whose
Aquiline Christian mind pursues
First, at *Portage deux Rivières,*
Distinctions sensuous yet severe?
Who was it first, between
Saskatchewan and Churchill
Rivers, where bare hills occur,
Asked himself what it could mean
For rock, mere unclothed rock, to stir
Such happiness? What questioner
Knew his idlest questions thus
The most momentous, least of use?

Whose the observances
The observations? Whose
Victorian rectitude
(He kept his sabbaths clear)
As soon would reason why about
The burden of a freighted mood
As what threw compass-readings out
Nearing the North? Who hunted down
Painfully the Magnetic Pole
Clocked through the months? The calendars
Of Keble's and of Humboldt's years,
Church's and Science's, confined
Doubly this least constricted mind.

Whose this enfranchised soul?
A much committed man's,
And straitly laced;
Would save the Cree for Christ.

An Anglican Lady

in memoriam Margaret Hine

Flattered at having no
less an authority than
Richard Hooker named
for my correction, I
had drawn, before I knew it, the
notepaper towards me for
the reference (Book Five:
sixty, three) when, live,
you sprang before me, Margaret.
                                I had chanced,
brought perhaps by sortilege or some
diviner leading, on
a sheet of your, the secretary's
notepaper. Oh my
poor Margaret, after how many
years, and since Hooker how
many centuries, does this
sad clod encounter, not in books but in
East Anglian blowing mornings, his
and Hooker's and your own, your decorous, God!

Mandelstam's Hope for the Best

1. *The Case Against*

'man must be the hardest thing on earth'

Stout and well-knit in fact,
But avian was the impression;
Skimming compacted bird-brain.
Everyone's ikon, martyred;
In life, not altogether
Lifelike, unless as a bird.

A bird that lives on bees!
No more classical emblem,
Gentile or Jew, will the age
That martyred him permit us
Than his own chirr of bees from
Stringent and high Taigetos;

Honeybees dried and strung,
Hard pellets, into a necklace
Of Russian words that he twines
And twines before us while
The deep blue Ovidian twilight
Purples internal exile.

Hard! As nails? No, harder;
Mailed with an unaltering
Assurance of redemption,
The Cross his *passe-partout*
To broad Parnassian fields
Under enamelled blue.

2. *Son of Isaac*

Ram caught in Stalin's thicket!
Rigged trials, typhus… Yahweh
Was Georgian, the 'I AM'
Expert in quickset mazes.

Though it is hard to say,
A Mandelstam's
Assurance of redemption
Huddles distress away.

The one-sided trade of man
With God has more of drama
Than his Parnassian
Enamel could gloss over.

His cupola, his cradle,
His ring (oh it is ringing
Home so bronze and true!)
All this settles nothing.

Much though it stirs us, still it
Forecloses on our hope
Too brutally. A harder
Trade earns wider scope

Than his so beautiful ring
Of memory, love and culture.
Wrestling with the angel
Pries the cupola open.

Jacob, the haunted child
Of him this surrogate
Saved by dying for,
Will not be reconciled.

3. *Hope Not Abandoned*

Hope so abstracted as
towards no temporal end
but 'a mode of address to facts,
to the world and to its persons',
however it be attested
by every grace of behaviour
sought for and found in language,
had better agree to be called
a living contradiction.

To avoid abuse of terms,
let poets say they are hopeless,
and this at whatever cost
in the self-approved dissenter's
brilliance of negation.
Better thus than to fox
ourselves by appropriating
a cardinal term to actions
by which, ourselves, we are baffled.

The alternative to the degrading
gibberish of the Gross
National Product is
known to, and hated by,
those who most gibber. It
is not the historical Church
but whatever asserts our ends
are, and therefore our hopes,
metaphysical, like our terrors.

4. *Sonnet*

As massive and dispensable as sculpture
Bees, dancing, point and utter their location.
Cotillions interspinning; monumental
Gossamer build-up of gnats' spiring wings
Punctuates space, commands it, by the river
Ephemerally, some evening. So a fly
Moves on the arm of Rodin's thinker with
No less weight than his effigy moves on earth.

Carve in that stone, Acmeist! Parian marble
You like to think so cold is all a-zing
With momentary fevers, and the scarp
Of language you would quarry, poet, whirls
Indeterminately shapely in
Helix on nebulous helix, not to be netted.

5. *Of his Armenia*

'Ararat has drunk the air' (Mandelstam)

Self-aggrandizing to say, and yet it is true:
When I went there in 1942,
Though I had read few of the books, and no one knew
All of the facts, the torn-apart suffering hung,
Suffusion or deposit of the years,
Glittering like mica or like tears
Around the Arctic toe-hold where we clung,
North of Murmansk, on to his mother-bear Russia.

Nothing was less like miasma. Mountainy air
It was, though there were no mountains. There was one
Mountain in our sense of it, hanging there,
Not to be dealt with by guides or expert advice,
No holiday chalets upon it nor excavators'
Trolley-lines disused among flowers at Delphi,
But there at our backs: a mountain that cast no shadow
Indeed, but excess of light – the Arctic ice.

Such he one time imagined, a serener
Than earth-bound mountain spilling the ice-flow Grace,
As pure and polar as music of Palestrina
He said, and pointed – where I cannot follow
Not now nor then, having too poor an ear.
Ox-like obtuse (though there are Armenian churches
Ox-like, he says), what can I do with a clue
Harder to grasp than what it sets out to construe:

The Eucharist? I had no way to know
The far other end of his lands, nor how he had
For those without an ear, without a head
For freezing heights, climbed an accessible mountain
As full of Grace, vineyarded, colour of ochre:
Ararat, earthenware mountain. It would be long
Before I could learn from him and in part for myself
The God-given mercy and warmth of terra-cotta.

Three Beyond

In memoriam Michael Ayrton, Claude Simpson, William Partridge

Judgement occurs, but is not
For the judged of much importance.
Who cares for the rank in which he
Utters his adorations?

Thinking of the blessèd
Company of the saints and
The army of martyrs, I find that
One friend of three absolves me.

Two artists and one scholar
I think of; and it is one
Of the artists, the less acknowledged,
Who comes through, solacing most.

One has to understand that
Over there, over the last
Hurdle, the race is over;
No one there is competing.

One has to understand that
The ranks, the armies are
Indeed there ranged in order,
But an order all will acknowledge.

Heavenly smiles from the two that,
Prayed to, gave limited comfort;
Delighted I should have reached to
Him of the highest standing.

A Garland for Ronsard

1

Green eyes from under cornsheaf curls
    Dart out at him, belated
Masks of alarming Orpheus, gaping
    And uncoordinated.

In dreams, in dreams... It is not true
    They haunt the familiar Loir,
Capering their black classics of
    Provence and Navarre.

Why then should laurels above the acclaimed
    Brow and the haggard face
Attest a restive Athenian, half
    In love with incult Thrace?

2

Dieu les tient agitez…

These – of whom only four or five are known
To have existed, mostly Greek – aspire
Not to the style of poet, but the stele
Erected in some secret glade nearby
Ancestral acres. Into these the god's
Sizzling probe pricks insecurity
At every turn. The common talk esteems them –
Not without some complacency – 'unsound',
Countryside crazies. It is thought they've much
Traffic with fairies, nymphs; with any not
Quite human *leman,* leaping the vales, woods, mountains.

3

Antres, et vous fontaines…

Caverns, and you fountains
That off the beetling mountains
Slide to this humbler place
    With stealing pace;

You also, forests; waves
whose gipsying current laves
These fields; woods, banks that bend
    Each side, attend:

When Heaven and my hour
Shall rule I be no more,
Reft from my happy stay
    In common day,

I make it your affair
No journeyman shall square
Marble to make ornate
    My entombed state.

Let my remains be hid
Under no marble lid,
But rather let the screen
    Be evergreen.

And earth-engendered from
Me may ivy come,
In which I may be wound
    Round and around.

The braided vine embellish
My sepulchre, and flourish
To cast on every side
    A speckled shade.

To that place shall repair
On my name-day each year
The droves of cattle and
    The drovers' band;

When, having made their fit
Oblation as is meet,
These words to the isle i' the river
    Shall they deliver:

'How widely are you known,
Who serve as tomb for one
Of whom the universe
    Intones the verse!

Whom Rancour, what is more,
In life consumed not, nor
Reduced to supplicate
    For grants the great;

Who'd not re-introduce
The aphrodisiac use
Of drams, nor yet have part
    In mages' art;

But rather to our own
Plains made the Sisters known,
Bending the grass to their
    Songs in the air.

For on his strings he knew
To winnow out such true
Accordance as adorns
    Us, and our lawns.

May the sweet manna rain
For ever on this terrain
That is his tomb, which let
    The May dews wet.

Grass crowns, and waters ring,
The site; the grasses spring
Green, and the fluctuant wave
    Brims round his grave.

To him we, mindful how
Glory redounds, will bow
As if to Pan each year
    Our foreheads here.'

Thus shall the rustic troop
Declare, while many a cup
Shall pour its votive flood,
    Milk and lamb's blood,

On me, who shall by then
Be gone to that domain
Where the blest spirits roam
    And make their home.

Not hailstorms nor the snow
Upon those quarters blow,
Nor ever thunder dare
    Break on them there;

But an immortal green
Adorns the constant scene,
And constant through all time
    Spring's at the prime.

Every solicitude
Kings care for, these elude:
They raze no world, the faster
    The world to master;

But live as brothers do,
And though they are dead pursue
The self-same trades they plied
    Before they died.

There I shall hear his lyre,
Alcaeus's, strung to ire;
And Sappho's chords, that fall
    Sweetest of all.

How much must those who long
Attend the diffusive song
Rejoice to be of those
    Who hear echoes

That the incumbent rocks
Rock back at, while what blocks
Old Tantalus fails for once
    His pain to advance!

Lyre! Sweet lyre! What more
Can heal our heartaches or
So far on us impose
    We hear repose?

4

End to Torment

At Ste Madeleine de Croixval,
housebound with gout, four sonnets;
October –
        'dusty air…
September's yellow gold that mingled fair
With green and rose tint on each maple bough
Sulks into deeper browns'.
             He died in that
same year at the other priory, St Cosme.

Hélène, Cassandre, Yseult
Is-hilda, Undine, 'O
swallow, my sister' – look
out for whom you
fatuously endow, though
posterity fail not desert perhaps.

Frenetic and protean
(One noted: double chin!)
'perched like a bird at dusk',
huge eyes, thin shoulders; or
the strapping one perched, shoes off
at the foot of his bunk. They are
no good, you know, these girls.

What did he write?
'Myrrh and olibanum',
gum-resin from incisions
in South Arabia: *dendron,*
cecily, chervil – and
AMOR, the palindrome ROMA.
Backward or forward it read
the same: she-wolf.

'There is a mellow twilight 'neath the trees
Soft and hallowed as is a thought of thee…'
'Whisper in the murmurous twilight where
I met thee mid the roses of the past
Where you gave your first kiss in the last…'

And which of them all did he, oh well,
'love'?
          The Lady Loba.

5

Living without Marie
Makes him, since he has tried,
Know what it is to live
Without the one illusion
That he has lived inside.

France, Orphic Greece Renewed,
Himself the Orpheus – all
Farrago, all mistaken.
Yes, but to be by her
He staked it on, forsaken…

Of course not celibate
For all his tonsure. Still
Rossignols' orisons
Could hardly compensate
For never having sons.

Though how much that amounts to
How could he calculate?
One has not, or one has,
Sons; and no one can
Know both alternatives.

Forget the brigade of his fellows
And the adoring pupils.
What he lacks in the end
Is not the bedmate even,
But the sulky spitfire friend.

6

Génèvres hérissez, et vous, houx espineux…

Bush-bristling juniper and you the thorn –
Enjoying holly, one the desert's guest
And one the thicket's; ivy-cover drawn
Across waste caves; sand-spiring spouts and freshets;

Pigeons that sip at them; you mourning doves
In your unending widowhood; nightingales
Who day-long night-long in appealing jargon
Rehearse the unvaried versicles of your loves;

And you with the red throat, non-indigenous swallow
If you should see *la Cara* in this Spring
Abroad for flowers, parting the young grasses,
Tell her from me I hope for nothing now
From her, no favours. Cut the suffering:
As well be dead as carry on like this.

'Pastor Errante'

for Robert Pinsky

'And you, Enscaldunac?' (Mary Austin, The Flock)

When you were explaining America, Robert, you did not
    – Why should you? – explain
To your small daughter there had been a time when the *pastor,*
    Meaning the shepherd in
Many tongues though not as it happens in Basque,
    Roamed the Sierra Nevada.

It would, you must see, have made a difference: not
    To have those alarmingly non-
Communicating Swedes or German-speaking
    Bohemians on
The Willa Cather prairies for your girl
    To grow wide-eyed at;

But instead in Inyo County Mary Austin's
    Long-gone shepherds who might
As well have been Hebrew or Greek or Sicilian as
    What they were largely – Basques,
Speaking their own impenetrable language
    And yet familiar.

What we seem to be speaking of, if you agree with me, is
    A sort of utterance
Made from out of earshot, the wonderful surely
    Lexicons of gesture
Though of implements also – Californian shepherds
    Even had crooks!

Is it only to us, and not to our children, that
    A shepherd's crook, which I
Doubt I have ever seen, is more comforting than
    That appalling threshing-machine
You imagined in which, like Berryman waving, your hobo
    Pitched head-first?

Imagine an America that was what
    At one time I infer
It might have been: the West not lost, a true
    Pastoral, sheep-bells ringing.
Would it have made a difference? Would it not, and
    Why do you think so?

I do not expect an answer. The lord Hermes,
    Tutelary deity
Of shepherds, no doubt patronizes also
    Hermetic poetry, ours:
Wherein we ask unanswerable questions
    To what man's profit?

Errant through why not America? although Asia
    Is what Leopardi
Too plangently imagined, that much nearer
    The god's faint trace. And

        'Moon,'
    He starts out, bald as that, 'what are you doing
    There in the sky? Unspeaking moon,
    What are you about? You come
    Up in the evening, and you go
    Looking at deserts; then you stop, stand still.
    What is this all about? Are you
    Pleased to be pacing these eternal alleys?
    Don't you get bored? Or is it
    Still to your liking, looking down on these
    Glens of ours? Ah well, your life is
    Much like a shepherd's. Up he gets before
    Dawn, and moves out
    His sheep to pasture, sees to
    Folds, to water, fodder; then,
    Tired out, snores through the evening:
    Hopes for no more, ever. Tell
    Me, you moon: what is it worth to
    The shepherd, this life of his,
    And what to you, your life? Tell me
    The ends they move to: his brief, vagrant life
    And yours, unending.'

                                        One perceives the question
        Looks for a no more
Reassuring answer than the worst we might
        Frame to alarm
Our daughters with, or else ourselves reflecting
        About our daughters. Where
Does it come in then, the incongruous sweetness?
        From an oaten reed and
Lyrical tortoise-shell? I wouldn't knock it,
        I tell myself
And tell you, Robert. Sicily, ancient Hebron,
        We cull their honeycombs.
Why should we not? And he goes on:

                                                'An old
        White and unable man,
        Half-dressed at best, and shoeless,
        A heavy bundle toted on his shoulders,
        By mountains, valleys and sharp boulders
        In wind, in storm, and when it
        Heats up and afterwards freezes,
        Keeps going, keeps, keeps going
        Through streaming and through standing
        Waters he falls, he gets up, bit by bit
        Quickens his going, he quickens it, torn and
        Bloody; and at last he reaches
        To where the road and where so much
        Overstraining stretched him to: to the
        Hair-raising gulch where he,
        Oblivious, pitches in. Immaculate moon,
        Immaculate, virginal, such
        The life of the dying, the mortal, the set to deadward.'

        Now why should we,
I ask you, derive any measure of consolation
        From such a cry, or from
The way of life that past all responsible doubt it
        Faithfully utters? I
Cannot explain why a pastoral life that I could not
        Pursue should
Figure for me as, however uncouth, still
        Human and proper, as
(To take a plain instance) the life of a rabble-rousing

Activist, though
He too has his classical prototype, the *rhetor*,
Emphatically is not.

'A man is born to
Painstaking, and his very
Birth is in hazard to death.
Trouble and worry are
The first things probe him. In his very
Setting out Mother and Father
Take on to console him
For having been born. And then
As he starts to grow up, the one
Takes over from the other
In heartening him, to come to
Terms with his human status.
This is the very best that parents
Can do for their children. But why
If that is the case donate them
To daylight in the first place? Why
Hold up at all in a life that
Crowds to such consolation?
If life is all misadventure,
Why does it keep going
Inside us? Untouchable moon,
This is the life of mortals, but
Mortal is what you are not;
And what I say perhaps
Very little concerns you.
        To you, you solitary, you
Moon, eternal vagrant
Brooding upon yourself, perhaps this
Life on earth comes clear, and this
Undergoing of ours, this breathing out
Of sighs, all this
That is, and happens; also what
Happens in this
Dying, this ultimate
Changing of colour in the way we look,
This perishing off
The earth, this coming clean of
All settled habits and good neighbourhood.'

Skip a bit then, and:

> 'So it is that I
> Cogitate, both on the grand
> Immeasurable heavenly mansions and
> On the uncountable kin. And then,
> After so long on the stretch,
> Coping with so many
> Each and every first celestial motion
> And each terrestrial, every one of them turning,
> Turning only to return to
> Where they started from, it is then I
> Can find no use nor fruit of it. To you,
> Undying bride, no doubt it is
> Comprehensible. But this I
> Both recognize and feel:
> From the eternal turnings
> Around, and my own unstable
> Being, whatever may come of
> Good or satisfying is
> For some one else. For me, my life is evil.'

What sort of a frigid monster would one have to
    Be, to derive consolation
From such a confession? How to deflect, by any
    Muster of formulaic
Muting properties, crook and staff, the brute
    Drive, and the justified pain?

What should we be, will we be, have we been doing, persuading
    Our daughters they would be safe with
For instance a hulking great villain once, flagging us down,
    Sheepskin over his shoulder in
Arcady if you believe it, in rain, and not without menace
    Cadging a smoke?
The justified pain, the justified brute... So
    Telling our daughters
Of pastoral idylls, what we might mean is this:
    There are some failures in
Life, and I mean in a life-long effort, one would not
    Soon confess to, Robert; and
Knowledge, foreknowledge of them (they are not the shepherd's
    Ineluctable hardships, though

One found no way to elude them) – such foreknowledge
     Is, you would surely agree,
What none of us has the heart or the gall to transmit to
     Our gullible daughters. Isn't
That the best reason for rubbing their dear snub-noses
     Into a shepherd's mishaps?

Summer Lightning

for Seamus Heaney, in imitation of Ronsard

'L'argument du Comicque est de toutes saisons.'

Heaney, one can get word-perfect at
Any profession. Law needs working at
But can be mastered; practice of Physic makes
Practitioners perfect; grind is what it takes
To come by effective public speaking or
Become a consummate philosopher;
Even the best computer-wallahs know it's
Close study counts. It's not like that with poets...
     Perfect is what the Art has up to now
Not been, and won't be, here; God won't allow
That much credit to Humanity.
Unfinished as we know ourselves to be,
Earthy by definition, could we reach,
Ever, to perfect energy of speech?
     The gift of poetry is like the fire
Seen of a summer's night: flames that transpire
Like a foreboding over a river, over
A field, or again there, flickering, hover
To silhouette some plume on a far coppice
Become a sacred grove. This randomness
Makes people jumpy; seeing the weird flame,
Souls for a moment batter against their frame.
And in the end it gutters down, all this
Dumb foundry-blast of clarification is
Suddenly dull, and then it dies away.
Because it's not predictable day by day
But jumps from place to place, never at rest,
No country gets this migrant on request

Or is bequeathed her. Some emergent state
Is (so one hopes) her current favourite.
    And so no Hebrew, Greek nor Roman hand
Can handle all of poetry on demand.
Germany she has visited, she advances
Her claim to England's coasts, to Scotland's, France's,
Vaulting over, wheeling, taking great
Pleasure in picking some unlooked-for state
And some unlikely person. The bright flare
Illuminates some province here or there,
Then just as soon evaporates in air.
The Muse, in short, is international;
She is put up by, she puts up with, all;
Peculiar to no property, no one breed.
But whom she picks on, him she clips indeed.
    Take me now, Heaney – and let this suffice:
If I have made it, it was at a price
Such as I'm not sure others would have paid.
What I know is this art of mine has flayed
Me, and still does. I'm skinned! So, after one
Death let me have another one, to stun
Into insensibility. I've had much
Fun in this life; and yet the undulant touch
Of the Parnassian flood, Permessus, meant
I would be, as I have been, somnolent,
Unhandy, useless; worse, I must admit
I cannot give it up, I'm slave to it.
    I am opinionated and embittered,
Inconsiderate, gruff, low-spirited,
Pleased and displeased at once, huffy and raw;
And yet I fear God, fear the Crown, the Law,
Am spry enough by nature, cordial,
Content to have vexed nobody at all.
So there you have me, Heaney... I suppose
All of our lot have vices much like those.
    Now if Calliope, to make up for this,
Had made me better than the best there is,
Star pupil in her class, star of the show,
Then all these feelings that I undergo
I could put up with. But it isn't so;
Since I'm at best a halfway poet here,
I'd rather like some less godlike career.
    Two sorts of business flourish on that hill

Of the nine Lovelies. One's compatible
With those who like to say that they 'compose',
Who tot up and keep tallies, who dispose
These many verse-lines here; beneath them, those.
(Tell off fourteen, and bless me, you've a sonnet,
Its subject: Time, a poet's reflections on it.)
By 'versifiers' (which these are) is meant
That verse on verse is all that they invent,
All cold too, ice-cold. Brought to bed, these brought
Out some small slice of life – which they abort!
Such verse does best as drapery for a pound
Of sugar or rice, ground ginger, screwed around
Cinnamon, say. And such work, if at last
It sees the light of print, is quickly passed
Over with 'What a drag!' So from the start
It goes unread. The Apollonian dart,
Corrosive and austere, has made no sores
Upon these creatures. They are sophomores
In painting or creative writing; no one
Taught them to write, or to put pigment on,
So ink and paint are squandered; both are laid
On so thick, the daub disgusts the trade.

    The other track provides for those who seem
In their sense of themselves, in an extreme
Consumption of the fire. Whatever odd
Sense 'poet' has, they pass it on the nod;
Fed, for their part, on Terror, and the God.

    Of these no more than four or five are known
To have existed, mostly Greek. Their tone
Is matter-of-fact and prosy – that's a blind;
Silly old tales on the surface, but behind
A beautiful science. That's the trick of it:
To be, while easy, cryptic. They could profit
In this way by the confident obtuseness
Of their much pampered public, and its less
Than open mind; its eyebrow raised, its jeer
Reserved for arcane verities made clear.

    These first made current whole theodicies
And abstruse astrological expertise,
While camouflaging this, by an astute
Highly developed use of anecdote
From a purblind public. God won't let them be,
His sizzling probe pricks insecurity

Into them always. Men like these are found –
Not without some complacency –'unsound',
Countryside crazies. It's believed they've much
Traffic with fairies (those!), and nymphs, and such.
    Cutting between these two tracks there's a third
Which, since it holds the middle, is preferred
As what God has supposedly designed
To satisfy the appetite in mankind
For culling an elect. This kind supports,
So runs the theory, the performing arts;
It's educational, irrigates the masses.
It spreads civility through evening-classes,
Where sinking selfhood in a common cause
Is a point much stressed. But then, our trip-wire wars
Or (worse) our big-time cosmos-splitters seem
Hardly at all to share a common theme
With Drayton's 'Agincourt'. Belligerent airs
Do wonders for morale, so long as there's
No chance we hear the enemy singing theirs.
So, if it comes to patrons, there's no doubt
Bellona and mad Captain Mars are out.
Which leaves us with the staged, or stagey; not
The happiest prospect…
                              Tragic plots are what,
So it was thought, some few great houses foster:
Plantagenet, Gore-Booth, Adams, Malatesta,
Atreus, Thebes. But ritual couplings, treasons,
Condign kills and shames are for all seasons
And all conditions. Thinking of your bog-queen,
Intact, tar-black when disinterred, I've seen
This calls for Comedy, never more demonic
Than when Divine, involved and unironic,
Painful and pitying. (This she also knew,
Your wife, who took the cannibal Ugolino
As type for poets: brain devouring brain,
One 'rabid egotistical daisy-chain'.)
Knowing what's out of joint is our dilemma
In Ireland, Denmark, England, the Maremma;
What is, what isn't. In your singing-school,
Dante's and yours, the dreadful is the rule.
    Dread; yes dread – the one name for the one
Game that we play here, surely. I think Sisson
Got it, don't you? Plain Dante, plain as a board,

And if flat, flat. The abhorrent, the abhorred,
Ask to be uttered plainly. Heaney, I
Appeal to you who are more in the public eye
Than us old codgers: isn't it the case
The Muse must look disaster in the face?
      Well, but – here comes the compliment, somewhat late
But sent with feeling – none should denigrate
Your early Georgics. None of us would steal
From your tin scoop plunged in a tub of meal
Its pre-Dantesque Homeric virtue. Those
English who prize your verse as rustic prose
Are not all wrong: Agricola is one
Hero persists. Farmer and farmer's son
Are two 'scape whipping. And the traveller,
Odysseus Weather-eye the navigator,
He's another. Both of them you've been,
And lover too; Apollo set the scene
And then these various provocations planned,
Providing that in ancient Ireland and
Historic England Heaney should rehearse
Cottage economies, curtness of good verse.

Death of a Voice

After Pasternak
and to him

1

Here is its mark left, thumbnail of enigma.
– It is late, you will sleep, come dawn you will try to read it.
And meanwhile to awaken the loved one, and to touch her
As you may do is given to no other.

How you have touched her! Though your lips were bronze
They touched her, as tragedians touch the stalls.
A kiss there was like summer, hung and hung
And only after that, your sound of thunder.

It drank, as birds drink; took till the senses swooned.
Long, long the stars flowed in from throat to lung.
Nightingales too, their eyes start, as by spasms
Drop by drop they wring night's arches dry.

2

Dawn will agitate the tapers,
Spark and propel house-martins to their mark.
Admonitory, in you dart:
Let life be always as bran-new as this.

Dawn, like a shot into the dark.
Bang, bang! – the wadding as it flies
Out of the rifle sees its spark go out.
Let life be always as bran-new as this.

Once more, outside – a puff of wind.
What night-long waited on us quivers.
With dawn came rain, and the rain shivers.
Let life be always as bran-new as this.

It is distinctly ludicrous!
Why should it bother with the man on guard?
It saw its own way in was barred.
Let life be always as bran-new as this.

Give us your orders, now, upon the drop
Of a handkerchief, the while you are still *seigneur*
While, for the while that we are at a loss,
The while, the while the spark's not blown upon!

3

In the unparented, insomniac
Damp and universal vast
A volley of groans breaks loose from standing posts,
And still the nightwind, self-aborted, idles.

And hard behind, in an unseeing scurry
Some slant drops fall. About a stretch of fencing
Damp branches quarrel with the pallid wind
Sharply. I quail. You, bone of their contention!

Mandelstam's 'Octets'

66

I love the way the weave, when two or three or
Four sometimes great gulps can't draw it tight,
Comes up, comes clear; when I achieve a more
Shuddering breath, and get it sounding right.
So much good that does me, yet I fetch
Much weight upon me, as the moment nears
When the arched breastbone, onerously a-stretch
Through my slurred mumblings, signals in your ears.

67

I love the way the weave, when two or three or
Four sometimes great gulps can't draw it tight,
Comes up, comes clear; when I achieve a more
Shuddering breath, and get it sounding right.
Meanwhile, by the arch of spinnakers beguiled
To open-form regattas, Space is idling
And adumbrating, half-awake – a child
That's never learned what would be meant by cradling.

68

When you have shoved aside the scribbled worksheet,
And what you hold in your intent mind is
Contentless, not to be glossed, just one complete
Arc on your inward dark, one sentence's
Periodic structure (eyes screwed shut
Upon itself, on the strength itself supplies) –
This had to do with the page that you will blot
As much as a cupola does, with vacant skies.

69

Advise me, craftsman of the drifting sands,
Geometer of wilderness, are these
Intractable alignments countermands
More clinching than the wind's voluminous scurries?
— Nothing to me such tremulous demurrers,
Judaic qualms! His baby burble builds
Experience out of babble, burble slurs
Imbibing the experience, modelling it.

70

Butterfly-girl of the Mussulman, all
In a cut-to-ribbons winding-sheet, who are
Livelong and deathlong, lifeling, deathling, tall
Insectile apparition, this same one
With the immense antennae and her chomping
Head hooded in a burnous, she has strayed
Out, at large. O, the flag of a winding-sheet, please
Furl it, and fold your wings — I am afraid!

71

Well, but the saw-edged maple-leaf can suffer
To have its claws drawn for it, in some fine
Perfected corner; butterfly-markings offer
Themselves that way, motifs for a mural design.
I have it now, of a sudden:
                                        mosques there are
That live and persist along with us. In our throes
We are perhaps ourselves Hagia Sophia,
That looks with our eyes out through innumerous windows.

72

Schubert from water, from birdsong's gamut Mozart;
Goethe, a trill down much-bewildered byways!
Hamlet's balked gait, itself his pensive part —
All took the crowd's pulse, banked on the crowded phrase.
Maybe, before we lipped them, lispings moved;
Where woods were not, already foliage flittered;
And those we propose experience to, have proved
In advance of experience fitted for it, and featured.

73

Those plaguy, needling games of ours, where stooks
Of jackstraws figure, phials whence we drink
Illusions of causality! These hooks
With which we touch on Quantities, we think,
Are deathly playthings; one small figure catches
On to another as the hook is cast
Over, and snags. The child, though, sleeps. The vast
Universe sleeps, where cradled Eternity watches.

74

I come in out of Space, and with a rake
In Quantity's garden that can do with tending
Grub up self-knowing Causes and the fake
Invariant there. My one book you, the Unending,
Wrote for me and I read it alone, in seclusion;
It is your leafless, your wayward Guide to Wild Herbs,
It is your book of difficult sums for solving,
Telling of massive roots, the squares, the cubes.

75

To get past harping on the laws of Nature
The blue-hard eye has pierced to the Law behind:
Lodged in the earth's crust, zany is God's own creature
And upthrust, grubbed from the breast, his groan is mined.
The aborted foetus, deaf, something can bend it;
Like a forge-ahead road it is bowed back, trooped to a horn
– The plenty of bent-in Space, to apprehend it
Takes up the pledge of the petal's, the cupola's form;

76

And of the sixth sense, the infinitesimal suffix;
Or else the minute sincipital eye of the lizard;
Cloisters of cochlea, cockles, the snail-shell helix;
And the cilia's small-talk, hairline flicker and hazard.
The unattainable, how near it comes!
No disuniting it, no scrutinies –
As with a message pressed into your hand, that is
To have an answer by return, at once!

Note: Of Mandelstam's 'Octets' or 'eight-liners', composed as a whole in Moscow in 1933 (though incorporating some writing from as late as July 1935), Clarence Brown has said: 'these poems are in no sense an isolated statement or a momentary excursus into metaphysics. They are central to an understanding of Mandelstam...' The text I have worked from is that established by Professor Brown in 'Mandelstam's Notes Towards a Supreme Fiction', in *Delos* (Austin, Texas, 1968), Vol. I, no. 1; the order of the poems in the sequence, and accordingly the numbers given to them, are those of Professor Brown – they have been printed in another order. In the case of poems so cryptic as these, translation cannot help but be at the same time interpretation; and I am greatly indebted to Clarence Brown's commentary (loc. cit.), though I have dared to differ from him somewhat, and the difference is registered in my versions. Though it must by no means be supposed that Henry Gifford approves of this enterprise, I am pleased to acknowledge that he assisted me crucially at several points.

TO SCORCH OR FREEZE

The Thirty-ninth Psalm, Adapted

I said to myself: 'That's enough.
Your life-style is no model.
Keep quiet about it, and while
you're about it, be less overt.'

I held my tongue, I said nothing;
no, not comfortable words.
'Writing-block', it's called;
very discomfiting.

Not that I had no feelings.
I was in a fever.
And while I seethed,
abruptly I found myself speaking:

'Lord, let me know my end,
and how long I have to live;
let me be sure
how long I have to live.

One-finger you poured me;
what does it matter to you
to know my age last birthday?
Nobody's life has purpose.

Something is casting a shadow
on everything we do;
and in that shadow nothing,
nothing at all, comes true.

(We make a million, maybe;
and who, not nobody but
who, gets to enjoy it?)

Now, what's left to be hoped for?
Hope has to be fixed on you.
Excuse me my comforting words
in a tabloid column for crazies.

I held my tongue, and also
I discontinued my journals.
(They accumulated; who
in any event would read them?)

Now give me a chance. I am
burned up enough at your pleasure.
It is all very well, we deserve it.
But shelved, not even with mothballs?

Hear my prayer, O Lord,
and please to consider my calling:
it commits me to squawking
and running off at the mouth.'

Benedictus

Importunately
inopportune,

blessed is he that cometh in
the name of the

splendour between
ice and pearl cover in
the clockless distance,

flying the polar route as
we did in those days
                    (We have been
                                modern
                                        so long!)

Poet Redeemed & Dead

Feeling good, green light, the earthly paradise,
where is it, poet? Not
in this or that inn, on this or that fell, supplying
this or that cheese, but in
old age, innoxious,
knowing its guilts and not
forgiving itself but assured,
you knew how, of pardon.

Attar of Roses

The mind (the soul) is not
a ghost in the box of the body or brain, although it
excusably seems so. For instance at times
recalling our priests who instructed us in
The Resurrection of the Body

– at Judgement Day, the cadavers out of their coffins,
boxes emerging from boxes! What nonsense,
he blindingly observed –

who was himself, it may be said, a little
fleshy, more than a little coarse,
and maladroit with it, not to say uncivil.

What female parishioner wants him resurrected,
if so in what shape, and for what fanciful purpose?
But all the same, do we live in a nest of boxes,
the nubs of ourselves, so tiny, secreted in
the innermost, most reclusive, most
cramped of the boxes? If not

we have to believe in, we already believe in,
the resurrection of the body

which is not a box, but a main
sweet-smelling part of what the box encloses.

Sing Unto The Lord a New Song

Cheerfulness in lordly
leisure; and
holiness in thunder and high wind.

The lordly thunder
cleaves out flakes of fire.

The lightning uncovers the woods,
making the roe-deer calve
untimely in the bracken.

It is the holiness thunders.

Do not ask for the storm to ease.
Spirits rise, the longer it goes on.
Imagine Him yawning, hear Him
crack His joints as He stretches,
magisterial!

Praise the Lord upon the harp,
sing to him on the damnable steel guitar!

'So make them melt as the dishousèd snail'

'or as the embryo, whose vital band
breaks ere it holds'.
                        As we grow old, the basics
(as you might say) emerge
with an uncanny force:
we and our siblings each day more alike.

'The ungodly are froward
                even from their mothers wombe;
as soon as they be borne they go astray;
born and perverted in one day,
lie, flatter, and betray.'

It seems there are such doomed creatures;
morally
spina bifida. But

as we grow old the features of one
or the other parent show up in the mirror
frightening and affecting, and we can

under the heavenly justice

be equalled with slug or snail but
hardly with the aborted
almost-brother who would have
been so like us. The psalmist goes too far:

Best not be born, he means.

Better be born a snail,
or lying and betraying,
so you be born.

God Saves The King

To the chief Chanters
upon the dumb Dove in far places:
 either your brows are knitted,
  or you whinny and smirk, such teasers,
  you take such pains.

Far the places
and you are in their hands
who feast on squabs.

But care for that other way
of being debonair:

the sauntering monarch's, David's,
whose vigorous warmth did variously impart
to wives and concubines, to chariot-wheels,
to realms and officers,

religious faith; that is,
light spareness, unconcern.

Meteorologist, September

We shall break out
into the mention of God's great goodness,
and the abruptness of it.

The year goes round,
yes, but with what ructions!
The violence of the turns!
Why else are Revolutions always bloody
except that seasonal change is the type of them,
calamitous though foreseen?

At the autumnal equinox
gales.
      Though the belief is
'unsupported by observation',
rationality and
superstition alike require it:
God does not make His changes
without some pother.

His steady counsels change the face
of the declining year.

He flings gross icy gobbets from His hand –
fire and hail, snow and vapours,
wind and storm, subduing the land.

By Him the rain
supples the clods of indurated acres.

His whirled-down snows are laid
like bleaching wool beside the streams
to clad the tender blade.

Breath steams on the sharpened air.
And who so hardy as to bear
the quickness of His frost?

He blows a cold too strong for strongest things.

His power declare,
you empty air,
and snow out of nowhere, suddenly.

Vengeance Is Mine, Saith The Lord

You that would bite the whole pie and
mell with the pack, yet pout yourself ill-used,

you have committed crimes
against the innocent for
no profit but self-promotion.
Mouse has a broken back by
the coarsest cheese in the larder.

The creaking scissors and the penman's knife,
derailed from their proper business, will do justice
in a *collage* of your cruelties.
                              'The children
wore their cagoules, but these were mortar-bombs.'

In the casinos most were vacuous, some
were fleshy and flaming, some profuse, some grasping,
far from Beirut.
                    Though I
address the mute, He hears, will testify.

Standings

'One Law for the Lion and Ox is Oppression.'

For Woman & Man, for White & Black, for Bent &
Straight, for Sick & Sane
one Law is Oppression?

Across the Albion of William Blake,
a tesselation of ghettos,
the traveller beds down at night in
a Fabian or Lesbian canton, in
a Rastafarian or Israelite republic,
crossing from jurisdiction
to jurisdiction, never
tyrannised, never chastened.

Divers waights and divers measures are
abomination to the Lord.

There is not the psychiatrist's truth,
and then the poet's;
the white man's truth, then the black's.

The Lord admits diversity of gifts,
but not disparity.
We need to know where we stand.

Happy the man or the brute
who stands corrected,
stands like that, helped like that to stand,
enabled to,

hungry for judgement always.

Church Militant

In the day of the mustering of thine army,
thy people shall be willing:

the young men come to thee as dew,
the dew of thy youth comes unto thee.

From everlasting to
God knows... But this is history,
vouched for over and over:

as dew from the sources of the morning
sparkles upon the grasses,
the Commander recruits His youth
repeatedly, the converts crowd
the rail and His army masses.

Always they all passed muster;
always they were triumphant.
Always, you would have it,
they were insincere or deluded.

Curtains!

The Lord is King, be the people
never so impatient; He
sitteth between the Cherubim,
let the earth stir as it will.

'And what if I
fall down and die?
Can the sun go down at noon?
His years are one perpetual day,
and shall His children die so soon?'

Soon is not soon. This earth grows old,
Auriga and the Bear shall be folded away
like the costumes for Act One.
The star-scene shifts at His command.
The Twins, the Southern Cross, the Scales
flap on their hangers, ungainly.

'Stars, far things…'
But in the reach of His arm.

For He is One, still One;
the clock-hand wavers, uncertain.
Whatever the next production, you
are there when the curtain rises.

Auriga and the Bear,
The Twins, the Southern Cross
show that He is there
for ever, as they are not.

'And Our Eternal Home'

Time like an ever-rolling stream
bears not its sons away,
but its own segments, years and days.

They fly forgotten, not as dream,
as thought:

'We have spent our years
as it were a thought',

few and short, or long and many
according as we think of them.
Keeping a tally is
little to the purpose.

'So teach us to number our days…'
Certainly number amazes.
Numberlessness however
astonishes mathematicians
more than the innumerate; they
live with it every day.

Suppose we counted our birthdays
by the difficult measure, *stasis?*

Fill us with gladness betimes
(betimes!) and we shall be glad
all our days,
seeing the calendar is
an illusion – and blissful at that,
if you can face it squarely.

Zion

Mired in it! Stuck in the various
rust-coloured, dove-coloured, yellowish
or speckled muds of history, you mistook
clarity, the dayspring from on high,
for a satisfaction of art, or the condition
of addressing the untutored.
                              (As you never
did, they were otherwise tutored.)

Once, stuck in the mud by the Capitol,
you thought of the ninth buried city,
Richmond, Montgomery, what you had built them for,
of Troy, and of Rome, of Richmond, of Rome, not Zion;

of Troy, of Troynovant, of London,
the West Country, sometimes Geneva,
never of Zion;

of New Caledonia, New
Amsterdam, New Zealand,
Rome (Georgia), other Romes
and Athenses of the North,

New Delhi, Athens, Syracuse, not Zion.

Tutored in computer-processing,
still they may learn of Zion.

Trained in marketing techniques they
may discern in that murk the clarity
of a city not built on seven hills,

not guarding a river-crossing
nor plugging a gap in the mountains.

Unskilled in Islamic culture, they
may still make a Mecca of Zion.

Having heard or not heard of Lindisfarne, Iona,
are not the lot of us pilgrims?

The variegation of muds,
the iridescences,
constitute for some
in youth a passion,
in age a distraction from boredom

which, if designedly aimless
for long enough, merits the name of
Zion or some say Eden.

Felicity's Fourth Order

Men of business, of pleasure,
too often men of learning,
must not be left at leisure.

Their satisfaction is
forgetting themselves in work.
Nothing else is diverting.

Concupiscence, though of knowledge,
is a debauch, and only
an art against thinking of ends.

Vacancy however, if
careful of its ends but
aimless, may earn the Fourth Order:

'Being gathered into their chambers,
and guarded by angels in profound quiet,
they understand the rest that they enjoy.'

Put Not Your Trust in Princes

Let them give up the ghost, then there is nothing but dust
left of their presumptions we were fools enough to trust.

Pin no more hopes on them, nor the promissory collective;
the light at that end of the tunnel is glass, the credit delusive.

In the presence of the authorities we spent our days
turning our caps in our hands, and the manful, inveigling phrase.

We combed our sparse hair in the mornings (silvered, we observed).
We regarded our consort sleeping, whom we had shabbily served.

They are lost among the histories, names of world-mastering heroes:
this, the peace-fixer; that, the cuckolded smith of Infernos.

Having the sceptre no more, no more the ambiguous terms
of an unbelieved spokesman parade them; their press-men too feed worms.

Their Rectitude Their Beauty

'The angels rejoice in
the excellencies of God;
the inferior creatures in
His goodness; sinners only
in His forgiveness.'

His polar oppositions;
the habitable zones,
His clemencies; and
His smiling divagations,
uncovenanted mercies,

who turned the hard rock into a standing water
and the flint-stone into a springing well.

The voice of joy and health is in the dwellings of the righteous;
my eyes are running with rheum
from looking for that health

in one who has stuck by
His testimonies;
who has delighted in
His regimen; who has run
the circuit of His requirements;
whose songs in the caravanserai
have been about His statutes,

not to deserve nor observe them
(having done neither) but
for the angelic reason:

their rectitude,
their beauty.

Except The Lord Build The House

A song of the degrees,
of the gradations,
the steps to the temple…

There is no need to insist;
it is enough to name them.

For Zion is a city
uniform in itself,
compact together.

Why are you so strenuous, my soul?
Vain to get up early,
to sit up late,
to bolt your bread in a hurry.

Short be your sleep and coarse your fare
in vain. The Lord shall turn
the key in the captivity of Zion,
and all go like a dream.

The grass grows over the ruins of Eblis,
nobody's hayfield;
you are loitering there, or studying
hard (you are a hard
loiterer) but no one
going by in the road calls out
'Good morning' or 'Good luck'.

No use of early rising:
as useless is thy watching.
No traveller bestows
a word of blessing on the grass,
nor minds it as he goes.

Climb the stair
manfully, and sing
a short song on each step of the stair.

It is not an arduous duty.
Eblis was hard, not Zion.

Inditing A Good Matter

I find nothing to say,
I am heavy as lead.
I take small satisfaction
in anything I have said.

Evangelists want your assent,
be it cringing, or idle, or eager.
God shrugs. We taste dismay,
as sharp as vinegar.

He shrugs. How can He care
what *billets-doux* we send Him,
how much we applaud? Such coxcombs
inclined to commend Him!

My heart had been inditing
a good matter. My tongue
was the pen of a ready writer
who had been writing too long.

Whoever supposes his business
is to commend and bless
is due for this comeuppance:
feeling it less and less.

But I find something to say.
I pump it out, heavy as lead:
'Buoy me up out of the shadow
of your ramparts overhead.'

Like one of those vanished performers
on an afternoon-matinée console,
I arise
        'Admit to your rock
this ready, this shriven, soul.'

The Creature David

The disposings of the heart in man,
and the answer of the tongue...
Not the domain of any
main poet's song;

not the halcyon, the mid-ocean range
where Ceteosaurus spouts, and Christopher Smart
numbers the streaks of the mollusc, where
the Spaniard is challenged for the Main
comradely, and Drake takes on the world,
a hirsute pirate. None of this
is documented history, it is not
fastidious, but dreadnought David's song.

Speech murmurs, and is always
forked, but this is song.
Nothing in this is talked.

There goe the shippes; there is
that Leviathan, whom Thou hast made
to play therein

upon the harp.

Saw I Never The Righteous Forsaken

I have been young, and now am old:

but I never saw Mr Worth
denied all reputation,
nor Mrs Worth and the children
go begging in the long run.

Reputations have
what seems when you get to my age
a shortish innings at best.
Remember the champion jockeys?
How many? From how far back?

'He shall bring forth thy
righteousness as the light,
thy judgement as the noonday.'

Banking on posterity
is an unwise investment.
Cold comfort, the little Worths!
Perpetual false dawn!

But merit is ascertainable as daylight;
unarguable justice follows
as certainly as noon ensues from dawn.

The Elect

Battle of Britain Sunday, RAF Gatow, Berlin

In their conventicles
stone-built or notional
they have withdrawn
from the life of the nation, or
have been excluded from it.

Strident, unaccommodating,
inelegant, sometimes smug,
they have despaired, and exchange
their Hosannas with each other.

An enclosed subculture,
they speak of such a one
no one has heard of, as
a guide to their devotions.

They comprehended, as
no others did, the fate
of the burned-up, scorched and screaming
sergeant-pilots:

*as
gold in the furnace has He
tried them, and received them
as a burnt offering.*

Luftwaffe pilots, also?
Don't fuss me. Yes, of course.

> They shall shine and run to and fro
> like sparks among the stubble,
>
> for though in the sight of men and in
> the sight of the unwise they seem to die,
>
> they are in peace and
>
> shall judge the nations.

'The just die young, and are happy.'

What sort of a nation is this,
bows its sleek head to these
outrageous obsequies,

born of a happiness in
the ghetto of the elect?

The Zodiac

> It won't stand up to the light;
> disgraceful, though
>
> *They fought from heaven, the stars in their courses fought*
> *against Sisera,* sang
> Deborah, and Barak the son of Abinoam sang,
> but Deborah in those days, saying:
>
> Star-crossed, ill-starred, oh ill-starred Sisera!
>
> Infirmity no doubt
> of our nature, that we guess at
> this nonsensical band in
> the heavens dispensing justice.

But that much should be allowed us.
Misfortune undoubtedly strikes
unequally, and to the worst
worldling one would not deny
the chance of blaming, rather
than God, a star-struck Nature.

In this way the sad Lorine
Niedecker, to explain
the ill luck of her father and mother,
remarked not once but often
Mars rising in Pisces, if
that is possible;
                              she,
raised and persisting in
a watery, piscatorial
district of Wisconsin,

assured the elemental
energies must have some
relation to the cosmos:
a God-enforced decorum.

'Just You Wait!'

To justify God's ways to man
like Eliphaz the Temanite
is a presumptuous folly;
it cannot be done.

Until the hurt comes I shall glorify
God on account of the ostrich,
hippopotamus, elephant,
crocodile, and whale.

(Zoological marvels:
King Edward the Seventh's racehorse,
his vertebrae fused together
from carrying a weight of jockeys.)

Who is confident though Jordan
rushes against his mouth,
who also lieth under the shady tree
in the covert of the reede, and fennes?

This is a riddle-me-ree.
'Hippopotamus' is the answer.
Until the hurt comes, and after,
play piously riddle-me-ree.

It comes, it is on its way, that hurting business;
it shall not be my affair until it comes.

Bowing The Head

Importunate for attention,
hanging around
the ante-rooms of Eternity,
the position of prayer, it must be
allowed, lacks dignity.

How much more, if it is not
hanging around so much as
hawking our goods, and the claim
we have by them, each howling
the loved one's, the needed one's, Name.

It is the position of love,
and which of us has not known it?
Lothario cannot gainsay it:
virility is the more
abject, the more we display it.

So, how to be manly in prayer?
'Hawking about for attention…'
It is a pungent phrase.
Getting down on your knees,
remember it all your days.

Widower

That sneaky Thomas Cranmer!
Turns out he had two
illicit marriages. One
cost him his fellowship at Cambridge.

Whence Matrimony, his
doing
in 1549:
'a remedy against
fornication'. (Other things also.)

Which makes ungrateful
sense for those
whose penis is a sacred member.

Poor Thomas Cranmer, his
doings in the dark!

'As Isaac and Rebecca gave
    A pattern chaste and kind,
To make domestic burthens light
    By taking mutual share,
    When we asunder part,
    It gives us inward pain.'

It is for you like tonsured
Ronsard, less
the bedmate you miss than the faithful,
the sometimes spitfire friend,

whatever the small hours' stress.

Master & Man

(Proverbs 19.22)

Chaste and kind... 'a pattern'
(Isaac and Rebecca)
'chaste and kind'. Such words!
What we have done to you
both long ago and lately...

For 'chaste', read 'pure'; for 'kind'
('The desire of a man is his kindness')
read, 'What is desired in a man
is loyalty.' Biddable man!

My lord, my liege lord, my dear
lord, what I desire is
my own and not your kindness.

A poor man is better than a liar,
dear my lord, suppose the
desire of a man is his kindness;

extended also
to the unthankful,
whose kindness is as a morning cloud
and as the early dew it goeth away,

milord.

Levity

What is man that you should weigh
the gravamen of his 'grievous unto me'?

The weight of his sins he must
profess intolerable;
'imponderable' comes nearer.

For he knows them light as a feather;
changeable, like history or the weather.

'Laïs, boy-prostitute, wife'
(he addresses them), 'were we not
all on the side of Life?'

The beam kicks: lift-off Man,
no counterweight in the pan,

no peise, no pondering, no
poise, no *avoirdupois,*

no slug of compassionate lead
to weigh him saved or convicted,

soars into and over the sunrise.
The angels are all eyes.

Oh slender, eternally youthful
balloonist, what you have missed!

For there He is, steadily weighing
your airy, your weightiest, saying.

Witness

Bearing and giving are different, it appears.

In the latter case (constrained)
one supposes, or may suppose,
a judge and a jury. In the case of
bearing

witness, there is a load
that has to be discharged
in physical fact, the weight
on the grieving shoulders
thankfully hefted off,
a sack into the shadows of God's barton.

No judge, no jury, but one,
that one incalculable, His
authority established by no statute.

'Come, O my guilty brethren, come,
Groaning beneath your load of sin.'

We bear like a weight in the gut
witness, a load that
must be evacuated
in the hedge-bottom or elsewhere.

Our Lady

The sea is all that they say: it wreaks death one way only;
it neither begins nor ends, nor ever suspends its motions;
indifferent as to racial stock and
era, it drowns
or does not drown, impartially, godlike in this,
not to be walked on.
One who
walked on the sea, though briefly,
walked also alone under olives also briefly,
seldom alone and always.
This his mother,
crude-painted odalisque, holds in her left hand
a seaport sacked, in her right hand a votive ship
tiny among trumperies, cheap mirrors.

She the recalcitrant sailor's
one and one only reached-after landfall, but under
an interdict he hymns, he worships instead,
and plumes with his perjured feathers
of spume and inconsequent waterspout, the faithless
indifferent non-god, Ocean.

The Ironist

'Sacred? or sacrosanct?
or sanctimonious, even?
Suppose you chose these topics
(which, you will say, chose you),
hoping to escape
the debilitating scope
of your kind in your time and place:

irony.'

It is Lord Haw-haw speaking;
it is Mephistopheles speaking,
the syphilitic; it is
Germany speaking.

A masterly ironist
of history knows
his subject inside out;
his dry wit drying out
a sop of sentiment from
the cerements of the West.

Lover of the mephitic,
of fog and stink,
his natural haunt the road by the chemicals plant,

his elegant strong suit
is tacit and total carnage:
the Devil's work, whose mark
(frivolity and distraction)
is on this page also

as on the best we can do.

'Thou Art Near At Hand, O Lord'

Or: *They are come near me that*
persecute me of malice.

How near was near? Were their camels
cropping his starveling pastures?

Or were they behind the skyline,
though they might be his 'nearest and dearest'?
Were they never in fact (though in truth)
shouldering for house-room?

It is thus with words on the page:
'Mephistopheles' and 'mephitic'
are more nearly juxtaposed
than two that are side by side.

Moreover, space is encoded
to signify lapses of time.
(One verse-line under another;
this one *after* that one.)

The nearness of God is known as
an aching absence:
the room the reception-desk
cannot locate nor account for,

in a fictitious or
analogous space that does not
answer to or observe
the parameters of Newton,

any more than a page of verse does.

The Nosegay

The roses of irony blossom
floridly on the trellis
of inexperience crossed with
a need for the fell and certain.

Seeing that irony is
the adolescent's defence,
'An end to irony!' means
death to most of our lyrics.

The objection to the God
of Islam and of Judah,
'He lacks a sense of humour',
means, He is not ironical,
He is not a lyrical God.

He does not come and go;
He is not glimpsed in gaps of
time. Alas, it is clear that
He claims to be omnipresent,
and had better be thus acknowledged.

He has His sense of fun
surely; He has even
(as we see it, who wait on deathbeds)
a mordant wit.

It is the bite of the wit
mauls our sense of humour.

Lyrists may proclaim their
intermittent visions;
ironists, their protective
clothing; but the surgeon

of Islam and of Judah
makes His incisions
justly, and He is not
deprecating about it.

Stepping along the Turl,
selecting a buttonhole
half mauve, half mustard-yellow,
what God and what men you malign!

Gripping Serial

Man fought against beasts, and won;
Man fought against priests, and won;
Man fought against kings, and won;
Now he fights the Collective.

This drivel is still believed.

Man fought against beasts;
Man fought against Man, and still does;

And there's the end of the series.

I Have Said, Ye Are Gods

And so you might have been:
a groaning light, a light that risked eclipse
and underwent it. Oh
luminaries, oh
sun and moon and stars of a low-browed heaven,

Enlighteners,

Captain Cook was the best of you,
bashing his bowsprit through
the gap between ice-floe and
a bruised cloud-ceiling, past
Bering's best, and may even have died for his friends.

But in twenty centuries,
not under the cove and whelm
of the *tsunami,* nor
splintered upon the wakes
of any nation's navy, breaks
the light that saves.

He maketh men to be
of one mind in an house,

and ye princes shall fall as one of the common sort.

David Dancing

Infrequently, dreams are heavenly.
How if the caustic 'Thou
dreamer!' excoriate those
hagridden by what, in a sleep
we learn to dread, comes often?

For dreams, most dreams, are hell.
Sundry authorities
exhort us to 'come to terms',
get used to our hells, distrust
the dull or brilliant daylight.

Neither to move nor console,
David dances before
the Ark. And the Ark is not
the dance, but what the dance
honours and accedes to.

Neither to move nor console
he dances, not in a dream
but exceptionally wakeful
in a recurrent morning.

Dancing Measures

Noah drunken, taking
his daughters in bed; a common,
seldom avowed occurrence.

How then for the dance, that is always
a self-abuser, glassed
in the pond of its own procedures?

The wrath of God! Yet Dance's
habitual incest seems
not to call down thunders.

Wrong! The penalty is
imposed in intimate places:
a rhythm imposed by no
more than proclivity, yet
prohibitively binding.

Measures, the prison of measures:
rumtitum, tumtitum, rum.
You know of a worse crucifixion?

What drunken stupor or
generative torpor sets
fingers or feet to tapping like Astaire?

Sometimes the drink implants it;
sometimes, God-induced, it
shakes free and runs loose, if the dancer's
executive will dispose it, to high meadows.

Being Angry With God

'Anger, yes. But God is God,'
the impious Pakistani
explained to V.S. Naipaul.
'God is not like people.'

Profound: God is not like people.

Shallow: He ought to be.

Indifference, if you can
manage it (youth can),
disposes of God well enough.

Imran runs up to bowl. The Rajput palaces
live not as art but as the youth
Imran, accelerating, is on the verge of losing.

Even with people, what did
anger ever dispose of?
It ties you in, like love.

Thanks to an undevout Muslim,
we recognize anger with God is
one more way to own Him.

The ex-Christian exclaims:
'But my angers amount to something!'
It is not at all clear that they do,

as Imran Khan
turns and begins his run:
poetry in motion.

The motion is unforgiving;
so is the poetry; so
(unless it is tempered) the Judgement.

The Comforter

St Patrick bound unto himself
the Trinity, but showed his practical sainthood
by playing down the third
member of the triad. No
anxious souls would be won by
that vaporous Holy Ghost.

'The whirling wind's tempestuous shocks'
registers Patrick's obeisance, but
no one is taken in, no one prays to the wind.

And indeed He is the strangest
of the Three Persons,
the most estranged.

For the Holy Ghost is nakedly a ghost.
Father and Son may be masks
compassionately adapted
to our capacities, but
Person is not *persona* and
the Ghost is a ghost, no fiction.

Integration, fulfilment
have nothing to do with this Person;
cure, or harmony – nothing
like that is intended.

Invasion is His note:
disintegration.
A wind from the outside corners
of the human map;
disorienting;

His strangeness for the comfort
of those not at home in the grid.

Cannibals*

As if to take in ocean
through a needle's eye,
a sundial divines
not why light moves, but when;

when, and how. He moves
now. And perhaps He loves us.
He moves in any case.
We trace, not chart, His passage,

like Uruguayan, defiled
prop-forwards and blind-side flankers,
iced up in the Andes,
cannibals, knowing Him near.

*My horne shalt thou exalt
like the horne of an unicorne.*

Presence, the nearness, is
the needle's eye;
not to make any more
proof of it, the trial.

* 'The Old Christians', a Rugby football team from Montevideo, was
isolated in a wrecked aircraft from October to December 1972.

Pray to the Holy Spirit, Let
not the most polluted
translation impede the witness:
ram's horn of unvarying plenty!

Woe Unto Thee!

Compunction at presumption
is a sentiment
conspicuous by its absence
from the college of prophets.

David the King, Isaiah,
Micah – what
regal or less than regal
prerogative gave them the right
to be so unforgiving?

Choked with the god, or blinded
by arrogance,
they were – by what right? – lifted
above being fair-minded.

Had they not thought of circumstance
extenuating?

'He that is free of sin, let him
cast the first stone.' Had they,
the fulminating,
nothing to atone for?

Baldly declarative,
their comminations live
on in the Scriptures like
an unacknowledged toothache,
bruising and assertive.

The nerve sings, and so long as
it sings, presumption calls for
no halter of compunction.

Kingship

It would have been because
they smelled so bad,
that the scriptural nomads and
city-dwellers made
so much of oils, of resinous
exudations
of Gilead; and we,
if our stick of deodorant is
jammed, what indignity!
The feel of that, and the fear

unfelt by the cheerful, the fearless
non-conforming whom
we hate accordingly with
olfactory revulsion.

The sweat of honest labour is
too honest for our noses.
And of dishonest?

Joy unto thee, if thou canst
muster a patience beyond
'The time will come.' It will not.
Idyllic earth where the hay smells of the dream
in Samuel Palmer's Shoreham
will not, it is certain, surface
in history, though a few
institutions hint of it: for instance

'the Lord's anointed',

sweating beneath his robes,
holding the orb and sceptre,
who would have been happier in
the malodorousness of Goodwood;
and over him Another
enthroned in majesty
'no sweat'.

Ordinary God

'Do you believe in a God
who can change the course of events
on earth?'
     'No, just
the ordinary one.'
       A laugh,
but not so stupid: events
He does not, it seems, determine
for the most part. Whether He could
is not to the point; it is not
stupid to believe in
a God who mostly abjures.

The ordinary kind
of God is what one believes in
so implicitly that
it is only with blushes or
bravado one can declare,
'I believe'; caught as one is
in the ambush of personal history, so
harried, so distraught.

The ordinary kind
of undeceived believer
expects no prompt reward
from an ultimately faithful
but meanwhile preoccupied landlord.

Nashville Mornings

Saint Cecilia:
          between
man as vehicle traversed
by constant, by unchanging
biological forces; and
his actions as reactions
solely to speedy changes –
where is the third term? Is it
what in the ghetto of letters
we least can stomach: Noise,
the appalling Rock and Country?
The damnable steel guitar?

               Cruising Canadian
               coaches pause
               by the patios of the stars,

               expensive silences, Olympus,
               Arcturus, a loft above tundra
               built by and out of
               clang, twang, nasalsong
               and corybantes? There is precedent:

               at Stonehenge, ululations,
               the nuptial hymn a disco.

               Dawdling the Franklin road
               Ontario plates;
               gardeners, sprinklers,
                         Elvis
               his platinum-plated Rolls
               garaged in splendour. Old
               Etonian freshman gawped
               along with the rest. There is
               spring on the world, and all the
               time in the yawning

               road for pleasurable
               memories, anticipations
               of strum and drum. The form is
               a rhythmical suck. The air-brakes
               ease from the sidewalk gently:
                     Homes of the Stars!

'thought I would like to
                    if it's all
right. On my way to Chicago.
You knew me when I was two.'
Youth on the road.

Graze the glass bowl, however
musically, the fish
in the fishbowl flick their tails
once, and are gone.

Flaw and withdraw, the
exquisite
accomplishments of flautists,
is that an achievement?

If we inhabit a gap
between the departure of gods and
their necessary return,

their absence is a salience
no doubt, as with
Chinese ceramics also,
a scrape on the ineffable. It
makes sense. Makes enough?

'What I had known, no one had known.
What I had seen, no one had seen.'
A man in love with silence, in
terror of silence, and in love with that:
tundra, snow-oceans. Rasp or whisper,
the wind outside.
                    'A silence fell between them.'

Celia, her music
confined in its operations
to a metaphysical annex,
irks on Nashville mornings.

If I Take The Wings Of The Morning

taking off at dawn
to circle *ultima thule,*

threading the splendours between
ice and pearl cloud cover,

God is not only also
there, but signally there,

who made the heavens skilfully,
who made the great lights
with a strong hand and a strained-out arm,

who brought forth clouds from the end of the world
and sent forth lightnings with rain
and out of His treasuries high winds.

When those who keep us in prison
ask of us mirth in our hang-ups
with 'Sing us a song of Zion',
what can we sing or say
under the mourning willows
of a common suffering in
the river-meadows of Babel?

It is our lingo utters us, not we.
Our native tongue, our endowment,
determines what we can say.
And who endowed us?

Speak if you cannot sing.
Utter with appropriate shudders
the extremities of God's arctic
where all the rivers are frozen,

and how He tempers our exile
with an undeserved planting of willows.

OTHER POEMS OF THE 1980s

Kavyria

Placatory pumice ledged
      against the exploding seas,
stone kettle of extinct fear,
Kavirios: and so little of it, drums
of lined-up stone shafts, six of them, all the rest rubble,
raw gravelly rubble that the fascist
Italian archaeologists
heaped over excavations
discontinued in the 1930s.

On the seaward slope of a desolate moorland, pungent
with thyme in Lemnos, that
single rank plant in the trash-filled court of
acccess perhaps, was it not (and
oh it was, they confirmed it)
asphodel!
       A field of it might have
been, we were told, a field of the dead like
Mudros behind us
           where we did not go,
war cemetery of Winston Churchill's dead.
But this was, if graveyard, a yard of the so
long dead, though by violence, horribly, and frightened,
thyme the great healer fragrantly expunged them.

George Seferis in '39, his
King of Asini, 'the landscape
       changed considerably since
       the poem was written',
              thrown
on the detritus
of a reader's exhausted life
as a golden burial mask
in the Athens museum might be. And
what but museums is it, all of it?

Including Mudros, him, and Clementine,
and all his dead, so many in the two
wars, and all over the globe.
                              Behind his
buried mask of beaten gold, what
stares but a void, a dark, a hole in space
labelled, perhaps in
fascist Italian, 'hero
of Malplaquet, of Blenheim'? The great Duke,
his ancestor, died drivelling.
                              Francis Hughes
has starved himself to death
in H-block. 'Something of
a legend: in a thicket lay
all night, wound packed with mud,
at daybreak found. For murder
and for attempted murder
sentenced to life, and on his
life-contemning features,
his, too, the golden mask
of Agamemnon, smiling.

Happy the people – how does it go? – who have
no heroes and no gods, or just no heroes.

Cameras slung, we tumble out of the coach
speaking the languages of northern Europe,
no heroes with us certainly, our fears
extinct on the flank of the once-volcanic island
of Lemnos, where the metal-worker god
inspired, one is told, among the initiates of
a murderous humble cult a terrified disaffection.

Sorting Old Papers

Old poems from long ago
Surface in memory or
In long-forgotten print.
A stranger's; let them go.

But note: one is reimbursed
For images left open
To a second application,
Time having quashed the first.

And one remembers how
Unnecessary it seemed,
How craven, hedging a bet on
Fallings away from 'Now'.

Let them go with the years!
They do that better now
For speaking double: what one
Wants to hear, one hears.

Well, hawkeye sees the green
Where we would least expect it:
Side issues, well enough;
Where growth is, there serene.

Sonnet

As massive and dispensable as sculpture
Bees, dancing, point and utter their location,
Cotillons interspinning; monumental
Gossamer build-up of gnats' spiring wings
Punctuates space, commands it, by the river
Ephemerally, some evening. So a fly
Moves on the arm of Rodin's thinker with
No less weight than his effigy moves on earth.

Carve out of that, Parnassian! Parian marble
You like to think so cold is all a-zing
With momentary fevers, and the scarp
Of language you would quarry, poet, whirls
Indeterminately shapely in
Helix on nebulous helix, not to be netted.

After Pasternak, in Byron's Manner

Oh had we known it turns out so
When I stepped up for my *début*,
How somewhat lively verses grow
A killing thing for me and you,

Pranks that provoke such vertigo
I would have, scandalised, repressed.
But starting was so long ago,
So boyish the first interest.

Growing old – that's Roman, though;
And from the accomplished raconteur
It asks not jests to zest the show
But a disaster *au sérieux*.

When feeling makes the verses go,
Feeling drives a slave on stage.
The art of it meets its Waterloo;
Earth gusts, our separate destinies rage.

from COLLECTED POEMS (1990)

North & South

for Emily Grosholz, who asked about metre.

Emily, you were sick
Of Arctic computations.
And you would go to Zen,
New Mexico, the Aegean,
Anywhere, to escape them.

The unfortunate Isaac Newton!
Philosopher of science,
You lived with his likes all day.
But herding them north of the Alps,
Weren't you carried away?

And poetry now, as for
Many another, must
Reconstitute, restore?
Well, sweet mole, you go
About it the right way:

Enjoying the lovely fibs,
But nosing the veins of the clay
Deep under the uttered fictions
Chambered and tunneled for: breath
Under the modelling thumb.

Breath, the sculpting of that!
Not synaesthesia, not
Spectacular mental pictures,
Not fables, not generous maxims –
Is this what you'd be at?

Well, and you are right;
Underground, groping and dumb,
Where there are no more rules
That schools can teach, but only
A trembling rule of thumb.

Emily… Persephone!
You see breath wreathe on the cold
Air of an arctic morning
Or fogging a southern glass;
In any and every landscape.

Its shape when it utters 'Eve'
Is as long as the edge of a roof
Or a day that seems never to end
On a Mediterranean island.
And yet, dear friend, we mine it.

If we would learn to scan,
We have to be exact;
Indeed, Newtonian.
The syllable's breath at the mercy
Of Apollonian measure…

Prosody has been thought
Also a science, and
A baffling one; for what
Kind habitat is built on
The count and crimp of breath?

Emily, I can only
Enter a plea for the north,
The sternness of long evenings:
Sun and moon together
In skies over the Orkneys.

They, to Me

'Life is over and you are its
        Memorialist. Such peace,
You ought to think, and be pleased.

You are not supposed to make
        More history. It is what
We have insupportably much of. Now lie still.

The frame, or the several frames
        Are sprained already. Let
"Already" be your quietus.

It would be nice to say:
        "Go on being yourself." But
Your selves were so mutably many.

Must sons and grandsons be
        For ever disconcerted
By a new or revised programme?

The self as elder statesman
        Is an acceptable posture.
But please, no further sorties!

The lack of any but wary
        Approbation is
Itself a kind of distinction.

You were always in the running;
        Earnest and talented fellows
Cannot say that, so be thankful.

How many, not less haughty
        Than you, have been loved? It is true.
But the shame of your need to be loved!

How many of us do you
        In fact recall? Not many;
Obliviousness your helpmeet.

In short you have made your bed
        And now you must loll on it. Patience:
A skill you have not acquired.'

Thus they, to me... Ah, they!
        In dimity gowns;
Pendulous breasts in bikinis;

Skinny in a black
        Bathing-suit, who now
Heaves herself round on two sticks;

Skeletal in a nightgown: 'Can't
    Be first and last, Don, can't
Be first and last...';

And her, incontinent
    In a fragrance of eau-de-cologne:
Mother at sea in Frinton.

By the Road to Upper Midhope

Tares make the corn to grow,
Tares make the corn to grow.
The sweetest hours that e'er I spent
Were spent beside the thistle-row.

Poppies make the corn to grow,
Winds have bared the barleymow.
The sweetest hours that e'er I spent
Were not where Boreas winters O.

Ill fares the winter wheat,
Ill fares the winter wheat,
The sweetest hours that e'er I spent
Were sportive in the summer's heat.

Tares make the corn to thrive,
Choked the more, the more alive.
The sportive hours that I have spent
Made corn and tares alike revive.

Poppies make the corn to grow,
Winds strip the barleymow.
The sweetest hours that e'er I spent
Were spent amang the lassies O.

Dule of a Dewsbury Matron

Why should we   defer   our joys?
While we may   the fruits   of love
Let us, lad   o let us   prove!
  Whistle and I'll come to thee, my lad.

Let us beware   the shepherd's warning:
Saturday night   brings Sunday morning.
  Whistle and I'll come to thee, my lad.

Cannot we   delude   the eyes
Of a few poor   household spies?
Here's my cabinet of joys.
  O whistle and I'll come to thee, my lad.

To be taken   to be seen
These have crimes   accounted been.
Pakistani brown ye be
  But whistle and I'll come to thee.

Cedarscented is this closet
I ope to thee, this cabinet
Of all the joys   that you'll disprize.
  O whistle and I'll come to thee.

Black Hoyden

Mary Jane, she's after me,
Mary Jane, black hoyden.
'Touch of the tar, lad,' says my Dad,
'Kitts Nevis or Tahiti'.

Mary Jane has been betrayed.
Don't meddle with Black Hoyden.
'Black eyes like that,' my father said,
'Would scythe a feller's garden.'

Black Hoyden's coming down the hill,
The sleet beginning to fall.
It wavers through the wintry air,
She wavers not at all.

Black Hoyden homing from the mill,
Black Hoyden, Black Hoyden.
Black honour coming tall and still,
A knife in her shawl.

Who is that knife for, Mary Jane?
But I know well, and I know why.
Black eyes lovingly have flashed,
This flash will leave a stain.

Harridan, black hoyden!

The Right Lads

To re-insert it in
The Yorkshire Post…
The venerable decorum
Of doughty drinking:
  For a'that and a'that,
  A staggering toast.

Shall we commend it to
The bullies of Leeds United?
Dear to the dumb, unlettered
And unemployable,
  A precedent shall be cited:
  A man's a man for a'that.

Is there for honest poverty
Wha hangs the head an a'that?
Hang loose, hang nail, hang dog!
Oh you are made of use,
  Acting the part assigned:
  Capitalism's refuse!

Grazia Deledda, *young*

*

How funny, she beat him, she
Beat him all through the week
And he knows we know it, and we
Giggle and don't know why
We choke when we learned to speak.

Our fists are balled against
Our treacherous mouths, our small
Handkerchieves screwed up tight.
Why are sadnesses funny,
Sad people such a fright?

Life is suffering, says
Mama, and Mama is right.
Mama, how does it happen
That laughing has to come when
Weeping might?

A crippled boy would be
A leggy girl's first lover.
What a disgrace she is!
She whistles, snorts, bows over
In agony, not to laugh.

Others have told, with almost
A giggle, stories of trees
That bleed, and girls that are birds
With tongues and without them,
Struggling short of words.

*

Don Sebastiano,
You speak of the not-quite-language
Of donkey, stone and cuckoo.
Stone? we say. But yes, you
Say, stone utters too.

A roll of thunder. Mountains
Lounge like big girls around
The dreadful horizon. Their
Languid and spiky eyes
Mutter over the playground.

Don Sebastiano,
How can I tell you? The hem
Hangs down in front and is
Rucked up behind, and because
They will notice, I hate them.

The unkind, stifled laughter
At cycle-rack and sickbay
And First Communion, is
This what explodes in the peacock,
The ass, the jeering jay?

Does all of the Creation
Deride us? Is it this that
The stone, the cuckoo, the stone-chat
Really intend? There are
So many questions I'd ask you!

A harder one, that I
Know your answer to
(You'll point to the Madonna):
Is girlhood a condition,
However we act, of dishonour?

Don Sebastiano,
Gravely you point your finger
Up to the heavenly blue.
That means you judge the gym-slips'
Horrible surmise true?

No, it is sadder than that:
Girl-geese, the hilly-billy
Goat, the demented ass…
Sometimes it seems the entire
Creation cries 'Alas!'

At last I am growing up:
Even our stories giggle,
Our sayings bray their dismay.
We are all of us aching to utter
More than we can say.

Hermes and Mr Shaw

The narrow backyard garden
    Of Mr and Mrs Shaw
Ran between us and, in its cutting, the railway;
    Ran right to left across the end of our,
Our and our neighbours', slightly more ample gardens.

Quite young, a childless couple,
    Mr and Mrs Shaw kept
Themselves to themselves; and so it was no light matter,
    When a ball had sailed over the fence, to
Go round and ask to retrieve it.

A minor clerk or else an artisan (I
    Never knew, I imagine), Mr Shaw
Kept mostly a kitchen-garden, though
    Next to his house a patch of lawn
Was where a mis-hit cricket-ball mostly pitched.

The grass there was of a deep, an Irish green,
    And not cropped close. I think it was grown from seed
Not sods. I have the impression lawns
    Grown from seed were thought to be second-rate
As most things were about Mr and Mrs Shaw.

Once, vividly, I saw from my upstairs bedroom
    A flock of white doves dense on that patch of grass
And in the midst of them, accusingly
    And neatly side by side, a pair of my
Canvas shoes, in the dream called quaintly 'plimsolls'.

And dreams – is it not so? – dreams are insistently verbal;
      Vocabulary is the key to them.
Not that I can, or care to, unlock this one:
      What did it guiltily mean, for things of mine
To show up there? Why shoes? Why a snow of doves?

Unlocking dreams is some one else's business.
      What comforts me is that in that
Year, as the *kristallnacht* splintered
      In Germany, or soon would, as Stalin moved
Elated to his Great Terror, dramas were

Enacted in my obscure pactfic boyhood.
      For was it not that, my dream undeniably proved?
Mr and Mrs Shaw are almost certainly dead.
      Their thin grass, they should know, once took the tread
Of what? Winged sandals? Settle for that: winged sandals.

Articulacy. Hints from the Koran

First lesson: Don't
get ahead of yourself, don't gabble.
For a pell-mell of syllables, is
that what it means to assemble,
as when He assembled our bones
like the articulated members of a saying?

Be sonorous.
                    Like a goose?
When the Writ is goose-like
(which will not be often), honk,
honk like a goose. And when
the text, as you may call it,
is plummy, gorge it with plums,
savour the vowels, give them,
each as it comes, full presence.

Next, imagine yourself
the privileged herald to
your chosen, not
chance-met companions;
with whom there is much that can be
taken for granted, since
they know all that you tell them,
though in an inferior fashion.

When the Writ runs into
consonantal crackle,
cacophonies, crackle with it.
This is the most of music:
thorn-hedges set round orchards.

Next you imagine yourself
the angel Gabriel who
divulges to the privileged
intermediary
what he shall relay.

And this is perilous, as
assuming the Angel is
always perilous. Now you
address a generality
of strangers, and there is
temptation, since you fear them,
to bully, or inveigle.

When Holy Writ quotes writ,
acknowledge the quotation-marks
by a doubled pause and poise,
keeping the voice lifted.

When the sense rides over
the end of a verse, accord it
enough and no more than enough
check, to gather its haunches
before the brush- or water-
obstacle that you,
no steeplechase-rider, will not
accelerate to get over.

Last (this not often attained)
you imagine yourself the Speaker
of what He divulged through angels.
So holy the act of reciting.

These are not prescriptions
on how to wow an audience,
but to diaphragm and pharynx
and parts more inward, how to
give body to the unbodied.

Man imagines his bones shall
not be reassembled.
He wants to be open-ended
as far as he can see:
one discrete happening after
another, all exclamation,
the palm of his hand unaware what his fingers are up to.

But the first, the second, the third
knuckles of every finger
are articulated more
closely than the best
reciter or singer can manage.

The act of reciting, however,
generates faith, done rightly.

Reminded of Bougainville

for Howard Erskine-Hill

'The rest is not our business.' Come the end or
a good deal sooner rest is
our only business. Up to
and battering that
a swarming
intelligence names the names, the
localities. Who is to say when
shearing the boom and in a way we
least expected H.M.S. Coventry shall

recuperate the Malvinas,
les Malouines, into renewed
restiveness and the wasps
of doubt, of self-doubt, of
resolution, of
intelligences swarm?

'a culture of regressive repetitions…'
Brave men and a gallant ship, her
namesake also sank
in World War Two
by bomber aircraft.
Carried aboard were
large mediaeval nails
from the bombed cathedral, formed in
the shape of a cross. She entered
the 1st of May the total exclusion zone;
3rd of May her Lynx
helicopter scored
direct hits, totally
with its Sea Skua missiles
destroyed one target.

Sheffield was sunk the 4th of May;
Glasgow out of action
by the 11th. In the last
week of *Coventry's* life, the
24th was a good day: three
aircraft down, and later another six.
The 25th, with *Broadsword,* in exposed
water, shortly after
six in the evening 'sprang
very brave and determined
at us from behind
the land' four aircraft, one
persistently with four
bombs, three in the portside,
exploded. Immediate flooding
and fire, very thick black
suffocating smoke. 'Get the ship…'

'Aye aye sir', though
no power, the ship on fire
listing to port some fifty degrees, in fifteen
minutes on her side, in thirty
her keel horizontal a few
feet above sea level. Later
she sank. Many brave deeds...

'In the Cathedral Three Great Nails once held
Hearts of Oak until in war they were felled.'
Nineteen dead.

The verse-line is commodious, has to be.
A sea-borne landing launched without
command of the air, a foredoomed operation
or not, as now appears. What is the rôle
of the term 'professional' in the expression:
'professional and brave men'? When did we last
hear: 'the profession of arms'? A stout, outmoded
or not, it appears, conception. Bloody business
is some men's business decently, as when
Bougainville made the Falklands briefly French
so now, and we may rest in that. It is
always our business, always.

A Measured Tread

for Kenneth Millar dead

Walking about the emptied house I
jangle softly at each heavyish step,
an old plough-horse, some parts of his harness upon him,
who strays, tired out but happy with that, through musky
honey-shot glooms of a barn where, though he
strays only idly towards it, sweet hay will be found in a crib.

Hello, Ken... I imagine, as everyone has,
the impossible: my living and my dead
looking in on the mote-shot Elysium they have emptied,
hearing the *ictus,* the chink of pocketed coins,
the household meter that my father once,
he from among the dead, both was himself and moved to.

I tread at my disoriented will
with a chime or a ding that, now I have emptied my pockets,
I if no other still hear and will attend to.
The hay in the bin will not be so sweet, after all?
No matter for that, it is sweet as I stumble towards it.
Such pacings of things seems all there is, sometimes, of wisdom.

Northern Metres

for Tony Harrison in Florida

Your grandad worked the signals
At Haworth, mine at Horton:
Old railwaymen.

Self-satisfied a little,
Their and our preference for
The overtly neat and tidy.

We have to be so overt!
The signals clack down smartly
Yes or No; no fudging

Unless it were… why yes,
As between fragrant cedar
And stinking, lasting cypress.

Done with a lovely touch, your
Emblem of that: the chairs
Standing opposed on your porch.

One cedarwood, one cypress,
I see them and yes, I smell them;
Together, but distinct.

No Old World sentinel
Of graveyards, but the bald
Cypress of the swamplands,

Of alligator-haunted
Original stews: a symbol
Of rationality taunted.

Symbols make at best
A puttering sort of logic.
Aerosol does the trick:

Obscenities spray-painted
On parents' headstones have
Made a morass of Beeston.

Pitiful understanding
Will not disperse that stench,
Nor tidy metres quench it.

Yorkshire's man-made swamps!
Cedar, a cedarn fragrance,
How plant it, how impart it?

Church of Ireland

for Barbara Hayley

Status indeed and protocol I pay
Too little regard to, since they rib our doings
To some ascertainable order. There's a mouthful!

Mouthful of rocks, of crags... which is as if
Equivalent to, or asked for by, small Sligo's
Dense knobbed hills. But it's not right, this language.

And yet it seems right, seems enforced by some
Home-made decorum, say, or protocol;
Except that home-made language never works.

What a rash thrust at being explicit leads to
Often is as little short of ugly
As the inside of the Yeatses' church, Drumcliffe;

Where things may happen that are beautiful,
But are so not by any or much decorum
But by their unavoidable and proper

Mismatches, incongruities: the bulky
Battered officiant, man of God, our Canon,
Out of his vestments such a good sort always

Holy behind his unreserve. One sees
The point of that in his less than elegant church,
Thirst though one may for an order more in keeping.

Knobbed hills, Ben Bulben, and the skinny Shee,
Phantasmagoria that englobed a poet
Once, and touchingly… and yet not there

The measured, the less abrupt, less adventitious
Fall of phrase I need when I think of us
Rain-dashed, in Sligo, walking to church together.

The Scythian Charioteers

'Black quadrigas reared
In veering triumphs'
(Mandelstam)

When it was found a fault
In Moscow that it lacked
Leningrad's Attic salt,

The charge was brought not in
The era of Peter the Great's
Contempt for Balt and Finn,

When every sucked-out mile
Of drained ground groaned to bear
Stoa and peristyle;

But rather when already
The sand was once again
Blood-slick, the ground unsteady,

Did the untimely Pindars
Of Russia acclaim the Olympic
Contests of brazen cars.

Not when each city-scape
Of Northern Europe cherished
Olive, acanthus, grape,

Did these wheel out the *quadriga,*
The jet-black four-in-hand
Dressed in the colours of Riga.

Now when it is known the modern
City of Athens is
Vociferous, vehicle-ridden,

When jerry-built prose and verse
Everywhere lethally topple,
The loftier the worse,

Now (and best so) they find
Occasion to exalt our
Lost Athens of the mind.

Mother

Taxis were beyond us
As ever beyond most
In Barnsley. So to attend us
Disembarkers, no
Limousines come and go,
No hackneys cruise and coast.

Well, from the station yard
In the now more affluent town
A mile's walk is no hard
Imposition on
A fat and prodigal son
As the summer day goes down.

How unlikely, though,
That there, unchanged, should stand
From twenty years ago
A structure that seemed meant
To be impermanent:
A shed with the blurred legend:

'TAXIS'. Thus it stood,
Locked and unattended,
When in fierce rain I would
Have found a car for her
Who with the hairdresser
Was having her wild hair tended.

Afoot I must pursue
In default of taxis,
Unpenanced pilgrim, two
Cousins whose stylish aunt
Shopped at the elegant
'Butterfields and Massies'.

No such pretensions were
Left to her that day
When I pursued for her
A non-available car.
There are who die, like her,
Puzzled, their wits astray.

At the Café Parnasse

for Turner Cassity

Sealed into the cocoon
Of light and water, face
And racked reflection, voice
And the nymph Echo answering, the grub
Narcissus throbs at high noon. Slapping
Languidly, the rocked
Wave on the bridge-piers means a speedboat passes
A half of a mile and all of a minute away,
Tensed for the seaway. Ah Narcissus, ah
Dreamboat of self! In Amsterdam the brick,
So I am told, abides no pulse but yours!

Perfection of the noon...
The waterfront *Café*
Parnasse safe harbours him, the smoke
Circling straight upward from his cigarette

(Always the same brand, with that special tang,
The Unfulfillable). He sits
Hour after hour, small glass or coffee-cup
Cold at his elbow; sees, as night comes on,
The knots of sailors speaking foreign tongues
Stream past him pell-mell, though as yet but idly,
Towards excess; then calls for the waiter; leaves.

Ensues his worst hour:
What if the grub he is
Should flap wet wings, and tower? What
If – the construction is unknown to him
Except in acquired and treasured English – this
Unfulfillable were
Fulfillable, in a high gale or a whorehouse?
A slowed-down speedboat! – ears that should
Hear their own memories of a pulse late heard
Repeated with some difference. Ah, free verse…
A scion of Narcissus, that one was!

And so he shrugs it off;
Prepares a frugal meal;
Recalls how there are carapaces more
Armoured than his – the dense, secure delusions
Of liberty, husks of so tough a rind
(The liberated seamen!) no one can
Tell if inside is a being alive or dead;
So falls asleep; and so sleeps through, against
The hour when he will take his seat again
At the *Café Parnasse,* the small waves slapping the brick,
His own blue smoke aspiring and dispersing.

Though dry, not dry

for Doreen

Dry season. Block. So, rain…
Why am I too proud
To pray for rain? Am I
The Muses' Lucifer
That I will not confess
A need so commonplace?

Truth is, I no longer care.
Rain would clear the air,
But foetid air suits well
My dozing in this chair.
Sloth; why is it always
Spoken of so ill?

It does no harm; it spares
The inattentive world
One more triumphant play
Out of my one strong suit,
Sardonic paradox:
This age's mask for Love.

A dancer's or an actor's
Mask, it is not dishonest;
Donning it, I do not
Betray myself to the age.
Deciding punctuation
Even, I mount the stage,

But it is an honest stage,
Mirror of men and manners;
This man, his manners. Why
Then, should the nice distinction
Of colon from semi-colon
That once absorbed, now bore me?

How merciful is our God,
My love, that it should be
Not Love but only love
In this abstracted mode
I cannot stir the will
To ask that I be stirred to!

To a Bad Poet

To break the pentameter, Pound's first heave
Sufficed where we were concerned. It was you
Who launched her again,
A foul old bottom, lurching,
Oars like trunks.

Was this, we said,
What once held spices,
Found the Americas
In ragged seas?
This tub?

(1951–75)

On a Proposed Celebration of Ezra Pound

for Clive Wilmer

He who proposes
Assembling those
Whose ear for verse is
Worse than for prose,

To celebrate
One whose least airs
Moved at a rate
To out-pace theirs,

Does him and us
Nothing but harm:
The infamous
Wish to disarm

Does no-one good.
When all is said,
He that could
Judge us, is dead.

Revenge for Love

Neither dead nor alive, neither asleep nor awake,
In a dreadful calm I drowse the night hours through;
No pride to nurse, no pains I need to take,
Not wanting you, and not not wanting you.

'Revenge for, or betrayal of
Love by change and death…'
'Revenge' is better, my
Love, 'revenge' is better:
I am certainly somebody's debtor
For you, and the debt it seems
Is paid this way. Not what
Any one had in mind;
Still, nobody is betrayed.

You and I, we have made
Very little of love, as it was
Sold by the big-band sound
That led me when I found
You in the 1940s.
Whose was the band? I remember
The startled glance we exchanged
When it turned out for our eldest
His discs were collector's items:

Glenn Miller! There was no price
We wouldn't have paid
In San Francisco for one
Of his to give our boy;
Paying over the odds
Already for whatever
Damage we did our children
By being so ready to move
On, and always on.

Neither dead nor alive, neither asleep nor awake,
These are the thoughts that float
Into and out of my mind, where once they might
Have taken me by the throat.

Vengeance is mine, saith the Lord. And surely it is
      A gentle revenge to take:
Nothing to fear, merely a lapsing away
      Neither asleep nor awake.

A Garland for Ivor Gurney

1

'God be praised that made
Gloucestershire...' The fool!
Gloucester or Avon – what
Administrative fiction
Shall God be praised for? Oh
For Crabbe and some sane depiction!

Gurney, whose burning need
And uninstructed eye
Were partisan for Gloucester,
Yet at St Albans too
Endowed mere masonry
With meanings out of true.

Of clouds and tower, he cried,
Of tower and cloud! ... and pointed
To Tewkesbury. The use of
Dilapidated altars?
Unhinged the text, disjointed.
'Lo Gloucestershire,' he falters.

2

Poor thing, perfection; he
Came to it though, at last.
Mother-of-pearl!

His lot were done for: not
On account of the War, which he
Knew made a poet of Ledwidge;

But because he would not,
Nor any of them, settle
For less than ecstasy.

Jacked up to that, its rough
And windy contours, nothing
But neurasthenia could

Cut him down to what
The Ancients settled for:
Krater and *patera*.

Ecstatic enough, the cup
Of red clay that
Sparkled with argent water,

We are happy to think. But he,
Unreconciled to that,
Committed himself to madness.

3

Whether Howells was
To die or not develop,
Beethoven wouldn't tell.
Bach was there but does not
Care for Gurney; Schumann
Also but Gurney's love
For him is less.
Oh, out of balance, oh
Too highly strung, poor Gurney,
What's to be done with you?
A ticket to the asylum?

Only a sufficient
Black surge of pain, he says,
Upon the fair thing standing;
Red block of power, St Albans,
Or Tewkesbury by Severn;
Mask above meadows in
Light that promised rain.

A promising composer
Stares at the stony mask
And cannot pierce it. What
Service is there like
The making of a great
Thing in stone? he asks;
And aches with promise of
Mask after mask, and veil
On drifting veil of rain,

And service not rewarded.

Wombwell On Strike

Horace of course is not
a temporizer, but
his sudden and smooth transitions
            (as, into a railway tunnel,
            then out, to a different landscape)

it must be admitted elide,
and necessarily, what
happens up there on the hill
            or hill-ridge that the tunnel
            of syntax so featly slides under.

I have been reminded of this
when, gratefully leaving my native
haunts, the push-and-pull diesel
            clatters into a tunnel
            under a wooded escarpment:

Wentworth Woodhouse, mounded
or else in high shaws drifted
over the miners' tramways.
            Horace's streaming style
            exhorts me never to pause;

'Press on,' he says, and indeed his
suavities never entirely
exclude the note of alarm:
            'Leave the unlikely meaning
            to eddy, or you are in trouble.'

Wombwell – 'womb well': it is
foolish and barbarous wordplay,
though happily I was
            born of this tormented
            womb, the taut West Riding.

Yours was solid advice,
Horace, and centuries have
endorsed it; but over this tunnel
            large policemen grapple
            the large men my sons have become.

After the Match

Hardly a one but here he is improved,
Long-legged, shell-chested, stepping to the bath.
The too long hair, the fatuous moustaches,
The fussy or the battered, beery face,
Do not, we see, do justice to the man

Who, naked, is quite free from all deception,
More simply strong and weak than in the scrum.
We felt them ardent then, but in a crowd,
Disguised in shirts and numbers; and the rank
Smell of them good, but not so spirited.

We now, however, having seen them naked,
Briskly and neatly towelling and stooping,
Seeing them flesh, see spirits in them walking,
The bridegrooms of some far-fetched metaphor,
Sophia or Idea, going crowned.

Mustered into the Avant-Garde

I am supposed to apologize
To you, old mumbler?
And to you, haughty reclusive
Master of the opal? And
To you, the not quite faithless
Friend and driving rival?
For being clear, if you please,
For making it seem as easy
As I can manage! Well
(At a summer-school in the Quantocks)
No, I will *not* be sorry!

A bugle-call to the Vanguard:
His Majesty's Light Horse?
You, with your plod-a-clollop!
(What have you got in those panniers?
What leaden inedible forage?)
You, phantom-like over the flanking
Hills where the enemy isn't?
And you, who appear in mid-column
Suddenly, here, and disorder
The main line of march with your sidelong
Bewhiskered and smiling troopers?

Such weight as they carry! Yes, even
Captain Phantom, back from
Another invisible skirmish
He isn't allowed to report on,
Look how he droops in the saddle!
See how the twitching and turning
To note who's in front and behind
Attenuates Colonel Driver!
And then of course poor old General
Mumble, encumbered with all our
Humanity, no less!

You know what does for them, don't you?
You know what that weight is, they carry?
Responsibility, trooper!
These are the antennae.
The whole damned army depends on

Them to know where it's going.
William Pitt and the Duke of
Wellington depended
For their intelligence on
A coterie at Racedown:
Coleridge and Southey! Wordsworth!

Sculptures in Hungary

A Hun turned sculptor spoke
Of the styles of Etruria. Under a basin-cropped

Black cap of hair, his drooping thick moustache
Was style of the First World War, style of Attila.

His toad-hipped plenteous nude
Pannonia bears

The name of a Roman province, but the art
His barber practised was

For art's sake also: more than a Magyar manhood
Spoke from the hairfringed lip wide in its welcome.

The closed still forms wear from his classic chisel
A smile like an enigmatic property,

But his hid nothing: human, it deserved
Better than I could rise to, when he spoke

Of the unfinished as a form of art,
Fragments entire. Not womanhood but through

Each woman's nub of breast and belly, stone
Spoke from a polished torso in the corner.

Pannonia! her bastion heaped the west
Outside the plateglass of a warm hotel

Against the luminous evening over Buda,
Still in bright cold gradations, grey and rose.

The frogged hussar
Curvetted there on terraces

And men alive in Germany have watched
Where plateglass glares from Pest

The Russian gunflash. When De Gaulle
Advanced upon Algeria

In armoured cars, the colonists
Howled, choking through the teargas, 'Budapest!'

He spoke through smiles. His hands braced up the air
Poising ideal objects. The matrix

Adheres a little, Istrian nor Carraran
Not of locale nor race but meaning, 'broken'.

Sounds of a Devon Village

1

Many compacted summers
Unpack for the ear
Viridities to come, as under
The watershed that wedges Culm from Exe
Long squeals of birdsong aggravate the eaves.

2

The long-haired husbandman forks hay;
Across an autumnal half-mile, solid-state
Blasts out his country, his some-other-country
Music, who will tend his little children
Devotedly tomorrow. The high branches
Crack on the hill-ridge, region of lichen and ivy.

High noise, no thud, but clash, moan, breaking clatter.
The wood's in trouble. Far below,
A jar of altercation in the lane
Signals his twin daughters are at hand
With pert expostulations home from school.

Companionably creaking, elm and oak,
Baucis and Philemon, bowed and feathered
In conjugal felicity in the hedgerow,
Hard-pressed, hard-earned, and blest at last by the gods.

The elms are shattered. It is not his fault,
Nor fault of a grinding gear-box, if Philemon
Be disjoint from Baucis in this end
Though they befriended gods. Dutch elm disease
By night and day travels in eerie silence.

Clatter of hooves, of iron-shod wheels over cobbles…
The ancients were not prone to understatement.
Stolidity has classic precedent
And so has noise. A Cynic schoolmaster
May think noise fevers, but his neighbours sweat
Most, and prickle, when a silence comes.

The church-bells clamour, the full-uddered heifer
Entreats the shuddering air, but is unheard
Above the inflexible thud. The human voice,
Strained to a scream to penetrate, is toneless
As if, what it is not, impassible.
'Your lunch,' she screams, 'your LUNCH!' and points to it.
He waves and nods, to show he's understood.
The binder-reaper curtains him with sound.

'Sylvan', from *silva:* a thesaurus of
Words and phrases is an unlikely meaning
Silva had, once. The greenest, most
Sylvan man is epicure of din,
Sorter of noises. *(Florilegium:*
A cultured nature, sedulously thinned.)

Woods: and to clear them, was that not his vocation;
Then to restore as windbreak, and plantation?

On Generous Lines

Hanoverian silverware, this jug
Though small amply dispenses cream
Out of the skin-tight flask of its silver belly;

Tunbelly never clumsy but as crescent
As there in Beverley
The Gothic font's Augustan cover, carved

In, would it be true to say, a settled age
That in a portly contour
Could safely read fecundity, not cancer?

Their resolutions – into hooking curves
Of a handle's poised relation, or to a darting
And avian grace the pouring lip – evince

A victory hypochondriac like ours,
Achieved against all odds
By battening on them, clamping down, provoking.

And would it be true to say:
'Be generous. Take risks. Give hostages'?
It would be true; incautious curves enforce it.

Equestrian Sestina

Horse, our poor creature, we treat as if elemental,
Stupidly. This is unfeeling. True, he is fabulous;
Goes, though, not like the wind, whatever his mettle;
Nor, much as he ripples in motion, is he conditioned
By a sky-god's whims, like a river. Not there did the Norman
Culture, that made him its talisman, ground its attachment.

Rather, he was their technology; unsentimental
Reasons made barons and bishops, bloodthirsty and emulous,
Curry, caparison into the finest fettle
Him their scout-car, halftrack, their efficient
Weapon-carrier. Dearer to them than Woman
The destrier trampling the Legate's obstructive parchment.

Why then so often, seeking a type for the gentle
And powerful, such as we once were, needing a stimulus
Even to think of that humanness lost, do we settle
On him, on the horse? Why are our horses commissioned
To stand in for what we think best in ourselves, for a yeoman
Sturdiness, or knighthood blurred in a lozengy hatchment?

Is it their having, except for holiday rental
Like jeeps or a sand-yacht, vanished, that now they compel us
Only as fluid, their hoofbeats soft as a petal
Floating to earth on a moonlit hill? A deficient
Sense for the civic has exiled even the Roman
Charger, all laurel and bronze, to eerie detachment.

This has us craning, to trace on a pock-marked lintel
The arms of Sir Hugo, the psychopath. Miscreant, infamous
Cavalier, his horsemanship counts for little
To earn him remission; yet that, no more, was sufficient.
Time, the sad torrent, has washed off his vices, and no man
Builds jetty or pier in that current, or measures its catchment.

There has to be reason why beings not elemental,
Divine, nor supernatural, soothe us as fabulous
Creatures moving among us. A horse of mettle
Or merest Dobbin ought to find us conditioned
To a sorry awe. Call it the flower of Norman
Or Saracen chivalry, this was a noble attachment.

Homage to George Whitefield

(1714–1770)

Born at 'The Bell' in Gloucester,
where you can go to this day
to sink a pint, and see
a piratical black beard
and fingers combing it and
a burly frame, all at sea.

Earth bound George Whitefield, not
a man to panic
at metaphysical terrors, having
a relish for them,
wanting his God to be
not oceanic but
earth-bound like him to the earth he knew,
shards and mosaic in it.

That Roman viniculture
in the Severn valley was
venal? He stands corrected,
considering: Well, perhaps.

He traversed the Atlantic.
This weeping day's corsair
is a second-order artist,
and womanish in his cups;

whereas this one was a hero,
dreadful and dreaded. Search
the Methodist roster now
in vain for such a pirate:
Bluebeard evangelist!

Two Widows in Tashkent

In, of all places, Tashkent
They were reading Keats; and were wrong
As the wives and widows of
Poets are always wrong:
'Each word is a self-confession.'
True; but not to the point.

To the point is how
It (his poem) measures
Up to, takes note of, departs from
Ovid or Dante. Ladies,
This is where he departs from
You, and you cannot abide it.

Helena Morley

★

In winter in Diamantina
(Which is in Brazil)
Does the wind blow keener,
December try you sorely,
Helena Morley?

In winter, in
Diamantina
(Which is in Brazil)
The month is June, and nothing
Stiffens the air or the will.

In high pure air in
Diamond-land
You have heard it said: 'A hundred
Minds the winter enamours
For one kind child that is summer's.'

This will vex you surely,
Helena Morley, Helena Morley,
Whose English cousins know
So lovingly ice and snow.

Disown them, Helena Morley.

★

Be sorry for those English
Cousins of Helena's dreams:

Their Daddies built the railways,
Their Daddies built the ships,
Their Daddies made their daughters
Their Ladyships.

Their gossamer wings whirr fast
At onset of winter weather.
Now they are summer's children,
Through the Green Park together
Crying, through or without
Tears: 'Here we are, we are dying.'

Pity those foreign cousins
Whom Helena could not know,
Accorded such esteem
So long ago.

★

'Every one in the end
In good time or in high time
Is summer's friend,'

You might have said, discovered
Late in life in your mansion
By the lagoon in Rio.

Instead you said, severely
Darning linen: 'Hours
To spare are spent on chores.'

Spend, or save... The words hang
Brightly in the air
If all time is to spare,

Waiting for Resurrection.

Sorting the Personae

Once the broom has started,
A cleansing of every corner
Of what has become a wide
Working-area is
A labour of anxious love.

None but old brooms here.
It cannot be called a rhythm,
The way I wield them, though
A certain jerky pattern
Does emerge from the proddings.

What odd inconvenient spaces
Some of the students prefer!
Consider the draughty landing,
Grand enough in its day,
Paul shares with grimy *putti*;

Or notice how Thomas and Trevor
Compete for the awkward angle,
Lit it is true by a bleak
Skylight, still an embrasure,
Burne-Jones glass in the casements;

Or Fiona and Frances,
One so disorderly, one
A furious miniaturist,
Side by side in the ballroom,
Easels together always.

Would it be better for them,
As the regretful committee
Is confident, were they allotted
Space in some custom-made
Airy and clean Polytechnic?

Or are they too old to change?
I am only the cleaning-lady,
But some of what Paul does, for instance
(And he has been at it for years)
Strikes me as *very* old-fashioned.

That dark little niche which no one
Since old Mr Housman died has
Been attracted to, still
Cannot be overlooked, must
Be given a lick and a promise.

Sometimes they dedicate,
Though never the way you'd expect,
Their unfinished works to each other.
Who'd thought that wild-bearded Trevor
Cherished a crush on Frances?

A lot of the time they quarrel.
They stamp around, waving their arms.
Bad days those are, when not
A stroke of even indifferent
Work gets done in this school.

They live and work in muck.
Yet 'clean' I have heard them give
As the highest praise to each other.
I am only the cleaning-lady
But anxious for them, and loving.

'1945'

A string of the scarlet rubies of Ceylon
Cheated the Customs in a re-sealed tin
Of boiled coagulate sweets... to which I turned
My officer's blind eye. The carillon
Was all 'St Budeaux' as I brought them in
By rail, the ship-boys, Devonport's draft returned!

Though not in fact: the halt at Keyham slept
In mild mid-morning and its signal-box
Absently clapped down its signal as
We, crawling from Southampton, smoothly crept
Home from Kowloon, from Trinco, from the shocks
And blithely endured alarms of the Moluccas.

My scapegrace sea-pups, what are the memories stir
In us, grown fat? A too white monument
Tall on the Hoe, ships' plaques, a name like 'Howe',
The shot-torn ensign of the 'Exeter' –
These are not what we want, nor what was meant;
Instead, the bells – in whose ears, then and now?

No one had said whom I reported to.
I skipped the train before the Dockyard, tore
In a lucky taxi up the marble-streeted
And marble-hearted town that Hardy knew,
In a bawdry of bells, the mess-deck's innocent roar
'Get up them stairs!' pealing for her I greeted.

Where's that West Country where each belfry peals,
Where no one's given cottonwool for bread,
Flowing with scriptural honey, milk, and wine;
Where the artificer guides the easy wheels
And no cranked labour blacks the overhead?
In women's arms, oh you who crossed the line!

Sheer hulk, Tom Bowling, I observe you climb
Staggeringly the Forder Valley tamed
Into industrial suburb. Novorossisk
Road, a sardonic legacy of wartime
Naively or duplicitously named,
Sees your arms flail at fame, betrayal, risk.

Somewhere a gross or ghostly woman plucks
At washed-out cottons, pats her hair behind
Absentmindedly, and measures on
Her bony breast something a battered box
Unopened in years has suddenly brought to mind:
A string of the pale small rubies of Ceylon.

GOODBYE TO THE USA

Sunday Morning

for Doreen

No point in looking. The
    Comanche were
A terror on this trail, the
Cimarron Cut-off. Now
The farmers' station-waggons
Feed at the gospel trough;
And while they worshipped, none
But you and I were astir.

Big mostly Baptist churches
    Crowned every hill.
Nothing to hear; if they
Sang, as no doubt they did,
Around us and above the
Noise of our engine, only
The gimlet larksong pierced
By snatches, fierce and shrill.

Eclogues of pick-up trucks!
    Georgics of
Jouncing springs, and the
Bucolic beer-can! Such
Good time we made, oh such
Good time, reeling off mile
On undistinguished mile that
Landscape of peace and love.

Not picturesque, although
    One hour ahead
Eastward the Cimarron,
Originating Lord,
Would round on us again
In pinkish buttes and vast
Eroded washes, where he
Coiled in a narrow bed.

Upstream New Mexico
    Makes much of his
Choked canyon, and the town
That on the Santa Fe
Trail was the famous last
Staging-post but one:
Cimarron, much reached for.
But here, few memories…

Such as they have, they would
    Sooner forget.
The past of this spread of land
Does no one credit: twice
Or many times evicted,
Cherokee, Choctaw, Chickasaw
Here were dispossessed
Once more, more brutally yet.

'Landscape of peace and love';
    And as construed
In the Chickasaw tongue? Who wonders?
Under whose past is there not
Greed, and injustice? We took
Nevertheless the blessing
Of the unjust at worship.
For once, then, gratitude!

For once, for once, the heart
    Can overprice its
Overt occasion. Over
The black-top streeling miles
Of the panhandle of
Oklahoma the heart hawks,
Remembering, baffled but
Convinced of benefits.

The University of the South

for Andrew Lytle, aged 80

That shrewd character Will Percy in
Lanterns on the Levee (that's pronounced
    'Levvy') lost his level
    Head over you, Sewanee.

Lammas House and Apthorp House and such
Or such a college housing a famous bell
    Were mellowed brick, but this
    Is the midwest, pretty well;

Aligned with Indianapolis although
Old, the old South. No matter for that, he peoples
    With clerics, with cavorting
    Dryads, your leafy mountain.

Grecian as saccharine as early Forster,
As Gothic too, in shattered Picardy
    Serving with Pershing he
    Preserved your episcopal stone.

An idiom we can hardly now remember,
Fatherly and white-supremacist,
    Sealed you, Sewanee, in
    Defaced, untenable amber.

So love is no preservative; Will Percy's
Enraptured idyll of you came apart.
    What youth now takes your bosky
    Artifice to heart?

Some, there's no doubt. Milan and Chattanooga
Are all one world, we have to think. The ghoulish
    Noble ambition after
    The shapely is universal.

Ghouls haunt the tombs of Will Alexander Percy
And Quintus Horatius Flaccus, sieving their dust
    For stanza-forms or the musty
    Adumbrations of myth.

And with them or not with them, seldom under
Your wintriest boughs, Sewanee, stalks the one
  Whose sharper hunger prowls
  That bone-yard, the Argonne.

His need of shapes more skeletal impels
Over the shattered carrion fields the last
  Exemplary monster. Now
  The veridical idyll emerges.

Savannah

for Alex Heard, administrator

Executive speed is poetry! Whereas,
Benevolently dallying, earnest Berkeley,
  Having his city planned,
  Abandoned it for Rhode Island,

Oglethorpe, philanthropist, had landed
A hundred and twenty souls to set in brick
  A philosophical blue-print
  Intended for Bermuda:

A pretty, rational city. And at Christmas
Incongruous with cane-brakes, we are grave:
  This was a place some thousands
  Died to take, or save.

None so murderous as geometers.
Quadrant, ellipse, short avenues beget
  Under their shade-trees furies:
  Claymore and bayonet.

And grave as we are, we are glad. The abrasive weather
Scouring the Factors' Walk, chill off the river,
  Gives us to think, engraves
  That solemn thought: the civic.

Proper but leaden piety of those
Amending generations! Thank the founder
For black-white hurly-burly,
Those streets your mother walked.

It is his act of mind we walk about in.
It is as one frequents a poem, gladly:
The reek of the initial
Implosion guarantees stillness.

Oglethorpe: magnanimous decision;
Then implementation, fast! His actions reek
Of nothing now but sweetness,
In Christ the Founder's week.

To an American Classicist

Shallow or deep, snows on Soracte won't,
if they ever did, deliver
an agreeable end for the means you expend on them;
nor Greek boys, dancing, dance themselves into a frieze.

Kentucky Bourbon, glossed as Caecuban vintage,
won't elevate, beyond
the gratification of a squalid hour, the squeamish
mistaken resolve never to sound like Whitman.

Because in all this you call on the ancient Roman's
precedent, do not
misconstrue him: a carnal indulgence is
one thing, and self-refrigeration another.

Mull the wine all you like, it will not warm you.
You know what will: your native
firewater, moonshine. Moonshine on Soracte
weave you a withering chaplet, leaves of grass!

H.D.

This lady was danger, this
lady was no lady;
authentic American poison.

The lady suffered, but
how many suffered for Lady!

Pussycat, lynx, and horse;
all the petnames were wrong.
'Lady', a name for bitches.

Ransacked Europe and
never noticed it, Europe.
Hysterical catamount.

This catamount, this
lioness of the mountains
of Pennsylvania, her
venom from mountain stills;
from the Moravian
hymns that appalled John Wesley.

Bestrid poor British
Havelock Ellis
like a colossus.

The Gardens of the Savoy

1

To be constant through a lifetime,
            not except in a very
            extended sense consistent,
does everyone some harm
not only in reputation but
more than conceivably in
sensibility also,
            that stiffens in self-esteem.

A curious freedom that
            feels like incarceration
is to recognise, at sixty,
            one has become an *exemplum*.

Should one have cast one's lot with
            gaiety,
the miscegenation of *verba*?
Positively Brazilian
            the leaping interlacements
            shuddered away from.

Cogitation be damned!
            And so it is, in the gardens
of the Savoy, but
come back to the point of pain:
            all the alternatives offered
once and again, and again and
            again repudiated.

It is long past midnight, in fact:
            birds begin to squeal their
            too little experienced chirpings
the other side of my drawn
            curtains in Tennessee.
Chirp, chirp, my little tyros who
            have fallen silent of late;
practice your amorous changes.

Chirp, loyal turtles, and
            cheep, libidinous sparrows,
each according to nature and
            I too have no choice in the matter.

The birds have begun again. The dawn
            reliably nears. How I
should take instruction from birdbrains?
I am to learn from them,
            from layabouts
feeding from garbage in the Savoy gardens?
From flitting sparrows, proved incompetents?

I am, I am; and let the time show how.

… rose and folded my blankets.
Both Eos and Hesperus have
waxed and waned unnoticed.

The sun all the same has risen
whose name is not Kuanon,
Helios, nor Apollo,
no thanks to me, on no
grounds of my beseeching

whether for eyes, for ears
to hear, or a nose for sunrise.
A cold in the head forecloses
most of the avenues,
inattention the rest.

The sun, notwithstanding, rises,
ball of fire, no less.
Charioteer would be more.

Challenger is the latest
space vehicle, named not christened
in Huntsville, Alabama,
the Wernher von Braun motel
in and against the sunrise.

The great sun rises;
flashes; it
cuts no ice
with or within me, approaching
in terror the cigar-shaped
bounties of Peenemünde.

Was at the receiving end
of those, my bride was, in
a long-ago war in London.
'There are no righteous wars':
            one more avenue closed
            to action by
            a cosmic cold in the head.

Pulaski, Tennessee
I pass by, where
Nathan Bedford Forrest,
a Christian gentleman,
created the Ku Klux Klan.
'There are no righteous wars.'

The defeated know it? Wernher
von Braun failed to know it?
Cold in the cosmos burns
the defeated but unvanquished:
        avenue into the blackest
        hot-cold hole in space.

Defeated but unvanquished
after a hundred years,
a Christian gentleman
blasts off against Mugabe.
He wanted Ian Smith
to go down fighting.
'There are no righteous wars.'
Avenues of perception
are choked with those to action,
my Alabaman says
and with some show of reason:
avenues closed to action,
perception suffers; even,
horribly, affections
        as, for three grandsons, shining-
        eyed, already recruited.

The great sun rises still,
though unregarded. Our
prayer at sunrise:
        Please
forgive our inattention,
it is enforced. Forgive,
morning and evening star,
our failure to follow you through
your heavenly motions. Wernher
von Braun attends you, we
are mesmerized elsewhere by
terrors that abort our

first and last mission:
                    worship.

That jinking centre-three
whose death in battle
discountenances still.
The killed-in-youth, with what an
ever-augmenting glow they
vindicate our envy

in an opaque midmorning
after a something less than
Brazilian aubade.

Nothing is exemplary about
                    fetching up here, in the tetchy unreconciled
South,
                    l'Amérique méridionale, as if
there were not, south of the border,
                    other and fiercer lingos
black for the most part, and curled. O Creole days,
'O minstrel galleons of Carib fire ...'

Aeneas of the adjective, Allen Tate,
Crane his Elpenor;
a loud moon buggy and a tinted visor
the gods my grandsons carry out of Huntsville
                    to Albion, third Troy.

Shadows begin to lengthen;
small boys start to be fractious.
Equinoctial storms had
in autumn flurried the Gulf of
Corinth, so we drove to
Olympia's weeping twilight.

Night comes down on the Cumberland
                    River some hours after
                    night comes down on the Thames.
Night comes, however; night
                    has fallen on Corinth also.

The Kyle of Tongue: the ancient
                castle, and the haycocks,
the treacherous channel between them;
                each of them, castle and haycock,
frailly against the odds

'where the salt hay'
                (Where did
he get that collocation
so far from literal?)
                'whispers
to tide's change'
                (When was Ezra
Pound at the Kyle of Tongue?)

This is a wonder, this is
                at last, at last the seed
of a sort of constancy better
                than churning cogitation.

It is not Ovidian nor
                Virgilian; it
could be the meths-induced
                dream of a derelict, a
                reprobate of the Strand in
the Gardens of the Savoy.

                2

Deeps in him
                (reprobate):
                                unemphatic,
happy to be brilliant as shallows;
Ovidian after all.
'It is only the cracked
                husk of the locust',
blown ... that is finished.
Consummatum est, not while
one line remains to be penned
light as a feather. It falls
short of contemplation
                as far as above
                                rumination. It

falls, however, floatingly: no failing
impetus, so long as
punctuation makes
a show of achieving order.

In him, it did not; whence
la grande faillite
           (of François Bernouard),
the grand or great
bankruptcy of the *Cantos*. Yet
to have that touch, the lightness
        of maybe meths-induced
or maybe not
release, disorientation. One
prays that from any grandson
the gift may be averted,
even as one honours
        the gift: non-emphasis.

'The hay ... at tide's change ...
        salt ...
                whispers.' It seems one might
disremember the perception
and rearrange it, yet
arrive at the same total.

Blind-drunk on the hill slope, on
conceivably dreams of power,
Archilochus is not
Archilochus only, singing
at once his spite, his desire of
the daughters of Lycambes.
        Drunk, *in ecstasis*
however artificially,
a man is reaching
for the ultimate
lack of emphasis: 'Gods
        or it may be one God moves
about us in bright air.'

'Brilliant. You always meant to be that.
And you were, and still are at times.

Brilliance, still you want it
impenitently. Truth, oh, as for ...'

You were not in love with the world
or never for long, and only with bits of it:

the usual bits. Trees in a forest? Not often.
Better in a vicarage garden

in the fens, a shelf of cedar
above two deck chairs, untenanted then and forever

at four o'clock of a summer afternoon.

Not brilliant enough, or not for long.

If that is the truth, you were never in love with it
or not for long, although you deceived yourself.

Diamonds, and still the blonde deserves them,
a whole tiara, festoons on the sky at night

or on the white page, black facets.

Impenitence, a diamond in itself,
unbreakable, breaking others.

Von Braun, Nathan Forrest.

Transcendent. Yes, such splendours;
out from the Kyle of Tongue
from the far north, northward.

A logic not for the many,
            for the upside-down *élite*,
            for the self-chosen, cropping
plastic and mineral fruit
of the garbage of the Savoy,
Proserpine's hell-side gardens;
not Nature, Art.

Purple heart, oak-leaf cluster
die in a shack off Main Street.
Red Biddy hymns their decease.

Consistent, but only in
resilience. Can the bounce
back of a rubber ball,
which dwindles in any case,
be thought exemplary?

Constant, but only in
the impenitent pursuit
of self-destruction – has
that little earned the garlands
of cadence and clear colour?

The alcoholic's delusion
that he controls his habit,
the warrior, his –
is this to be esteemed and
heroically lamented
                in Dylan Thomas, in
                a broken Coriolanus?

If to be free of delusion
is the worst delusion of all,
are we to save our applause
for those whose delusions are noblest;
for instance, loving the world?

Granted, the noble is
unarguable, known as
soon as apprehended;
still, Delusion limes his
limp nets also for eagles.

Brilliance is known in
what the tired wing, though
it never so crookedly towers,
wins at last into: air
diamond-clear, unemphatic.

Brilliance, then, is noble;
not in the subject but
in what the subject attains to:
a metaphysical, not
in the first place human, property.

'Can you tell the down from the up?'
The unthinkable answer: No.
God moves about us, and
brilliance is His preferred
supernal way of moving.

Alzheimer's Disease

for Kenneth Millar (Ross Macdonald)

It is said that he laughs at himself,
Betrayed into such grotesque
Non-sequiturs. I am told he
Powerfully still plies his
Breast-stroke across the pool
That was the arena or focus
Of his most disturbing fictions.

Focus, a pool; a fluid,
A watery hearth he found
For any of us, this
Californian-born and
Canadian-raised, this unfathered
Quester after arenas
Familial and stable.

The chlorinated hearth
He swims and swims has not
Held his mind together;
Keeping his head above
Private waters he
Absently-mindedly earned
A world-wide reputation.

Non-sequitur! No wonder
If, now his mind is gone,
He chuckles at the bizarre
Concatenation of
Circumstances that a private
Eye can disentangle
Retrospectively always.

Wonderful all the same, or
Wondrous, there in the thresh
Of the directionless lengths
Of days, how the artist snorted
And seal-like turned himself round
To plunge upon the next
Pitiless, pitiful fable.

Ken, you were a powerful
Swimmer always, tireless.
Not you tired, but your brain.
When you wrote *The Galton Case,*
I fiddled with *Pan Tadèusz*.
(Sons sought fathers in both.)
Those days won't come again.

Recollection of George Oppen
in a letter to an English friend

'This lime-tree bower my prison'
(Coleridge)

That lime-tree – no, what is it? mulberry? –
bower at combe's bottom, your Brook Cottage
where the light sleeps so evenly in silence
one would not say even in summer's heat
it pulses ... there you have entertained
George Oppen, along with Mary who survives him;
of whom, and just there, you and I have talked
not without malice while George Oppen lived.

That we should do that, should make mock of his
style of public reading (which he hated),
his unpretentious chuntering monotone
that could not mark when a poem began or ended,
would have dismayed them both. Such vipers, such
English ingrate stingers as they had
taken to their bosoms! How could they
understand how that milk-candid, flowing
bosom it was, that armed and drew the stings?
Too good to be true, such nice Americans – we
had to pink them, that way to pinch ourselves!

Hearing in due course of his mindlessness
(Alzheimer's, terminal) that Mary could
towards the end not cope with, were we not
happy to have them down on our grubbing level?
And on that level, ours, Poetic Justice
I swear made her appearance in a toga.
Alzheimer's, yes – the diagnosis was
all very well, but surely George's dealings
with language had for years anticipated,
almost provoked, the visitation? Such
pains as he had been at – in verse, in prose,
in conversation – to subvert, discount,
derange articulation. Destiny
strikes, and for months before he dies
he's inarticulate. A hideous justice.

I've not the energy nor the confidence
for playing God like this with George's shade,
his fragrant shade my prison. For indeed,
often as I have settled George's hash
to my own satisfaction, proved him wrong
– my spare and handsome gaoler with the cropped
moustache, so Jewish when one thought of it
yet on a first impression soldierly,
frontiersman even – still he shoots the bolt;
won't go away, nor let me be, reproachful
as always the dead are, though in life indulgent.

'Friends, whom I never more may meet again,
On springy heath, along the hill-top edge,
Wander in gladness, and wind down, perchance
To that still roaring dell, of which I told;
The roaring dell...' Dells round Brook Cottage must,
and that whole dell itself, defile or vale,
roar when the wind is up, undoubtedly.
Did it, when George was with you? Hard to think so
of him whose scenes for preference were
wind-scoured indeed but wide and open, hills
in and about the city of San Francisco,
or else the flowing and unsteady bosom
of off-shore Maine. That semblance, the frontiersman,
was not unearned by such a small-boat sailor,
no messer-about. Pathfinder, though? Trailblazer?
Never for me, threading the roaring dells
and snapping branches of morose
inspirations, aspirations, habits
held up to the weak light, scowled at. Not a bit
of help to me was George, or George's writing;
though he achieved his startling poignancies,
I distrusted them, distrust them still.

But hope, such hope he had, such politics
always of hope! Hope is a strenuous business;
I hope the roar of it enlivens your
west-country dell, as a whisper of it mine.

West Virginia's Auburn

'Sweet Auburn, loveliest village of the plain'
(Goldsmith)

Ejected Indians haunt the lawns
    Where Alabama's youth
Loud on the Auburn campus yawns
    At Goldsmith's mournful truth.

New Hampshire's lakeside Auburn keeps
    A little faith with him
But is, agreeably though it sleeps,
    Too vigorous, too trim.

But West Virginia, rural slum,
    The idyll! Only there
In our excursions did there come
    Such silence on the air

As, we were surprised to learn,
    We had looked for more and more:
Placidities we could not earn
    And were not fitted for.

Silence of hopes foreclosed, foregone –
    That, we'd already found
In derelict installations on
    Lost capital, lost ground,

First in Maine, then in New York,
    Whose indigent Auburns drift
Under grime-blackened dates that talk
    Of once effectual thrift.

No thrift nor thriving ever was
    Invested in this green
Corner of West Virginia's
    Dilapidated scene.

It would be wrong to think it prinked
    Ever as right or pretty;
It has at best the indistinct
    Unpruned amenity

That topers in a village inn
    Might unconcernedly share,
Who found no project to engage in
    Worth their hope or care.

The poet who in Meath or West
    Virginia hails this breed
As his own congeners, justly blest –
    He rusticates indeed!

Yet across oceans, once again
    Old adages still mutter
Adagios of the plangent strain
    We are ashamed to utter.

Keen-eyed, the idyll has no salve
    To ease the throb in the verse:
'You can't go home again. You have
    Gone further, and fared worse.'

Through Bifocals

This you have heard before;
Have heard to the point where it serves
Only to numb, of the insult
Historical markers invite
With such inconsequence: Battle
Of Murfreesboro, of Franklin...

Two hours ago a boom
And a brief billow of pink
Dust was how a small
Recalcitrant bluff was cleared for
'A Planned Community in
The Williamsburg Manner.'

Earth-movers on that hillside
Lie still now, and a jiggle
Of off-and-on orange flashes
Seemed, when I looked over there
Through reading-glasses, a pulse
Of pain in the pink earth's wound.

My trustier bifocals
See lights atop the blazon,
Red on yellow, of
'Country Store' in this
Uncomplaining tract of
Tennessee disembowelled.

Among the supposedly fine
Arts, one at least has weaseled
Out of the tatterdemalion
Rearguard, and puts its trust in
The double focus: 'plan'
Enforced; then (optional) 'manner'.

Architects! Co-workers
With Louis Sullivan once, you
Wink at as foolishly 'dire'
My warning to your consumers:
The wider the range of manners,
The more inhumane the enforcement.

from POEMS AND MELODRAMAS

After a Change of Régime

A DRAMA IN THREE ACTS & FOR THREE VOICES

for Don Stanford

Synopsis: The time is c.1953. The Head of State has been manipulated by conspirators, headed by the Count, a war-hero; when the time comes, the conspirators require of the Head of State, suicide 'for the cause'. By the succeeding *régime,* Count and Head of State are alike found 'enemies of the state'. But the son of the Count and Countess, a lyrical poet, becomes a principal apologist for the new *régime,* and is applauded accordingly. The Minister for Culture observes all this sardonically, but is not adroit enough to conceal his contempt. The context is one Cold War; but the pattern persists through many.

There is also, sketched in, a *whodunnit,* but that's the merest device.

I

From the Widow of the Head of State
The Countess Remembers
Soliloquy of the Minister for Culture

II

Frankness of the Minister for Culture
The Countess Gives an Interview
From the Widow of the Head of State

III

The Countess Points a Finger
The Minister Disgraced
The Widow of the Head of State, as Ready Reckoner

I

FROM THE WIDOW OF THE HEAD OF STATE

He was never above the mêlee
Of four bare legs in bed.
But what did the Countess say,
The groomed black head
Over the military typewriter?
I had gone there by mistake.
I saw her lips go tighter
And her hands pause, then take
A cigarette from her case.
Did she seek manhood
In the assassin's face
Of her own man of blood,
The mutilated colonel with the bomb,
As I did in the bed
Of one whose time would come
To be his figurehead?

I ought to have found it more
Difficult to forgive
The rôle they cast us for:
Removed, contemplative,
Statesmanlike. We paid
The heavier price, all told.
For Heinrich was afraid.
'Will no one help the old
Gentleman?' they said,
Meaning, to press the trigger
He held against his head.
Did he have to cut their figure?
A statesman has to fail
If the wife of a statesman needs
To judge her man by the scale
Of the crippled man of deeds.

They were planning it even then,
At the machine the Countess,
A network of hard-pushed men
And Heinrich. I counted for less
Than she did, less than I thought.

My contemplative man is dead
By violence, who taught
Civility instead.
Those professorial lips
He sealed against me earned
Honours and fellowships
Years ago. I had learned
From him, I had understood
How manhood is in the mind.
Then came this spilling of blood,
And manhood still to find.

THE COUNTESS REMEMBERS

I told him enigmatically: 'You need
Ventilation.' After a pause (he was
Famously imperturbable) he said:
'You mean, after all this, Canada?'

                                   His wound
Had sobered him so far as not to attempt
The quizzical. 'Why, my dear,
Who'd rule it out? Kicking Horse Canyon for
Ever!'

       My limbless horseman
Had ruled out being amused, and yet amusement
Affectionately flickered in those tawny
Eyes that should have been Prussian. Easily he
Indulged me:

                'Yes, Saskatchewan. Why not?'

And yet he knew that, notable horseman though
He was on the sands of Pomerania, his
End had to be in the claustrophobic
Bunker, his bomb, asphyxiation by cordite.
No prairie airs for him.

                     Nor for me. And indeed I knew it.

Soft cats in public places ogled their cream
In the dish of him limping, laurelled by the *régime*.

'Where, where is justice, when the sacred gift,
When deathless justice comes not to reward
Perfervid love and utter self-denial... ?'
(Pushkin, *Mozart & Salieri*)

Salieri to his Mozart – poisoner,
The sterile rival. If that Muse of his,
So bare and truthful, took it upon her
To know her peers, why here the parallel is,
Exact and banal. Calling him 'immature'
Gives me away; my lost youth makes the claim,
Wasted and Moscow-nipped. His never-worked-for,
Free, ambiguous mastery, all the same
I have the edge of – he should have a more
Responsible, a more adult concern.
He manages the thing with too much ease.
Expert in skills he never had to learn,
What can he see in them except caprice
Or self-indulgence? But there's more than this:
What Pushkin couldn't know, what this *flâneur*
Ought to know but doesn't, is
The right our guilt affords us. If I were
Free to tell this faithful party-member
All that the Party knows, were I to confess
The cost I know and choose not to remember,
I'd see his golden and unnatural youth
Age on the instant. And his truthfulness!
How cheap that comes, until one knows the truth...

Bored tonight, I took down Pushkin's trifle,
'Dubrovsky'. Does he know it? Poet's prose,
Bare narrative *résumé,* beautiful.
It made his much-praised spareness look verbose.
And yet I thought of him. Yes, reading through it,
I saw him cast just that cold classic light
On us, on the Revolution. If he knew it,
If only he knew... He can't be told outright.
But he's no fool. He ought to know me better
Than to interpret all my talk of 'conflict'
According to the letter.
I've tried to tell him, underneath the strict

Seal of our barbarous jargon, what the truth
Is, that he needs – not that he may tell it
(That he may not), but that its resonance
Tell for him. The elegance of the tacit
Informs the life we lead, and reticence
In art reflects it. Therefore all my planned
Exclusions should be seen as right
By a taste like his. Insufferably bland,
His blindness strips me. How unfair it is
That I, who know the truth, am bored tonight,
And he alert among complacencies!

II

FRANKNESS OF THE MINISTER FOR CULTURE

'Know your enemy.' I know him,
Can whistle Dixie and
The Battle Hymn of the Republic.
I did not waste my time in Washington.

Because their kids are good kids, what their kids
Are avid for, they have to like as well;
Prompt action (swift compliance) has
Earned commendations. BCM (US):
Battle Communications
Maintenance. Crucial in Combat.

Or if their kids are bad kids by
Calvinist definition, what
Their kids have been inured to has to be
Endured by them for patriotic reason,
For Uncle Sam's sweet sake. Complying, their
Abnegation gets to like the diet.

Parentage in America – there's a study!

AAA (triple A),
Atrocities Awareness
Agency: a boon to every age-group.
Of course it is their arts that are atrocious.

Americans live by acronyms.
And so I fear do we – a distasteful interim measure.
The measures of verse must be that much more cherished and
    honoured.

Since we, not they, are the heirs
Of the Enlightenment, an enlightened
Fatherly concern for artists is
A high priority for the Revolution.

I should not need to spell this out, and would not
Except for the dolts among us. Turnip-heads!

THE COUNTESS GIVES AN INTERVIEW

Surviving was his business as a schoolboy
During those years of our sleazy triumphs, before
It came to be every one's business. Huge eyes under
The always thin thatch of his straight straw hair, he
Questioned: 'Was it not terrible?' I
Embraced him of course, said No, abstractedly;
Pleased by his sensitivity and yet
Uneasy with it, plagued by even then
In his piping treble the note of options kept
Open, and channels open, though of course
In the case of a mere child thinking so was absurd.

The mereness of him, of his or of any childhood
In those years and for people of our rank
Is hard to imagine. His father and I
Interacted so intensely... pah,
Where did I learn such gibberish? Our love,
Mine and the Count's, could find no room for him.
And that's no crime. We found superior nurse-maids,
Then *mademoiselle,* then tutors. It was the pattern
In our world that was passing, not yet past.

He has favoured the public with precocious memoirs
In which – I have skimmed them – he accounts for
Father and Mother briefly indeed but with
Tenderness even one might say if one
Could so far trust him.

Yes, I am a tigress,
But not as you see in defence of her cub. I speak of
My son the poet who is having a great success;
On whose account you interview this non-person.

His patronage, or theirs who for now protect him,
Permits these indiscretions. You have been
Indulgent, comrades. You know better
Than I can do what character best projects him
Before a public that I have no truck with.

FROM THE WIDOW OF THE HEAD OF STATE

The English it was, he relied on.
A frail reed! Who was I
To tell him not to confide in
Their so amusingly drunken
Cultural attaché, their
Embassy spy?
           I had little
To go on beyond what I heard
(One could hardly avoid it indeed): their
Journalists uproarious at the bar –
         'Sister Wragg
         will carry the flag...
         Sister Barker
         will be right-hand marker...'
(My English is good.) I heard them
Commending some one:
         '... would as soon
         miss Christmas or the Queen as
         the glorious First of June.'
(The anniversary of a naval action,
Heinrich, I researched it.)

More I half-heard, wafted in and out
Of the Danubia's tea-time strings over cream-cakes,
The bar's increasingly loud and intemperate voices:
         'The mind of Europe stops...'
         'The ideologies rattle...'
         'Nobody's easy touch,
         Guy Burgess thought

Old England's winding-sheet
ought to have been sewn
by sailmakers and such…'

                    'Lest we forget!'

A ragged roar came. Then:
                'One who sold as much
                small dirt as he could get.'

The Danubia's tea-room emptied. There came through
one slurred discontinuous prattle:
                'This is a common market,
                trams continue to rattle.
                This is the way the mind
                of Europe stops, has stopped.'

                'With a hey, jolly Jack, with a hey
                and hearts of oak come home,'
the voice said, then went dumb.

Heinrich, they spoke of one
Who had betrayed their secrets.
Leibchen, you should have known
Better. Perfidious English,
They trawled to catch only their own;
Their splotched own trout-farmed fish!

III

THE COUNTESS POINTS A FINGER

Who tipped them off about the bunker? Not
Istvan, not Karl… The field is appallingly narrow
Seeing that all who knew, who were in the network
Were rounded up and 'dealt with', there and then.
Quite in their style to kill their own informant,
That would be thorough. Istvan? Oskar? Karl?
François?… I would have let the question go
If it would let me. Some one said the leak
Could have been nearer home: the Count's *factotum*.

That loyal blockhead? Never! Nearer home
Even than that? That's paranoia speaking,
That must be chained and kenneled. Even so
I sniff our gate-posts
                          and come back with what
I cannot prove nor ever could: that drunken
English charmer whom I know my son
At times fell in with, in the Danubia bar.

Timid old Heinrich's Ganymede
A double agent? It's conceivable.

THE MINISTER DISGRACED

Slowly destroying each other in transports
Of joy and rage the Count and Countess
Tolstoy lately stalked the stage.

Sheets were over the circle where children's
Voices would chant oh the song of the golden
Goose the principal boy of Panto,

And Claus or Nicholas all the grosser
Gods of the Christmas hissed the holy
Boyar and approved his Countess.

★

At blood-warm Christmas booby Joseph
Feels a fool since pap and sleepy
Parturition seem the rule.

But I could wait. Their child the poet
Was mine, no other's. Children of my loins
Are not so dear; their several mothers know it.

Slowly destroying each other in torments
Of rage and appetite male and female
Mankind wrote the pre-war page,

Pre-Revolution. But paternity now
Is a considered, not a carnal matter;
Not once for all, but a perpetual Easter.

The spirit of Revolution easing
Out of that blasphemous egg, a mother's ardent
Good of coincident animal goes beg.

★

I told his mother: It was not for me
To legislate for poetry, nor for her
Tainted by certain 'ill-advised connections'.

Some pride I took at the time in that
Civilized manoeuvre. Now the light
Leaks into my cell, accusing me over and over:

'Romanticized conception of the poet,
Hectic or pale *naïf*!' He took a leaf
Out of my shrewd book, and impaled me on it.

I was the golden goose. This pantomime
Enacts the goose I was, and golden is
The price he has had for me, who dared to choose.

The time will come… It may, but I don't think so.
Thirty years on, he'll star in freedom-loving
Congresses where I'll be a dirty word.

THE WIDOW OF THE HEAD OF STATE AS READY RECKONER

As a researcher I'm no longer tireless;
Tenacious, though. It's not
The highest virtue, Heinrich let me know,
But has its usefulness. 'My little bloodhound,'
He called me once or twice, those years ago,
Smiling. I have my own techniques: I
Never let go,
And – here's a professional secret – I let chance
Work for me; meek short-lived gusts that blow
Crumples of information down the gutter
Bring what I could have slaved for years to know
And nowhere found. My swan's nest of grey hairs,
My reticule and sandwich, are well known
In the Academy of Sciences. I am not

Often saluted there, am seldom noticed,
A corpulent old biddy, but
I know my trade, and I am not afraid.

This time it was the merest air, not in
Metaphor but quite literally, blew
The crimped clue to me. It was the Tannoy
System one learns how not to listen to:
A bad mistake, a failing. Blaring from
Each tenement's or public building's corner
Came to us, day by day, what the *régime*
Thought proper for us. And this summer morning
It was, I perceived belatedly, a poem
Excited, high-flown, urgent. This was not
Anything new. For poetry too was the workers',
The ideology said, if they would only
Reach out and take it. And perhaps they did
For all I know; perhaps in the lonely *puszta*
Some herder of long-horned cattle half-remembered
What the Tannoy had blared as he scuffed his feet
Stumbling at dawn in his mired village. My
Allegedly muddier origins
In the small *bourgeoisie* had muddied me.
In our circles poetry was permitted,
Was even at time extolled: it fabricated
Idylls one might day-dream in. But this
Poetry made an idyll of our present
And thereby lied, it lied. I have been made
Indignant on this account – which will not do
For a researcher who should always be
Dispassionate, who very nearly this time,
Pulled by her passions, missed the straw in the wind.

The exalted diction, once and then again,
Swooped on to 'turnip-heads': not a locution
Altogether current yet, it seemed
(The poetry was ambiguous, as usual),
A slogan of class-division and resistance
In some one or other's mouth.
                                    For the researcher,
States like ours present a special problem:
Much that is said is said in code. Decoded,
This drop from aureate diction signalled, if

I may be excused the vulgarism, some one,
And some one of some eminence, 'for the chop'.

My cattle-herder on the *puszta,* what
Could he have made of it? It was not meant
For his decoding. The researcher knew
And knew right: fall of some one eminent.

Scholarship? No, hardly scholarship;
A matter of life and death. But it's on this –
What some one said, what some one else let slip,
The coral-insect's inching edifice –
That erudition grounds its hierarchies.

The obtuse researcher gets there after all
Or rather, first of all. The annalist
Sees in the tyrant's circle this one rise
And that one, who was more deserving, fall.

A Heroine of the Academy

President of the Academy
First Academician
Second Academician
Academician Fùrtseva

PRESIDENT:
        Elections to the Academy: referred from
        Section Eleven – Madame Fùrtseva
        Spokesperson – T. Afanasy Miliescu
        Is nominated. I invite your comments.

FIRST ACADEMICIAN:
        The Academy is a learned body. Where
        Miliescu's learning is, we have been told:
        In versions made from Pahlavi and Turkish.
        Academician Fùrtseva's command of
        These tongues I suspect is no more certain than mine,
        But never mind. The case, we all know, rests on
        Quite other grounds. The candidate in question
        Is an idol of our youth, some sections of it

And those most bravely prominent in our late
Costly upheavals. It would do us good
Therefore to recruit him. Should we not, though,
Proceed on what we know? And what we know is
A ubiquitous bar-fly, clown, and womanizer,
Whose writings call for blood to run in the streets.

PRESIDENT:

That remark will not be minuted.

FIRST ACADEMICIAN:

I beg your pardon, Mr President.
Let me be impersonal, if I can:
We might as well elect the late Dictator
Who killed, who tortured, with such hardihood.
A writer's killings are all notional;
Does that absolve him?
Academician Fùrtseva thinks it does.
The Muse that she is or exalts, she exalts as exacting,
Extreme of its nature, not to be qualified.
Academicians, the atrocious Muse
(I grant she is atrocious) isn't what
We can or should be legislating for.

FÙRTSEVA:

Academies exist to succour eunuchs?
The cruelties of art we batten on,
Yet wash our hands of? That's despicable.

SECOND ACADEMICIAN:

Come, colleagues, let's remember who we are:
A faun and hamadryad in
Gardens of the receding Ottoman
Engendered us. And now we are to be
Severe of a sudden, so many impeccable Catos?
Danubian history doesn't permit us that,
Least of all now. We are ill-placed to open
Questions of art and art's morality.
All that we have to fudge, if we'd survive.

PRESIDENT:

Isn't that a little... cynical?

SECOND ACADEMICIAN:
             No sir, it's merely prudent. For consider:
             The emergent *régime* will not, any more
             Than the fallen one, fail to secure
             (If we are prudent) the Academy's
             Fall-back position in
             Public disturbances.
             What more placatory, then,
             Than for the Academy to designate
             What drove despair on to our streets as
             Acceptably 'problematic'?
             We serve a purpose, colleagues;
             Best we acknowledge that. Small price to pay,
             Electing some innocuous demagogue.

PRESIDENT:
             I will not put the question while such passions
             Rage in the chamber, though we have other business.

FIRST ACADEMICIAN:
             'Rage in the chamber...' Always chamber-music:
             The best we manage here is closet-drama.

SECOND ACADEMICIAN:
             And just as well. Drama out of the closet
             Means, we have all seen, corpses in the streets.
             All nationhood is mythical. Every nation
             Began, and in part persists as, a mere notion.
             Start from there, not where the myth says we
             Once were, but where we might be. Honoured friends,
             Between the February and October
             Revolutions a window opens.
             Look through it while it's there: this Miliescu,
             So widely loved, might be our Mayakovsky.

FIRST ACADEMICIAN:
             Perish the thought! Anyhow Mayakovsky,
             That demagogue, didn't have to deal with
             The *demos,* woman, whose emergence muddles
             All our already dangerously muddled
             Models of politics. Miliescu is
             Patently the women's candidate;

On that score alone I'll vote against him,
And if the bullets fly, so much the worse.

FÙRTSEVA:

The bee in some bonnets
Brave among bullets
Seems more of a harpy
Than my poor virago
For all her exactions.

Talk of the Muse is
Gender-determined.
A shame; since she flames with
Equal injustice
On women and men.

Friends and dear brothers,
All that we asked was
(And was it so taxing?)
A straight, even-handed
Acceptance of bondage.

But everywhere, hatred;
Women mismated
Struggle for freedom
In un-free assemblies.
Ridiculous matrons
Playing Cassandra!

Hearing the hierarchs'
Tongue of the tribe
Clipped to encode the
Will of the elders,
What can they speak but
The programmed diatribe?

A harmless male person –
Voice of the many –
Is axed from contention
Because of a chorus
Of womankind's ringing,
Too fevered endorsement.

Fevers? We shake with
No fever that did not
Equally warm such
Heroes of freedom
As Rousseau or Burke.

Limed in the nets of
Partisan prudence,
Burke was a woman!
Singing a nation
Not his, nor in being.

Academicians!
Harridan songsters,
Birds of Burke's feather,
Crow over, bespatter
Your tacit procedures.

Rather than flatter
A paste-board consensus,
Here we abjure what
Token transvestite
Is foisted upon us.

I have heard colleagues
Debate Revolution
Through its two stages.
We would have fed it
Dry wood by bushels.

PRESIDENT:

T.A. Miliescu then
No longer has supporters.

Bella & Rosa

& AN OLD LADY

for Harriet Wanklyn, author of
The Eastern Marchlands of Europe

OLD LADY:

> Voices, such voices ... They assail me now;
> No, not assail, assuage. Did I ever hear Admiral Horthy,
> King Carol? Oh I think not. And not theirs
> Voices to oil my wheel-chair. Leave aside
> Dear dead Stanley's that is with me always,
> The voices that float in and out are *most*
> Unexpected: one just now a station-master's
> In I think Debreczen – such
> A courteous man, in 1931
> Or 1932, it must have been. And then,
> Just as surprisingly, a choked-up voice
> From a reception in say Nottingham,
> Somewhere like that. Now why
> Should that voice come? It had no foreign accent
> Although the name was Portuguese, I'm sure;
> Naturalized for centuries, it could be.
> Anglicist in fact, with a solid
> Reputation, Stanley said he'd heard.
> He asked, with emphasis and urgency
> Under the bland convention of those times:
> 'What are the poets of Poland up to?' Now
> How should I know? Poetry was not
> My interest nor my business, then or now;
> Was happier with my station-master. Still
> The urgency, it must be, brings it home
> Across this tonic Northern air I can
> Profit from for thirty-minute spells.
> Now I am drifting off again. So good,
> Those times, so good... Tonic. I'm drifting off ...

BELLA:

> Unhappy Daddy, drifting off
> In an alcoholic haze we knew about
> And wouldn't acknowledge. He was still
> For all of that a clean old man, to the end.

ROSA:

It was that stupid poetry did it to him.
Once his delight, said Mother. I don't believe it.

OLD LADY:

Budapest no by-line; Prague was not
'The most beautiful city in Europe'.
I hadn't seen them all. And then, who has?
Such loose hyperbole! Poetical!
The press today is all such poetry.
That Portuguese-ish man, so keen on it,
Can he have been a reputable scholar?
Stanley knew as little of that as I did,
Hardbitten scholar but not hard,
Oh no not hard at all. Hyperbole is.
Could it be said that I hate poetry?
Old, a woman has no time for hatred,
No energy for it; young, I loved
Geography and history. Dear dead days
Of amateur and solitary travel
To and beyond the Iron Gate of the Danube...
A vanished world, the world the poorer for it.

BELLA:

Rosa, that new old lady in
The Garden Wing, she saw my name
Pinned to my shirt and she said,
Smiling: 'Portuguese.' I said
No, it was originally Spanish.

ROSA:

You were wrong there. Daddy when he was jolly
Would – don't you remember? – call us *portingales,*
What Shakespeare would have called us.

BELLA:

If you say so. Point is: she met Daddy
Or thinks she did. Do you believe she could have?

ROSA:

What does it matter? I suppose she could have,
Being in English or some sort of Slavist.
All of them live in the past, as Daddy could have.

BELLA:

      Why must you think so bitterly of Daddy?
      I don't reproach you, but it makes me sad.

ROSA:

      'I don't reproach you, but it makes me sad.'
      Bella, do you want another quarrel?
      Our father had no right to be unhappy
      But was, and the blight of it has hurt us both.

OLD LADY:

      Learning the languages… well, of course one couldn't.
      A few stock phrases, for politeness' sake.
      Mostly one's English, failing that one's French
      Served. (No, that's wrong – the *lingua franca,* German:
      Significant I shouldn't want to think so.)
      Surprisingly often, in obscure small places
      The Hotel Bristol, named
      For a peripatetic Bishop, there before Thomas Cook.
      'Cocooned', the so-called scholars of today
      Have said of me: cocooned in privilege,
      Milady, if you please. The funds that sent me
      Were ironmasters' dividends. And bright eyes,
      An eager heart, a scholarly conscience – my
      Sirs, the young forager had flown, for all
      Your one more heedless metaphor.
                           Baroque
      Small country towns, tiled roofs and cobbled streets,
      Storks in their season everywhere, on belfries
      With onion cupolas. Still bringing babies?
      Are there storks still in the – wait a minute –
      The *Alföld ? I* am glad to think so, yes.

ROSA:

      Bad enough, the queer outlandish name.
      But then having nothing to back it up with, in
      School, I mean. Portuguese – did he ever
      Teach us a word of it? Had he a word to teach?
      Too much like hard work!

BELLA:

                        It's true I sometimes
      Dreamed of a castle in Leon, Aragon,

Coimbra, is it? Or at least a parchment's
Dubious claim to some such. I confess I
Sometimes said there was, to satisfy
You know, the young men.

ROSA:

                                    The one satisfaction
They ever got from either of us, my dear!

BELLA:

Rosa, that affair of our not having
Married, or had the chance of it, is not
(Remember, dear) worth speaking about. At our age!

ROSA:

Yes, yes, I know. And whether it was his fault. But, Bella,
Remember his castles not in Spain but in
Bukovina, Bosnia, I don't know.
Not that we ever went there, nor did he,
Nor tried to. It was all –
Here we go again – poetical.
Damn poetry that has damned us
To being what we are, a pair of spinsters
Running a nursing-home for the decayed
Gentry of the islanded North of England.

BELLA:

Rosa, you've been drinking again though where
You find the money for it I don't know. However,
Never mind. He had a mind like that;
He dreaded things, dreaded them for himself
And Mother, and for us. Now mostly I
Forget about him, I don't thank
That new old thing in the Garden Wing for bringing
Him back in his oh yes clean, his upright, vaguely
Soldierly, saddening presence. Best forget him.

OLD LADY:

Nothing I'm more inured to: punctuating
My days by the recurrent, wearisome
'Soon I shall have to eat' (to 'force it down'),
Then sleep when I don't want to. Stanley dear,
You knew this under my bleared but eagle eye

Those last years. I pouted: 'You
Don't like my catering? I'll not cater for you.'
Bravely you pretended: 'Savoury'.
Hunger it must be, though it doesn't seem so,
Sharpens my memory: how the wagons tooled
Briskly behind the fair-haired (Can
Horses be blonde?) horses in *troika,* whipped
By tow-haired Slovaks, always Lutheran
There, in Hungary. That much I manage.
Here comes the clatter of the approaching tray;
And after that oblivion comes, as always.

BELLA:

The new one in the Garden Wing, she had
A visitor: fat, crumpled, but quite clean,
Polite too, one might even venture courtly;
Old of course but not so old as she is.
It left her quite unmanned – I don't mean that:
Quite in a tizzy. And he signed
Our Visitors' Book not with the usual scrawl
But bold and clear: such-or-such PAKULL
(I wrote it down), then unmistakably
'Yugoslavian Embassy', and yet
With an address in Harrogate! I tell you
After a fashion it quite made my day.
We're not so out of the swim, dear. Such queer capers!

OLD LADY:

I didn't like him, though it was
Exceptionally kind for him to come.
It was Pakull, who wrote (But who'll remember?)
'Réforme Agraire en Yougoslavie et
les Provinces de Bachka et de Srem.'
'The dreaded rock-sill of the Iron Gate',
He quoted at me, paused and smiled, and said:
Not any more. Of course I'd heard about it:
Downriver the barrage that made the great
River a pond (he brought it home to me),
One hundred and thirty miles unruffled pond
Drowning the underwater spikes, the tortuous narrows,
The races and of course the riparian homesteads.
And thus you see, he said to me, again
Quoting my words and smiling, though I thought

This time slyly, the Danubian nations
Attain at last to economic
Maturity.
                    Yes, but the cost of it!
The downstream island, harbour of the marooned
Turks where, Apollonius Rhodius says,
The argonauts anchored on their return from Colchis
(Gold panned in the upper Carpathians to this day
Or to my day), drowned necessarily –
The ancient inbred Turks of course re-settled
'Humanely'. He was undeniably gracious,
Come, so he said (his English very good) to
'Pay his respects'. A vanished world indeed!
So vanished it might never have been, one might as
Well have dreamed it up and never gone there,
Declaring it to begin with as it were
Vanishable, adumbratable
(If there were such a word), a world
That, since it never was, can never vanish,
Invulnerable to time and change. Unhappy,
Yes but unhappy in the frame of things.
That's harder than hyperbole. 'Dreaded sill.'
Stanley, I will not think such things. I won't!
Still, dread all gone, what else incorporates us?

Three Pastors in Berlin

for Rosanna Warren

NEMETH:

I was the Nazis' padre, you might say;
Magyar, you see, not Slav. Hungarians
Served with the *wehrmacht*. Did you know that, padre?

COLLINS:

I don't quite see what that...

NEMETH:

                    Of course not. And quite right.
Magyars were by courtesy Aryans,
All that in the long ago, before you were born.

'His beauty to consume away like a moth',
The psalmist says. But to the point: my claim.
It is by right of, don't you say, *the cloth* ?
Pastor, I need a pastor; need him now!
And not with a German name, for various reasons.
I come to you. Confession and absolution
By a protestant rite, from some one who's not German:
That's what not I but one of my sometime flock is
Parching for; drools for it, and from me won't do.
You're chaplain to the Occupying Forces,
And English too. Your chrism he'll think sterling.

COLLINS:

Oh my Lord – I don't mean that, but oh
Gosh! I'll be glad to oblige. It's rather
Out of my line (which is dealing with kiddies, mostly),
But I expect the drill is in the Prayer Book.
As everything is, if you look. It calls for some
Study though, and prayer. The penitent
Is not, I suppose, available just now.
Oh he is? Well, give me twenty minutes.
The church is two doors up, by the football-field.
Goodness me… But wait! you say he is
Protestant, I think my Free Church colleague…
There are sects, you know, that differ quite a lot…

NEMETH:

Pastor, all he asks is to be forgiven.
In twenty minutes he'll be primed for you.

[Departs.]

COLLINS:

Primed for it… like a bomb. Oh Christopher,
Thank God you're here. This is a weird one. Listen,
It's some Hungarian comes for absolution.
I thought they were all Arcees in any case.

THOMSON:

No, that's wrong. Plenty of Lutherans and
Calvinists too – I can't remember how.
It's in the histories of the Reformation.
Except you'll miss your jogging, what's the problem?

COLLINS:

Chris! Just think what this chap might confess to,
What I shall have to absolve him from. Oh Brother!
Pray with me.

THOMSON:

What? Oh all right. But no talking.

[Silence.]

COLLINS:

Thanks.

THOMSON:

That's all right. But tell me, Dicky:
What if you hear things you can't forgive?

COLLINS:

There aren't such things.

THOMSON:

Well no, that's true, there aren't.
Good luck, chum. Rather you than me, I tell you;
But our lot's not empowered, as you know.

[Interval]

THOMSON:

Well, you look perky. How did it go, then? Oh
Seal of the confessional, I suppose?

COLLINS:

Yes, but I'll tell you one thing: he was not
Hungarian, he was English-speaking Russky.

THOMSON:

Russky? But that's incredible. Wait a minute.
Fought with the wrong mob, did he?

COLLINS:

Very canny;
Something of that. But set your mind at ease:
He wasn't the butcher of Lôdz or Lidice
Or if he was, he didn't tell me. Mostly

Fornications, blasphemies, run of the mill;
And something more, that I can't tell you.

THOMSON:

                                       Dicky,
I have to admire you, could have been hearing confessions
All your pastoral life.

NEMETH:

                        Excuse me, sirs.

COLLINS:

Pastor, come in. Can I present my colleague:
The Reverend Christopher Thomson?

NEMETH:

                           Ah, delighted!
Three pastors in one place, three hoodie-crows
(Your Scots might say) perched on one withered bough,
Or rather on one withered, two quite green.
PASTOR Thomson, I am pleased to meet you.
Nemeth's the name. Yes, I am Pastor Nemeth.

COLLINS:

I was just brewing up a cup of tea.
Won't you join us?

NEMETH:

                     Why, that's very kind...
And as for the hoodie-crows, you must forgive me:
I spent some time in the Kingdom of Fife, you see.
While we're about it, the title 'Pastor' is
Dubious in my case, I must admit,
Like most things else about me. Pastor Collins,
I am most grateful to you. As for that
Brave friend I brought, he has departed quite
Overjoyed – I'll risk that, over-joyed.
[Silence.]

THOMSON:

Pastor Nemeth, do you perhaps not owe us,
Me and my colleague, a word of explanation?

NEMETH:

You think so, do you? Let's see; after
My years in the Kingdom of Fife (I passed for Polish),
Back to Berlin. To men of my
Generation (I could have fathered you,
Not many of us left), Berlin's the place.
'Fought with the wrong mob. Can't go home again' –
Epitaph here, unwritten, on many a grave-stone.
For instance in your cemetery one
South African Air Force grave-slab, the inscription
In Afrikaans. You fancy that equation?

THOMSON:

Not much. And Dicky and I are not so green.
You push us hard.

COLLINS:

I'll go and refresh the pot.

NEMETH:

He's gone to alert the guard-room, I imagine.
Very proper. Your security
Was always lax, I should have been stopped at the gate.
Your people know me, though: a small-scale nuisance.
A few hours' inconvenience is all.

THOMSON:

And what about that friend of yours whom Pastor
Collins so much obliged?

NEMETH:

His being here
Was out of order, obviously. However,
He's even less of a threat: a man of honour
Such as I wouldn't claim to be. And brave,
I said he was brave. I'll offer you an instance:
You've been through Checkpoint Charlie, I suppose?
Yes. Well, it's harder for us twilight people.
For him it was unconscionably risky.
He went through, and came back. And you know why?
He'd got it in his head he had a brother
Interred in the Red Army mausoleum.
You've seen it? It's impressive. Forty or

Sixty times over, I.V. Stalin lauds
The Russian dead. Not Pushkin even once?
No, not once. Nor Lenin. He came back
Appalled, distraught. Fought in the wrong mob, see?
Him and his brother, both; no help for it.
And, pastor, that's irreparable Berlin
East and West: a happy Babylon
For your young soldiers and their gravid wives.

THOMSON:

In Babylon the pastoral office is
Harder than in encircled Stalingrad.

NEMETH:

Ah, very true. I seem to taunt you, pastor,
Because you have the authority I once had.
That I envy you, but not your mission;
Just as, unlike the brave old friend I came with,
I want confession, but not absolution.
– Which I'm to get. A corporal's detail
Is stamping underneath us, and high time.
Pastor, goodbye. And thank you. It's not often
I get to have some clerical conversation.
'His beauty to consume away like a moth',
You might remember; and remember me
Possibly in your prayers from time to time?

Chernobyl. A Disaster

for Thom Gunn

Chernobyl: a *defecting author*
Overculme: his *English translator and at need interpreter*
Dignitary
Interviewer
Assassin

AT THE AIRPORT

OVERCULME:

      Mr Chernobyl is
      Tired and despairing. Besides
      As a classical poet, he is
      In any case sparing of words.
      He hopes you will understand.

INTERVIEWER:

      Sir, while respecting Mr
      Chernobyl's unwillingness
      At this time to venture
      Remarks of a political nature,
      Could he favour us with his reaction
      To the just announced award
      Of the Nobel Prize for Literature
      To an East European author?

CHERNOBYL:

      Eh, what? What? Oh the so-called
      Minimalist, it must be. (Stupid Czech!)
      It is all of it costume-drama. Look, we are as good at
      Turning things round and upside down
      As any of you are. Having, you might say, fewer
      Pieces in play we overturn the chessboard
      Sooner than you do. We can better afford it.

      A *genre*-painting: board gone sprawling
      Over the dirt-floor in the dirty light,
      Indigenous, you are meant to understand.
      No Flemish draperies, viols, virginals; no!
      Slick boards, bare crusts, and sticks of furniture…

OVERCULME:
>   Mr Chernobyl says …

CHERNOBYL:
>   I haven't finished.
>   Every penurious nation has its one
>   Accredited monument: the national bard,
>   Crammed down the gullets of gymnasiasts
>   Whatever the régime. To denigrate him
>   By parody and impudent distortion
>   Costs nothing, and goes down well, and is
>   The merest child's play: coarsen
>   His metres to begin with…

INTERVIEWER:
>   I haven't understood him, not a word.

OVERCULME:
>   Mr Chernobyl has not heard
>   News of the award;
>   When he does, he will be happy
>   To speak of it for the record.

INTERVIEWER:
>   Let us be the first to tell him:
>   It is a Slovakian lady;
>   Her name is hard to pronounce.

CHERNOBYL:
>   What did he say?

OVERCULME:
>   Oh nothing.
>   It's some Slovakian tart. You guessed it wrong.
>   Now get into the car.

CHERNOBYL:
>   A woman!

OVERCULME:
>   Mitya,
>   Save it for now. Remember where you are.

ASSASSIN:

> He is, I submit, irrelevant: a one-off
> Disaster waiting to happen. History,
> Finding no earthly use for him, writes him off.
> Why should we help history along?

DIGNITARY:

> Daughter, I am in charge here – don't
> Assume too much. Still, I approve your gumption:
> Chernobyl, an ill-aimed missile, will
> Undoubtedly self-destruct. Why then destroy him?
> The answer, I fear, is metaphysical.
> And metaphysics wasn't in your training.

ASSASSIN:

> With all respect, economy in
> Means to ends, I was taught. And isn't that
> (I beg your pardon) metaphysical?

DIGNITARY:

> No, it is a principle of aesthetics,
> And though a key one, not I'm afraid conclusive.
> 'Say what you have to say, then stop':
> The rule rebukes the bureaucrat, but also
> Such as him, freewheeling into saying
> What he had not known he meant to say
> Until he said it. Therefore you mistake him,
> You and whoever sent you. Merioneth
> Sheep make tainted mutton for his sake
> And spruces brown in Norway. Do you think
> A pistol-shot eradicates his persistence,
> Maker of stanzas, rooms and cyclotrons?
>
> The God of Hosts, of all the hosts of creatures,
> Underwrites him, don't you see? And though you
> Wish, I perceive, that he be quarantined
> In a canton of 'Who cares?' (Who cares Derzhavin had
> Metres to fox the prosodist?), I care.
> And therefore, daughter, you will take the gun
> That will be slipped you after you pass the screening
> And you will use it, as you have been taught to.
> You give the signal; it's 'Slovakia'.

DIGNITARY:

  In the Alice-in-Wonderland language
  That I find on these occasions
  Inescapable, every one
  So far has won a prize.
  But let me remind the Congress: our remit
  (A grievous one, I'll be the first to admit)
  Is to make 'the classical'
  Propitious to modern eyes.

  Mr Chernobyl, would you care to lead us
  Into our second session… ?

OVERCULME:

  It's all yours, Cherners. Now remember:
  Slovaks, you think, are renegade seceders
  From a Pan-Slav Federation. *But don't say so!*

CHERNOBYL:

  What I would say to you, our dear
  Colleagues from the liberated West,
  Is that our emptied larders pre-empt yours.
  Our ikons are up for sale as yours are not;
  Though yours are too. We have much less to lose.
  Our canon's so discredited we can
  Overturn it and make mock of it
  As you must sweat a little to unseat yours.

  Let me recount an anecdote: on my
  Transit here, some months ago, I stayed
  With a Berliner friend. One afternoon,
  Dodging the Press, my comrade-writer took me…
  To what a wonderland! My friends, what riches!
  Netherlandish, early German treasures…
  And shall I tell you what entranced me most?

  The furniture! The Fleming couple, their
  Uxoriousness, fastidiously severe,
  Ought to have moved me; but I fell
  In love instead with a downfall of green fabric
  Behind their unbending backs. Conspicuous

Consumption. Vulgar. But a vulgar Russian
Conceives this as the classical: the costly.
(The sumptuous, not the expensive.)

Our pinched poor writings elevate the bare;
In this, you emulate us. But I ask
Luxuria: metre, assonance, orchestration.
Short of that rhetorical surplus nothing
But comes out mean. Crystal, majolica-ware,
Entablatures, and hyperbolical scroll-work –
All that I crave. I hunger for those bounties.

Frugality, you will say to me: a terse
Economy in fitting means to ends –
Nerve of the classical! My friends,
I have survived the labour-camps. The lice
Are not so frugal there, and not so nice:
Them we must emulate, if we would survive them.

ASSASSIN:

I am a delegate, Mr Chairman. How
Can any of us here refuse
Mr Chernobyl's wrenching paradox?
Frugality is one felicity
Known only to the profuse.
The classic husbanding of means to ends
Means having first sufficient choice of means;
Infinite, ideally.
                        I've a question
For Mr Chernobyl: who was ever,
Or is, the national poet of the Slovaks?

Pause. Then a storm of gunfire. Yells. Screams. Turmoil.

DIGNITARY *(breathless):*

She got the signal wrong, the wretched girl.
Eight guns at least, where two would have done the trick.
As always, metaphysics turns out messy.
This could have been an elegant operation.
Instead the disaster walks, sedately frantic;
Chernobyl lives, to alarm another day.

Balancing Acts

A SMALL DRAMA IN THREE SCENES

Seamus
Shelagh
Eamonn

Donovan

SCENE ONE

SEAMUS:

> *Traditore, traduttore* – spare us!
> Of course the harsh Italian makes good sense
> Though nothing but an easy rigmarole.
> Translator/ traitor, yes; but how if we
> Reversed the proposition? Treachery
> Would come to seem a civilised occupation,
> Facilitating traffic over frontiers,
> Bringing what's dark to light (by selling secrets).
> That's what my Granda did, translating us
> From Herzegovina to County Louth.
> (Not that he sold us; I've no cause to think so.)

SHELAGH:

> You with your Italian! I don't mind it.
> Is it that same old Gramshie?

SEAMUS:

> Gramsci! Shelagh,
> You astonish me: you move around,
> Heeding my talk with half your mind at most
> And something lodges. No, love, it's not Gramsci.

SHELAGH:

> Just as well; he was a communist.

SEAMUS:

> Not in the sense you mean, but never mind.

SHELAGH:

> It's true I only give you half my mind,

There's chores to do. When you go muttering
Half to yourself and half to me, it's homely.
You're like a kettle simmering on the hob
And when you're boiling dry I have to wet you
With an ignorant question. So what's *Herze...*
Herze – whatever-it-is? It's news to me:
I thought your Da was Yugoslavian.

SEAMUS:

He was, we are; for all we are –
True Irish, Irish-born, the three of us,
Me and Siobhan and Eamonn. Don't you see?
That shows what a translator Granda was.
(Not Da, he was but a schoolboy.) Not
A stitch or a snag in the one of us, to show
There was an original we're translated from.

SHELAGH:

That's great, I'm sure. But what about this *Herz...*
Isn't it Yugoslavia?

SEAMUS:

         Yes, it is:
As Connacht's Ireland.

SHELAGH:

         And as Ulster is.

SEAMUS:

Ah yes, very like indeed, or so I'm told.
There's Herzegovina and Bosnia,
Macedonia, Serbia, Montenegro,
Slovenia, Croatia... that enough?

SHELAGH:

More than enough. Ireland has only four
Provinces, and they can't fend together.

SEAMUS:

If you attend, I'll tell you something else:
Not all Mohammedans always had brown faces.
Bits, large bits, of Yugoslavia were
Hungarian, Austrian, Turkish. And the Turks

Were there the longest. Can't you see
How, like the potato Protestants in this country,
A Bosnian might see benefits in the mosque?
Apostasy! The acme of translation!

SHELAGH:

Ah get away with you! You want to scare me,
Mister Schoolmaster. You are as good
A Catholic as most people in this town,
Though your brother and sister are better, and despite you
Study atheists like your precious Gramshie
Who was (yes, I attend more than you think)
A traitor, wasn't he? Went to prison for it?
– Enough of nonsense! On the morrow you
Visit your Granda. You want sandwiches?

SEAMUS:

I do, but I… Shelagh, don't walk away!

SCENE TWO

EAMONN:

So, and you've seen the ould disgraceful fella
Lately, have you?

SEAMUS:

     He's had visitors.

EAMONN:

Has he now? And much good it may do them.

SEAMUS:

Depends what good they looked for. I don't like it.
I visit him quite regular; you don't.
There in the Home he has perked up a bit
Thanks to the Sisters, talks quite lucidly
For minutes at a time. At least he seems to.
And that's what I don't like.

EAMONN:

      He talks of us?

SEAMUS:

Not at all. Of long before we were thought of;
Of Niko this, of Slobodan
Such and such. He talks of partisans,
Chetniks and Ustachi, Klagenfurt…
What's weird is that he talks of them in English.
And there's the trouble: strangers at his bedside
Might get him wrong. He's very prompt with names,
At his best he'll even answer questions.

EAMONN:

What questions would those be? Who'd care at all
Digging up all that ancient fol-de-rol?
Doesn't he talk of Da?

SEAMUS:

                Well now, he does;
And that's the worst of it. He said to me
That you and I by a mere miscarriage missed
The cyanide Da had for the six of us.
What six? Don't ask me. Last time I was there
He said to me: 'My son, your father was
Corrupt from the day he was conceived, too clever.'

EAMONN:

That's horrible, you could have prepared me for it.
Let me think… He's bad things on his conscience
That he won't own, but fathers on some one else?

SEAMUS:

Yes, on some one else, and that's our Da.
Cyanide ampoules – hard to find, I'd think,
In a Saxon gentleman's toilet-case when he,
Our youthful Granda, unbelievably lounged,
Austrian-Saxon in the height of fashion,
Through spas and gardens.

EAMONN:

                Now you've lost me, brother.

SEAMUS:

It doesn't matter. Eamonn, don't you see?
He's fantasizing what an attentive stranger

Either won't see, or won't be prepared to see
Or hear, as fantasies. What that stranger gets
Is names, and some names maybe lately famous
Set to be blackmailed.

EAMONN:

                      Now *you* fantasize!
And yet not more than I have: you suspect,
As I have, that our dear old Granda (not
So dear at that, if the truth be known), he might be
What's known as a war-criminal?

SEAMUS:

                              He might be.
Younger ones, or untimely dead like Da,
Might suffer for that still, although he won't.
Who talked to him? By what authority?

EAMONN:

Leave that to me; I think I can arrange it.
I have some influence in this diocese.

SEAMUS:

Ay, and across the Border, I believe...
The harm is done. I had a call from Dublin:
I am to hold myself available
All this week for interview. And as for
Authority, what do you say to INTERPOL?
That scares me, Eamonn, as it should scare you
Though you've the Bishop there to call upon.

SCENE THREE

SEAMUS:

Mr Donovan, now the investigation
I gather is over, what was the point of it?

DONOVAN:

God bless you, Mr Burkitt, none at all!
You have, if I may say so, a distorted
Notion of the police. We do not, as
Policemen, judge of treachery, or treason

Or (what's a more inclusive term) betrayal.
We gather names, we work out circumstances;
Our betters bury or else brandish them.

SEAMUS:

A humble trade, so. Tell me, did my Granda
Provide what you had looked for?

DONOVAN:

                                        Pretty well.

SEAMUS:

You know he's senile! What construction can…?
Well, I remember: it's your betters judge
What weight, or none, to give his maunderings.
Are they your betters?

DONOVAN:

                        It's a way of speaking.

SEAMUS:

A way of passing all the bucks upstairs!

DONOVAN:

You need no lessons, Mister Schoolmaster,
On passing bucks without the staircase creaking.

SEAMUS:

What does that mean? You've investigated
My classroom schedules, and my reading-lists?
Interviewed my pupils and their parents?

DONOVAN :

Of course we have. What do you think we are:
Ton-ton macoutes or a Praetorian Guard?
It's hard work, Mr Burkitt: drudgery.
You think I care what homework you've prescribed
These many years? And yet there's some one cares.

SEAMUS:

A small obedient cog in the machine
Of a police-state…

DONOVAN:

                Come now, that may serve
The Lower Sixth, or Trinity College even;
The stupidest *garda* knows the difference,
And knows a clapped-out metaphor when he sees it.
I don't serve a State, as the *garda* does.
You can be assured no pupil nor
Parent knows he's been interrogated.
Some basic skills we have, enough for instance…

SHELAGH:

Wait a minute! Here's Saint Francis,
Him of Assisi, Hymn of the Creatures, done in
Beautiful Irish by me husband. I'll
Read it, I will.

SEAMUS:

              Ah Shelagh, Shelagh…

DONOVAN:

                      Mrs Burkitt?
Donovan's my name, Pierce Donovan.
I hoped I'd get to meet you, Mrs Burkitt.

SHELAGH:

And now you have. I don't know what you're after.

DONOVAN:

After, ma'am? Not after, but before:
Beforehand, you might say. Whereas your husband,
He's 'after', isn't he? That poem of his is
After Saint Francis. And that's proper but
Perilous, Mrs Burkitt. Seeing that your husband
Has left the room to show that he's annoyed,
I offer you, although I go beyond
My brief in doing it, a word of warning:
Those we would call war-criminals, by others
Are thought war-heroes, worth the re-assembling;
And being a good Catholic means something
Different at the other end of Europe.
It all comes down to problems of translation,
Mrs Burkitt; and your learned husband
Is very well aware of that, I reckon.

You lose your balance, even thinking of it.
Prudent policemen don't learn languages.
Italian now, I'd have thought was a difficult language;
And yet my daughter tells me it comes easy.

Another Old Bolshevik

for Philip Edwards

A MELODRAMA FOR THREE VOICES

DR P:

'Alamein to Zem-Zem' – have you read it?
Ah but forgive me! Always I
interrogate at first meeting. Such bad manners.
The book was under your arm, is not well known.
Myself I was a bookseller for a time.
You want to hear of that, I think? My daughter
told me: no more of all that stupid stuff
from years ago, but how it has been since –
'Reflections of a Fortunate Survivor'.
Start me off with a question…

                                        Oh,
that one: the office that I hold in
the government-in-exile. Deary me!
My office? It's a lowly one. After all I
collaborated, did I not, and at
a not inconspicuous level? One does not
live that down, not with the intransigents.
So I lick stamps, and sometimes lick their boots,
and am a lucky creature, always was.

My nation never was. You know the record,
our tiresome history: an imperial duchy
six hundred years before Versailles; and there,
to satisfy President Wilson, nationhood!
What a joke! Our representative
a coterie French poet, with a name
beyond reproach of quite the bluest blood in
the reedy reaches of the Pripet or the Dniester,
I can't remember which. And this was what

had earned one's – what's the charming word – one's
fealty?

My dear young man, imagine it if you can!
I'm loyal to this gas-fire, this
malodorous bed-sitter in West Hampstead,
and to whatever pays the rent of it,
just about pays it, sometimes. Oh the farce,
you can't imagine. Do you know there is
a Wendish government-in-exile? Yes;
somewhere in Putney, sends out invitations
once a year. And what a stir of conscience
among the greasy sports-coats, when we meet to
draft our reply! Turns out there are, you see,
unsavoury squads at large in unlikely Sweden
blowing up travel-agencies. Of course
they are disowned, a tall frock-coated old
head of a non-state spreads his fluttering hands.
But how can we (such statesmen!) risk our good
relations with your tolerant H.M.G.,
your well-policed Great Britain? No, we think;
the Putney Wends must swallow their dismay!

You are surprised to find me so
jolly, you say. Well, it's a jolly business
don't you think? Now Mrs Mackay, my daughter,
who vouches for you... that's a jolly business
too: that I seem to have fathered
an excitable Gaelic Jacobite. She alarms,
you must have noticed, her compliant husband.

But now I have embarrassed you. Oh dear.
That Scotch you brought (so kind of you) it rather
went to my head, I'm so unused to it
nowadays, and at my age. Now when
you come again, I'll be as talkative
but more to the point perhaps, or more in earnest.

★

LYUDMILA MACKAY:
Wendish? In Putney? Oh he pulled your leg,
how naughty he is! You'll get to know my father

but it takes time. He'll go to any lengths
not to appear embittered, which he is.
It's sad of course, but saves his dignity.

ALEX MACKAY:

Mackays were Hanoverian, he knows that;
it's just his mischief, making out he doesn't.
The history of our clan is very boring.
I don't mean that the way he would, I mean it.
Now, my wife's history – Polish – that's eventful,
full of pathos. Oh, not Polish, he'd
have you believe, but something more exotic?
If he says so, then it must be right.
And yet the name, you know for yourself, is Polish.
Lyudmila thinks the name Mackay has lodged her
in Fingal's Cave, to strains of Mendelssohn,
and why not? He and she alike
are more enraptured by a dripping wave
in Wester Ross than all its stupid natives.
Let the old gentleman have his fantasies.

*

DR P:

'The Captive Mind' … but there I go again,
the allusive bibliomane. I meant to say
the captive and the captivated mind
are not so different. Mendelssohn
enthralls some people, some are enslaved by Wagner.
The unenthralled, the unenslaved, who envies?
He ought to jostle with the cut-off jeans
and captivating maidens I encounter,
as doubtless you do, in the Underground.
Every one would be in thrall to something
given the chance, a chance that's free for all.
Who's in the Top Ten? It's of no account,
that's just the point. Oh that Enlightenment dream!
These are the unenthralled, who hoot and scream
for a tooled-up ensemble gone tomorrow.
They are not deceived; in fact, these are the free,
these are the hoped-for freedom-fighters of
here today and gone tomorrow. Freedom
in a consumer society is to be free of the market,

that's to say, enslaved by it, to be sure.
But what a painless, unperturbed enslavement!
I've come to love and envy it, such freedom.

No, I am not ironical. I am not,
as I did last time, making mock of you;
I mean it. I can see now what I meant by,
or should have meant by, the dictatorship
of the proletariat. Here you have it, in
glorious undiscriminating London.
And I aver, or rather I repeat,
I love it. It was what we laboured for,
killed for in fact. It was worth killing for?
Yes, and worth dying for, if Freedom is.

None of this of course must you report
back to my daughter and my son-in-law.
And yet why not? They'll only put it down
to the old gentleman – so they speak of me –
finding his feet at last. And they are right.

★

DR P:

I am Lithuanian on my mother's side,
does that content you? I confess I do not
care to be quizzed about my ancestry,
however deprecatingly. You
want to know what it was like, though you pretend
not to. Well. Very well, I will try to tell you:

The village wife, the greying civil servant,
the crazy gutters and the nervous birds
cried out for him: Mamai,
the little man with the enormous gun
in the hideous cap. Mamai!
Wind out of Asia with a horde of horses,
once the magnificent, now from a peeling pent-house
toting a sudden gun.
                    And in the stallion
seamen's pea-jacketed patrol
ranging, the sudden angels
of every Revolution, the wild horses

tethered to every lamp-post, and stampeded
by a little spur.
         And you, you too have seen them,
obsequious querist that I dally with:
the liquid eyes, the trembling
flanks, the saliva docile
after the ritual clap-trap or a casual
pass of the hands.
         It is always Fingal's Cave
for them in the West, but for us who have known the
                             Tartar –
Lithuanian, White Russian, what's the odds? –
it is the gong of Asia, wizard-god,
Mamai the Great. The fragrance brims
the latticed alleyways,
a sherbet spiked with Terrors.

Now do you see? Of course not. Why I should,
my dear young fellow, burden you with my
specially cherished nightmares, I do not
well understand. It must be, that I like you.

                 ★

ALEX MACKAY:
         Finding his feet? He found them long ago,
you ask Lyudmila. It's his tragedy,
if that's the word, to have found the spectacle
of human doings, here or anywhere else,
a puppet-show of Folly.
How with that background – there are documents
from his pre-war youth as a would-be *avant-gardiste*
(in print, I assure you: poems, even a play)…
how he became a Revolutionary, now
that's the absorbing question. Mr
Ashraf, you study politics, I think;
in my way, so do I. But isn't it
remarkable, and falls within our field,
how many revolutionaries started –
Hitler's the obvious case – as failed
avant-garde artists? It's the 'failed'
that commentators fasten on. But with my
father-in-law as instance, it's the

'avant-garde', the varieties of it,
I'd like to know more about. My wife can help you.

LYUDMILA MACKAY:

Poor Daddy! Far from finding his
always findable feet, it's being swept
off them, so firmly planted as they are,
he's always looked for. Odd that, as you tell me,
he's never fixed upon your being Asian,
Asian (not ancient!) Briton. In the past,
Asia it was he looked to, to redress
his European rationality. If he's
stopped dreaming of that – and you assure me he has –
I'm glad of it, yet sorry for him, a little.

*

DR P:

Our friends the Wends have hit the headlines,
Mr Ashraf! You have seen the papers?
Kurds and Croats are the touted suspects
for the atrocity in Gothenburg
but you and I know better: hail the Wends
though in a splinter-group... And we know who
the Wends are, don't we, my Iranian friend?
I drink (he'd disapprove) to the Ayatollah.
Desert ascetics purge the bloat of the West –
of rationality? No! Of bloat and blood.
Tell your masters I am at their service.

Bits and Pieces

Harmonious first and last,
a classical composure,
is what the republican mentors
ask of a verse in your honour.

For them to accredit it,
bits here and pieces there
knocked together aren't
sufficiently severe.

And no doubt they are right.
Clear-eyed accommodations
don't measure up to our sessions;
neither do porticos.

Composites, inspired
improvisations on
the one part and the other,
make up the script of our love.

Ah my Isotta, I'd
raise you a temple not
less ramshackle than
the one in Rimini.

The Knave of Hearts

for Vikram Seth

The accomplished *hetaira* toys for this Knave of Hearts.
Though he writes his poems as often in English as Urdu,
He speaks for a culture where the courtesan
Is the honoured exponent of more than one of the arts.

Imagine a bimbo as conversant with
Fanshawe and Waller as with Tennyson!
She would attract a different clientele,
Not more in love with her than with Purcell.

Seductive magic of the Knave of Hearts,
Lovely and winning, but impossible…
He cannot trump the Ace of deadly Spades:
A rule in our game and in his as well.

The Lost Bride

(Arkhangelsk, 1943)

'Versify it, Donald,'
I hear one of them say;
'Put it in rhyme, if I'm
To give it the time of day!'

And level-headed you
See the force of that:
'Unable to join the dance,
Keep still and sit it out.'

Dear vanished one, alive
As I have to imagine, your
Booted foot beats out: 'Not
Up to it any more.'

It is the dancer's verdict
On the irredeemable clown,
His feet all asplay, although with
A clumsiness all his own.

Younger grizzled men
In Spain and Morbihan
At this very hour take drams
To greet the unwelcome dawn.

Hours later, the concerned
Seeking a fuddled answer
Get only this: 'In youth
I loved a dancer.'

Orvieto. The King of Clubs

If I should riffle a pack
Of playing-cards in sight
Of the Duomo's façade
(Angular Gothic, three-gabled),
It should be the King of Clubs
Turns up, and answers back.

Nowhere except in untrue
Photographs is it a wall,
Not even a screen. From whatever
Angle you look at it close,
It is all of a ripple, three
Dimensions, nowhere two.

And this you take for *richesse*.
But it is more disconcerting:
There are in the end no walls,
Nothing to screen us. Whatever
We took to be safely outward
Implicates us no less.

Once he was King of the rustics,
His clubs were staves. Now trefoil,
Three knobs on a whistling stalk,
They smite us out of the blue as
In an archaic, armoured
Affray of singlesticks.

Sidelong or in wristy backlash
This Gothic emperor bruises.
Come close; in his gilt, his marbled
In-and-out, there is no
Place to escape his buffets.
You owe, though you paid in cash.

Serpentine is the edge
And hazard of it. That
Enemy, the serpent,
Has our measure, as
Card-players in the gardens
Of the *fortezza* acknowledge.

Clubs take the rubbers, mostly.
Drubbed, the King of Hearts
Meekly, modestly sweeps
The board under his coat as
Night comes in. The game
He covertly wins is ghostly.

On the Final Day

for Charles Tomlinson, concerning Ivor Gurney

No, there will be no explanations then:
Not mine of myself to God (who knows me through)
Nor God's of Himself to me concerning (say)
Ivor Gurney. He will not explain;
Illuminate sometimes, but not explain.

You'd have 'illuminate' equal to 'enlighten'.
The etymology bears you out, but not
The history of those two English words.
The land, the language – they are not the same;
And Eden isn't either one's right name.

Eden is what we forfeited, once for all:
His first illumination, ground of the rest.
Read, for 'Gloucester', England; read, for 'English',
Catalan, Hebrew, Navajo. Which is best?
Too plain our answer spells self-interest.

Foredoomed, poor flailing Gurney! Mostly we
Aren't, but seek out a doom not meant for us.
The muddy flash – our brief flame soon eclipsed –
Flares out, reveals it. His, in the madhouse, flames
To glorify God, and all our exploits tames.

See Charles Tomlinson, *Jubilation* (1995), p.60

To C.T.

We have shown each other the tricks
Of an abstruse trade
For fifty years, old friend;
Now to an attentive
Third party, did such exist,
An array of certain tics
In the deployment of words
Would amount to a common style,
Disconcertingly similar
From your hand and from mine.

Will he even notice,
This improbable person,
That at your hand and mine
The style serves a different end?

Hearing the same promise
Made on behalf of a godchild,
Will he notice our gods
Cannot be reconciled?

See Charles Tomlinson, *Annunciations* (1989), p.55

To a Staffordshireman, from a Devon Villa

I went to war once, I'm not sure for what
But not for Eden. I'd no thought of that,
Religious or irreligious. I was glad
To go, for what till then I'd never had,
The heedlessness of youth. From Staffordshire,
Yorkshire and Gloucester, Devon, for the mere
Adventure of it 'in a righteous cause',
The unlicked levies came to earn applause.
The blamelessness of that, the poignancy,
Has never ceased, and will not cease, to move me;
But Eden, Avon? Come, we knew the date,
Raw though we were; we knew it was too late
For moonlit meadow umbels. War kept sane
Gurney, whose chromosomes played him up again

Only when peace came. Do I have to say
That war, however garlanded with may
And Tewkesbury towers, prefigures our perdition?
Its therapy, though, can manage a remission
In a woe that, once the armistice lets it loose,
Drives the sufferer out of civic use.

Such harsh sentiments are bold and loud;
Nothing umbrageous niceties can't cloud
With a good conscience. But, clipped or ornate,
Horatian diction cannot mitigate
Horrors reserved to crown a later date.
Horace was shrewd, but knew of nothing fit
For Edward Thomas's death or the manner of it.
My door swings open for you always, but
In another's mouth 'Sabine' might keep it shut.

See Charles Tomlinson, *Jubilation* (1995), pp.43–44

Jottings, not so Random

1

'He's a sad sack. So's he.'
Does the 'sad' a little
Mitigate the 'sack'?
No; I meant to belittle.

2

Infinite Wisdom and Pure Mind
Are not even distant cousins;
The one advises prudence,
The other cozens.

3

One thing you can say
For the Devil Incarnate:
The embodiment means you can
Rub him the wrong way.

4

Pure Mind and Satan are,
Paul Valéry observes,
Near kin. Can Theory say
Which serves, and which subserves?

5

Pure Mind. Never mind that it is
Demonstrably impure;
It keeps its promises,
Like Mephistopheles.

6

Though what we've a mind to is
For the most part muddle,
Most lethal among our toys
Is not that, but ill-will.

7

Rubbing the wrong way
Is an allowable mischief,
I judge: it is undertaken
To nettle, not belittle.

Sea of Tiberias

'Prevalent, his death he pleads.'

The man on the foreshore cooking a fish breakfast
Was a King Arthur or a Deadwood Dick,
Not false and yet not actual; between
The Resurrection and the Ascension, Christ
Had turned into (what couldn't be right) a legend.

The man on the foreshore might have seen the shoal
Break surface in an unregarded quarter.
By trawlers of a sterile night he might
(Given the dawn's eleventh-hour draught of fishes)
Be credited with legendary know-how.

Revenants are not unheard of, nor
Are the uncanny masters of a trade;
Every locality has wind of them.
But what was designed for Him was such a transfer
As makes the hairs at the back of my neck stand up.

The ghost that was a revenant departed
Along with its localities. Succeeded
A sort of Ghost that would be known as Holy:
Prevalent, but not as Error is;
Prevailing for us sufferers everywhere.

Seeing through Me

'The dead shall look me thro' and thro''
(In Memoriam)

'Mesmerized eyes on one's
Dead fathers, not on one's
Unborn sons': a verdict
Stage-managed to convict
This line of Tennyson's.

It happened no longer ago
Than 1969;
'A foul proposition', opine
The worthies of that era.
So little did they know.

Now men choose to be sterile,
They do not know their sons
No, nor their daughters, each
A threat to a life-style out of
Fortunate Tennyson's reach.

'The dead shall know me through
And through.' Not shall, but do.
Is it Mesmer's, is it Freud's
Client most lightly avoid what
Eternity amounts to?

The forebears, whose defaced
Gravestones endure the tread
Of sceptical visitors,
Are vindicated, seeing
They see though they are dead.

See John Fowles, *The French Lieutenant's Woman* (1969), chapter 48

Toby to Aguecheek

My mountain belly and incontinent girth
That strutted, more than trod, the groaning earth

Have, in some questionings of saluted merit
Worried that sheer bulk balks the encroaching spirit.

Carnality. But we worship the Incarnate:
Buried in the ageing flesh, or blossoming in it?

I who cull those blossoms know the truth:
Gross age engrosses all we risked in youth.

A fat man is as like to be a saint
As any hermit skeletal in paint,

I tell myself, and with more confidence
Now, in advanced age, needing her carnal presence

Whom no, my lean fastidious friend, you have
Not so much as entertained a thought of.

War Criminal

He had the gift of being pitiless;
Rare he thought it, though in that he was wrong.
It was his only talent, and I picked
Away at it I cannot say how long.

Bride to one past saving, him I bridled;
And he (poor dear) came bit by bit to function
Shorn of the one citation that he cherished,
The serving soldier's: 'Served without compunction'.

Vengeance is mine, mine only, saith the Lord;
That is to say, past our capacities.
We do, however, wreak it as we can,
And that is allowed, but do not call it Justice.

Ecclesiastical Polity

(The Laws of... by Richard Hooker, 1597)

'Not what's done, but what
Is done religiously...'
Hooker proposed. Accounts
That credit him with Laws
Of Pusillanimity
Pretend that this amounts to:
'It is the thought that counts.'

His long book of short views
(Short as he was with profaneness),
Because he was deferential
To long-established use
Has made him seem to profess
'Nothing succeeds like success',
That sorriest of long views.

The *via media,* that
Anglican offer to trimmers,
Was not his style of play.
Marrying Rome with Geneva
Would always tax the Believer
Sorely, he thought; no grimace
Nor smirk would blow it away.

Unread, he is still co-opted
To shore up the C. of E.,
Though long ago that adopted
Expediently a more
Beguiling polity
That keeps abreast of the times.
(What else are Synods for?)

Against the rigorist Cartwright
Hooker was in the right.
But now, since he sought to construe
The Laws in a liberal light,
He is thought to set Law on its head;
So little is a true
Liberality admitted.

Women and War

Rebuke the company of spearmen
Trampling in wedges of silver.
Scatter the peoples that delight in war,
The Seventh Fleet and the Sixth.

They are not in pains as other men
And they are not gorged as other men,
Therefore the pride wind about them as a chain.
The apparel of violence hath covered them so that
                they feel little.

Their eyes pop. Affluent princes,
They have overpassed the thoughts of their heart,
They swim afloat and talk, they speak from aloft
Saying 'sanctuaries', they have no thought of Zion.

But the Lord shall give matter of talk
To the concourse of women reporters.
Miriam and her sisters who sang the praise upon timbrels,
Daughters of the Confederacy and of recaptured Zion,
                    and of the Primrose League,
Distributors of white feathers.

He maketh men to be of one mind in an house.
He shall have pity upon the poor
And shall save the lives of the poor,
And precious shall their blood be in his sight.

'Our Father'

I *On a hint from Bertolucci*

Passed from you, mother, to the custody
Of another, and that other, though a Muse,
Acerbic, limited, can I think I am
Worth your nine months' indignity and labour?
The Muse you may have vowed me to was not
The one I find I'm serving. In the clear
Service of dream you come to me, forgiving
Although unsmiling:
                  'Look, your father's here.'

II *On another*

'venne il padre'

He is the delineator, here he comes,
Diffident porter of the primal hues
To the palette of his endowed but ailing
Child, the devoted homemaker who scumbles
To glories of old rose, of Cambridge blue,
Of less than Irish green to pin the wilting
And waxing indeterminacies of verdure.

Comes the Father, the delineator,
Master of line and of the primary,
Behind the scenes the guarantor of Nature,
Not the all-round factotum that he seems.

III *Green*

Issue of yellow's intercourse with blue,
Green is no primary hue. Though every Spring
Persuade us of its primacy, it is not
The unmediated progeny of the Father.

'Father, saddest of all my brethren, father.'
Franco Fortini, what were you thinking of?
Brothers have all one father. Are there no
Odds between filial and fraternal love?

Lincoln green, fraternity of the greenwood ...
But blue or yellow is His blazon, he
Sired King John no less than Robin Hood.
Being the Father, he is no man's fellow.

IV *Alfieri*

Tragedian of an Italy then unborn,
He cudgelled himself for having prostituted
The buskin to the tiara; that's to say,
His play to the scrutiny of the Holy Father.

Later he learned how much more tolerant an
Unpolished pontiff was, than a godless State
That asked a theatre for Everyman,
The man first dulled, then frivolously diverted.

Later again (we look beyond him now)
The buskin throve by dirtying – the tiara
And then the Cross; which lives by seeing how
Unwearyingly the Father's sons revile him.

V *To a Neophyte*

Do not fancy that the 'oh' and 'ah'
Which may escape me signify the cut
And smoothing face of the Father's chisel are
Soon or blithely suffered. They are not.

From me, although acerb, no epigrams.
Much as I'm enamoured of the terse,
Frauds self-confessed, self-interested scams...
Shameful, the in-house dailiness of verse!

The mother of all battles, and the father
Of every cock-up... that's an issue reckoned
By a superior calculus. Would you rather
Side with the first, or sign up with the second?

Whichever daunting parent gets your voice,
Recollect:
              To start with, you'd no choice.

VI *After Whittier*

('Dear Lord and Father of Mankind')

Carnival-master, Father, god of the glitch,
Functionary of the out-of-phase,
Apparent fumbler tripping the wrong switch,
Dear gremlin Lord, frustrate our foolish ways.

VII *After Watts*

Behold! what wondrous grace
        The Father has bestow'd
On sinners of a mortal race –
        To call them sons of God!

We would no longer lie
        Like slaves beneath the throne;
My faith shall *Abba* Father, cry,
        And Thou the kindred own.

It does not yet appear
    How great we must be made;
But when we see our Saviour here,
    We shall be like our head.

VIII *Good Friday*

'God the Son is our brother.'
Not true, but let it pass;
It's not for a splendid sibling
Good Friday cries, 'Alas!'

For also it cries, 'All hail!'
'Papa!' it cries, and is
Thereupon desolate
Past help of therapies.

Not how we are begotten,
That prurient 'primal scene',
But how it is to be fathered
Is what our tremblings mean.

IX 'That he should be so severe'

That he should be so severe
In what He asks of us
(For so it seems) – is this
Love, so onerous?

True, it springs of an action
Beyond engendering;
But it is felt as some
Less amiable thing.

On our idea of 'father'
Fed, if we're lucky, by
Memories of indulgence
(Kicking a ball in the alley),

Ancient Israel leaves
Its inexpungible mark:
A Father no less father
For being patriarch.

X *Freedom*

A patriarch prone to cock-ups
Is not what we would choose;
But we have no choice in the matter
Any more than the Jews.

And would it be fun in the alley,
Trying to out-shoot
A preternatural marksman,
Dad's infallible boot?

Omnipotent, oh yes;
Not omni-talented.
See Him walk back to his mark,
Shaking a worried head.

What can it be but love
That He is tendering,
Possessed of so much power
So much surrendering?

On Edmund Spenser's House in Ireland

Every so often, Lord, the wanton muse
– So, or in some such strain, the mantled stump
Kilcolman semaphored unwelcome news
Across a mile of bog and Munster damp,
Harrier-haunted… Not as we would choose
(For we would go, Lord, where you set your stamp)
But every so often still, the unruly muse
Yearns for the flowery noon, the midnight lamp.
Elysiums out of nowhere: compositions!
The workaday exigencies of prose
Serve best, in us and Spenser, the tame missions
You seem to have assigned us. Only those
Who famously once were prey to faerie visions
Flag home to you. Ourselves we must compose.

Two Intercepted Letters

in memoriam Philip Larkin,
ob. 2 December 1985.

1

'Southey! Alas, my writings
Are not on slate: no finger,
Not Time's that is
Dipped in the clouds of years,
In freezing rains that split
The monumental stone,
Rubs out the written. Byron
I had avoided, slighted; he
(Byron) knew it; he did not
Love Landor; he could not.

Injurious print
Outlasts all slate, although
What's said should be unsaid
Of Byron dead.'

'A ghoulish, ghoulish, ghastly business this,
Mr Nollekens! No one when I
Was 'prenticed mason, rustic archivist,
Told me the verb I'd conjugate was "die".

Epitaphs are very well. But, sir,
Tell me by what wise exercise of will
The elegist in need of custom jibs
Short of where "die" shades over into "kill".

Here in Northampton I have traffic with
Lord Byron and such spectres. I declare
Grave-robbers, monsters, had recruited me.
From that morne service spare, I plead, John Clare.'

Immortal Longings.
Before Surgery

So now we know the worst.
We start to count it up
And it is not so bad;
We have an almighty thirst,
As always, for a cup
That is not to be had.

And this is nothing new.
Such croaking throats as we
Communed with, even at best!
The thirst – me wanting you,
You half-possessing me –
Always distracted, vexed…

Whoever it was that thought
We needed scaring, erred.
Whichever first must die,
The one and the other throat
Will always answer a word
Together: 'Dry… I'm *dry*.'

For this is almighty thirst.
This is the all-availing
Unsatisfied demand.
We always knew the worst,
And always this unfailing
Remedy was at hand.

Thomas and Emma

Not deaf to ghosts yet not expecting them
I paced the hill-rim's shadowy belvedere
At Shaftesbury, when from the abbey ruins
An old thin voice pronounced, for me to hear:

'A levelled, levelling culture leaves no room
For amorous or other compliment.
Analogy and allusion are ruled out;
Our happiness can have no monument.'

A voice returned: 'The happiness alleged
To have obtained between us never was,
Or else so seldom that a truthful culture
Rightly discounts hyperboles like yours.'

In the event I heard both voices falter.
Hyperbole, analogy, allusion
Build up what is no lie, although so wishful:
Conspiratorial, conjugal collusion.

This, though unsettled, was a summer's day –
I took another turn along the grass
And gravel of the rampart. Overhead
The boughs soughed something. It was not: 'Alas.'

NOTES

Most of these notes are Donald Davie's own, from *Collected Poems* (1972). I have added a number of brief quotations from *These the Companions* (1982), which supply useful background information about specific poems: these are marked [*TC*]. And I have provided some short notes of my own – marked [*Ed.*] – on the sources, and in a few cases the circumstances, of hitherto uncollected poems.

Pelican; A Song for These Crusaders; Glaphira III; Kites; Duplicity in Prayer. From *Poetry from Cambridge in Wartime*, ed. Geoffrey Moore (London, 1946). [*Ed.*]

Tiger at the Movie-Show. From *Prospect*, Summer 1949; published in *Poems and Melodramas* (1996). [*Ed.*]

Landfall among Friends; Condolence. From *Poetry London*, September 1949. [*Ed.*]

Christmas Week, 1948. From *Poetry London*, August 1950. [*Ed.*]

Protesilaus and Laidamia. From *Poetry London*, Summer 1951. [*Ed.*]

Homage to William Cowper. Cowper's poem, 'On the Death of Mrs Throckmorton's Bullfinch', in its controlled hysteria, is surely one of the most frightening poems in English.

The Poet-Scholar. From *Essays in Criticism*, January 1955. [*Ed.*]

Elders and Betters. From *Essays in Criticism*, July 1955. [*Ed.*]

Among Artisans' Houses. 'The house in this poem is the home of Doreen's parents, in Peverell … The question which the poem raises has become for me ever more naggingly unanswerable over the many years since. It nags at me whenever and wherever I am in England, but particularly in the West Country where, since 1976, I have had a little house of my own. It is the question: at what point do the signs of civility, as the poem adumbrates that quality, become so rudimentary or so vestigial that one can no longer defend them, or applaud them, or invest any hope in them?' [*TC*, p.69]

Hypochondriac Logic. Written 5 October 1951, this poem was probably written earlier than any other poem in this collection, except for 'Pushkin. A Didactic Poem'.

Creon's Mouse. I commented on this poem, in relation to one by Kingsley Amis, in *Encounter*, October 1969. It was written in November and December 1951.

Mamertinus on Rhetoric, AD 291. See Burckhardt, *The Age of Constantine the Great.*

Pushkin. A Didactic Poem. 'It is extremely prosaic, and was meant to be; for already then I had conceived, from my reading of *Four Quartets*, an enterprise which I suppose I have never since given up – the incorporating into verse of more and more of the prose virtues, so as to see how near to prose poetry can come while still remaining poetry. But in that pursuit it matters greatly what *sort* of prose your poetry is borrowing from and alluding to. And in my "Pushkin", it is clear to me now that the prose in question is the prose of *Scrutiny* – not Leavis's own prose, which is distinctive, but the sort of prose, at all events of vocabulary, which Douglas [Brown] and I expected from the undergraduates we had begun to supervise.' [*TC*, pp.81–2]

Remembering the 'Thirties. I have amended this poem in one place. When I first printed it, I gave it an epigraph from Paul Tillich: 'Courage is an ethical reality, but it is rooted in the whole breadth of existence and ultimately in the structure of being itself.'

Hawkshead and Dachau in a Christmas Glass. I seem to remember that this poem is connected with an essay I contributed to the Dublin periodical, *The Bell,* entitled rather quaintly 'Professor Heller and the Boots'. The poem was written in imitation of Coleridge's 'Dejection. An Ode'.

Woodpigeons at Raheny. The house at Raheny, near Dublin, was Myles Dillon's.

Jacob's Ladder. 'Jacob's Ladder' is the name of a spur of the mountain Kinderscout in the Derbyshire Peak.

Dream Forest. Written 19 October 1954, this poem is earlier than others in *A Winter Talent.*

At the Cradle of Genius. Suggested by Fromentin in *The Masters of Past Time,* on Rubens and (especially) Vandyck.

The Wind at Penistone. 'From Barnsley there runs north and south an unbroken chain of squalid little townships, the meanly built and hastily improvised barracks of the Industrial Revolution, all the way from Sheffield up to Leeds and beyond. But west and east it is a different, more hopeful story. Westward in particular – and we lived on the west side of town – the land begins to rise at once, through Dodworth and Silkstone and Hoylandswaine; and then, after a dip into Penistone, which is already a windy upland town, it rises steeply again to become after a few miles uncultivated and largely trackless Pennine moorland.' [*TC*, p.19]

A Baptist Childhood. The echo of Dylan Thomas was intended.

A Gathered Church. 'But in the areas of personal morality and the arts, realms where I expect principles more rigorous and absolute, I cannot see, much as I should like to, how to rule the prig, the precisian, out of court. And indeed this dilemma was, I now recognize, predictable and inescapable; son of a Baptist deacon and grandson of a Baptist lay-preacher, how could I not have felt some sympathy, however sneaking, with the prig as the eighteenth century defined him? According to the Oxford Dictionary again, "prig" in the late seventeenth and early eighteenth century was "applied to a precisian in religion, *especially a noncomformist minister*" (italics mine). The Dissenters' conception of "a gathered church", gathered *from* the world and in tension with it, cannot help but be the model for Leavis's minority culture. But it was some years later that I worked this out for myself, and documented it in a handful of poems.' [*TC*, pp.75–6]

Corrib. An Emblem. Suggested in part by a plate of Tiepolo's 'Apollo pursuing Daphne', in Berenson's *Italian Painters of the Renaissance.*

The Pacer in the Fresco. Inspired by Andrea del Sarto's wall-paintings of the life of John the Baptist, in the Chiostra dello Scalzo, Florence. The painted panels run round four sides of a square, which is small enough for one to stand in the middle and, by a turn of the head, see the Baptist's end in his beginning, and his whole career simultaneously present as in a strip-cartoon.

The Fountain. Berkeley uses the figure of a fountain at the end of his *Dialogues of Hylas and Philonous.*

Under a Skylight. I have amended the last four lines.

The Forests of Lithuania. A prefatory note to this volume read:

> This poem, like the *Pan Tadeusz* of Mickiewicz, from which it is adapted, is set in Lithuania in the years 1811 and 1812. At this period Lithuania was under Russian occupation, but the sister Kingdom of Poland had been liberated by Napoleon, and Lithuanian patriots frequently escaped to join the Polish legions fighting with the Napoleonic armies as far afield as the West Indies. In 1812, when the French launched their march on Moscow, Lithuania was also briefly liberated. The poem is to be supposed written, as Mickiewicz's poem was written, by a Lithuanian in exile, twenty years later.

I have no Polish and, as some astute reviewers realized, I rely for my knowledge of Mickiewicz's masterpiece on the excellent prose translation by G.R. Noyes in the Everyman Library. Since my poem is thus not a translation, I was (and am) at a loss how to describe it. Neither 'imitation' nor 'paraphrase' will meet the case. I have always cherished the advice of Charles Brink who, being told of my quandary, affirmed that what I had written was, strictly speaking ... a travesty.

To a Brother in the Mystery. The poem arose out of a visit to Southwell Minster, and a reading of Nikolaus Pevsner's *The Leaves of Southwell.* But the relationship explored in the poem is in some sort that between myself and Charles Tomlinson.

With the Grain. The poem is obscure. Completed on 24 July 1957, it appears to be related to a note written three days before. Though this is a vulnerable piece of writing, I transcribe it here:

> It is true that I am not a poet by nature, only by inclination; for my mind

moves most easily and happily among abstractions, it relates ideas far more readily than it relates experiences. I have little appetite, only profound admiration, for sensuous fullness and immediacy; I have not the poet's need of concreteness. I have resisted this admission for so long, chiefly because a natural poet was above all what I wanted to be, but partly because I mistook my English empiricism for the poet's concreteness, and so thought my mind was unphilosophical whereas it is philosophical but in a peculiarly English way.

Most of the poems I have written are not natural poems, in one sense not truly poems, simply because the thought in them could have been expressed – at whatever cost in terseness and point – in a non-poetic way. This does not mean however that they are worthless, or that they are shams; for as much can be said of much of the poetry of the past that by common consent is worth reading and remembering. Nevertheless I have taken a decision to write no more poems of this kind, only poems which are, if not *naturally,* at all events *truly* poems throughout.

For a true poem can be written by a mind not naturally poetic – though by the inhuman labour of thwarting at every point the natural grain and bent. This working against the grain does not damage the mind, nor is it foolish; on the contrary, only by doing this does each true poem as it is written become an authentic widening of experience – a truth won from life against all odds, because a truth in and about a mode of experience to which the mind is normally closed.

My 'Obiter Dicta' is a poem which wins through to sensuous immediacy, to poetic concreteness, by asking what sort of abstractions appeal to me, and answering that question in the only possible way, by a concrete fantasy. Instead of discriminating attractive ideas from others less attractive (which is the sort of operation to which my mind lends itself most readily), I ask in that poem by what criterion I find some ideas more attractive than others. I answer that I like ideas which are *stony*. This represents (I hope) a true poem won out of precisely that which is most inimical to it, free play among abstractions.

'A Gathered Church' actually follows out the process of thus winning to the concrete though the abstract – the church I was brought up in represents itself to me in the first place as a pattern of doctrines and doctrinal cruxes; only after giving these their head, in a free play and snip-snap of ideas and distinctions, can I win through to an apprehension of Dissent as embodied and made concrete in the personality of my grandfather.

'Under St Paul's' by contrast conceals the true movement of my mind, presenting as a deduction from concrete experience what was in fact the source of the poem (the idea of Candour), to which the concrete experience of the cathedral as a building was subsequently attached, not without difficulty. Yet perhaps this is to be less than fair to myself. As in 'The Fountain' and 'Killala', the idea and the sensuous experience struck me independently, and only in the process of writing did I recognize a harmony between them, and a rightness about splicing them together in the poem. All the same by and large it is certainly true that the idea comes into my mind more readily than the sensuous experience which not only can stand, but must stand, as its symbol.

Now I am meditating an essay on the relationship between poetry and painting. Yet I feel that I shall not express in the essay what makes this complex of ideas so interesting to me. What takes my interest is something behind the ideas, something which can be expressed only, as in 'Obiter Dicta', by finding a concrete fantasy which not only expresses but truly *is* the common element in the ideas which attract me. I have a hunch that this common element has something to do with the distinction in painting between hue and tone. This distinction is still a distinction between ideas, but the ideas are a good deal less abstract than those I started with …

The 'Sculpture' of Rhyme. The title comes from Pound's *Hugh Selwyn Mauberley.* Some of the notions and sentiments packed into this little epitome were teased out by me years later in an essay on Michael Ayrton's 'The Maze Maker', in *The Southern Review,* Summer, 1969.

A Sequence for Francis Parkman. When this was first published, Philip Larkin in an amiable review speculated that Francis Parkman was 'one of Mr Davie's American friends'. The historiographer Francis Parkman (1823–93) was the author of *France and England in North America,* in many volumes. A large portion of each of these poems is a cento of passages snipped from Parkman's distinguished prose. The marginal notes were designed to be an integral part of the total composition. Unlikely as it may seem, the sequence represents my response to North America on my first visit, from September 1957 to August 1958.

Barnsley Cricket Club. An early version of this poem is one for which I have some affection. (Like many in the first half of *Events and Wisdoms,* it has a remote source in Pasternak.) I give it here under its title 'July':

For work like mine, fine weather is inclement.
'Know when to stop,' breaches hoarse July,
A stalk in his blistered mouth. 'Whatever end
You seem to reach this month is fraudulent.'

He would be cool: I see his bushy tufts
Toss in their hanging ranks, or inky single
In steeps of corn promise a stone-cold shade;
And all such ovens, funnels of hot draughts!

Frigidity can every day outwit
And stone-cold stone outstrip him. But to freeze
Distress and torpor in a finished gesture,
Hard as it is, is not the half of it.

Whatever would be natural is begun
With a more troubled feeling: we've a duty,
If nothing natural bears with finishing,
To leave our work dishevelled and half-done.

Hornet. 'At any rate, the poems that I wrote from or about Italy in these years characteristically defined that Italy by contrast with the East Anglian England that we had departed from and returned to. One of these poems is called "Hornet".' [*TC*, p.139]

The Cypress Avenue. 'The "she" of this poem, "my companion", is our old Dublin friend Helen Watson, who (bless her!) has never objected to, but rather embraced, the poem's making use of her in the way it does. And there are things in the poem – for instance, my ignorance of the gardener's practical knowledge of botany – which lay around in my head to be taken up and dealt with only many years later. But the poem at any rate … raises the question whether the philistine, in music or poetry or whatever else, has not access to legitimate pleasures which further education and refinement would only close to him.' [*TC*, p.11]

Homage to John L. Stephens. I have suppressed the second half of this poem.

The Vindication of Jovan Babič. I read about Babič in Vladimir Dedijer's *Beloved Land*. I visited Yugoslavia in 1962. 'Across the Bay' belongs to that visit, as does 'Poreč'.

Bolyai, the Geometer. The Hungarian mathematicians Bolyai, father and son, I first encountered in the script of a play *The Two Bolyais* by Laszlo Nemeth, and an essay by the same hand in the *Hungarian Review*.

After An Accident. The landscape is that of Friuli, in the north east of Italy, behind and around the city of Gemona.

Fairy Story. Of the original poem by Pasternak, George Katkov remarks:

> The story of St George, as it spread through the oral tradition of the 'Religious poems' *(dukhovnoye stikhi)*, sung by the Russian equivalent of minstrels, is a fusion of the Byzantine story of the martyrdom of St George and the western version of the liberation of the 'maiden' from the dragon. This explains the mixed style of imagery in which the Russian landscape combines with a somewhat westernized medieval style.

In my version I have tried to reproduce this 'mixed' and 'Westernized' style, by drawing on the diction of Spenser's *Faerie Queene* which itself is modelled in part on that of the English medieval romances. I like the metre to which the Russian prompted me.

Back of Affluence. Written in Iowa in 1965, this poem was suggested by a short story by Hamlin Garland, to which I was directed by a reading of Wallace Stegner's *Wolf Willow*.

Or, Solitude. 'Or, Solitude' is the sub-title of Wordsworth's 'Lucy Gray'. Wordsworth said of his poem: 'The way in which the incident was treated and the spiritualizing of the character might furnish hints for contrasting the imaginative influences which I have endeavoured to throw over common life with Crabbe's matter-of-fact style of treating subjects of the same kind. This is not spoken to his disparagement, far from it …'. The source of my poem is Hamlin

Garland's *Boy Life on the Prairie*. The poem however was written in England.

To Certain English Poets. 'Surly pluck' is what Whitman allows to the English – in 'Song of Myself', XXXV:

> Our foe was no skulk in his ship I tell you, (said he),
> His was the surly English pluck, and there is no tougher or truer …

Landor, however, in 'Alfieri and Metastasio' (1856) makes Alfieri say:

> The English are innately vulgar, with some few exceptions. Noblemen, suspicious and invidious of untitled gentlemen, whose families are more ancient and more honorable than theirs, and who perhaps lost their fortunes and their station by the wars of the Plantagenets, have no reluctance or dislike to walk and converse with jockeys and boxers; from those they gather the flowers of their phraseology …

– and he goes on to instance, as such a 'flower', the slang novelty 'pluck', meaning 'courage'. If we think of E. M. Forster in *Two Cheers for Democracy* extolling the 'plucky', might we not think that the Englishman's diminished sense of himself and his own possibilities is accurately graphed in the different inflections given to 'pluck' and 'plucky' by Landor, and by Forster? (Landor and Forster, however, have nothing to do with my poem.)

To Helen Keller. This was commissioned by the Friends of the Library of the University of Southern California, and was read at the annual dinner of that Association in 1969, by Mr Charlton Heston.

An Oriental Visitor. A Japanese girl visiting England is provoked by her experiences into recalling some of the classic *haiku* of her own poetic tradition. I found them in Henderson's *Introduction to Haiku*.

England. Among the sources for this poem are Beckles Willson, *The Life of Lord Strathcona and Mount Royal* (2 vols, 1915); Thomas Simpson, *Narrative of the Discoveries on the North Coast of America; effected by the Officers of the Hudson's Bay Company during the Years 1836–39* (London, 1843); John Henry Lefroy, *In Search of the Magnetic North*, ed. G.F.G. Stanley (Toronto, 1955); D. Geneva Lent, *West of the Mountains. James Sinclair and the Hudson's Bay Company* (Seattle, 1963); Alexander Simpson, *Life and Travels of Thomas Simpson;* Vilhjalmur Stefansson, *Unsolved Mysteries of the Arctic* (New York, 1943); Douglas MacKay, *The Honourable Company* (New York, 1936).

Trevenen. For Trevenen, see Rev. John Penrose, *Lives of Vice-Admiral Sir Charles Vinicombe Penrose and Captain James Trevenen* (London, 1850), and *A Memoir of James Trevenen*, ed. Christopher Lloyd and R.C. Anderson (Navy Records Society, 1959). Burke's tributes to Trevenen and James King are in 'Edmund Burke's Character of his Son and Brother', Appendix I in *The Correspondence of Edmund Burke*, Vol. VII (Cambridge and Chicago, 1968). I also consulted *Letters of Anna Seward, written between the Years 1784 and 1807* (Edinburgh, 1811); James Prior, *Memoir of the Life and Character of the Right Hon. Edmund Burke* (1st ed., London, 1824); *The Life of George Crabbe, by his*

Son; Percy Colson, *Their Ruling Passions* (London, n.d.), pp. 39–90; and various volumes of *The Correspondence of Edmund Burke.* These materials and others were assembled in the thought that I might write a closet drama; but finding, not much to my own surprise, that I had no talent for that sort of composition, I threw the subject into the only form of writing that I know about and am practised in.

Vancouver. The modern biographies of Vancouver are by George Goodwin *(Vancouver, A Life. 1757–1798,* New York, 1931), and by Bern Anderson *(The Life and Voyages of Captain George Vancouver, Surveyor of the Sea,* Toronto, 1960). Anderson describes Gillray's caricature, 'The Caneing in Conduit Street'. For Camelford, my source is *The Farington Diary,* Vol. 2, ed. James Greig (London, 1923); I have not seen *The Life, Adventures, and eccentricities of the Late Lord Camelford* (anon., London, 1804). I consulted also *Writings of Fermiǹ Francisco de Lasueǹ,* tr. and ed. Finbar Kenneally (2 vols, Washington, 1965); John Carswell, *The Old Cause* (London, 1954); James Dugan, *The Great Mutiny* (London, 1966); and the *Dictionary of National Biography* (1896–7), articles on David Samwell; on Thomas Pitt, 2nd Baron Camelford; and Alexander Wedderburn, 1st Baron Loughborough.

Commodore Barry. John Barry (1745–1803), called the father of the American Navy, was born in Ireland and came to America about 1760. 'Rodney's Glory' by Eoghan Ruadh O'Suillebhain is printed by Daniel Corkery in *The Hidden Ireland.*

England, for Ezra Pound. From *The Guardian,* 30 October 1965. [*Ed.*]

T.S. Eliot (1928). From *Encounter,* February 1966. [*Ed.*]

Cowper's 'Yardley Oak': A Continuation. From *The Listener,* 14 March 1968. [*Ed.*]

Midsummer's Eve. From *The Listener,* 8 August 1968. [*Ed.*]

August, 1968. From *The Listener,* 19 September 1968. This poem, in obvious ways a companion-piece to 'July, 1964', alludes to the 'Prague Spring' of 1968 and to the subsequent Soviet invasion of Czechoslovakia. [*Ed.*]

Energies. From *The Listener,* 12 December 1968. [*Ed.*]

Boyhood Misremembered. From *Times Literary Supplement,* 26 December 1968. This is a substantially different version of 'Looking out from Ferrara'. [*Ed.*]

Fatherhood; Reticence. The typescripts of these two poems, evidently dating from the mid- to late-1960s, were discovered by Bernard Bergonzi in a book by Donald Davie; they were previously printed in *Poems and Melodramas* (1996). [*Ed.*]

Six Epistles to Eva Hesse. In an introductory note to the first publication of the Six *Epistles,* I explained about Eva Hesse:

> Miss Hesse, Ezra Pound's German translator and an erudite champion of Pound's poetry, was the editor of *New Approaches to Ezra Pound* (London

and Berkeley, 1969), in which was reprinted some of my own writing about Pound. Because I have more reservations about Pound than Miss Hesse and the other contributors to the book, I told her so in a private letter which I found it amusing to put into verse; and this is the first Epistle that follows, in which I also have some fun with another of the contributors, my friend Christine Brooke-Rose. Both, I'm glad to say, detected the affection behind my mockery; and so I'm sure would Charles Olson have done, if he'd lived to see the use that I make of him in the Second Epistle. It's a grief to me that he didn't. One other contributor to the Pound book, Guy Davenport, is being mocked in the later Epistles when I talk about myth.

The poems were all written, light-heartedly, between September 1969 and March 1970. A main objective was to show that, despite current assumptions on both sides of the Atlantic, as much variety of time, space and action can be encompassed in one of the traditional forms of English verse as in the much vaunted 'free form' of an American tradition originating in Pound's *Cantos*. The source of the Third Epistle is *Letters of Letitia Hargrave*, ed. by Margaret Arnett MacLeod (Toronto, Champlain Society, 1947).

In the Stopping Train. 'The years were 1972 and 1973; when we lived, much of the time, in a rented "particulier" in Tours, in rue Jolivet. It all should have happened long before, since French is the only foreign language that I can speak and read with confidence and tolerable correctness; it was the merest chance that postponed my French experiences until so late. Several poems came out of it – notably, one of thanks to old Fiery Evans of Barnsley Grammar School, who inculcated the language that gave me access to the lives and landscapes I lived among ["To a Teacher of French"]; and another longer piece in several sections called "In the Stopping Train", which originated in a miserable journey by rail from Tours to Paris and back, through heavy rain much of the time, on a fruitless attempt to keep a rendezvous with the Irish poet John Montague.' [*TC*, p.143]

Mandelstam in the Crimea; Robinson Jeffers at Point Sur. From *The Listener*, 1 March 1973. [*Ed.*]

Berryman. From *Times Literary Supplement*, 29 June 1973. [*Ed.*]

Replying to Reviewers. From *The Listener*, 19 July 1973. Davie's review of *The Oxford Book of Twentieth-Century Verse*, edited by Philip Larkin (*The Listener*, 29 March 1973), had opened with an analysis of Brian Patten's 'Portrait of a Young Girl Raped at a Suburban Party'. 'How Patten got to the point of thinking that this sort of thing was a poem,' wrote Davie, 'is a good and appalling question.' The review provoked lengthy and heated controversy in the magazine's correspondence columns; Brian Patten did not join in. [*Ed.*]

Kavyria. From typescript dated May 1981. [*Ed.*]

Sorting Old Papers. From *The American Scholar*, Summer 1981. [*Ed.*]

Sonnet; After Pasternak, in Byron's Manner. From *Scripso*, Summer/Autumn 1982. [*Ed.*]

The Gardens of the Savoy. From *Parnassus*, Spring/Summer 1986. This long poem includes two much shorter pieces: 'Brilliance', published in *To Scorch or Freeze* (1988), and 'The Trip to Huntsville', published in *Collected Poems* (1990). The author explained the title in a footnote to the poem's original publication: 'In London, between the Strand and the Embankment, frequented by winos and worse.' [*Ed.*]

Thomas and Emma. This was the last poem Donald Davie wrote, in July 1995, two months before his death. [*Ed.*]

INDEX OF FIRST LINES

A boy turned to a newt! 371
A brutally sheared-off cliff 322
A carving on the jamb of an embrasure 54
A cuckoo in the singing nest betrays 10
A farm boy lost in the snow 199
A glass in a Liverpool drawing room cracked across. 117
A Hun turned sculptor spoke 508
A knowledge of history fetches 149
A lift to the spirit, when everything fell into place! 301
A poem is less an orange than a grid; 17
A poet's lie! 368
A queer thing about those waters: there are no 150
A room designed by Orrery receives 71
A shrunken world 208
A song of the degrees, 451
A string of the scarlet rubies of Ceylon 517
A thin brown orphan in his washed-out blue 72
A thin green salient aimed at the heart of London, 300
A village of kite-flyers, we 2
A wind I know blows dirt 194
Above a stretch of still unravaged weald 22
Adam had found what was not his to seek, 72
After two months, already 146
Age is a pale bird, gilm of ice on the sea 162
Alfred, this couple here – 392
Already running, sprang from the womb; met, 60
'Alamein to Zem-Zem' – have you read it? 579
All the soft runs of it, the tin-white gashes 133
All these love-poems...! 39
Americans are innocents abroad; 58
Among the serviceable mills and 147
An arbitrary roll-call 314
An island cast 327
And so, the retraction. 404
And so you might have been: 465
'Anger, yes. But God is God,' 467
Angry and ashamed at 204
Antennae of the race, 318
Appendicitus is his worst 16
Aquitaine, England's loss 253
Arable acres heave 182
Arkansaw's westernmost county 408

Arthur Allen, when he lived   163
As a horn of the high moon veers in clear skies over Main Street   212
As if to take in ocean   469
As massive and dispensable as sculpture   479
As when a ruined face   356
At home with my infirmities I fare   32
At Hay, or near it, 1944   308
At that time, two friends stood   4
Atheist, Laodicean or   354

Bearing and giving are different, it appears.   460
Before me a far-off time arises   383
Behind the grid, the radiant   334
Behind the hills, from the city of an Etruscan gateway   161
Below us all day, a mile away, in a flashing   388
Beware the ball-point lens: 205
Bideford! Nothing will do   381
Blackbird of Derrycairn   402
Born at 'The Bell' in Gloucester,   512
Break it off? Listen! we have left a jagged edge,   231
'Broad acres, sir.' You hear them in my talk.   8
Brush of a raven's, not an eagle's wing!   20
Bunyan, of course. But Potton it was, or Sandy,   299
Burly, provincial France,   212

Called out on Christmas Eve for a working-party,   405
Certainly, Lean-shanks, you have forced the pace –   43
Chaste and kind ... 'a pattern'   459
Chatham was my depot,   310
Cheerfulness in lordly   441
Chemicals ripen the citrus;   152
Chiddingly, pronounced   320
Chrysanthemums become a cult because   62
'Collapse of a civil privacy of manner   363
Come rain down words as does   184
Compunction at presumption   470
Conquistador! Live dangerously, my Byron,   346
Constant the waterman   385
Cornwall, the unreality   302
Creon, I think, could never kill a mouse   17
Curé and pastor, dead at the one time   127
Curtis, you've been American too long,   134

Daisy and dandelion, speedwell, daffodil   15
Danger, danger of dying   202
Dark ages, calm and merry   206
Day by day, such rewards,   143
Deacon, you are to recognize in this   52

Dear language, English, whose	389
Decaying teeth, before they start to ache	24
Deep-sea frost, and	148
Dim in the glimmering room	200
Discharged upon the body of the world	304
'Do you believe in a God	472
Don John of Chesterton was riding to the wars	74
Don't care for it.	299
Driving up from Tees-side	305
Dry season. Block. So, rain ...	499
Each of us has the time,	143
Eight hours between us, eight	216
Ejected Indians haunt the lawns	536
Elections to the Academy: referred from	551
Emily, you were sick	480
Envisage it: the Atlantic	203
Every so often, Lord, the wanton muse	601
Excellence is sparse.	185
Executive speed is poetry! Whereas	522
Eye on the object, eye on the congeries	321
Feathers up fast, and steeples; then in clods	61
Feeling good, green light, the earthly paradise,	440
First lesson: Don't	489
Flattered at having no	411
For such a theme (atrocities) you find	37
Forlorn indeed Hope on these shores,	119
Four close but several trees, each green, none equal.	207
France of the poujadiste!	157
From a view to a kill in pursuit	311
From easterly crepuscular arrivals	30
From thirty years back my grandmother with us boys	140
Germans, she said, were sometimes independent;	313
Gina, I saw you walk	349
'God be praised that made	503
Gold is not autumn's privilege;	56
Green eyes from under cornsheaf curls	416
Green silk, or a shot silk, blue	141
Hairless and worse than leathery, the skin	56
Hanoverian silverware, this jug	511
Hardly a one but here he is improved,	506
Harmonious first and last,	585
Having no ear, I hear	407
He fared from Bethany to Jerusalem,	175
He had the gift of being pitiless;	594

'He's a sad sack. So's he.'   590
He was never above the mêlee   541
He who proposes   501
Heaney, one can get word-perfect at   428
Hearing from some how the Sierra answers   130
Hearing one saga, we enact the next.   28
Her father's brother rapes her!   364
Here is its mark left, thumbnail of enigma.   432
High above Plymouth, not so high   12
His themes? Ah yes he had themes.   344
'History, not wanted yet,   255
Horace of course is not   505
Horse, our poor creature, we treat as if elemental,   511
Housman came, savage recluse,   300
How funny, she beat him, she   486
How many memories, what long sorrow   115
How often I have said,   139

I am supposed to apologize   507
I could not live here, though I must and do   141
I discover in myself   256
I find nothing to say,   452
I get, surprisingly, a sense of space: 391
I had to assure myself: 380
I have a photograph here   325
I have been young, and now am old: 453
I have got into the slow train   337
I like the sidewalks of an American city,   151
I look a long way back   192
I love the way the weave, when two or three or   434
I remember the scarlet setts   154
I said to myself: 'That's enough.   438
I saw brown Corrib lean upon his urn,   69
I see the low black wherry   142
I smell a smell of death.   180
I tend to suppose the part I know least   303
I was never impressed, when they presented   3
I was the Nazis' padre, you might say;   561
I went to war once, I'm not sure for what   589
I wish for you that when you wake   70
Iced with a vanilla   160
I'd have the silence like a heavy chock   21
If distance lends enchantment to the view,   36
If I should riffle a pack   587
If music be the muses' paragon   24
Importunate for attention,   457
Importunately   439
In Candiac by Nîmes in Languedoc   131

In days of old 172
In lilac trained on the colonnade's archway, what 139
In, of all places, Tashkent 513
In the day of the mustering of thine army, 445
In their conventicles 454
In winter in Diamantina 514
Infrequently, dreams are heavenly. 466
It is not life being short, 189
It is said that he laughs at himself, 533
It must make a great difference, having friends. 401
It needs there to be no one 213
It needs there to be no one 259
It was agreed we would not mount by those 39
It will not help, my heart 3
It won't stand up to the light; 455
It would have been because 471
Italian prisoners of war still haunted 309

Joe, little serpentine white boy, 1
John Fowles's book, *The French Lieutenant's Woman*: 305
Johnson's pentameters, nailed by the solid *ictus*; 315
Joke county, smallest in England, 317
Judgement occurs, but is not 415
Judy Sugden! Judy, I made you caper 156

Kendal ... Shap Fell! Is that in Westmorland? 321
King's Cliffe, in the evening: that Northampton stone 314

L'avenir de l'intelligence 254
Let him rehearse the gifts reserved for age 398
Let them give up the ghost, then there is nothing but dust 449
'Life is over and you are its 481
Lighting a spill late in the afternoon, 65
'Live-in-ease', and then to wash 378
Look there! What a wheaten 147
Looping off feline through the leisured air 73
Loose lips now 116

Making the best and most of a visitation 123
Man fought aginst beasts, and won; 465
Man with a scythe: the torrent of his swing 66
Many compacted summers 509
Mary Jane, she's after me, 484
May's, whose mouth was 189
Men of business, of pleasure, 449
'Mesmerized eyes on one's 592
Mired in it! Stuck in the various 447
Mr Chernobyl is 567

Mrs Throckmorton's bull-finch sang a song.   8
'My brethren ...' And a bland, elastic smile   29
My companion kept exclaiming   145
My dears, don't I know? I esteem you more than you think   207
My father was born in Horton   310
My mountain belly and incontinent girth   593

named them   335
Names and things named don't match   306
Natuire? No, not Nature.   361
Nebulous, freezingly moist   390
Neither dead nor alive, neither aslseep nor awake,   502
New every morning is the love   350
New surprises? No. No new surprises: 362
Night frost glitter glazes   258
No moss nor mottle stains   386
No point in looking. The   519
No ripening curve can be allowed to sag   63
No, there will be no explanations then: 588
Noah drunken, taking   466
Nobody's hero, George Vancouver, ever;   244
Noon. And as from the hawk   85
North Sea, Protestant sea,   179
Northwood I came, and knocked in the coated wall   178
Not architecture, not   307
Not deaf to ghosts yet not expecting them   603
Not deerpark, royal chase,   194
Not, I keep being told, the Time   261
'Not the action of rowing: 410
'Not the least enviable of your many gifts,   44
'Not what's done, but what   594
Now I am afraid for a child,   256
Now the heat comes, I am demoralized.   137

'O happy skies of Italy!   92
Obtrusive and absurd, the guilty mind   1
Of this aspiring burgher who disdained   128
Oh had we known it turns out so   479
Oh I can praise a cloistered virtue, such   13
Old Glory at halfmast   190
Old oak, old timber, sunk and rooted   377
Old poems from long ago   478
Once the broom has started,   515
'One Law for the Lion and Ox is Oppression.'   444
One simple and effective rhyme   37
'or as the embryo, whose vital band   441
Or: *They are come near me that*   463
'Our argute voices vied among the bracken.'   307

Pacific: in Russian as   181
Passed from you, mother, to the custody   596
Pennies of sun's fire jazzing like silver foil,   155
People spruce themselves for a party.   176
Persone seek provisional assent.   19
Placatory pumice ledged   476
Pluming himself upon a sense of sin   51
Pontiac fires Detroit!   132
Portland, the Isle of Portrland – how I love   335
Potter nor iron-founder   126
Pragmatical old Capulet, the head,   9
Presences are always said to be brood;   58
Provided for! Provided for,   260

Red mills and farms clumped soothingly here and there.   144
Rebuke the company of spearmen   595
Riparian origins ... did you know   196
Rococo compositions of decay,   59
'Room for manoeuvre,' I say,   196
Rose late: the jarring and whing   352
Rosebay willow herb pushing   315
Russian Jew, for you   332

'Sacred? or sacrosanct?   462
Saint Cecllia: 473
Sealed into the cocoon   498
Seeing his stale vocabulary build   64
Seneschal leaving the wood   104
Service, or Latin sorbus, European   125
Shallow or deep, snows on Socrates won't,   523
She thinks she was hurt this summer   376
Simpering sideways under a picture-hat   312
Sir, you were a credit to whatever   353
Small boy in a black hat walks among streaky shadows   209
Smashed, and brought up against   164
Snow-white ray   182
So many nights the solitary lamp had burned;   327
So now we know the worst   602
Some I perceive, content   406
Some quickly-weathering rock, perhaps,   14
Something gone, something gone out with Nelson,   319
'Southey! Alas, my writings   601
Spring pricks a little. I get out the maps.   357
St George's, Hardwicke Street,   55
St Patrick bound unto himself   468
'Start such a fire in England, Master Ridley,   316
Status indeed and protocol I pay   495
Stillness! Down the dripping ride,   186

Stout and well-knit in fact,   411
Strange walkers! See their processional   45
Sunlight so blurred with clouds we couldn't tell   137
Surely it has some virtue, having none,   122
Symmetries, harmonies   361

taking off at dawn   475
Tares make the corn to grow,   483
Taxis were beyond us   497
Thanks to industrial Essex   188
That a toss of wheat-ears lapping   348
That Christmas quite the animal   6
That honoured name!   249
That lime-tree – no, what is it? mulberry? –   534
That proper ghoul, the scholar, may exhume   10
That shrewd character Will Percy in   521
That sneaky Thomas Cranmer!   458
That time of the early year   198
That, true to the contours which round it   49
The accomplished *hetaira* toys for this Knave of Hearts.   585
'The angels rejoice in   450
The best way in (not that I've checked the map)   322
The best, who could, went back – because they nursed   329
The blanched tree livid behind   197
The blank of the wall is over against you; which   181
The Boyne at Navan swam in light,   19
The chief of the civil administration   234
The circle of her arms could be   2
The colonist's 'they' that needs no antecedent   313
The disposings of the heart in man,   453
The Duke insists you stay; you could do worse.   59
The graces, yes – and the airs! To airs and graces   323
The hideousness of the inland spine of Cornwall!   377
The 'I have' poem   204
The jaunty style of Arnold Bennett's 'Card' ...   318
The light wheels and comes in   184
The Lord is King, be the people   446
The man on the foreshore cooking a fish breakfast   591
The mind (the soul) is not   440
The muse that makes pretensions to discourse,   21
The narrow backyard garden   488
'The rest is not our business.' Come the end or   491
The roads getting emptier, air in a steadily purer   70
The roses of irony blossom   464
The sea is all that they say: it wreaks death one way only;   461
The scroll is defaced; the worm   354
The shuffle and shudder of Autumn   169
The streaming simile, the plume,   7

The sun works up to a lather 172
The time is at an end. 385
The weather of living in an island 230
The wind meets me at Penistone. 46
The world of God has turned its stone faces 118
There came, for lack of sleep, 153
There has to be a hero who is not 162
There is a heigh-ho in these glowing coals 68
These have I set up, 40
They see his face! 327
Thinking how it is 400
Thirty years unremembered, 215
This has to be for my school-chum Billy Greaves 317
This head meant to be massive and therefore, 27
This lady was danger, this 524
This place is so much 201
This West! this ocean! The bare 331
This you have heard before; 538
Those Cambridge generations, Russell's, Keynes' ... 22
Though love is the word a mother 259
Though painters say Itallian light does well 57
Through a wide window all Somerset might look in 65
Time like an ever-rolling stream 446
Time passing, and the memories of love 40
To a bell in Lincoln Cathedral 214
To be constant through a lifetime, 524
To break the pentameter, Pound's first heave 501
To flex in the upper airs 387
To justify God's ways to man 456
To re-insert it in 485
To the chief Chanters 442
Traditore, traduttore – spare us! 572
Trying to understand myself, I fetch 41

Unimaginable beings – 326
Unsettled again and hearing Russian spoken 63
Up and down stairs of the inner ear, 201

'Versify it, Donald,' 586
'Via Portello,' I wrote, 167
Visiting Belfast at the end of June, 21
Voices, such voices ... They assail me now 556
Vying is our trouble; 171

Walk quietly around in 336
Walking about the emptied house I 493
'Warm hands, cold heart,' they say; and vice versa. 170
Was it, I wondered, some freak 309

We have a lawn of moss. 136
We have shown each other the tricks 589
We have written to Giulia, saying 348
'We last of Yugo-Slav 395
We never made it. Time and time again 303
We shall break out 443
What is man that you should weigh 459
What we do best is breed: 150
What with hounds and friends and, in the winter, 25
Whatever is said to be so 188
When all my hours are mine, 206
When Bradbury sang, 'The Roast Beef of Old England' 50
When does a town become a city? This 358
When he came back from saying good-bye 5
When I think of you 211
When it was found a fault 496
When Owen Roe 247
When some were happy as the grass was green, 50
When it is cold it stinks, and not till then. 55
When you were explaining American, Robert, you did not 423
Whenever I talk of my art 138
Where depths are surfaces 170
White walls shone from far 75
Who does not remember his boyhood, gun on shoulder, 79
Who now reads Thomson or Collins? 319
Why, by an ingrained habit, deviate 120
Why should we   defer   our joys? 484
Will it be be one of those 154
Wind-claps of soot and snow 193
Winds from Cook's Strait cannot blow 235
With the actual the illusory 187
With the effect almost of carving the hillside 124
With you to Bideford 379
Worry hedges my days 169
Wren and Barry, Rennie and Mylne and Dance 47

X, whom society's most mild command, 67

Year well remembered! Happy who beheld thee! 107
You may be right: 'How can I dare to feel?' 67
You remember Rossignano 159
You saw the sunlight ripen upon the wall 382
You that would bite the whole pie and 444
Your grandad worked the signals 494
Your special witness, as I recollect. 36
Yours was the original freak-out: Samuel Beckett's 210

INDEX OF TITLES

'Abbeyforde' 215
Across the Bay 150
Admiral to his Lady, The 379
Advent 406
After a Change of Régime 540
After an Accident 164
After Pasternak, in Byron's Manner 479
After the Calamitous Convoy (July 1942) 327
After the Match 506
Against Confidences 116
Agave in the West 151
Alzheimer's Disease 533
Amazonian 196
Among Artisans' Houses 12
'And Our Eternal Home' 446
Anglican Lady, An 411
Another Old Bolshevik 579
Apparition, An 349
Ars Poetica 336
Articulacy. Hints from the Koran 489
Artifex in Extremis 398
At Knaresborough 8
At the Café Parnasse 498
At the Cradle of Genius 44
At the Synod in St Patrick's 27
Attar of Roses 440
Aubade 70
August, 1968 257
Autumn Imagined 169

Back of Affluence 198
Balancing Acts 572
Barnsley and District 156
Barnsley Cricket Club 137
Barnsley, 1966 193
Battered Wife, The 376
Battlefield, A 144
Bedfordshire 299
Behind the North Wind 203
Being Angry With God 467
Belfast on a Sunday Afternoon 21
Bella & Rosa 556

Benedictus   439
Bent, The   400
Berkshire   299
Berryman   362
Bits and Pieces   585
Black Hoyden   484
Blank of the Wall, The   181
Bolyai, the Geometer   163
Bougainville   133
Bowing the Head   457
Boyhood Misremembered   259
Brantôme   212
Break, The   231
Bride of Reason, The   9
Buckinghamshire   300
By the Road to Upper Midhope   483

Cambridgeshire   300
Cannibals   469
Castle, The   79
Catullus on Friendship   401
Chernobyl. A Disaster   567
Cherry Ripe   63
Cheshire   301
Christening, A   150
Christian Hero, A   410
Christmas Syllabics for a Wife   211
Christmas Week, 1948   6
Chrysanthemums   62
Church Militant   445
Church of Ireland   495
Cold Spring in Essex   209
Comforter, The   468
Commodore Barry   247
Conditioned Air, A   194
Condolence   5
Cornwall   302
Corrib. An Emblem   56
County Durham   305
Cowper's 'Yardley Oak': A Continuation   255
Creature David, The   453
Creon's Mouse   17
Cumberland   303
Curtains!   446
Cypress Avenue, The   145

Dancing Measures   466
David Dancing   466

Death in the West. A   189
Death of a Painter   334
Death of a Voice   432
Demi-Exile, Howth   15
Democrats   207
Departed, The   327
Depravity: Two Sermons   329
Derbyshire   305
Derbyshire Turf   49
Devil on Ice   405
Devonshire   304
Dissentient Voice   50
Dorset   305
Dream Forest   40
Dublin Georgian   71
Dublin Georgian (2)   72
Dudwood   70
Dule of a Dewsbury Matron   484
Duplicity in Prayer   3

Ecclesiastical Polity   594
Eden   72
Eight Years After   36
Elders and Betters   10
Elect, The   454
Emigrant, to the Receding Shore   230
Energies   258
England   216
England, for Ezra Pound   253
English Revenant, An   30
Epilogue   115
Epistle. To Enrique Caracciolo Trejo   208
Equestrian Sestina   511
Essex   306
Evangelist, The   29
Evening on the Boyne   19
Except The Lord Build The House   451
Expecting Silence   188
Ezra Pound in Pisa   185

Fairy Story   172
Fare Thee Well   381
Father, the Cavalier   325
Fatherhood   259
Feeders, The   147
Felicity's Fourth Order   449
For an Age of Plastics   124
For Doreen. A Voice from the Garden   136

Forest, The	92
Forests of Lithuania, The	74
Foreword. Mickiewicz in England	74
Fountain of Arethusa, The	371
Fountain of Cyanë, The	364
Fountain, The	61
From the New World	190
Frontenac	129
G.M.B.	377
Garden Party, The	22
Gardens no Emblems	66
Gardens of the Savoy, The	524
Garland for Ivor Gurney, A	503
Garland for Ronsard, A	416
Gathering of Mushrooms, The	85
Gemona-del-Friuli, 1961–1976	348
Glaphira III	2
Gloucestershire	307
God of Details, The	184
God Saves the King	442
Going to Italy	57
Grace in the Fore Street	382
Grazia Deledda, young	486
Green River	141
Gripping Serial	465
Grudging Respect	456
H.D.	524
Hampshire	307
Hardness of Light, The	167
Harrow, The	326
Having No Ear	407
Hawkshead and Dachau in a Christmas Glass	32
Hearing Russian Spoken	63
Heart Beats	24
Heigh-ho on a Winter Afternoon	68
Helena Morley	514
Herefordshire	308
Hermes and Mr Shaw	488
Heroine of the Academy, A	551
Hertfordshire	309
Hill Field, The	147
His Themes	344
Homage to George Whitefield	512
Homage to John L. Stephens	162
Homage to William Cowper	8
Homestead, The	79

Horae Canonicae	350
Hornet	139
Hot Hands	170
Housekeeping	140
House-martin	142
Humanly Speaking	146
Huntingdonshire	309
Hyphens	159
Hypochondriac Logic	16
I Have Said, Ye Are Gods	465
Idyll	212
If I Take The Wings Of The Morning	475
Immortal Longings. Before Surgery	602
In California	152
In Chopin's Garden	154
In the Stopping Train	337
Inditing A Good Matter	452
Intervals in a Busy Life	196
Iowa	197
Ironist, The	462
Jacob's Ladder	39
January	182
Jesuits in North America, the	127
Jottings, not so Random	590
July, 1964	180
'Just You Wait!'	456
Kavyria	476
Kent	310
Killala	119
Kingship	471
Kites	2
Knave of Hearts, The	585
Lady Cochrane	249
Lancashire	310
Landfall among Friends	4
Lasalle	128
Late Anniversary, A	385
Leicestershire	311
Letter to Curtis Bradford, A	134
Levity	459
Life Encompassed	139
Life of Service, The	125
Lily at Noon, A	148
Limited Achievement	64

Lincolnshire   312
Liverpool Epistle, A   392
Livingshayes   378
Looking out from Ferrara   213
Lost Bride, The   586
Love and the Times   148
Love-Poems: for Mairi MacInnes   39
Low Lands   141

Machineries of Shame   24
Magdalene   176
Mamertinus on Rhetoric, AD 291   19
Mandelstam in the Crimea   361
Mandelstam, on Dante   332
Mandelstam's Hope for the Best   411
Mandelstam's 'Octets'   434
March   172
Master & Man   459
Measured Tread, A   493
Meeting of Cultures, A   160
Mens Sana in Corpore Sano   43
Metals   161
Meteorologist, September   443
Method. For Ronald Gaskell   37
Middlesex   313
Midsummer's Eve   256
Miracle, The   175
Monmouthshire   313
Montcalm   131
Morning   352
Mother   497
Mr Sharp in Florence   58
Mushroom Gatherers, The   45
Mustered into the Avant-Garde   507
My Father's Honour   200

Nashville Mornings   473
New Year Wishes for the English   205
New York in August   153
'1945'   517
Nineteen-Seventeen   117
No Epitaph   386
Nonconformist, The   67
Norfolk   314
North & South   480
North Dublin   44
North Sea, in a Snowstorm, The   206
North Sea, The   179

Northamptonshire 314
Northern Metres 494
Northumberland 315
Nosegay, The 464
Nottinghamshire 315

Oak Openings 204
Obiter Dicta 41
On a Proposed Celebration of Ezra Pound 501
On Bertrand Russell's 'Portraits from Memory' 22
On Edmund Spenser's House in Ireland 601
On Generous Lines 511
On Not Deserving 169
On Sutton Strand 69
On the Final Day 558
Or, Solitude 199
Ordinary God 472
Orford 187
Oriental Visitor, An 214
Orpheus 335
Orvieto. The King of Clubs 587
'Our Father' 596
Our Lady 461
Out of East Anglia 181
Owl Minerva, The 23
Ox-bow 385
Oxfordshire 316

Pacer in the Fresco, The. John the Baptist 60
'Pastor Errante' 423
Pelican 1
Penelope 404
Pentecost 201
Pietà 182
Pilate 234
Poem as Abstract 17
Poet Redeemed & Dead 440
Poet-Scholar, The 10
Pontiac 132
Poreč 155
Portland 335
Preoccupation's Gift 206
Priory of St Saviour, Glendalough, The 54
Prolific Spell, The 143
Protesilaus and Laodamia 7
Pushkin. A Didactic Poem 25
Put Not Your Trust in Princes 449

Quarrel, The   104

Rain on South-East England   201
Recollections of George Oppen in a letter to an English friend   534
Red Rock of Utah   122
Reflections on Deafness   123
Rejoinder to a Critic   67
Remembering the 'Thirties   28
Reminded of Bougainville   491
Replying to Reviewers   363
Resolutions   138
Reticence   260
Revenge for Love   502
Revulsion   204
Right Lads, The   485
Right Wing Sympathies   157
Robinson Jeffers at Point Sur   361
Rodez   178
Rousseau in his Day   327
Rutland   317

Samuel Beckett's Dublin   55
Savannah   522
Saw I Never The Righteous Forsaken   453
Screech-owl   380
'Sculpture' of Rhyme, The   126
Sculptures in Hungary   508
Scythian Charioteers, The   496
Sea of Tiberias   591
Seeing Her Leave   331
Seeing through Me   592
Selina, Countess of Huntingdon   36
Seur, near Blois   348
Short Run to Camborne   377
Shropshire   317
Siloam   408
Sing Unto The Lord a New Song   441
Six Epistles to Eva Hesse   261
Skelpick   388
Some Future Moon   383
Some Shires Revisited   354
Somerset   318
'So make them melt as the dishousèd snail'   441
Song for These Crusaders, A   1
Sonnet   479
Sorting Old Papers   478
Sorting the Personae   515
Sounds of a Devon Village   509

Spring Song, A 357
Staffordshire 318
Standings 444
Stratford on Avon 192
Strathnaver 389
Suffolk 319
Summer Lightning 428
Sunburst 184
Sunday Morning 519
Surrey 319
Sussex 320
Sylvae 194

T.S. Eliot (1928) 254
Thanks to Industrial Essex 188
Their Rectitude Their Beauty 450
They, to Me 481
Thirty-ninth Psalm, Adapted, The 438
Thomas and Emma 603
'Thou Art Near At Hand, O Lord' 463
Though dry, not dry 499
Three Beyond 415
Three Moral Discoveries 13
Three Pastors in Berlin 561
Through Bifocals 538
Thyestes 20
Tiger at the Movie-Show 3
Time Passing, Beloved 40
To a Bad Poet 501
To a Brother in the Mystery 118
To a Staffordshireman, from a Devon Villa 589
To a Teacher of French 353
To an American Classicist 523
To C.T. 589
To Certain English Poets 207
To Helen Keller 210
To Londoners 391
To Thom Gunn in Los Altos, California 346
Toby to Aguecheek 593
Townend, 1976 358
Trevenen 235
Treviso, the Pescheria 143
Tunstall Forest 186
Tuscan Brutus, The 59
Tuscan Morning 58
Twilight on the Waste Lands 14
Two from Ireland 401
Two Intercepted Letters 601

Two Widows in Tashkent   513

Under a Skylight   65
Under St Paul's   47
University of the South, The   521
Utterings   387

Vancouver   244
Vengeance Is Mine, Saith The Lord   444
Via Portello   59
Vindication of Jovan Babič, The   162
Viper-Man   154
Vying   171

War Criminal   594
Warwickshire   321
Waterfall at Powerscourt, The   73
Wearing of the Green, The   56
Well-found Poem   385
West Virginia's Auburn   536
Westmorland   321
Where Depths are Surfaces   170
Wide France   137
Widower   458
Widowers   354
Wild Boar Clough   368
Wiltshire   322
Wind at Penistone, The   46
Winter Landscape near Ely, A   189
Winter Landscapes   202
Winter Talent, A   65
Winter's Talents   390
With the Grain   120
Witness   460
Woe Unto Thee!   470
Wombwell on Strike   505
Women and War   595
Woodpigeons at Raheny   37
Worcestershire   322

Year 1812, The   107
Yorkshire   323

Zion   447
Zip!   21
Zodiac, The   455